# How Theory Influences Treatment and Prevention Practice with the Family

### THOMAS P. GULLOTTA

## INTRODUCTION

Like a serial from a 1930s Saturday matinee, the reader was left in the preface wondering about the meaning of the word *family*. In this next installment that question is addressed further. To do that, several theories of family behavior are selectively examined to discover an understanding of family. Choosing elements from those theories, a definition of *family* is fashioned. Later, using family theories again and explanations of individual behavior, their usefulness is explored in establishing interventions that promote health, prevent illness and treat illness to return the child to a healthier state.

## FAMILY THEORIES

### Social Biology

Times were that the word *family* was inexorably intertwined with the word *marriage*:

> Marriage was a union, institutionalized and publicly recognized, between a man and a woman. Accompanying this union was a set of traditional societal assumptions that the couple would share economic resources, produce offspring, and stay married, A family provided the structural setting in which these assumptions were carried out. It offered a framework by which married individuals shared a residence and economic resources and reproduced. Further, it was in the family that children were raised, socialized, instilled with values, and protected. (Gullotta, Adams & Alexander, 1986, pp. 5–6)

But long ago before "times were," another pattern of behavior existed. Living in small groups, where speech was a grunt, the dominant male in this group would impregnate a female. She would bear his child and have responsibility for the child's upbringing. From a social biological view, this pattern of behavior was both beneficial and problematic. Oh, what is social biology? Social biology understands human behavior to be overwhelmingly influence by our genetic evolution such that instinctual thoughts (unless very consciously controlled) dominant the more recent cognitive thought processing abilities developed over the past 15,000 years (Wilson, 1978). It is the selfish-gene view of life with the carrier of that gene pool (that is you and me) seeking two essential circumstances in life (Dawkins, 1976). First is our self-continuation in the here and now. Next is our self-continuation in the hereafter—no, not heaven in this case but the spreading of our genes by propagation to ensure that we continue through our descendants. So, what is problematic about the dominant male impregnating females? From his perspective, he was increasing the odds that his genes would achieve longevity. The greater the number of offspring with as many females as possible extended his family tree. On the other hand, the female in this relationship was at a decided disadvantage. Whereas his moment till ejaculation lasted minutes, her role in this process lasted months. Unlike most other animals, the offspring of this chance mating required extended care, limiting not only her contribution to the survival of the group but also her ability to conceive another child. Thus, her evolution and the behaviors emanating from that evolution strove to limit the male to fewer mates and to establish a bond among the male, the impregnated female and, ultimately, the child. As this evolutionary pathway benefited the survival of the species, new behaviors like emotional attachment and romantic love developed to coexist with older behaviors like jealousy and physiological arousal. Eventually, this coupling became institutionalized as marriage. But do not mistake this coupling for monogamy (one man and one woman). Many societies permitted polygamy (one man to more than one woman), and some even practiced polyandry (one woman to more than one man) or group marriage (the union of several women to several men).

## Structural Functional Theory

Rather than using the gene as the unit of analysis to drive our view of behavior and the family, we might choose the social system and a theory called structural functionalism (Parsons, 1949). Teasing apart those words, *structural* is understood as a clearly defined element of a pattern or organization in which the general character of the whole emerges and is maintained. *Functionalism* speaks to the contribution of each element to the development and maintenance of the whole. Thus, "society is made up of a number of structures, each serving a useful function that maintains and/or further develops the whole" (Gullotta et al., 1986, p. 31). From a structural functionalist perspective, the family needs to clothe to the extent weather demands, to shelter and to nourish its members. Now, depending on the complexity of the society in which the family lives, other needs may exist. For example, living alone a family stumbling upon a beehive in a tree hollow may act as freely as the bees permit to remove that sweet nectar. However, that same family acting as freely in a group of people where one individual is a beekeeper will create group turmoil. Their action of honey taking is now considered stealing from another group member. Thus, as the complexity of the surroundings increase about the family, their function enlarges to encompass nonkin group socialization—that is, teaching family members appropriate behaviors for larger group membership, which in turn is an attempt at maintaining group harmony (balance) or, as the structural functionalist would say, homeostasis.

## Social Exchange Theory

Another way to conceptualize the family is through an emotional cost–benefit analysis. The word *social* in this theory implies the interaction of the individual and the group. *Exchange* is understood to mean the giving of one thing for something else of near equal value. In social exchange theory, life is seen as a marketplace where emotions, relationships and all other behaviors are traded. Here are its four operating principles.

First are rewards. These are the satisfactions, pleasures or attainments resulting from an exchange. To be told, "I love you," by someone you love is a pleasure. To see your beloved child succeed is a satisfaction. To be surrounded by loved ones in old age is a satisfying, pleasurable attainment.

Next is cost, which represents the actions, feelings or interactions that are either unpleasant or are rewards lost. In a reward lost, the principal is that choice entails loss. For example, to choose pie for desert costs you ice cream. Yes, you can have pie à la mode, but that costs you the cake as a choice and adds 350 additional calories to your already bulging belly. The point is that everything costs something.

The third element to social exchange theory is profit. In the marketplace of life, decisions are made to make one's life as profitable as possible while limiting life's losses. To illustrate, social exchange theory is often used to explain the phenomenon of older men marrying much younger women. For the male, it is suggested that the much younger wife is a statement of continued vitality, attractiveness and masculinity at a time when reproductive ability likely is measured in days rather than minutes. For the female, she is thought to be trading her youth for the security the older male brings to the relationship. This security might be emotional or financial or might be found in his maturity. Regardless, if asked, both male and female would express satisfaction at their decision for reasons of love, of course.

Last, there is the norm of reciprocity. This means that over time rewards and costs should roughly equalize in the eyes of givers and takers. As the saying goes, "Do unto others as you would have them do unto you." Sharing among your group is good. Hoarding is bad. Continually taking advantage of others jeopardizes the longevity of the relationship with those others and thereby places your own longevity in question.

## DEFINING FAMILY

What can be gleaned from these three schools of thought about the family? From social biology, the primary function of the family is reproduction and continuation. From structural functionalism, the maintenance of the family is dependent on the establishment of rules (i.e., structures) that enable the family to function (i.e., behave successfully) in the circumstances in which the family finds itself. From social exchange theory, those rules or structures over time should balance profit and loss, favoring gain if possible but not at the expense of violating the norm of reciprocity. Now, a nuance from symbolic interaction theory could be added in that family members perform numerous roles like mother, wife, lover, employee, homemaker, den leader and the list goes on, each with its own socially approved behavioral script. Or, from general systems theory, concepts could be added that define the openness of the family to change (i.e., boundaries) or how it achieves change through transformation, cybernetic control and, ultimately, morphogenesis, but for these purposes I think a useful definition of the family can be offered without these. Oh, there is one more factor to consider: This is a book about children in families; thus, the definition of family must include children.

Thus, a family provides a structural setting in which individuals share a residence and economic resources. It is in the family and other institutions that children are raised, socialized, instilled with values and protected. This definition is remarkably similar to the definition at the beginning of this chapter, with three exceptions. The first is the omission of the word *marriage*. The second is the omission of the word *reproduction*, and the third is the addition of others in raising children. Let us examine those exceptions more closely against my thinking and that of Gerald Adams and Sharon Alexander more than two decades ago.

## Marriage and Its Variations

Consider the ways people might live together. They could cohabitate—that is, two unrelated individuals sharing a common dwelling. Should this male and female remain together for several years, the legal argument could be made that a common-law marriage occurred. The strength of this case would depend on the conditions described earlier like the sharing of economic resources. Or the couple—male and female or, in some states, of the same sex—could pursue a civil union that entitles them to certain legal conditions, for example, coverage under their partner's health insurance. Last, in the eyes of the state that is the entity issuing a marriage license, the male and female couple can declare an intention to live together till death do they part or to divorce, whichever comes first. Currently, no state issues marriage licenses for same-sex couples. In each of these arrangements children have been reared less or more successfully to adulthood. The success of those experiences was independent of the form the couple relationship took but is dependent on factors such as respect for family members; fairness and consistency; parenting behavior toward offspring; financial, emotional and social resources; and other behaviors discussed in the next chapter.

## Reproduction and How the Child Arrives in Its Living Circumstance

Earlier we shared the reality that children arrive in a variety of ways beyond the female (mother) and male (father) mating. A child may be conceived with donated sperm or a donated egg. The fetus may gestate in the womb of a surrogate mother. The child may be adopted or may be placed by a governmental entity in a foster home. Out of these five possibilities, only one is the result of the mother and father mating. Although it was not possible to identify data on sperm and egg donations or surrogate births, the following was discerned. Approximately 4% of children (2.9 million youth in 2002) under the age of 18 in the United States do not live with a parent. The majority (1.3 million youth) live with grandparents, with other relatives (802,000 youth) or in foster-care placements (235,000 youth) (Fields, 2003).

## Family

Searching the census records reveals that in 2003, 5.5 million couples reported living together (i.e., cohabitating) as unmarried partners. This is an increase of more than 2 million couples since 1990, and the number may be even higher due to suspected underreporting (Fields, 2004). The number of children living in cohabitating relationships is unknown. Children might find themselves living in a single-parent household with their mother, as 16.5 million did in 2002. Of this number, 1.8 million children lived with their mother and her unmarried partner. Or children might find themselves living with their father, as 3.3 million did in 2002. One third (1.1 million) of these children lived with their father and his unmarried partner. Together, these single-parent family variations accounted for 28% of the housing arrangements for all children under the age of 18. As noted earlier, 4% of all children live with grandparents, other relatives or in foster-care placements. The remaining 68% live in two-parent households. But before celebrating this last remark as proof that the nuclear family is alive and well, consider this: Within that 68% are remarriages. In census department lingo, the two-parent family could be biological, step- or adoptive parent (Fields, 2003). Thus, the percentage of families with Mom and Dad matching the *Ozzie and Harriet, Father Knows Best, Leave It to Beaver* or *Donna Reed Show* on Nick at Night is quite lower.

From a historical perspective, two parents raising their biological children from birth till 18 is of recent vintage. Mind you, male and female coupling was occurring sometimes within the context of marriage or a village custom akin to marriage. Yet, because of early and frequent death, family structures were as and even more complex than those found today. For example, consider that in the Plymouth, Massachusetts, colony of the 1600s one third of men and one fourth of women remarried after the death of a spouse (Demos, 1970). With death arriving in 1900 for Black men at 33 (48 for Whites) and for women at 35 (51 for Whites), families could have children with neither biological parent alive (U.S. Bureau of the Census, 1975).

Today, it is not death that dissolves the family but divorce. But although the legal marriage of the two adults may be severed, the growth of joint custody and visitation privileges leave in place other roles (remember symbolic interaction theory) connected with the family—namely parenting. This circumstance can become complicated should the former spouses remarry, as most do when they are less than 40 years of age (Gullotta et al., 1986). The new family can be complex, and the confusion and ambiguity of the role of parent offers rich opportunities for difficulties to arise.

But divorce is not the only way children find themselves in new living circumstances. For a variety of reasons—some good and some not so good—grandparents increasingly are finding themselves as the primary caretaker for their grandchildren; when grandparents are not available other relatives are filling that role, and, in still other cases, a nonrelative or foster parent is expected to fill that role. Thus, child in a nuclear family finds itself as common as child in a blended, remarried, step-, single-parent, grandparent, extended kin, adopted or foster family, and I am sure the list goes on. One outcome of this reality is, to twist a phrase from Christopher Lasch (1977), that the nuclear family is no longer the *only* haven in a heartless world. Rather, in this new millennium, the responsibility of the community in child-rearing has reasserted itself.

## Community Child-Rearing

Our functional definition of the family includes the phrase, "It is in the family and other institutions that children are raised, socialized, instilled with values, and protected" (Gullotta et al., 1986, pp. 5–6). Is this a cloaked reference to that now overused phrase, "It takes a village to raise a child?" Simply put, yes.

Interestingly, before the mythic rise of the nuclear family that blossomed with the start of the industrial revolution, family historians like Edward Shorter (1977) described the family as more community centered than family centered. Evidence for this position was found in townsfolk demonstrating outside a village home where community norms where violated or with European villagers halting family-arranged marriages.[1] With the transformation of Western society from an agrarian to an industrial society, from village to city life, from self-producing family unit to employee for others, the cult of domesticity emerged in the mid 19th century. Loving, faithful keep-the-house-spotless wife with adoring, well-behaved seen-but-not-heard children and faithful pet welcomed income-producing father home each night not from the field but from the factory to his home where in framed needlepoint hung the words "A man's home is his castle." This popular image of American family life continued to the Second World War when a cluster of factors like women entering the labor force to replace husbands off to war, highways that gave rise to suburbia and a slowly growing divorce rate that rocketed upward in the 1960s challenged males, homes and castles, in that order.[2]

With the historically recently emerged nuclear family morphing into single-parent, remarried (or, if you prefer, blended, reconstituted, merged), extended kin and other family variations, the expectations for socializing and moralizing offspring needed revamping. Each of the family theories previously mentioned offers a unique view of this revising process. To offer a few examples, structural functionalists would say that unable to undertake its duties (functions) successfully, alterations to the structure like dad taking on a child-rearing duty in a dual-worker family or additions to the structure like the creation of child-care centers develop. The symbolic interactionist would say that if the script (role) is too difficult to master then revisions occur expanding the roles of others like schools, churches and youth groups teaching social skills. The social exchange theorist would weigh the contribution of the family member—say, as an employee against the value of child-rearing. Depending on the values assigned to those behaviors, one behavior would be encouraged through incentives like increased pay or employer subsidized child care over the other.

To these theories, let me add the thinking of Hirschi (1969), who, in the midst of these changes, offered social control theory to explain the misbehavior of youth and reintroduced, theoretically at least, the community into this equation. In contrast to viewing the family as solely responsible for youthful indiscretions, Hirschi views youth misbehavior as the result of incomplete socialization and moralization. Poorly socialized youth feel no moral obligation to belong to the wider law-abiding society. Not attached, not committed, disbelieving, nay scornful, of the community around him or her, the young person acts out against that world. Fault for this misbehavior rests not only with the family but also with schools, churches, youth groups and neighbors who fail in their societal responsibility of socializing and moralizing this young person.

Today, this community responsibility extends beyond sharing duties of socializing and moralizing youth to other aspects of family life. But first, consider two brief moments in history. In 1630 the Massachusetts Bay Colony passed a law akin to the commandment that children should honor and obey their parents. The habitually disobedient child could be brought before the court and punished up to and including death (Bremner, Barnard, Hareven & Mennel, 1970).[3] Now fast forward to 1967, when the U.S. Supreme Court overturned the conviction of Francis Gault for a lewd and obscene phone call stating that Gault was denied his rights by the juvenile court acting in *parens patriae* and *loco parentis* (U.S. Supreme Court, 1967). Incidentally, that is the Bill of Rights, and this legal decision extends to youth—all youth—those rights for the first time. What are we to make of these two actions?

The first partially affirms the ancient common law that the child is the property of the parent. Why partially? Unlike Job, who apparently could attempt to sacrifice his son without legal recourse, only the community could authorize such an action in Massachusetts. In the second instance, the child no longer can be treated as property but must be treated as a person—a person with certain societal rights. More than any other, the Gault decision gives impetus to the fledging children's rights movement that shortly sees an expansion in child protective legislation. This and other acts redefine the relationship between parent and child and expand the responsibility of the community for the health, education and welfare of the child. With family definition in hand and a brief introduction to several family theories and one social psychological theory, let us briefly examine how psychology understands child behavior.

## PSYCHOLOGICAL THEORIES

Psychological explanations for child behavior can be grouped into four schools of thought (Parloff, 1977), with a fifth school recently added. The first derives from the work of Sigmund Freud (1935, 1949) and is called psychoanalysis or analytically oriented therapy. Freud built this theory on two instinctual urges (i.e., sex and death instincts), and a developmental process that begins at birth with the emergence of the id, at two the ego and at a somewhat later age possibly the superego. Concurrent with this personality evolution, all individuals experience three stages that shape the personality—the first at birth (oral), the second at roughly age 2 (anal) and the third shortly thereafter (Oedipal). For Freud (1949, p. 310), "the little human being is frequently a finished product in his fourth or fifth year, and only gradually reveals in later years what lies buried in him." Here, Freud is referencing the role of the ego's defense mechanisms in insulating the individual from the desire of the id expressed by the libido's (sexual energy) fixation. Freud (1949, p. 316) expresses dysfunctional behavior (neurosis) in the following formula:

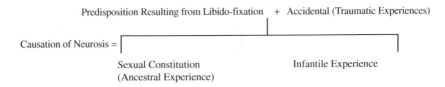

**Figure 1.1**   Freud's formula for expressing neurosis.

Thus, dysfunctional behavior results when one or more distressful (traumatic) experiences trigger earlier oral, anal or Oedipal experiences that were not successfully resolved before the "fourth or fifth year" of the child's life (Freud, p. 310).

The next school of thought draws from social learning theory and is referred to as behavioral therapy. Major contributers to this school of thought are Ivan Pavlov (classical conditioning), B. F. Skinner (operant conditioning), and Albert Bandura (cognitive behaviorism). Social learning theory can be expressed as, "What you see—is." To alter undesired behavior, "Change what you see to what you want to see." To continue or develop desired behavior, "Encourage what you see or want to see." The straightforwardness of this approach, which some consider mechanistic, has been softened with Bandura's (1977, 1986) work. He maintains that learning occurs as we model our behavior after others. Learning occurs as we observe the consequences of our behavior and that of others. Learning is environmental meaning that the reinforcement following a response will increase or decrease the probability of its reoccurrence. Last, we are active participants rather than passive recipients in this process, meaning that we partially control our environment by our reaction to it. Thus, dysfunctional behavior is the result of learning. Dysfunctional behaviors can be replaced with new socially acceptable (functional) behaviors.

The third school of thought developed by scholars like Charlotte Buhler, Abraham Maslow, and Carl Rogers draws not from instinctual urges or learned patterns of behavior. Rather, humanism emerges from a philosophical belief that humans are innately good and that, if given the right opportunity, goodness will emerge. Further, although instinct is not dismissed, attention focuses on the untapped capacity of the higher-functioning elements of the brain associated with empathy, generosity, reciprocity and kindness. In this model dysfunctional behavior is the result of the individual not realizing his or her potential as a human being. Thus, attention centers on self-acceptance, self-satisfaction and achieving one's inner potential. This client-centered discovery process results in that inner good emerging (Rogers, 1961).

Parloff (1977, p. 8) calls the fourth, but not last, school transpersonal therapy: It is "not content with the aim of integrating one's energies and expanding the awareness of oneself as an entity separate from the rest of the universe." Rather, the goal is to become one with the cosmos, to achieve a transcendental plane of awareness, to invoke powers beyond those of Western medicine for the healing process. With a growing awareness of medicine and philosophy from non-Western countries and with a corresponding increase in the U.S. population from the people of those nations, transpersonal approaches are on the increase.

Parolff's (1977) paper did not mention biological or psychopharmalogical approaches for treating problems in living. Though social biology was discussed earlier in this chapter, it is important to revisit genes and say hello to brain chemicals as our growing understanding of how both function have and will continue to change the methods used by helping professionals to ease the problems of livings discussed in this book.

## Genes

Genes are long strings of deoxyribose nucleic acid (DNA) that are the chemical building block of all living matter. Each gene contains a set of instructions that enables it to replicate one type of protein molecule. Proteins exist in thousands of variations. Incredibly, each protein has a specific function. Correctly assembled and working together, these proteins result in life. To get to that life, 23 pairs of chromosomes[4] (the egg) combine with 23 pairs of other chromosomes (the sperm) to result in a one-celled zygote that with time and under proper conditions develops into a fetus.

Some genes are called structural genes. A structural gene generally ignores the environment and performs its specific function of producing proteins or enzymes. A second gene that is sensitive to the environment is called a regulator gene. The activity of these genes can be widely influenced by a variety of factors including heat, exposure to heavy metals like lead, or viruses.

To understand how genes operate it might be useful to imagine each gene as a food recipe enabling signaling molecules to copy the ingredients and the step-by-step process to assemble and create new material. A flawed recipe—that is, flawed DNA—missing some vital information or providing misinformation is believed by some to explain behavioral and emotional problems. The question is whether this flaw is solely genetic or is genetic and environmental. Selectionists like Michael Gazzaniga (1992, p. 3) believe that all behavior is hardwired—that is, genetic: "For the selectionist, the absolute truth is that all we do in life is discover what is already built into our brains. While the environment may shape the way in which any given organism develops, it shapes it only as far as preexisting capacities in that organism allow. Thus, the environment selects from the built-in options; it does not modify them."

Representative of the interplay between environment and genes is the work of Robert Plomin (1990, 1994). Instructionists favor a dialogue between nature and nurture. For example, some human characteristics like height are highly inheritable. Of your height, 90% can be attributed to the genes you received from your parents. But other characteristics or behaviors do not have this effect on size. As Plomin states, "[Genetic research] provides the strongest available evidence for the importance of environmental influence. That is, twin and adoption studies usually find more than half the variance in behavioral development cannot be accounted for by genetic factors. For example, if identical twins are 40% concordant for schizophrenia, as recent studies suggest, no genetic explanation can account for the 60% discordance between these pairs of genetically identical individuals" (Plomin, 1994, p. 28).

To Plomin's example of schizophrenia, let me add this example. Some young people experience epilepsy to such an extent that it cannot be controlled through medication. To reduce the severity of damage to their brain, a heroic operation is performed to remove parts of the brain that are responsible for their seizures. Regrettably, this operation can result in damage to areas of the brain affecting speech, coordination and movement. If Gazzaniga (1992) is correct, then once these areas of the brain have been destroyed their function should be lost forever. Fortunately, that is not the case. Other parts of the brain appear to reprogram to imperfectly compensate for this loss. The younger the child, the greater the compensatory effect appears to be. The brain is malleable within certain parameters that diminish with age. This is further evidence that the environment matters from partially reconstructing a damaged brain to triggering the release of chemicals that determine behavior.

### Brain Chemicals and Behavior

How is chocolate like running or sex like a turkey sandwich? Each of these activities stimulates the release of brain chemicals that in some people bring pleasure. These and other actives like progressive relaxation, laughter, anger—in fact, any activity—produces brain chemicals like dopamine, norepinephrine, serotonin and others that influence our mood and behavior for good and bad.

This discovery has revolutionized the treatment of individuals with serious and not-so-serious mental health issues across the planet. From this perspective a chemical imbalance explains the behavior problem. Correct that imbalance, and the problem behavior, at least theoretically, disappears. This imbalance may be the result of solely genetic factors, solely environmental factors, or the interplay between the two.

Psychopharmacology and its interest in understanding brain functioning is an exciting and promising development in both the prevention and treatment of those with concerning behaviors. It is a field in its infancy with only a beginning understanding of the brain and the effects of drugs on the brain. This is especially true for children and adolescents, for whom virtually no evidence-based testing has occurred. This is in spite of the fact that these medications are prescribed for both.

Does the future of helping reside in a pill? Likely never. As the reader of this volume soon discovers, the human touch is essential to achieving the desired outcome of improved behavior. The human touch is capable of exciting the same neural pathways and chemical transmitters to encourage healthier behavior. Further, the issues chosen for examination in this volume are not solely intrapersonal but are interpersonal as well. That is, an event like childhood cancer, or removal from one home to live in another with different guardians, or acquiring a new adult figure in your life through the remarriage of a parent interacts with numerous other factors to result sometimes in a lessening of successful functioning or, as Thomas Szasz (1974, p. 1) once so eloquently stated, "problems in living."

## HOW THEORY INTERPRETS PROBLEMS IN LIVING IN TREATMENT

If there is a truism in mental health then it is that good helping behavior is undertaken intentionally. This means that the helping person conceptualizes the client's needs through a theoretical lens that interprets the problem in living and offers an approach to ease the discomfort, thereby enabling the person to return to a healthier state of functioning. This scientific approach works with some success in the arena of physical medicine because in some areas the theories of physical medicine have evolved beyond theory into law.

To illustrate, some infections are caused by invading small harmful bacterial organisms. If the body's immune system is unable to destroy or to learn quickly to tolerate these organisms, then that body expires as it did from the beginning of time till recently when antibiotic drugs were developed to destroy these pesky bacteria. A medical theory, appropriately enough called germ theory, led to a belief that evil bacteria caused illness. Repeated use of the intervention, this theory suggests, defined the parameters of the appropriate application of this theory to those little organisms.[5] Those repeated trials gathered evidence to sometimes support, at other times to refute, but always to refine this theory soon to become a law. In this discovery process, physicians learned that some bacteria are helpful and that other little pesky devils even smaller than bacteria existed. These devils called viruses can be just as deadly as bacteria but are immune to antibiotics. Thus, new interventions must be developed to treat viral infections and must be repeatedly tested to identify those that work, and protocols must be developed for their optimal effectiveness. By the way, this is the essence of evidence-based practice: From repeated use of an intervention derived from one or a combination of theories, identify those interventions that have the most success and eventually discard those that are worthless.

Unfortunately, not only have our colleagues in physical medicine been at this longer than we have in mental health, but also few serious mental health issues have markers as clearly discernable as those found in bacterial or viral infections.[6] Indeed, none of the issues examined in this volume have the genetic or biological markers that, say, pediatric autoimmune neuropsychiatric disorders associated with streptococcal infections (PANDAS) presents for obsessive compulsive disorder (OCD).[7] Thus, we are left with an interesting set of theoretical explanations from which therapeutic interventions are descended.

It is vital to understand that theories are not laws but assumptions, and these assumptions may or may not be correct. Further, there is no diagnostic condition known as remarried, adoptive, or single-parent family. These family arrangements and others, including the nuclear family, are part of complex ever-changing environments in which children can either prosper or languish at any given moment. What directs our attention to these family arrangements or other circumstances examined in this volume is a body of research and clinical observations suggesting that the members of these families are at increased risk for a problem in living that does carry a diagnostic code. What theory does is provide an explanation for that risk and suggest an intervention. If administered successfully, that intervention should produce improved functioning (better health).

For example, very young children are at high risk for physical abuse if cared for by the boyfriend of the biological mother. Why? Social biological theory suggests that these offspring present a barrier to reproducing with that mother by that boyfriend. As this theory goes, the removal of that child dissolves any past connection with a previous mate and enables the reproduction process to begin anew (Daly & Wilson, 1999). Of the family arrangements described in this volume, sexual assault is most likely to occur in a stepfamily. Why? Psychoanalytic theory suggests that the incest barrier that naturally exists in a biological family is missing in the stepfamily. In its absence, sexual activity is a possibility. As hostility creates such a barrier, psychoanalytic theory explains the anger (even hatred) by the child toward the stepmother or stepfather as the child's attempt to establish an incest barrier (Goldstein, 1974).

Children living with a single parent appear to become sexually active sooner than children living in a nuclear family with their biological parents. Social learning theory suggests that the child observes the parent dating behavior and all that it entails (e.g., grooming, new clothes, possibly a new persona and sexual activity with someone other than the previous partner). Seeing this behavior, the young person models the parent's dating behavior. Children living with a mentally ill parent are at risk for depression and other problem issues. Symbolic interactionism maintains that the role of a parent is to provide guidance and nurturance in a fair and consistent manner to off-spring. However, the seriously mentally ill parent frequently is unable to ful-fill this role and thus creates family turmoil if the family attaches importance to this unfilled role. Using the same circumstance from a general systems per-spective, it assumes the family undergoes a transformation process in which the mother's or father's inability to parent is determined (input in systems lan-guage). With this determination, the family engages in morphogenesis—that is, a family's search for or creation of new responses to that circumstance. Thus, if the mother or father because of illness cannot parent adequately, can another perform this vital need?

Children living in and out of home situations experience turmoil in their lives. Whether due to family circumstances, individual reasons or both, the young person not living at home is at risk for mental health issues. Note that the origin of these issues is not the new living situation. The new living situa-tion is a stage from which these problem issues may be seen. From a structural functionalist perspective the creation of this new living situation (struc-ture) is in response to the inability of the existing structure to adequately perform its function—that is, to care for the child according to the expecta-tions of the community. From this perspective, new structures like foster care evolve to undertake functions that others, in this case the family, perform inadequately.

From these brief examples, the reader can appreciate the multiple direc-tions a clinician might take in preparing a treatment plan in partnership with a child and his or her family. There is another way of conceptualizing these issues. Preventive interventions rest on stress theory.[8]

## PRIMARY PREVENTION: AN OVERVIEW

Primary prevention can be understood as the avoidance of illness and the promotion of health. Though it would be nice to stay healthy forever and for-ever well, the reality of that is not possible. So, let us set our sights simultane-ously on lowering the number of people who become ill in a population and improving their overall health status for a period of time. How long should that period of time be? A tetanus shot is good for 10 years; five years after can-cer treatment, a cancer-free individual is declared cured; a flu shot protects against some flu strains but not all for a mere four months. Might we say that a preventive intervention lasting for three years, in the words of my garage mechanic, "owes us nothing." That is, it worked and worked well to prevent illness and to promote health during that time. To accomplish this, primary prevention is group focused, encourages social support, is proactive in building new coping resources and adaptation skills and thus promotes emotional healthy people (Albee & Gullotta, 1986). Prevention is an active strategy willing to identify dysfunctional activities in institutions and on a societal level (Gullotta & Bloom, 2003). Finally, prevention activities are planned interventions that can be observed, recorded and evaluated for effectiveness (Cowen, 1982b; Klein & Goldston, 1977).

Prevention is not done to someone. Rather, prevention involves each of us as an active participant in preventing illness and promoting health not only for ourselves but for others as well. Recognizing the bio-psycho-social-environmental complexity of mental health problems, prevention takes the position that psychological states, social conditions and environmental circumstances are alterable. Further, although we may be unable today to reprogram that thin DNA thread, we can create supportive nurturing humane circumstances in which the script nature may have handed to us is altered. The theoretical framework to achieve this goal is stress theory.

## Stress Theory: A Model for Preventive Interventions

Unlike some of the other theories mentioned earlier, stress theory is family and person neutral. It is not a deficit within the person or family (e.g., bad genes, inadequate parenting, unresolved childhood experiences); rather, it is external and internal pressures that combine to precipitate a crisis that may be either of short or long duration.

Stress is any change in life (McCubbin, Cauble & Patterson, 1982). The life events that mark off the life cycle carry with them positive stress (eustress) and negative stress (distress). Life can be filled with boredom and a lack of challenge (hypostress), or it can be filled with excessive demands on time, labor and energy. These stressful situations mark transition points that, if coped with successfully, facilitate a healthier individual and family environment.

Understanding how stress affects organisms is credited to Cannon (1939) and Selye (1974). Selye's laboratory work with animals found that stress-producing agents called stressors create a reaction that he called the general adaptation syndrome. When stress exceeded some threshold, Seyle found, laboratory animals enter into a stage of alarm. During this stage the organism is on alert, calling on its defensive systems to combat the stressor. The period during which the body fights the noxious stressor is called the stage of resistance. If the body cannot defeat the noxious stressor, it enters the stage of exhaustion. Unable to overcome the damaging virus, bacterium or other adverse stimulus, the body surrenders to the stressor and dies.

## The ABCX Model

Although a number of models have drawn on the pioneering research of Cannon (1939) and Selye (1974), one of the most useful and elegant of these is Hill's (1949, 1958) ABCX paradigm. Intended to explain the behavior of families, it is just as applicable in explaining individual behavior. The letter A represents some event that brings discomfort, such as divorce, illness or removal from the home (e.g., foster care). B stands for the internal and external resources the individual can use to fight the discomfort. These can be wealth, close friendships, level of self-esteem, internal locus of control, coping abilities, spiritual belief, community involvement and so on. C is the meaning the individual attaches to the event. X is the crisis. Together A, B and C result in X. That is, the magnitude of the crisis, its duration, and the individual's level of reorganization after the crisis are determined by the sum of A (the event) + C (its meaning) – B (the available resources).

The second part of Hill's (1949, 1958) model predicts how individuals and families react in a crisis. The crisis (X) trips the individual and his or her family into a period of disorganization in which that child and family marshals their resources—those existing and those created in response to the event to meet the crisis. The angle of recovery reflects the time necessary for the child and family to find a solution to the crisis. The level of reorganization is the child and family's success in returning to a precrisis state.

## Functional and Dysfunctional Responses to Crisis

Some adaptations in response to a crisis are dysfunctional. For example, parental overuse of alcohol or other drugs may numb the pain associated with a seriously ill family member, but most of society would find unacceptable this means of coping with a family member's sickness. Most of us would judge it destructive to the parent, the ill family member and other family members.

Other adaptations can be considered functional. Using the same example, if that parent in that family turned to friends and other positive adult role models like the clergy for emotional support and found that support so that the relationship among these individuals were strengthened, most of us would judge this coping process leading to adaptation as constructive—that is, beneficial to the health of the individual and the family. Such constructive, or functional, methods of coping and adaptation in mental health are called primary prevention or, in lay terms, wellness.

## PREVENTION'S TECHNOLOGY

Prevention makes use of five technologies to prevent illness and to promote health. It should be noted that prevention is not done to us or for us. Rather, it requires us to accept responsibility for our health and that of others in society (Gullotta, 1987, 1994; Gullotta & Bloom, 2003). Prevention's tools are education, community organization, systems intervention, competency promotion and natural caregiving. No one tool will promote health or prevent illness. Rather, tools must be combined to create successful preventive interventions.

## Education

Education is the most widely used of prevention's five tools. The premise is that by increasing our knowledge we change attitudes and ultimately the behavior that does harm to oneself or another. Education can be used to ease the passage from one life event to another, and it can be provided to individuals to enhance their well-being. Education is the spoken word, a visual image and printed material. This information can take three forms.

The first of these forms is public information. This information excites, alerts and opens us to circumstances that can adversely affect our lives. For example, public service announcements about excessive alcohol consumption are attempts to enlighten the public and to promote healthier behavior in regards to this powerful drug. Education includes written material like this book that encourages individuals to take responsibility for their life while sharing with them the findings the social sciences can offer about individuals, relationships and the family. Here, the intention is to inform the reader not only to potential health hazards but to health-promoting activities as well. Public information includes DVDs, role plays, and group learning experiences that provide the learner with new or improved skills for managing life.

Research is clear on the point that humans want some warning about an event before it happens. The time between the warning and the actual occurrence permits us to gather emotional resources—Hill's (1949, 1958) B factor—to handle the event and to understand it within a personal context (Hill's C factor). Preventionists call the educational technique that builds these resources anticipatory guidance. Anticipatory guidance can be as simple as a booklet that explains an upcoming life event, like "Caring About Kids" by the National Institute of Mental Health (NIMH), which explains divorce to young children, or it may involve a mixture of print, film and lecture material, like that used by health organizations to explain health procedures to young children undergoing treatment for cancer and other health issues.

Some educational approaches use behavioral techniques to promote increased self-awareness. This includes approaches such as biofeedback, progressive relaxation and Eastern meditation philosophies. These techniques provide informational feedback that enables individuals to manage stress, to control certain bodily functions and to relieve pain.

Finally, readers should understand that although education is the most commonly used of prevention's tools, it is also the weakest. Studies have repeatedly shown that educational approaches increase knowledge, occasionally alter attitudes, but rarely change behavior (Durlak, 2003). It is when education is combined with each of the following technologies that its effectiveness increases. The importance of this last statement cannot be more strongly stated. Used together, prevention's technology can reduce the incidence of illness and promote health. Used separately, the effectiveness of prevention's technology diminishes dramatically.

## Systems Intervention

Consider the following: Institutions are dysfunctional, rules are made to be broken and open institutions are healthier than closed institutions. Recall if you will social exchange theory, and remember that in that theory everything costs something. There is no action that is universally benevolent. Every decision will result in some profiting and others losing. Now in a card game without stakes among friends this might matter for little, but as the stakes grow being on the losing side can be problematic.

If one is a child with cancer in a hospital with practices that increase the child's fear and reluctance to undergo lifesaving treatment, the costs are unacceptable, as Ciporah Tadmor (2003, p. 816) describes for children with leukemia:

> [Imagine a respected leading medical center, where] children with leukemia were not aware of their diagnosis, the chemotherapy protocol, or its side effects.... Frightened children of all ages waited in a long, narrow

corridor with adult patients.... At every clinic appointment, a different nurse treated the child.... Invasive medical procedures ... were performed without premedication. ... The parents waited outside the door, listening to their child screaming, feeling helpless, guilty, and desperate. Some parents reported that their children woke up in the middle of the night screaming, as waking from a nightmare.

The prevention tool of systems change sees this institutional behavior as dysfunctional, unacceptable and needing change, as Tadmor brought to that oncology department: change to help children anticipate the treatment, to have control to the extent that is possible over the treatment, to wait in a child-friendly area for the treatment and to invite direct involvement of parents during the medical procedure. These changes focused not on the client's mental health status but on the hospital's dysfunctional behavior toward the client. Changes in the institution's behavior produced positive changes in the children and families undergoing this painful but necessary treatment.

Institutions exist not for themselves but to serve the needs for which they were established. Rules, though necessary, should be administered carefully and should ensure flexible decision making so that care is administered in a respectful and health-promoting manner. Exceptions are good practice. The involvement of families in the creation of the treatment program for their child encourages higher compliance and better outcomes. This reality has led to the "Systems of Care" movement in the United States. It is a recognition that bad institutional decisions are made in isolation. Better decisions result from a process in which openness prevails.

## Community Organization

The phrase *social capital* is synonymous with the prevention technology of community organization. Individuals invested in their community live in neighborhoods, towns and cities that are cleaner, are lower in crime and are healthier. To be invested in one's community means to be invested in the welfare of one's neighbor or, to steal a phrase from Putnam (2000), it is not "Bowling Alone." The ability to live a healthy life is at times obstructed by irrational beliefs and flawed practices in the community and society in which one lives. Where obstructions exist because of societal factors, individuals can work to modify or remove those barriers. This prevention tool is focused on achieving a more equitable distribution of equality of opportunity to improve the standard of living of a group of people within a community. Vocal, active, well-attended neighborhood associations, civic clubs, community groups like the parent–teacher association (PTA), or child sport leagues and 4H organizations that behave in a civil manner are examples of activities in vibrant healthy communities.

Another example is legislative or judicial action. This is the most controversial of prevention's tools because it involves a change in the balance of political power in the direction of politically enfranchising the weak or correcting legislative injustice against them. If one of the keys to explaining dysfunction is a lack of power, then organizing and mobilizing a group for the purposes of acquiring power in a free are necessary and legitimate functions of prevention activity. Initiatives undertaken by the American Civil Liberties Union, Mothers Against Drunk Drivers, Mothers of Murdered Sons, and the

National Association for the Advancement of Colored People provide examples of such action. These organizations are attempting through legislative and judicial means, to put teeth into the phrase equality of opportunity. Court and legislative activities like the equalization of per-pupil school expenditures, mental health parity legislation, and the increased regulation of the sale of handguns illustrate possible activities in this area.

## Competency Promotion

To belong, to be valued, to make a meaningful contribution to your group—that is the essence of social competency (Gullotta, 1990). Activities that promote competency lead to a feeling of being a part of, rather that apart from, society. They encourage feelings of worth, care for others and belief in oneself. Encouraging such pride promotes self-esteem, an internal locus of control and community-interested rather than self-interested citizens. Activities that promote the development of social and emotional learning, that teach assertiveness training and that encourage respect for oneself and others nurture interpersonal and community relationships or, as Hill (1958) would state, the B factor of personal resources.

## Social Support

Hardly an issue exists that adults and youth do not turn to friends or others (e.g., coaches, teachers, youth leaders, the parents of friends, the clergy) for advice and guidance before professionals. Natural caregiving recognizes the ability within each of us to help a fellow human being. Natural caregiving extends beyond activities like those of helping another in similar straits (mutual self-help groups) to acknowledge the responsibility each of us has to fellow human beings (Cowen, 1982a). Natural caregiving involves behavior such as the sharing of knowledge, the sharing of experiences, compassionate understanding, companionship and, when necessary, confrontation. Such caregiving is a reference point for people to acknowledge that they are an important part of an emotional network (system) that extends beyond family members and friends to all people.

Some of us may choose professions in which we become trained indigenous caregivers, such as teachers and the clergy. Others of us will sometime in our lives join a mutual self-help group to give and receive help from others who find themselves in similar straits—for example, Alateen. Regardless of the circumstance, it is vital to remember that each of us is an indigenous caregiver with a responsibility to assist his or her fellow human beings.

## CONCLUSION

Like the Flash Gordon movie serial of our parents' childhood, this chapter concludes with observing that family form can take a variety of shapes. Its responsibilities remain unaltered but occur in a time when society has redeclared an active interest in the ability of the family to successfully undertake those functions. A variety of theoretical models offer a multitude of perspectives to explain behavior. Although all are useful, none are necessarily true in any given circumstance. Finally, it is possible to promote health and to prevent illness within a population. The technology, when used as a whole to achieve the objective of healthier behavior, exists. It remains for us to use it to fashion a healthier environment for children and their families.

## ENDNOTES

1. Now you know the origin of that part of the marriage ceremony that asks if anyone present wishing to oppose the union of these two people speak now or forever hold your peace.
2. The popular media chose not to focus on African American families in which the mother was as important a wage earner as the father.
3. It should be noted that Massachusetts was not the only colony to pass such legislation and that although young people were punished by fines and whippings no child was ever put to death under this statute.
4. These are rod-like structures that carry the genes.
5. That intervention is the use of antibiotics.
6. Before one goes off believing that physical medicine is vastly superior to mental health, recall that for hundreds of years Galen's four humors (blood, phlegm, yellow bile and black bile) dominated medical thinking much to the chagrin of the purged, bled, blistered and evacuated patient.
7. PANDAS is a specific form of OCD behavior caused by a streptococci infection (Bessette, 2005).
8. I would be remiss not to note that stress theory increasingly is finding its way into the clinician's conceptualization of the problem issue and is used to address that issue.

## REFERENCES

Albee, G. W. & Gullotta, T. P. (1986). Facts and fallacies about primary prevention. *Journal of Primary Prevention, 6,* 207–218.

Bandura, A. (1977). *Social learning theory.* Englewood Cliffs, NJ: Prentice-Hall.

Bandura, A. (1986). *Social foundations of thought and action: A social cognitive theory.* Englewood Cliffs, NJ: Prentice-Hall.

Bessette, A. P. (2005). Obessive compulsive disorder. In T. P. Gullotta and G. R. Adams (Eds.), *Handbook of adolescent behavioral problems: Evidence-based approaches to prevention and treatment* (pp. 255–282). New York: Springer.

Bremner, R. H., Barnard, J., Hareven, T. K. & Mennel, R. M. (1970). *Children and youth in America,* vol. 1. Cambridge, MA: Harvard University Press.

Cannon, W. B. (1939). *The wisdom of the body.* New York: W.W. Norton.

Cowen, E. L. (1982a). Help is where you find it: Four informal helping groups. *American Psychologist, 37,* 385–395.

Cowen, E. L. (1982b). Primary prevention research: Barriers, needs, and opportunities. *Journal of Primary Prevention, 2,* 131–137.

Daly, M. & Wilson, M. (1999). *The truth about Cinderella: A Darwinian view of parental love.* New Haven, CT: Yale University Press.

Dawkins, R. (1976). The selfish gene. New York: Oxford University Press.

Demos, J. (1970). *A little commonwealth: Family life in Plymouth colony.* New York: Oxford University Press.

Durlak, J. A. (2003). Effective prevention and health promotion programming. In T. P. Gullotta and M. Bloom (Eds.), *Encyclopedia of primary prevention and health promotion* (pp. 61–68). New York: Kluwer/Academic Press.

Fields, J. (2003). *Children's living arrangements and characteristics: March 2002* (Current Population Reports, pp. 20–547). Washington, DC: US Census Bureau.

Fields, J. (2004). *America's families and living arrangements: 2003* (Current Population Reports, pp. 20–553). Washington, DC: US Census Bureau.

Freud, S. (1935). *An autobiographical study.* London, England: Hogarth Press.

Freud, S. (1949). *A general introduction to psychoanalysis.* New York: Perma Giants. (Original work published 1920)

Gazzaniga, M. S. (1992). *Nature's mind: The biological roots of thinking, emotions, sexuality, language, and intelligence.* New York: Basic Books.

Goldstein, H. S. (1974). Reconstituted families: The second marriage and its children. *Psychiatric Quarterly, 48,* 433–440.

Gullotta, T. P. (1987). Prevention's technology. *Journal of Primary Prevention, 7,* 176–196.

Gullotta, T. P. (1990). Preface. In T. P. Gullotta, G. R. Adams & R. Montemayor (Eds.), *Developing social competency in adolescence* (pp. 7–8). Newbury Park, CA: Sage.

Gullotta, T. P. (1994). The what, who, why, where, when, and how of primary prevention. *Journal of Primary Prevention, 15,* 5–14.

Gullotta, T. P., Adams, G. R. & Alexander, S. (1986). *Today's marriages and families: A wellness approach.* Monterey, CA: Brooks/Cole.

Gullotta, T. P. & Bloom, M. (2003). Primary prevention at the beginning of the 21st century. In T. P. Gullotta and M. Bloom (Eds.). *Encyclopedia of primary prevention and health promotion* (pp. 116–120). New York: Kluwer Academic.

Hill, R. (1949). *Families under stress.* New York: Harper & Row.

Hill, R. (1958). Social stresses on the family. *Social Casework, 34,* 139–150.

Hirschi, T. (1969). *Causes of delinquency.* Berkeley: University of California Press.

Lasch, C. (1977). *Haven in a heartless world.* New York: Basic Books.

Klein, D. C. & Goldston, S. E. (Eds.) (1977). *Primary prevention: An idea whose time has come* (National Institute of Mental Health ADM 77-447). Washington, DC: U.S. Government Printing Office.

McCubbin, H. I., Cauble, A. E. & Patterson, J. M. (1982). *Family stress, coping, and social support.* Springfield, IL: Charles C. Thomas.

Parloff, M. B. (1977). Shopping for the right therapy (National Institute of Mental Health, DHEW Pub No. ADM 77-426). Washington, DC: U.S. Government Printing Office.

Parsons, T. (1949). *Essays in sociological theory: Pure and applied.* New York: Free Press.

Plomin, R. (1990). *Nature and nurture.* Pacific Grove, CA: Brooks/Cole.

Plomin, R. (1994). *Genetics and experience.* Thousand Oaks, CA: Sage.

Putnam, R. D. (2000). Bowling alone. New York: Simon & Schuster.

Rogers, C. R. (1961). *On becoming a person.* Boston: Houghton Mifflin.

Selye, H. (1974). History and present status of the stress concept. In L. Goldberger & S. Breznitz (Eds.), *Handbook of stress* (pp. 7–20). New York: Free Press.

Shorter, E. (1977). *The making of the modern family.* New York: Basic Books.

Szasz, T. (1974). *The myth of mental illness.* NY: Harper.

Tadmor, C. S. (2003). Perceived personal control. In T. P. Gullotta and M. Bloom (Eds.), *Encyclopedia of primary prevention and health promotion* (pp. 812–820). New York: Kluwer/Academic Press.

U.S. Bureau of the Census (1975). *Historical statistics of the United States colonial times to 1970: Bicentennial edition part 2.* Washington, DC: U.S. Government Printing Office.

U.S. Supreme Court (1967). Re Gault. May 15, 1967. Washington, DC.

Wilson, E. O. (1978). *On human nature.* Cambridge, MA: Harvard University Press.

# 2

# Childhood Growth and Development within a Family Context

**KRISTIN N. WILLIAMS-WASHINGTON,
JOANNA MELON AND GARY M. BLAU**

## INTRODUCTION

There are numerous factors that impact child development, but the most important is the influence of families. Family influence is widely interpreted as parents or caregivers instilling their values onto their child, whether purposefully or unintentionally. However, as children develop, this dynamic becomes reciprocal.

Although child development is heavily weighted on the contribution by parents and caregivers, children play an active role in their development. As parents and caregivers communicate certain values to their children, children incorporate this new information with their own existing values. Children do not merely absorb information presented by their parents; rather, they integrate it into their already existing body of knowledge (Bush & Peterson, 2008).

As children develop, their moral schema increasingly becomes their own interpretation of their social environment and less that of a parent or caregiver. Depending on the age of the child, a direct correlation between parental influence and certain child development outcomes can be made. The older the child, the more influence the child may possess over his or her social environment and the less influence the parent or caregiver may contribute. The opposite is true of younger children, especially infants, as parents and caregivers influence nearly all stimuli encountered. The child at this point is much like a sponge and absorbs all information presented. As a child moves from infancy to early childhood, parents impart their views and means of existing upon their child. The child then integrates these views to fit his or her expanding world. A child becomes more proactive in his or her development particularly during the school-age years when his or her world expands beyond the home and family to include school and peers.

When children become adolescents, they receive further external stimuli that may conflict with the previously accepted views of their parents. Familial conflicts may arise between parents or caregivers and the developing adolescent. Thus, for the parent–child dyad to persist, it becomes a necessity

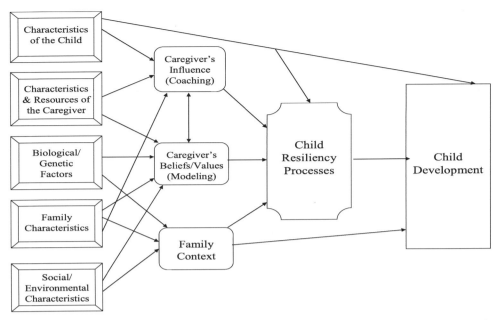

**Figure 2.1**   Model of familial socialization of child development. This figure has been adapted from a theoretical model of the socialization of coping by Kliewer, et al. (2006).

for both parties to be willing to coexist along a developmental continuum, both acknowledging that from time to time they may have opposing views and that compromise may be necessary. The many facets of child development are depicted in Figure 2.1.

Although not tested within the context of child development, there are reasons to believe the model would apply. Research supports the many mediating factors of the model and indicates that all aspects contribute to positive or negative outcomes in child development. The main factors in a child's development are characteristics of the child, characteristics and resources of the caregiver, biological and genetic factors, social and environmental characteristics and family characteristics.

These bio-psycho-social-environmental factors provide a foundation for a child's development, which are further influenced by factors such as caregiver coaching, modeling and the wider family context. Coaching refers to explicit suggestions made by parents and caregivers regarding thinking, believing and feeling about specific situations. Modeling is the manner in which parents and caregivers respond to certain stimuli and the child or adolescent then imitates. The family context is the way the family operates and fills the specific roles as a cohesive unit.

The bilateral arrows in Figure 2.1 between caregiver's influence and caregiver's values exist because caregivers model their beliefs and coach those beliefs to their children through their influence and vice versa. If all factors operate in a protective and prosocial manner, the child's development likely will be positive and successful. However, if many problems exist, the child's development may be impacted negatively.

This chapter provides an overview of risk and protective factors with those contextual and family factors that are integral in child development.

## RISK AND PROTECTIVE FACTORS

As children move through the stages of development, their genetic, physical and emotional identities change. As this occurs, different physical, environmental and emotional factors may become risk factors. These factors increase the possibility of adverse development. As a result, there may be an increased chance of undesirable genes expression. On the contrary, other bio-psycho-social-environmental factors may serve as protective factors and may impede the expression of undesirable genes. Table 2.1 demonstrates risk and protective factors that may occur in different aspects of development.

It is important to note that these risk and protective factors are not always indicative of a positive correlation with respect to developmental outcomes and that results may vary. For example, siblings can be raised in the same envi-

**Table 2.1**    Risk and Protective Factors in Child Development

| Physical Development | | Cognitive Development | | Socioemotional Development | |
|---|---|---|---|---|---|
| Risk Factors | Protective Factors | Risk Factors | Protective Factors | Risk Factors | Protective Factors |
| Prenatal viral infection | Prenatal care | Low socioeconomic status | High IQ | Poor parent–child bond; insecure attachment | Close and secure attachment to parent or caregiver |
| Prenatal exposure to harmful substances (e.g., drugs and alcohol) | Proper diet | Low maternal education | Effective parenting | | |
| Malnutrition | Enriched environment | Single-parent household | High self-esteem | Poor coping and emotion regulatory skills | Internal locus of control |
| Premature birth | Routine medical care | Maternal mental health illness (e.g., anxiety and disorder) | Secure socioeconomic status | Attention deficits | Effective parenting |
| Low birth weight | Secure socioeconomic status | Premature birth | Social supports | Low birth weight | Strong religious identity |
| Early or late onset of puberty | Social supports | Suffer from pervasive learning or developmental disorders | | Marital discord | High Self-esteem |
| Aberrant physical development or maturation | High self-esteem | Poor parenting skills | | Poor temperament | Secure socioeconomic status |
| | | | | | Social supports |

*Source:* Adapted from de Voursney, D., Mannix, D., Brounstein, P. and Blau, G. M., in T. P. Gullotta & G. M. Blau (Eds.), *Handbook of childhood behavioral issues: Evidence-based approaches to prevention and treatment,* New York: Routledge Press, 2008 (with permission).

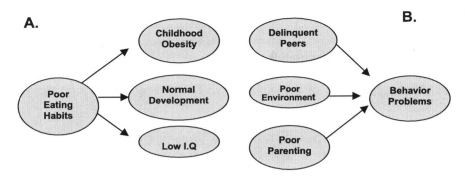

**Figure 2.2** Multifinality versus Equifinality in Childhood Development. A. represents the concept of multifinality. B. represents the concept of equifinality.

ronment and have similar genetic coding, but only one of them may develop behavioral problems. This concept is known as multifinality. Simply put, multifinality is one pathway that may lead to different outcomes (Cicchetti, 2006). On the other hand, two children who are not related and are raised in different environments can both have the same outcome. This is equifinality. Equifinality refers to multiple pathways leading to the same results (ibid.). Figure 2.2 demonstrates the concepts of multifinality and equifinality.

## BIOLOGY AND GENETICS

A prevailing controversy has persisted within the realm of psychology: Which is the biggest contributor to development, nature or nurture? Does a person's genetic make-up define who he or she is? Genes are the building blocks of every human being. For example, a person's genes dictates to a large extent his or her eye color, height and weight. In addition, certain disorders, both physical and emotional, have been linked to genetic mutations. However, this is not to say that genes dictate every aspect of a person's development. In most circumstances genetic expression is the result of a combination of influences.

A person's genetic make-up is constructed at the moment of conception. When a woman's egg is fertilized the X chromosome pairs with the male's X or Y chromosome to form a zygote. This zygote has a total of 46 chromosomes (23 from the mother and 23 from the father), each containing thousands of genes. Each of these genes makes up a person's genotype (de Voursney, Mannix, Brounstein & Blau, 2008). However, genes are only one part of the puzzle. A cyclical relationship exists between a person's genotype and his or her environment, in that both a person's environment and his or her experiences affect genetic expression (Perry, 2002). In turn, the genes that are expressed affect how people interact with their environment and respond to their experiences. The physical expression of genes is referred to as a person's phenotype (de Voursney et al., 2008). Genetic factors interact with risk and protective factors at every stage of development from the fetus in the womb to the infant at birth through and beyond adolescence. At or around the time of birth, the brain is initially mapped and cells are in their appropriate place. This initial prenatal hardwiring provides the foundation for brain development; however, development is far from complete at this time. Nearly two thirds of the brain's cortex develops during postnatal development, and many of the brain's

structures are malleable into adulthood (de Voursney et al., 2008). Some structures, such as the hippocampus, retain their plasticity across the life span
(Cicchetti & Walker, 2001). However, because the foundation for brain development is essentially laid out during gestation, the prenatal environment plays a
vital role in the future of brain development. During this time the developing
fetus may be exposed to an array of toxic risk factors including lack of nutri-
ents or harmful substances such as drugs and alcohol that can impede and
have detrimental effects on development (de Voursney et al., 2008).

Following birth, an infant's brain seeks all the stimuli present in his or her
environment. Research suggests that an enriched environment is extremely
beneficial in stimulating brain development. Toys made for children ages birth
to three are often rich in color and require tasks, such as pressing buttons or
placing shapes in appropriate places to stimulate coordination. Additionally,
aspects of physical development (e.g., learning to crawl and walk) also facilitate brain development (de Voursney et al., 2008). On the contrary, a harmful
environment may have adverse effects on brain development. For example,
the habitual presence of stress may have adverse effects on the brain and may
alter structures such as the hippocampus (Bremner, 2006; Carrion, Weems &
Reiss, 2007; Fletcher, 2003).

In terms of size, the brain is nearly fully developed by age six. However,
the density and structure of brain development is ongoing throughout adolescence and into adulthood (Giedd, interview with *Frontline PBS*, retrieved
June 1, 2007). With puberty the brain undergoes further change. The release of
sex hormones activates the appearance of secondary sex characteristics, such
as body hair and breast development. Other changes such as the growth spurt,
the deepening of the voice for males and the widening of hips for females
occur. The onset of puberty varies from adolescent to adolescent and may be
genetically determined (de Voursney et al., 2008; Sisk & Foster, 2004).

During the years of puberty, the electrochemical connections (Carlson,
2002; Kolb & Whishaw, 2003) responsible for processing and relaying information mature, and the formation of the frontal lobe, which is responsible for
complex thought, fully develops (Giedd, 2004). Up to this point, the brain has
an abundance of cells. Beginning in adolescence, the brain starts pruning,
a process hypothesized to trim the cells that are not used by the individual
(ibid.).

Recent research focuses on how brain development during adolescence
affects youths' ability to make decisions, to learn and to engage in other
activities (Reyna & Farley, 2006). Additionally, the use of magnetic resonance
imaging studies allows researchers to better map the areas of the brain and to
outline key areas associated with specific functions. Other areas of research
now focus closely on the genetic aspects of mental health disorders by using
family, twin and molecular genetic studies (Barkley, 2003). For example, the
Autism Genome Project (AGP) is an ongoing study designed to examine the
genes associated with the onset of autism spectrum disorder (Autism Speaks,
Inc., 2007), a pervasive developmental disorder. Since the launch of AGP,
researchers have linked possible causes of autism to specific chromosomes
and have begun to closely examine heritability factors (ibid.). Likewise, there
are possible genetic factors related to the onset of other mental health disorders. Research points to genetic involvement with attention deficit hyperactivity disorder (ADHD) (Biederman & Faraone, 2005; Price et al., 2005),

schizophrenia (Sullivan, Kendler & Neale, 2003; Tsuang, Stone & Faraone, 2001; Van't Ent et al., 2007), bipolar disorder (Smoller & Finn, 2003) and separation anxiety disorder (Cronk, Slutske, Madden, Bucholz & Heath, 2004).

## ENVIRONMENTAL FACTORS

Five major realms of environmental factors may influence child development:

1. The prenatal environment
2. The physical environment
3. The learning environment
4. The emotional environment
5. The social or cultural environment

Though not all of these environments are experienced simultaneously, overlap does exist in the way one environment affects another. For example, a person's physical environment (e.g., neighborhood) has a great effect on his or her social environment (e.g., peers). Regardless of the level of intermingling between environments, each plays an integral role in shaping the child's current and future well-being and functioning.

### Prenatal Environment

The prenatal environment is the first contextual factor encountered and thus serves as the impetus for a child's development. When considering the prenatal environment, two main types of environmental conditions need to be considered: maternal characteristics and external harmful agents. Maternal characteristics include conceiving under the age of 17 (Jolly, Sebire, Harris, Robinson & Regan, 2000) or over the age of 35 (Fretts, Schmittdiel, McLean, Usher & Goldman, 1995), as this increases the possibility of a failure to carry the unborn child to full term or the possibility of birth complications. Furthermore, an inadequate diet and the presence of diseases, conditions or toxic substances also increases risk and alters developmental processes.

External harmful agents such as chemicals, drugs, radiation and viruses have a negative impact on prenatal development. Harmful agents of this kind are known as teratogens. Exposure to teratogens cause birth defects such as mental retardation, heart defects, brain damage, cancer, spina bifida and low birth weight or increase the risk of negative developmental outcomes of the unborn child. Specific causes and outcomes of exposure to teratogens include the following:

- Lead-based paint may lead to mental retardation.
- Smoking may lead to a lack of oxygen, low birth weight and problems with brain development.
- Alcohol use may lead to fetal alcohol syndrome, problems with learning and memory during adolescence and a correlation with ADHD.
- Cocaine use may lead to miscarriage or infant drug withdrawal.
- Maternal diabetes may lead to cardiac defects and spine and limb abnormalities.

This list is in no way exhaustive of all possible teratogens. Rather, it serves as a brief overview of common teratogens encountered. To prevent harm to an unborn child, it is recommended that all teratogens be avoided. For teratogens that cannot be avoided (e.g., maternal diabetes), close monitoring with a doctor during pregnancy is suggested.

## Physical and Learning Environments

Successful development relies on the basic needs to support and sustain life; among these, an environment that is conducive to positive outcomes is instrumental. Environmental risk factors and their accompanying effects are closely linked to social and economic conditions. Thus, specific attention is paid to those factors surrounding socioeconomic status (SES), such as income, neighborhood and homeownership, and the impact each has on a child's physical and cognitive development.

Socioeconomic status typically encompasses family income, parental education and occupational status (Bradley & Corwyn, 2002). SES is a contributing factor to child development outcomes that is often exhibited in the impact of SES on parents and its expression within the family dynamic (Bush & Peterson, 2008). The stress of raising a family under low SES standards is thought to negatively affect the mental health and behavior of parents and, in return, to be detrimental to a child's well-being (Gershoff, Aber, Raver & Lennon, 2007).

Parents with higher SES levels are able to provide their children with additional opportunities, thus increasing the likelihood for positive development. In contrast, parents with lower SES levels are less equipped financially to provide additional pathways that may increase the chances for positive developmental outcomes for their children. For example, poverty is related to increased neonatal and postnatal mortality rates. Being poor increases the possibility of injuries due to accidents, physical abuse or neglect and heightens the risk of acquiring asthma (Aber, Bennett, Conley & Li, 1997).

Leventhal and Brooks-Gunn (2000) researched the beneficial effect of high SES on young children's intelligence quotient (IQ), verbal ability, and reading recognition scores, finding that lower SES hinders these abilities, due to a lack of exposure. Hoff (2003) reported that maternal speech that differed as a function of SES is a cause for variance in early vocabulary development. The higher the SES generally indicates that the mother will have a larger vocabulary, which predicts positive child developmental outcomes.

The same results have been found true when neighborhood is considered in terms of SES and child development outcomes: the higher the neighborhood SES, the greater the association with adolescent achievement. Homeownership has also been found to be associated with lower levels of child problem behavior (Boyle, 2002). Thus, environmental factors, particularly those related to living in poverty, increase the risk for childhood behavior issues (Halpern & Figueiras, 2004).

## Emotional Environment

Much has been written about ways children develop emotionally. Sigmund Freud, Erik Erikson, Jean Piaget and others have posited that children advance through various stages of development and that within each stage a child's ability to manage and regulate emotions becomes solidified (Gullotta, 2008).

Erikson's psychosocial model provides a useful framework from which to understand the interaction between a person and his or her environment, and in particular the way a child develops within a social and familial context.

Erikson originally hypothesized eight stages of development that begin in infancy and end in late adulthood. In each stage the individual confronts a specific challenge; for example, in infancy the challenge is whether or not the child develops trust or mistrust of the environment, and between the ages of 1 and 3 the challenge is whether the child develops autonomy versus the development of shame and doubt (Rosenthal, Gurney, & Moore, 1981). Later challenges involve the development of initiative, industry and identity.

Central to these ideas is that the emotional life of children develops early in life and is heavily influenced by families and caregivers. Lieberman (1995) and Spock (2001) did much to popularize this notion. In fact, consistent with Erikson, these authors wrote that an important component for positive emotional development is a nurturing family environment in which a child is allowed to achieve autonomy and to develop a personal identity. Autonomy is the ability for an individual to function independently in an emotionally supported environment.

Autonomy is acquired as a child develops and begins to integrate external information into his or her world and form an identity. A child's personal identity begins to form once he or she is permitted to gradually express autonomy and individuality through means that are tolerated or supported by his or her parents or caregivers. For example, one's identity is expressed through the type of music listened to or what one watches on television. As children age in a nurturing environment, they are encouraged to be more of an individual than just products of their familial structure.

A positive emotional environment is effective for establishing autonomy and personal identity, thus providing the ability for a child to successfully complete one stage of development and transition to the next. The ability to have autonomy and to exist as an individual strengthens protective factors and increases a child's coping skills through fostering a healthy self-perception that is reinforced and encouraged by the family dynamic.

## Social and Cultural Environment

As children age, they move from simply absorbing their environment to taking on a more interactive role. Children become more aware of their surroundings and learn how to extract resources and to communicate. As a result, various social factors such as the family's religious beliefs, culture and peer relationships play an integral part in childhood development.

As children grow, they become more active in defining their environment and themselves. From birth, children learn to interact with their world, crying in different ways to indicate the need to be fed or changed. As children progress, they learn to communicate with the use of eye movement, pointing and eventually using words. Throughout the preschool years a child's social environment is somewhat limited, because parents and caregivers mostly control environmental factors, save for those encountered if a child attends a child-care facility. Children absorb the information their parents or caregivers provide and integrate this information into their own worldview (Bush & Peterson, 2008). As development continues, more factors contribute to their identity. For example, children begin to identify themselves by their gender and their role within the family (e.g., child, brother, sister). Additionally, their religious and cultural identity begins to take effect. These new identities can be positive contributions to healthy development. For example, research suggests that religious identity promoted constructive childhood development and that there is a positive relationship between religious identity and perceptions of one's self such as personality and meaning in life (Furrow, King & White, 2004).

Once children enter school, their social system expands to include peer groups, other adult authority figures and an altogether different environment. Identities are further solidified through friendship formation and an expansion of information from sources such as television and the Internet. During this time, children transition from integrating information into their definition of the world to deciphering which information to accept or reject. In addition, firm opinions about likes and dislikes develop.

The manner by which children develop likes and dislikes is culturally influenced. Children learn how to communicate and act in a manner that is acceptable to their given culture. For example, there are implications depending on whether a child is raised in an African American, Asian, Latino or American Indian culture, as each of these has distinct norms and traditions. Culture has been conceptualized as a developmental niche in which children acquire knowledge and skills. This developmental niche includes both the physical, social and cultural and emotional features of the child's setting, the nature of the community and child-rearing customs and the caregiver's beliefs about child development (Cole, Bruschi & Tamang, 2002; Super & Harkness, 1993). Thus, cultural characteristics serve to shape child developmental outcomes.

A potentially troublesome gap between individualist and collectivist cultures exists. In individualist cultures, individual uniqueness is valued, whereas in collectivist cultures, people are expected to identify with and work well in groups that often protect them in exchange for loyalty and compliance. For example, in Asian societies anger is discouraged because it is seen as threatening to authority and relationship harmony (Barrett, 1995; Cole et al., 2002). In contrast, in the United States the development of individuality, autonomy and self-expression in children is highly regarded (Chao, 1995; Cole et al., 2002).

Potential conflict arises when children act in a manner that is acceptable in their native culture but not in the nonnative culture (Mejia-Arauz, Rogoff, Dexter & Najafi, 2007). If one cultural background has been deemed as the preferred, the participation of individuals from other cultural backgrounds may be excluded due to unfamiliarity or unwillingness to conform.

## FAMILY SYSTEM

Today, the traditional nuclear family composed of biological parents and their biological offspring is no longer the primary family system. Stepparents, adoptive parents, foster parents, grandparents and others also are family systems. However, what has remained constant is the role of children as members within these family systems.

Family systems theory suggests that members of a family are all believed to be operating under one system—that of the family—and the role of the individual is deemphasized (Bowen, 1978). The concept of a family system can be better understood through the notion of a mobile. Congruent with general systems theory, when any part of a mobile is moved, the other parts will also move. In regard to a family system, any action taken on behalf of one member will affect the entire family system.

The notion of a family system is one in which members of a family are interpreted not as exclusive on one another but rather as a combined unit related to each other by some means of interdependence. Family systems interact in cyclical patterns that serve to maintain equilibrium within the family structure and to provide insight into their specific way of functioning. The manner in which a family functions is determined by the boundaries expressed, be they open or closed. An open boundary allows external stimuli to affect their day-to-day functioning. A closed boundary attempts to isolate its members from environmental factors. Family systems do not operate in solely a closed or open boundary system. Instead, behavior occurs along a continuum where both concepts function as required.

Family systems are usually broken down into subsystems in which individuals within the same subsystem form alliances. An example of this can be interpreted as parents forming a united front about a particular issue with the children or children within the same family unit sticking together to avoid getting into trouble. Specific characteristics and rules vary according to the dynamic of the subsystem.

According to one family system model (Bowen, 1978), there are four relationships patterns that suggest where problems might develop:

- Marital or caregiver conflict
- Emotional or behavioral challenges in one caregiver
- Impairment of one or more children
- Emotional distance

Marital or caregiver conflict is one of the most universal problems children face (Katz & Gottman, 1996). Such conflict, both direct and indirect, affects child adjustment and may be associated with child problem behavior (ibid.). Conflict between caregivers may lead to ineffective parenting practices. As the couple's ability to successfully parent is compromised, children tend to exhibit elevated levels of both internalizing and externalizing behaviors. These behaviors further strain the caregivers, leading to more conflict and parenting challenges (Kaczynski, Lindahl, Malik & Laurenceau, 2006). This conflict encourages a maladaptive developmental process by the children within the family system.

Impairment of one or more children often strains the family system because remaining family members feel neglected due to the impaired child receiving the majority of the family's attention. Emotional distance also presents a problem as it deters the family from operating as a unit because one or more members are not vested in the interests of the family.

## PARENTING STYLES

Just as family dynamics, values and culture play roles in child development, parenting styles are important. Parenting style is defined as the end result of an amalgamation of different parental behaviors (Chao, 2001). The types of parenting styles implemented affect several areas of child development: the child's behavior (Aunola & Nurmi, 2005), academic performance (Spera, 2005) and autonomy (Baumrind, 2005).

Baumrind (1971) identified three parenting styles: authoritarian, permissive and authoritative. Authoritarian parents believe their children should not question authority figures and expect respect and compliance. Punishments for lack of adherence to stated rules are often punitive (Baumrind, 1968). Children of authoritarian parents have lower opinions of themselves (Lamborn, Mounts, Steinberg & Dornbusch, 1991) and poor academic performance (Bush & Peterson, 2008; Dornbusch et al., 1987; Steinberg, Mounts & Lamborn, 1991).

Permissive parenting is a passive means of interacting with one's children. A parent who uses this parenting style does not use punitive forms of punishment, nor does he or she have high expectations for impeccable conduct. Rules are openly discussed with input from the child, and the parent or caregiver often serves as a resource to be used as the child deems necessary (Baumrind, 1968). Permissive parenting can be further categorized as permissive-neglectful and permissive-indulgent. Whereas permissive-neglectful parents show minimal parental support of and control over their children, permissive-indulgent parents are very supportive and nurturing but have minimal control (Bush & Peterson, 2008). Children with permissive parents tend to be more delinquent, to associate with delinquent peers, to have little interest in school and to display external behavior problems (Bush & Peterson, 2008; Maccoby & Martin, 1983).

Authoritative parenting is defined as a parent who rules by example. This style equates an understanding of the child's autonomy, values obedience and time, and provides explanations for the rules (Baumrind, 1968). Children who have authoritative parents have fewer behavior problems (Steinberg et al., 1991) and high academic outcomes (Bush & Peterson, 2008; Dornbusch et al., 1987; Steinberg, Lamborn, Dornbusch & Darling, 1992).

Maccoby and Martin (1983) expanded on Baumrind's (1968) typology by examining parental control, demanding nature and responsiveness. This resulted in the development of four parenting styles: authoritative, authoritarian, indulgent and uninvolved. Authoritative parents and caregivers are highly controlling and highly responsive. Authoritarian parents and caregivers are highly controlling but display low to minimal levels of responsiveness. Indulgent parents and caregivers are very responsive but are not very demanding. Last, uninvolved parents and caregivers are neither very responsive nor demanding (Simons & Conger, 2008).

To determine the parenting style of parents and caregivers, Baumrind (1971) and Maccoby and Martin (1983) considered parenting behaviors (e.g., control and responsiveness). Thus, parenting styles evolve from a combination of behaviors from the parent or caregiver. If researchers study parental behaviors in addition to parenting styles, more direct predictors of a child's behavioral outcomes can be identified (Bush & Peterson, 2007). These behaviors can be divided into supportive, behavioral control, psychological control and autonomy granting.

Supportive parents and caregivers exhibit warm feelings and are accepting of their children, whereas parents and caregivers who exhibit controlling behaviors are much more demanding when it comes to their children (Bean, Barber & Crane, 2006). For example, parents/caregivers who exhibit behavioral control create a more structured environment for their children and additionally reward good behavior and punish bad behavior. Parents/caregivers who exhibit psychological control affect their child's psychological world through a lack of validating their feelings and limiting their child's self-expression (Bean, Barber & Crane, 2006). Parents and caregivers who exhibit autonomy-granting behaviors are on the opposite end of the spectrum from parents and caregivers who exhibit psychological control (ibid.) in that they accept their children as individuals.

Research demonstrates that authoritative parenting has the most positive outcomes on child behavior (Baumrind, 1991; Bush & Peterson, 2008; Dornbusch et al., 1987). This conclusion, however, must be treated cautiously because most studies that examine parenting styles look solely at those styles employed by the mother (Simons & Conger, 2007). For example, one study examined the parenting styles employed by both the mother and the father, indicating a possible 16 combinations of styles (ibid.). In this instance, the researchers found that in households with two authoritative parents, children had the lowest level of depression and highest level of academic commitment. The presence of one authoritative parent did prove to be better than a household without an authoritative parent present. Further research indicated that better outcomes are attained when the mother is an authoritative parent and the father is uninvolved than vice versa. The most detrimental combination was found to be that of two uninvolved parents.

Results are influenced also by racial and ethnic factors. For example, research by Chao (2001) found the effects of an authoritative parenting style more positive for European Americans than Asian Americans. A study by Dwairy, Achoui, Abouserie and Farah (2006) with 2,893 Arab adolescents found that authoritarian parenting does not have the same adverse effects on adolescents for the Arab culture as it does on European Americans. Therefore, although parenting style plays an integral role in childhood development, it is important to consider ethnic and racial factors as well.

## FAMILY MEMBER ROLES AND RULES

Family roles generally dictate the expectations of members. Typical roles include mother, father, son and daughter. To these roles, one may add other roles such as "the reliable one," "the emotional one" or "the bad one." In reality, the list of roles and accompanying scripts is endless. For example, a child's behavior problems may serve in some families to distract parents from their marital problems (Kaczynski et al., 2006; Minuchin, 1974). This role maintains the family's equilibrium, or typical way of being.

In these specific roles, unspoken rules are created that indicate how the family will operate. These rules tend to be unspoken because they come into existence following patterns of previous behaviors and responses to those behaviors:

- Who is the final decision maker in the household?
- Can the child verbally disagree with a punishment given?
- Are feelings (e.g., anger, love) expressed within the family?

The responses to questions serve as guidelines for how future similar occurrences will be handled within the family system. Thus, the rules never have to be dictated because they are understood by all members. Roles and rules vary from family to family, but every family has a set organization by which the structure persists. Whether the family operates with conventional or novel roles and rules, the critical factor is whether the family system is fostering a healthy environment for successful child development.

## SOCIALIZATION

The family provides a child with his or her first interaction with the world. Until a child is approximately three years old, the family is the core of the child's social world, save for those experiences at a child-care center. Regardless, the social interactions a child encounters are ultimately guided by the family and the way they are taught.

Socialization—the process by which people learn and develop through culture, identity and societal norms—begins at birth. Consider this truth: Infants are able to recognize their mother's voice. Babies are also able to interact with their environment by smiling, forming eye contact and pointing. Before age one, children are engaging in social play, enjoying the presence and contact of others and recognizing when their caregivers leave the room (American Academy of Pediatrics, 1998; Shonkoff and Phillips, 2000).

During this first year, the formation of healthy attachments with parents and caregivers is essential for positive development (de Voursney et al., 2007). According to attachment theory, it is a system that interacts with other systems, such as those that produce fear and respond to a caregiver's availability (Bowlby, 1982). For example, at different developmental points varying systems are triggered when the caregiver is absent. One of the most notable examples of this is the "Strange Situation" procedure conducted by Ainsworth and Bell (1970). In their experiment, 56 babies under one year old were observed. A situation was created in which a mother would be in a room with her child. The mother would then exit the room and be replaced by a stranger. Upon the stranger's departure, the mother would return to the room with her child. Changes in the child's behavior were observed, and researchers found that when the mother was in the room the children expressed more exploratory behaviors than when the mother was not present. When the stranger was in the room, the infants engaged in more fearful behaviors such as crying and avoidance.

A child's type of attachment is an important predictor for success in later developmental tasks (Bates, Maslin & Frankel, 1985). For example, during the preschool and school-age years, children with healthy attachments do better playing with others, become more independent from their parents and learn to solve their own problems and compromise with friends (American Academy of Pediatrics, 1998).

Children who fail to form healthy attachments early in life are at risk of developing social anxiety and attachment disorders later in life. Studies suggest that a lack of healthy attachment may result in the child's inability to regulate emotions and to self-soothe. Finally, poorly attached youth are at higher risk for developing behavior problems (Shaw & Vondra, 1995), anxiety disorders (Muris, Mayer & Meesters, 2000) and antisocial behaviors (Aguilar, Sroufe, Egeland & Carlson, 2000).

## SUMMARY

This chapter examined several factors that contribute to child development. From fertilization through childhood and adolescence, a child's growth and development are influenced by a complex ever changing bio-psycho-social environmental set of factors. Within this world, children begin to identify themselves and to integrate external information with their internal definition of the world to establish an identity. As children move from reliance on their parents to autonomous beings capable of making their own decisions, familial support, genetic factors, good socialization skills and a healthy, enriched environment are key elements for a child achieving positive child developmental outcomes.

## REFERENCES

Aber, J. L., Bennett, N. G., Conley, D. C. & Li, J. (1997). The effects of poverty on child health and development. *Annual Review of Public Health, 18,* 463–483.

Aguilar, B., Sroufe, L. A., Egeland, B. & Carlson, E. (2000). Distinguishing the early-onset/persistent and adolescence-onset antisocial behavior types: From birth to 16 years. *Development and Psychopathology, 12,* 109–132.

Ainsworth, M. D. S. & Bell, S. M. (1970). Attachment, exploration, and separation: Illustrated by the behavior of one-year-olds in a strange situation. *Child Development, 41*(1), 49–67.

American Academy of Pediatrics (1998). *Caring for your baby and young child: Birth to age 5* (S. P. Shevlov, Ed.). New York: Bantam Books.

Aunola, K. & Nurmi, J. (2005). The role of parenting styles in children's problem behavior. [Abstract] *Child Development, 76*(6), 1144–1159.

Autism Speaks, Inc. (2007). *The autism genome project.* Retrieved June 1, 2007, from http://www.autismspeaks.org/science/programs/autism_genome_project.php.

Barkley, R. A. (2003). Attention-deficit/hyperactivity disorder. In E. J. Mash & R. A. Barkley (Eds.), *Child psychopathology* (pp. 75–143). New York: Guilford Press.

Barrett, K. C. (1995). A functionalist approach to shame and guilt. In J. P. Tangney & K. W. Filcher (Eds.), *The psychology of values: The Ontario symposium, vol. 8: The Ontario symposium on personality and social psychology* (pp. 299–328). Mahwah, NJ: Erlbaum.

Bates, J. E., Maslin, C. A. & Frankel, K. A. (1985). Attachment security, mother–child interaction, and temperament as predictors of behavior-problem ratings at age three years. Monographs of the Society for Research in Child Development, 50(1–2), 167–193.

Baumrind, D. (1968). Authoritarian vs. authoritative parental control. *Adolescence, 3,* 255–272.

Baumrind, D. (1971). Current patterns of parental authority. *Developmental Psychology Monograph, 4*(1), 1–103.

Baumrind, D. (1991). Effective parenting during the early adolescent transition. In P. A.Cowan & M. Hetherington (Eds.), *Family transitions* (pp. 111–163). Hillsdale, NJ: Lawrence Erlbaum.

Baumrind, D. (2005). Patterns of parental authority and adolescent autonomy. *New Directions for Child and Adolescent Development, 2005* (108), 61–69.

Bean, R. A., Barber, B. K. & Crane, D. R. (2006). Parental support, behavioral control, and psychological control among African American youth: The relationship to academic grades, delinquency, and depression. *Journal of Family Issues, 27,* 1335–1355.

Biederman, J. & Faraone, S. V. (2005). Attention-deficit hyperactivity disorder. *Lancet, 366,* 237–248.

Bowen, M. (1978). *Family therapy in clinical practice.* New York: Jason Aronson.

Bowlby, J. (1982). Attachment, stress and psychopathology: A developmental pathways model. In D. Cicchetti and D. J. Cohen (Eds.), *Developmental psychopathology, vol 1: Theory and method,* 2d ed. (pp. 333–369). New York: John Wiley. (Original work published in 1969).

Boyle, M. H. (2002). Home ownership and the emotional and behavioral problems of children and youth. *Child Development, 73*(3), 883–892.

Bradley, R. H. & Corwyn, R. F. (2002). Socioeconomic status and child development. *Annual Review of Psychology, 53,* 371–399.

Bremner, J. D. (2006). The relationship between cognitive and brain changes in posttraumatic stress disorder. *Annals of the New York Academy of the Sciences, 1071*(1), 80–86.

Bush, K. R. & Peterson, G. W. (2008). Childhood growth and development. In T. P. Gullotta & G.M. Blau (Eds.), *Handbook of childhood behavioral issues: Evidence-based approaches to prevention and treatment.* New York: Routledge Press, pp. 43–67.

Carlson, N. R. (Ed.) (2002). *Foundations of physiological psychology.* Boston: A Pearson Education Company.

Carrion, V. G., Weems, C. F. & Reiss, A. L. (2007). Stress predicts brain changes in children: A pilot longitudinal study on youth stress, posttraumatic stress disorder, and the hippocampus. *Pediatrics, 119*(3), 509–516.

Chao, R. K. (1995). Chinese and European American cultural models of the self reflected in mothers' childrearing beliefs. *Ethos, 23,* 328–354.

Chao, R. K. (2001). Extending research on the consequences of parenting style for Chinese Americans and European Americans. *Child Development, 72*(6), 1832–1843.

Cicchetti, D. (2006). Development and psychopthaology. In D. Cicchetti and D. J. Cohen (Eds.), *Developmental psychopathology, vol 1: Theory and method,* 2d ed. (pp. 1–23). New York: John Wiley.

Cicchetti, D. & Walker, E. F. (2001). Editorial: Stress and development: Biological and psychological consequences. *Development and Psychopathology, 13,* 413–418.

Cole, P. M., Bruschi, C. J. & Tamang, B. L. (2002). Cultural differences in children's emotional reactions to difficult situations. *Child Development, 73*(3), 983–996.

Cronk, N. J., Slutske, W. S., Madden, P. A. F., Bucholz, K. K. & Heath, A. P. (2004). Risk for separation anxiety disorder among girls: Paternal absence, socio-economic disadvantage, and genetic vulnerability. *Journal of Abnormal Psychology, 113*(2), 237–247.

de Voursney, D., Mannix, D., Brounstein, P. & Blau, G. M. (2008). Childhood growth and development. In T. P. Gullotta & G. M. Blau (Eds.), *Handbook of childhood behavioral issues: Evidence-based approaches to prevention and treatment.* New York: Routledge Press, pp. 19–39.

Dornbusch, S. M., Ritter, P. L., Leiderman, P. H., Roberts, D. F. & Farleigh, M. J. (1987). The relation of parenting styles to adolescent school performance. *Child Development, 56,* 326–341.

Dwairy, M., Achoui, M., Abouserie, R. & Farah, A. (2006). Parenting styles, individuation, and mental health of Arab adolescents. [Abstract] *Journal of Cross-Cultural Psychology, 37*(3), 262–272.

Fletcher, K. E. (2003). Childhood posttraumatic stress disorder. In E. J. Mash & R. A. Barkley (Eds.), *Child psychopathology* (pp. 330–371). New York: Guilford Press.

Fretts, R. C., Schmittdiel, J., McLean, F. H., Usher, R. H. & Goldman, M. B. (1995). Increased maternal age and the risk of fetal death. *New England Journal of Medicine, 333*(15), 953–957.

Furrow, J. L., King, P. E., and White, K. (2004). Religion and positive youth development: Identity, meaning, and prosocial concerns. [Abstract] *Applied Developmental Science, 8*(1), 17–26.

Gershoff, E. T., Aber, J. L., Raver, C. C. & Lennon, M. C. (2007). Income is not enough: Incorporating material hardship into models of income association with parenting and child development. *Child Development, 78*(1), 70–95.

Giedd, J. N. (2004). Structural magnetic resonance imaging of the adolescent brain. *Annals of the New York Academy of Sciences, 1021,* 77–85.

Gullotta, T. P. (2008). From theory to practice: Treatment and prevention possibilities. In T. P. Gullotta and G. M. Blau (Eds.), *Handbook of childhood behavioral issues: Evidence-based approaches to prevention and treatment.* New York: Routledge Press, pp. 3–17.

Halpern, R. & Figueiras, A. (2004). Environmental influences on child mental health. *Journal de Pediatria* (Supplement), *80*(2), 104–110.

Hoff, E. (2003). The specificity of environmental influence: Socioeconomic status affects early vocabulary development via maternal speech. *Child Development, 74*(5), 1368–1378.

Jolly, M. C., Sebire, N., Harris, J., Robinson, S. & Regan, L. (2000). Obstetric risks of pregnancy in women less than 18 years old. *Obstetrics & Gynecology, 96,* 962–966.

Kaczynski, K. J., Lindahl, K. M., Malik, N. M. & Laurenceau, J. (2006). Marital conflict, maternal and paternal parenting, and child adjustment: A test of mediation and moderation. *Journal of Family Psychology, 20*(2), 199–208.

Katz, L. F. & Gottman, J. M. (1996). Spillover effects of marital conflict: In search of parenting and coparenting mechanisms. *New Directions in Child Development, 74,* 57–76.

Kliewer, W., Parrish, K. A., Taylor, K. W., Jackson, K., Walker, J. M. & Shivy, V. A. (2006). Socialization of coping with community violence: Influences of caregiver coaching, modeling, and family context. *Child Development, 77*(3), 605–623.

Kobak, R., Cassidy, J., Lyons-Ruth, K. & Ziv, Y. (2006). Attachment, stress and psychopathology: A developmental pathways model. In D. Cicchetti and D. J. Cohen (Eds.), *Developmental psychopathology, vol. 1: Theory and method,* 2d ed. (pp. 333–369). New York: John Wiley.

Kolb, B. & Whishaw, I. (2003). *Fundamentals of human neuropsychology.* New York: Worth Publishers.

Lamborn, S. D., Mounts, N. S., Steinberg, L. & Dornbusch, S. M. (1991). Patterns of competence and adjustment among adolescents from authoritative, authoritarian, indulgent, and neglectful families. *Child Development, 62*(5), 1049–1065.

Leventhal, T. & Brooks-Gunn, J. (2000). The neighborhoods they live in: The effects of neighborhood residence on child and adolescent outcomes. *Psychological Bulletin, 126*(2), 309–337.

Lieberman, A. F. (1995). *Emotional life of the toddler.* New York: Free Press.

Maccoby, E. E. & Martin, J. A. (1983). Socialization in the context of the family: Parent–child interaction. In P. H. Mussen (Ed.) and E. M. Hetherington (Vol. Ed.) *Handbook of Child Psychology Vol. 4. Socialization, personality, and social development* (4th ed., pp. 4–101). New York: Wiley.

Mejia-Arauz, R., Rogoff, B., Dexter, A. & Najafi, B. (2007). Cultural variation in children's social organization. *Child Development, 78*(3), 1001–1014.

Minuchin, S. (1974). *Families and family therapy.* Cambridge, MA: Harvard University Press.

Muris, P., Mayer, B. & Meesters, C. (2000). Self-report attachment style, anxiety and depression in children. *Social Behavior and Personality: An International Journal, 28*(2), 157–162.

Perry, B. D. (2002). Childhood experience and the expression of genetic potential: What childhood neglect tells us about nature and nurture. *Brain and Mind, 3,* 79–100.

Price, T. S., Simonoff, E., Asherson, P., Curran, S., Kuntsi, J., Waldman, I., et al. (2005). Continuity and change in preschool ADHD symptoms: Longitudinal genetic analysis with contrast effects. *Behavior Genetics, 35*(2), 121–132.

Reyna, V. F. & Farley, F. (2006). Risk and rationality in adolescent decision making: Implications for theory, practice, and public policy. [Abstract] *Psychological Science in the Public Interest, 7*(1), 1–44.

Rosenthal, D. A., Gurney, R. M. & Moore, S. M. (1981). From trust on intimacy: A new inventory for examining Erikson's stages of psychosocial development. *Journal of Youth and Adolescence, 10*(6), 525–537.

Shaw, D. S. & Vondra, J. I. (1995). Infant attachment security and maternal predictors of early behavior problems: A longitudinal study of low income families. *Journal of Abnormal Child Psychology, 23*(3), 335–357.

Shonkoff, J. P. and Phillips, D. A. (Eds.) (2002). *From neurons to neighborhoods: The science of early childhood development.* Washington, DC: National Academy of Science.

Simons, L. G. & Conger, R. D. (2007). Linking mother–father differences in parenting to a typology of family parenting styles and adolescent outcomes. *Journal of Family Issues, 28*, 212–241.

Sisk, C. L. & Foster, D. L. (2004). The neural basis of puberty and adolescence. *Nature Neuroscience, 7*(10), 1040–1047.

Smoller, J. W. & Finn, C. T. (2003). Family, twin and adoption studies of bipolar disorder. *American Journal of Medical Genetics Part C, 123C*, 48–58.

Spera, C. (2005). A review of the relationship among parenting practices, parenting styles, and adolescent school achievement [Abstract]. *Educational Psychology Review, 17*(2), 125–146.

Spock, B. (2001). The first two years: The emotional and physical needs of children from birth to age two. New York: Simon & Schuster, Inc.

Steinberg, L., Lamborn, S. D., Dornbusch, S. M. & Darling, N. (1992). Impact of parenting practices on adolescent achievement: Authoritative parenting, school involvement, and encouragement to succeed. *Child Development, 63*(5), 1266–1281.

Steinberg, L., Mounts, N. S. & Lamborn, S. D. (1991). Authoritative parenting and adolescent adjustment across varied ecological niches. *Journal of Research on Adolescence, 1*(1), 19–36.

Sullivan, P. F., Kendler, K. S. & Neale, M. C. (2003). Schizophrenia as a complex trait: evidence from a meta-analysis of twin studies. *Archives of General Psychiatry, 60*(12), 1187–1192.

Super, C. M. & Harkness, S. (1993). The developmental niche: A conceptualization at the interface of child and culture. In R. A. Pierce & M. A. Black (Eds.), *Life-span development: A diversity reader* (pp. 61–77). Dubuque, IA: Kendall/Hunt.

Tsuang, M. T., Stone, W. S. & Faraone, S. V. (2001). Genes, environment and schizophrenia. *British Journal of Psychiatry, 178* (supplement 40), s18–s24.

Van't Ent, D., Lehn, H., Derks, E. M., Hudziak, J. J., Van Strien, N. M., Veltman, D. J., et al. (2007). A structural MRI study in monozygotic twins concordant or discordant for attention/hyperactivity problems: Evidence for genetic and environmental heterogeneity in the developing brain. *Neuroimage, 35*(3), 1004–1020.

# 3

# Families Matter

TRINA W. OSHER, DAVID OSHER AND GARY M. BLAU

## INTRODUCTION

Being a parent and raising a child with an emotional, behavioral or mental health challenge is a full time job without pay, vacations or nights or weekends off. We should know because two of the authors of this chapter (Trina and David Osher) have more than 30 years of personal parenting experience that included navigating the mental health, education, social service and criminal justice systems. Based on this experience, we can say that, despite the stress and strain of raising a child or children with complex mental health needs, families typically serve as an anchor or "home base" as their child encounters various systems and services to address their mental health needs.

Families are the backbone of our society (just ask any politician who regularly promotes family values), and no matter the problem, and no matter the level of stress, families do matter in the lives of children. We use the term *family* broadly to include all types of family arrangements and compositions. Whether the family involves adoption, stepparents or foster parents, the influence and importance of families cannot be understated. For this reason it is critical that families are respected and included in the care of their children.

There has not always been agreement with this last statement. There are those who would blame families for problems in their children, and there are some who would disagree that families should be a major decision maker in treatment. However, in the past 20 years there has been a national movement to ensure that families are at the heart of mental health treatment decisions. Recently, this has led to the belief that families should drive the care delivered to their children (New Freedom Commission on Mental Health, 2003).

## WHAT DO WE MEAN BY *FAMILIES MATTER?*

In 2003, the president's New Freedom Commission on Mental Health issued *Achieving the Promise: Transforming Mental Health Care in America*. Goal 2 of that report called for "consumer and family driven care." The report cited research showing that hope and self-determination play a key role in recovery. The commissioners insisted that families "must stand at the *center* of the system of care." They also said that the needs of children, youth, and families must "drive the care and services that are provided." Consumers and families told the commission that "having hope and the opportunity to regain control of their lives was vital to their recovery" (p. 35).

Notwithstanding this realization and emphasis on family involvement, the report did not say how families should matter or what family-driven care should look like. However, the commission did make five recommendations offering clues about what they meant (New Freedom Commission on Mental Health, 2003).

1. Develop an individualized plan of care for every adult with a serious mental illness and child with a serious emotional disturbance.
2. Involve consumers and families fully in orienting the mental health system toward recovery.
3. Align relevant federal programs to improve access and accountability for mental health services.
4. Create a comprehensive state mental health plan.
5. Protect and enhance the rights of people with mental illnesses.

Families, youth consumers and family-oriented practitioners echo the findings and recommendations of the commission, giving further legitimacy to the concept that families matter. One reason for this is a growing body of evidence that treatment outcomes are better when families have a key voice in decision making (Dunst, 1997).

Typically, families know what works for them. Their experience is holistic and not compartmentalized into a mental health segment, a child welfare slice, a juvenile justice piece and so forth. By necessity families focus on the concrete challenges they face each and every day. Families know their strengths and limitations. They know the difficulties they face. On a daily basis they can see change in themselves or their child. They know whether a program, agency or system works or does not work for them. And of no small consequence, without family buy-in, young people will not participate in services. Families matter, because their voices are listened to by politicians and public officials, and it is their passion and persistence on behalf of their children that ultimately transform mental health services.

Understanding that families matter and that partnerships with families are critical for mental health services to work effectively, is perhaps best viewed as a road trip. Picture a car filled with good traveling companions. The main passenger is a child who has a mental health need. The driver is the child's family. The rest of the passengers are along because they know at lot about child development, education, health, family support, psychology, literacy, housing, employment and other things families need for a good quality of life. The family knows where they want to go but need help choosing a good route to get there safely. The traveling companions share what they know and discuss all the options with the driver. The traveling companions may have to negotiate and accommodate everyone's perspective about the best way to make the trip, but the family chooses the destination and makes the final decision about the route. The family then takes the wheel and drives the chosen route. If needed, the driver gets help along way and may even let someone else take the wheel at times. Destination achieved. Everyone celebrates the success of the arrival together.

Families matter because family-driven care leads to success by overcoming fear, stigma and prejudice, lack of support and encouragement, resource limitations, ignorance or misunderstanding, resistance and cultural dissonance. It is the right thing to do, and the data support this. Family-driven practice fulfills the promise of "nothing about us without us." It supports a professional code of ethics and enables professionals and providers to "start where their client is at." Furthermore, funding streams are increasingly mandating family involvement and family-driven care.

Providing family-driven care requires a major shift in how people think and act. There must be administrative support to change behaviors and relationships. Developing, promoting and supporting a commonly accepted definition of family-driven care is a necessary step in helping people change both attitudes and behavior. This chapter reviews the history of the family movement in the United States, provides evidence for the practice of family-driven care, demonstrates mental health practices that embrace family support, describes ways families can be included in policy and practice decisions and offers resources for practitioners and families to use to implement this approach to service delivery.

## HISTORY OF THE FAMILY MOVEMENT IN CHILDREN'S MENTAL HEALTH

Two national organizations have been prominent advocates in the mental health arena: Mental Health America (MHA), formerly the National Mental Health Association, and the National Alliance for the Mentally Ill (NAMI). MHA, founded in 1909, has 203 affiliates and a mission to promote mental health, to prevent mental disorders and to achieve victory over mental illness through advocacy, education, research and service. MHA sponsors the "Children's Mental Health Matters" campaign and hosts "mpower," a Web site especially for teens and young adults.

NAMI, founded in 1979, has 110 affiliates and a mission to the eradicate mental illnesses and to improve the quality of life for all whose lives are affected by these diseases. NAMI's education programs include "Family-to-Family," the "Provider Education Program," "Peer-to-Peer," support groups, and various state and local programs. Although both of these organizations have addressed children's mental health, their historical focus has been on adults with mental and behavioral health problems and mental illness.

The family movement in children's mental health is relatively new, but it has developed rapidly due, in part, to funding from federal, state and, in some cases, community agencies that recognized the importance of family involvement and set an example by investing in developing family-run organizations. Family organizations typically started informally when a few families in an area banded together for mutual support as they struggled with the challenges of raising a child with emotional, behavioral or mental health needs. Organizations coalesced when the group discovered a common cause or became involved in responding to a community crisis or issues related to mental health service delivery such as a budget cut or the establishment or closing of a facility or program. At the beginning, they worked passionately on systems change, rarely planning for the future of their organization. They capitalized on their grassroots origins to focus on system change, operated on a informal basis and relied on volunteers to provide peer-to-peer support.

Without a sustaining source of funding many organizations did not survive. Thus, only a handful of family organizations are more than 20 years old.

## Child, Adolescent and Service System Program

Federal funding for community-based mental health services began in 1963 when the Mental Retardation Facilities and Community Mental Health Centers Construction Act (Public Law 88-164) provided states with funding to build and staff community mental health centers. However, it was not until 1988, 25 years later, that the National Institute of Mental Health funded the first five statewide family networks with federal funds from the Child Adolescent and Service System Program (CASSP). Although growth has been gradual, federal support for statewide family networks has been critically important. For example, in 2007 the Center for Mental Health Services awarded 42 statewide family network grants and supported a national technical assistance center to provide grantees with training and technical assistance, to facilitate networking and to collect data. Without that support fewer family networks would have been established and none with as strong a supportive network as those with CMHS underwriting.

In addition to supporting independent statewide family-run organizations, the CASSP initiative gave impetus to the development of the national family movement by holding the first Families As Allies conference in April 1986. The purpose of the meeting was to promote families and professionals working together—a novel concept at the time. For the first time, a handful of family-run organization leaders and family advocates met with each other, shared experiences and discovered commonalties.

## Federation of Families for Children's Mental Health (FFCMH)

Although it is the newest organization advocating for children with mental health needs and their families, the Federation of Families for Children's Mental Health is the only national family-run organization focused on children's mental health with an emphasis on family support, education, training, and involvement in all aspects of family-driven care, influencing national and state policy and actively participating in local and state system development, operation and improvement. The federation is a national network linking thousands of families through state chapters that in turn connect families to policy makers, agencies and providers to child serving systems.

## Promoting Family Involvement through Systems of Care

From its inception, the Comprehensive Community Mental Health Services for Children and Their Families Program (more generally known as the federally funded systems of care) required grantees to involve families more actively than ever before. Starting in 1993, states and communities that received systems of care funding began to actively recruit family members to help them implement these requirements. As a result new family-run organizations emerged largely supported with funds from these grantees. Training and technical assistance provided by system of care communities and their family-run organization partners lent further strength to the family's voice of serving individual children and youth collaboratively as well as of promoting and achieving system change (see http://www.systemsofcare.samhsa.gov for more information).

## FEDERAL POLICY ON FAMILY INVOLVEMENT

Society holds parents responsible for making decisions that are in the best interest of their children. However, systems that serve children traditionally have expected families to support professional decisions without question. Engaging families in planning their children's services and in making decisions has not been typical practice. Several federal agencies have, however, initiated projects where family involvement is either encouraged or required.

### Special Education

With the passage in 1975 of the Education of the Handicapped Act, Congress took the first step toward seriously engaging families in decision making about their child's care: special education in this case. The statute specified rights and responsibilities for parents of students served under the act, established advisory councils that had to include parents of enrolled students as well as adults with disabilities and provided funding for training and technical assistance to help families understand their rights and participate in the special education process for their own children. Subsequent reauthorizations of the statute changed the name of the program to the Individuals with Disability Education Act (IDEA) and expanded the range of activities and decisions in which school special education teams were required to include the student's parent.

### No Child Left Behind

No Child Left Behind (NCLB) places a priority on family involvement in education policy and practice. It establishes school-linked or school-based parental information and resource centers that provide training, information and support to parents (and to individuals and organizations that work with parents) to implement parental involvement strategies that lead to improvements in student academic achievement. For the more intensively parents are involved in their children's learning, the more beneficial are the achievement effects. Researchers also have reported that the schools with the most successful parent involvement programs are those that offer parents a variety of ways to participate (U.S. Department of Education, Office of Elementary and Secondary Education, 2002).

### Medicaid

In 2007, the Center for Medicare and Medicaid Services (CMS) initiated a demonstration project to develop community-based alternatives to psychiatric residential treatment facilities (PRTFs) for children and youth. The goal of program was to test the effectiveness in improving or maintaining a child's functional level and the cost effectiveness of providing coverage of home and community-based service alternatives to PRTFs for youth enrolled in the Medicaid program under title XIX.

Since 1993, and in keeping with the values and principles of systems of care, the federal Center for Mental Health Services required the systems of care it funds to commit to meaningful family involvement including collaboration with family-run organizations. The specific requirements have evolved and expanded with each subsequent cycle of grants.[1] The original Guidance for Applicants had two requirements about family involvement. First, applicants had to explain how there would be full involvement and family-professional partnership in planning, implementation, management, delivery and evaluation of the system of care and in the planning and delivery of care for individual children and families. Second, applicants had to explain how they would ensure consideration of the existence of and collaboration with local family support organizations or a statewide family network organization that has the potential to rapidly create such an organization in the community served by the community.

The 2005 Request for Applications promoted full participation of families and youth in service planning and in the development of local services and supports. Importantly, it directed applicants to articulate how they would incorporate the values and principles of family-driven care. Applicants' narratives needed to be detailed and explicit with regard to strategies and tactics for ensuring real family involvement—especially with respect to partnership with family-run organizations.

## WORKING DEFINITION OF FAMILY-DRIVEN CARE

*Family-driven care* means families have a primary decision making role in the care of their children as well as the policies and procedures governing care for all children in their community, state, tribe, territory and nation. This includes choosing supports, services, and providers; setting goals; designing and implementing programs; monitoring outcomes; partnering in funding decisions and determining the effectiveness of all efforts to promote the mental health and well-being of children and youth.

### Guiding Principles of Family-Driven Care

1. Families and youth are given accurate, understandable and complete information necessary to set goals and to make choices for improved planning for individual children and their families.
2. Families and youth, providers and administrators embrace the concept of sharing decision making and responsibility for outcomes.
3. Families and youth are organized to collectively use their knowledge and skills as a force for systems transformation.
4. Families and family-run organizations engage in peer-support activities to reduce isolation, to gather and disseminate accurate information and to strengthen the family voice.
5. Families and family-run organizations provide direction for decisions that impact funding for services, treatments and supports.
6. Providers take the initiative to change practice from provider driven to family driven.
7. Administrators allocate staff, training, support and resources to make family-driven practice work at the point where services and supports are delivered to children, youth and families.
8. Community attitude change efforts focus on removing barriers and discrimination created by stigma.

9. Communities embrace, value and celebrate the diverse cultures of their children, youth and families.
10. Everyone who connects with children, youth and families continually advances his or her own cultural and linguistic responsiveness as the population served changes.

## Characteristics of Family-Driven Care

1. Family and youth experiences, their visions and goals, their perceptions of strengths and needs and their guidance about what will make them comfortable steer decision making about all aspects of service and system design, operation and evaluation.
2. Family-run organizations receive resources and funds to support and sustain the infrastructure that is essential to ensure an independent family voice in their communities, states, tribes, territories and the nation.
3. Meetings and service provision happen in culturally and linguistically competent environments where family and youth voices are heard and valued, where everyone is respected and trusted and where it is safe for everyone to speak honestly.
4. Administrators and staff actively demonstrate their partnerships with all families and youth by sharing power, resources, authority, responsibility and control with them.
5. Families and youth have access to useful, usable and understandable information and data as well as to sound professional expertise so they have good information to make decisions.
6. Funding mechanisms allow families and youth to have choices.
7. All children, youth and families have a biological, adoptive, foster or surrogate family voice advocating on their behalf.

## THE EVIDENCE BASE FOR FAMILY INVOLVEMENT IN CHILD AND ADOLESCENT MENTAL HEALTH SERVICE DELIVERY

The previous information makes a philosophical case for why families matter in child and adolescent mental health service delivery and provides both a historical context as well as examples of how this conceptualization has influenced funding and policy decisions. Additionally, there is an evidence base to support family involvement. This includes research on the following:

- The importance of family involvement and the family–professional partnership
- The factors that limit or facilitate family involvement and the family–professional partnership

The evidence base comes from research in many fields—early childhood, general and special education, mental health prevention and treatment for children and adults, physical health, child welfare and juvenile justice. It includes experimental and quasi-experimental research, cross-sectional analyses from national survey data, ethnographic research and focus groups with family members and providers as well as from practice wisdom synthesized in reports. The evidence base includes information on what does not work (e.g., ignoring the barriers families face in accessing services) and what works (e.g., providing families with the support they need to participate in services).

## Importance of Family Involvement

Children with emotional and behavioral problems and disorders experience poor school, community and mental health outcomes, and there are great disparities between the better outcomes experienced by middle-class Caucasians on the one hand and the poorer outcomes experienced by individuals of color, first-generation Americans and economically disadvantaged individuals on the other hand (U.S. Public Health Service 1999, 2000). Factors that underlie these problems include interventions and services that are sometimes aversive or culturally inappropriate, are often not matched to family and child needs and are frequently ineffective (Castro, Barrera & Martinez, 2004; Garcia & Weisz, 2002; Jensen, Hoagwood & Trickett, 1999; Kazdin, Mazurick & Bass, 1993; Weisz & Hawley, 1998). Families and youth do not always have access to adequate service, and they often withdraw prematurely from services and school (Owens et al., 2002). This is particularly the case in poor neighborhoods and for families of color (Balfanz & Legters, 2004; Bischoff & Sprenkle, 1993; Dumka, Garza, Roosa & Stoerzinger, 1997; Griffin, Cicchetti & Leaf, 1993; Kazdin, 1996; Kazdin & Mazurick, 1994; McKay, Gonzales, Quintana, Kim & Abdul-Adil, 1999). In addition, the greater levels of family stress and parent or child mental health needs contribute to attrition (Kazdin & Mazurick, 1994; McKay et al., 1999; Miller & Prinz, 1990) and poor outcomes (Kazdin & Wassell, 1999).

Family involvement, as well as partnerships between families and professionals, is key to improving school and mental health outcomes and reducing disparities (Christenson & Havsy, 2004; Christenson, Rounds & Gorney, 1992; Henderson & Mapp, 2002; Osher, 2000). For example, Hill et al.'s (2004) longitudinal study, which followed 463 adolescents from 7th through 11th grade, found that family involvement (e.g., volunteering, attending parent–teacher association [PTA] meetings, parent–teacher contact and communication, involvement in academic-related activities at home) in 7th grade was associated with fewer school behavior problems in 8th grade, higher achievement in 9th grade, and stronger academic aspirations in 11th grade.[2] Family involvement depends on the quality of the relationships that are established between and among families, professionals, schools and agencies (Christenson, Godber & Anderson, 2003), which, in turn, is related to organizational culture and structure (Hoover-Dempsey, Bassler & Brissie, 1992; Glisson, 2002; Griffith, 1998; Osher, 2002). Parental contributions as well as the barriers to and facilitators of parental contributions can be categorized into four areas.

### 1. Parents have special knowledge that can enhance the design of interventions and treatments.

Because parents see their children in different contexts, they can help professionals overcome the challenges of visibility and observability—what the professionals cannot see or know (Merton, 1957). Because families often possess cultural and local knowledge, which professionals often lack, families can help contextualize interventions (American Academy of Pediatrics

Committee on Hospital Care, 2003) and in so doing can contribute to filling the gap between efficacy and effectiveness studies (Weisz & Jensen, 1999). Because parents have this knowledge, they can help design and adapt effective interventions and treatments as well as improve the ability to monitor and evaluate interventions (Briar-Lawson, Wiesen & Lawson, 2001; Bruns, 2004; Kendziora, Bruns, Osher, Pacchiano & Mejia, 2001; Osher & Osher, 2002; Ross & McLaughlin, 2006; Rzepnicki, 1987). Although the failure of parents to participate in planning is often attributed to parental factors, research in medicine suggests that the strongest predictors of patient participation in medical consultations about their care are the clinical setting and the physician's communication style (Carlsen & Aadvik, 2006; Harrington, Noble & Newman, 2004; Richard & Lussier 2007).

## 2. *Parents can promote healthy development, can prevent problems from developing or exacerbating and can implement effective treatment protocols and educational interventions.*

Parents can foster their children's healthy development (e.g., Hoagwood, 2005; Lynn et al., 2001), for example, by how they interact with their children and by what they do (or do not) expose their children to. Parents can also reduce, buffer or even eliminate risk factors. Finally, parents can implement or support treatment plans, but their ability to do so is mediated by their belief in the effectiveness of the treatment (Spoth & Redmond, 1993, 1995; Spoth, Redmond & Shin, 2000).

The ability of parents to participate in interventions depends on their knowledge, their willingness to hear and listen to professionals and agency representatives who suggest changes in their behavior and their ability to understand and remember what is communicated. It also depends on the ability of professionals to understand and address parental needs that often interfere with the ability of parents to follow through. In a number of studies, Prinz and colleagues have demonstrated the importance of the parent-professional relationship in sustaining preventive and treatment interventions (Prinz & Miller, 1994, 1996; Prinz et al., 2001). Similarly, Kazdin, Holland, and Crowley (1997) found that parent perceptions of treatment obstacles and poor relationships with therapists influenced who dropped out of parent management training. Two longitudinal studies of the family-driven Regional Intervention Program (RIP) suggest the power of a program that asks parents what they need to succeed, responds to their needs, and employs trained parents (who have been through the program) to train and educate parents of children of children with severe behavioral problems regarding positive child development and positive behavioral approaches, and provides opportunities for practice and coaching. These two studies document impressive long-term impacts for children who displayed behavioral problems when compared with their more typically developing peers (Kendziora et al., 2005; Osher & Hanley, 2001; Strain & Timm, 2001). The impacts included grades, attendance, disciplinary referrals, grades and graduation. The RIP results are consistent with Snell-Johns, Mendez, and Smith's (2004) literature review, which, in part, synthesizes research on family training interventions that have been successfully broadened to address individual family needs such as the Incredible Years' ADVANCE Program (Webster-Stratton, 1994).

Parents are key to accessing and sustaining mental health treatments for their children, and their relationship with providers affects their behavior. Although services are often insufficient, even when services are available, they may not be accessed by children, and even when accessed, children and youth may drop out of services prematurely. A number of experimental studies suggest that parents are key to children's accessing these services and continuing with them through the course of treatment. Hawley and Weisz (2003) found that the parent–therapist alliance, but not the child–therapist alliance, was associated significantly with greater family participation, less frequent cancellations and no-shows and greater persistence in therapy. Families who attended an outpatient community clinic but dropped out were more likely to indicate problems in the therapeutic relationship compared with those who completed treatment (Garcia & Weisz, 2002). Although family characteristics are often blamed for a lack of parental participation, research in education and early intervention suggests that professional and organizational practices, which are changeable—not parent characteristics—are the key factor in parent participation (Dunst & Trivette, 1994; Eccles & Harold, 1996; Snell-Johns et al., 2004; Szapocznik et al., 1988). Studies of multisystemic therapy (MST) and wraparound are suggestive here. Huey, Henggeler, Brondino and Pickrel's (2000) study of the mechanisms of change in MST found that this efficacious treatment realized poorer outcomes when clinicians were highly directive and families were not fully engaged with the therapist, and Schaeffer's (2001) examination of mediators of MST outcomes found that parent engagement mediated the relation between high family adversity and drop-out. Finally, as family-driven approaches are key to wraparound (Bruns, 2004; Bruns, Walker, & Penn, in press) and its mediators (Paulus, Larey & Dzindolet, 2001; Suter, 2007; Szapocznik et al., 1988; Williams, 1988), the results of experimental examinations of wraparound suggest that family-driven approaches can help improve child-welfare, school and juvenile-justice indicators (Bruns, Rast, Walker, Peterson & Bosworth, 2006; Carney & Buttell, 2003; Clark, Lee, Prange & McDonald, 1996; Clark et al., 1998; Rast, Bruns, Brown, Peterson & Mears (in press).

Parent efficacy and empowerment play key roles in the mental health interventions. Self-efficacy and empowerment are important variables in a caregiver's ability to participate in his or her children's education (Hoover-Dempsey, Walker & Sandler, 2005) and mental health treatments, as well as in treatment outcomes. For example, McKay, Pennington, Lynn and McCadam (2007) found that parental efficacy and positive attitudes toward mental health services significantly correlated with children's attendance at an initial intake appointment and a parent's assessment of his or her ability to meet an improvement goal. Similarly, Resendez, Quist, and Matshazi (2000) found that caregivers who perceived themselves as more competent, knowledgeable and efficacious and as advocates of the service system had children who functioned better and were more satisfied with service compared with parents who were less empowered.

Self-efficacy beliefs involve a parent's assessment of their capacity to learn or perform behaviors (Bandura, 1986, 1997). Although self-efficacy is important for parental participation in general, it may be particularly important for parents who are confronted by many challenges (Bandura & Cervone, 1983) or who struggle with depression or anxiety disorders (Maddux, 2002).

Professionally or agency-driven interactions between professionals and families can work against self-efficacy and empowerment, particularly for caregivers who already feel socially stigmatized or marginalized. For example, Dunst and Trivette (1994) showed that service integration that is not consumer driven is more likely to be dependency forming than competency enhancing. Surveys of professionals and interviews with families document that some professionals have attitudes that blame families, particularly families of color. These attitudes, and behaviors that flow from them, are incompatible with empowerment (e.g., Harry, Klingner & Hart, 2005). These interactions may also serve a de-skilling function, where family capacities that may be adaptive to the families' context (e.g., greater protectiveness of children in high-crime areas; Furstenberg, Cook, Eccles, Elder & Sameroff, 1999) are devalued and ways of handling simple matters are mystified by overly technical jargon (Freire, 1985; Harden, 2005, p. 211; McKnight, 1985). These behaviors contrast with Dunst's (1997, p. 86) studies of interventions that were "consumer driven, proactive strengths based, and health-promotion oriented" and that contributed to parental empowerment and psychological health. Similarly, Taub, Tighe and Burchard's (2001) study of 131 children and caregivers who received wraparound services found that family empowerment increased significantly over time during services; parents' reports of children's adjustment correlated significantly with both family and service system empowerment at follow-up; and family empowerment over time was a significant predictor of change in children's externalizing problems while in services.

Changing the attitudes and behaviors of family members and providers are key to improving mental health outcomes. Attitudinal and behavioral change is not easy. Families and providers both need help to do the following:

- View the decision-making process differently
- Act and interact in new ways
- Feel comfortable with shared responsibility for decision making
- Own and believe in a family-driven approach as the right way of working together

Research suggests that family-driven approaches can support these attitudinal and behavioral changes (e.g., Bullock & Gable, 1997; Huey et al., 2000; Maddux, 2002; McDonald, 1998; Morrissey-Kane & Prinz, 1999; National Council on Disability, 2004; Osher & Hanley, 1997, 2001; Osher & Osher, 2002; Williams, 1988).

## FAMILY-DRIVEN CARE IN ACTION: WRAPAROUND AND FAMILY SUPPORT

Wraparound is a manualized process for making decisions that recognizes the importance of long-term connections between people, particularly the bonds between family members. Family voice and choice is the first principle of wraparound. It acknowledges and affirms that the people who have a long-term, ongoing relationship with a child or youth have a unique stake in and commitment to the wraparound process and its outcomes and should have the greatest influence over the wraparound process as it unfolds. Family voice is realized by providing opportunities for family members to fully explore and to express their perspectives during wraparound activities. Family choice is facilitated by structuring decision making so that family members can select, from various options, the ones that are most consistent with their own perceptions of how things are, how things should be and what needs to happen to help the family achieve its vision of well-being. Family and youth or child perspectives are elicited and prioritized during all phases of the wraparound process.

Wraparound is a collaborative process, and within that collaboration family members' perspectives are typically the most critical. Team procedures, interactions and products—including the wraparound plan—should provide evidence that the team is indeed engaging in intentional activity to prioritize the family perspectives. Wraparound is intended to be inclusive and to manage disagreement by facilitating collaboration and creativity. Special attention to the balancing of influence and perspectives within wraparound is especially necessary when legal considerations restrict the extent to which family members are free to make choice (e.g., when a youth is on probation; when a child is in protective custody). Regardless of the competing interests, the principle of family voice and choice is a constant reminder that the wraparound process must place special emphasis on the perspectives of the people who will still be connected to the young person after agency involvement has ended—namely their family (see http://www.rtc.pdx.edu/nwi for additional information).

## FAMILY PARTNERS IN WRAPAROUND

The team's capacity to ensure family voice and choice throughout the process can be enhanced by having a family partner on the team. By providing peer support and education, family partners promote self-empowerment and nonadversarial advocacy, which leads to more productive teamwork and better outcomes for children, youth and families. By representing families in system level decision making and by providing training for all members of the wraparound team, family partners enhance overall understanding of the family experience and promote family professional partnerships throughout the wraparound system of care.

The family partner is a paid and formal member of the wraparound team with access to the organizational supports necessary for them to do their work effectively. Their role is to serve the family by helping them engage and actively participate on the team and make informed decisions throughout the process. Family partners have a strong connection to the community and are knowledgeable about resources, services and supports for families. The family partner's personal experience in raising a child with special needs is critical to their earning the respect of families and establishing a trusting relationship that the family they are helping values. Family partners typically, though not universally, are employed by a family-run organization under a contract with the entity that is managing the care provided by the wraparound system of care. This arrangement helps maintain their connection to the family movement and keeps them grounded in real family experiences, hopes and dreams.

# HOW FAMILIES SHOULD BE INCLUDED IN IMPLEMENTATION AND POLICY

How can we know that the principles of family-driven care are, in fact, being implemented through policy and practice? Here, we offer an approach and a tool to help family members, practitioners, administrators and policy makers examine the context in which they are working and assess the extent to which it is family driven.

There are seven factors to consider in creating the conditions and capacities necessary for real collaboration to occur. Further, the definition of family-driven care mentions six activities in which responsibilities for decisions should be shared by families and practitioners. Mapping the factors necessary for collaboration against the decisions making activities in the definition provides a framework for documenting how families are engaged in these activities (see Figure 3.1 for a template).

Completing the template concurrently from the different perspectives of the various partners allows the sharing of ideas, opportunities and constraints. Using this framework can help all partners find common ground and shared expectations as well as point out and clarify where and why significant differences exist. To illustrate how this template could be used, we provide a hypothetical example of how a family-driven practice might complete the first row of Figure 3.1 if it was examining its efforts to enhance culturally competent services (Figure 3.2).

Any state, system, agency, tribe, organization or provider that is serious about being family-driven makes a deliberate and strategic effort to develop strong partnerships with individual families as well as family-run organizations. Key among these are building relationships, mentoring and providing tangible support for family participation, encouraging autonomy in decision making, communicating effectively, sharing power, providing quality services and following through reliably and consistently on responsibilities, decisions and agreement.

# WHAT FAMILIES AND PRACTITIONERS CAN DO TO DEVELOP MEANINGFUL PARTNERSHIPS

## Ways to Get Started

- Ask and explain about the steps ahead and what to expect along the way.
- Ask and tell about including other agencies involved with the child and family and getting relevant information from them (e.g., an individualized education program, or IEP).
- Ask for and offer referrals for services to meet the child's needs.
- Ask for and give explanations of all options and ask for the support the family would need to make things work for the child.
- Request and offer services that teach the child how to adapt successfully in his or her school and community.

| | Choosing Supports, Services and Providers | Setting Goals | Designing and Implementing Programs | Monitoring Outcomes | Funding Decisions | Promoting Mental Health and Well Being |
|---|---|---|---|---|---|---|
| Perspective | | | | | | |
| Bottom Line | | | | | | |
| Expectations | | | | | | |
| Strengths | | | | | | |
| Barriers | | | | | | |
| Supports Needed | | | | | | |
| Resources | | | | | | |

*(Left vertical axis label: Factors that Create the Conditions and Capacities for Collaboration)*

**Figure 3.1**  Mapping Collaboration with Shared Decision Making—Template for Strategic Planning. [Osher, T., Blau, G., & Osher, D. *Family Driven Practice: How Families Can Collaborate with Professionals and Youth to promote and Influence It.* FFCMH Conference, St, Louis, MO, December 2006.]

| | | Choosing Supports, Services and Providers | Setting Goals | Designing and Implementing Programs | Monitoring Outcomes | Funding Decisions | Promoting Mental Health and Well Being |
|---|---|---|---|---|---|---|---|
| Factors that Create the Conditions and Capacities for Collaboration | Perspective | Families desire services that are congruent with their cultural values and spiritual beliefs and providers who are culturally competent

Providers typically deliver services according to dominant culture models in which they were trained | Within on year, 25% of the array of services and staff will be considered culturally competent by families – and this will increase annually

Within one year, a study will be designed and funded to evaluate services nominate as effective but for which there is no scientific evidence base | Families will be asked to train current staff to understand and respect cultural values and practices

Families will participate in recruiting new staff to ensure they reflect the cultures and ethnicities of the community

Families will participate in designing and implementing research on services they believe to be effective | Data will be collected from families about how culturally competent they find the service array and staff

Data will be collected from families about which services and provider staff they find to be most effective and culturally competent | Family expertise has great value and they are paid accordingly for training they do for staff

Family members are paid a fair wage to collect evaluation data and participate in special research studies

Family members share in decision making about financial incentives paid to staff to reward and encourage delivery of services in a culturally competent manner | Families report increased participation in community life when there are culturally competent mental health services available to their children

Children attend school more and parents miss fewer days of work due to a child's physical or mental illness or behavioral disorder |

**Figure 3.2** Example: Enhancing Culturally Competent Services—Mapping Collaboration with Shared Decision Making.

## Ways to Keep Moving Along

- Find out and tell about all opportunities for families to participate in planning and advocating for their child's and the family's services and supports.
- Talk and connect with professionals to learn the evidence about the kinds of treatments, services and supports that can help achieve the family's and youth's goals.
- Seek and offer opportunities to develop new skills to build (or rebuild) and to sustain good relationships between the family and his or her child.
- Insist on making and providing discharge and after-care plans for reintegration into the community at the outset of out-of-home care.
- Ask and offer for help to find the right services and providers and funding to pay for them.

## Ways to Sustain Gains

- Request and provide services that support the child's gains and will help ensure he or she continues to adapt successfully in his or her school and community.
- Ask and offer for supports that can help the family cope with the stress at home—including support for siblings.
- Seek and offer services that promote wellness and resilience.
- Insist on and provide services that build on the child's and family's strengths and counterbalance risk factors.

## Additional Ways to Partner in Judicial Proceeding

- Find and provide a family advocate attached to the court or other knowledgeable and trustworthy person who can help other families learn what they need to know and prepare for court.
- Ask and provide for a description of the courtroom and the court proceedings beforehand—including any security measures family members are likely to encounter.
- Get and offer help for families to prepare any statements they wish to make during the proceeding.
- Request and provide transportation, child care, and qualified, professional translators (if necessary) so families can fully participate in the hearing.

## CONCLUSION

Families matter—no ifs, ands or buts. All families deserve respect and a voice in the care of their children—even the most challenged. Families with lived experience should have a primary role in the development and implementation of policy and budgets and in those decisions that impact the service delivery system affecting them. Evidence supports these statements. Mental health service delivery is a business of relationships, and it is through these relationships that the field will advance.

# ENDNOTES

1. Readers who wish to trace this evolution step by step are referred to Figure 3.2, which contains a table showing the Evolution of Family Involvement Requirements in System of Care Grant Program.
2. Although this finding was for parents with higher parental education levels, specific positive effects were also found for other subgroups.

# REFERENCES

American Academy of Pediatrics Committee on Hospital Care (2003). Family-Centered Care and the Pediatrician's Role. *Pediatrics, 111*(suppl): 1539–1587.

Balfanz, R. & Legters, N. (2004). Locating the dropout crisis. Baltimore: Center for Social Organization of Schools, John Hopkins University. Retrieved 16 August, 2007, from http://www.csos.jhu.edu/tdhs/rsch/Locating_Dropouts.pdf.

Bandura, A. (1986). *Social foundations of thought and action: A social cognitive theory.* Englewood Cliffs, NJ: Prentice Hall.

Bandura, A. (1997). *Self-efficacy: The exercise of control.* New York: Freeman.

Bandura, A. & Cervone, D. (1983). Self-evaluative and self-efficacy mechanisms governing the motivational effects of goal systems. *Journal of Personality and Social Psychology, 45*, 1017–1028.

Bischoff, R. J. & Sprenkle, D. H (1993). Dropping out of marriage and family therapy: A critical review of research. *Family Process, 32*(3), 353–375.

Briar-Lawson, K., Wiesen, S. & Lawson, H. (2001). What hurts and what helps: Listening to families to build 21st century child welfare reforms. In A. Sallee, H. Lawson & K. Briar-Lawson (Eds.), *Innovative practices with vulnerable children and families* (pp.229–244). Dubuque, IA: Eddie Bowers Publishers, Inc.

Bruns, E. J. (2004). The evidence base and wraparound. *Wraparound Solutions Newsletter*, 3(1), 4–10.

Bruns, E. J., Rast, J., Walker, J. S., Peterson, C. R. & Bosworth, J. (2006). Spreadsheets, service providers, and the statehouse: Using data and the wraparound process to reform systems for children and families. *American Journal of Community Psychology, 38*, 201–212.

Bruns, E. J., Walker, J. S. & Penn, M. (in press). Individualized services in systems of care: The wraparound process. In B. Stroul & G. Blau (Eds.). *The system of care Handbook: Transforming mental health services for children, youth, and families.* Baltimore, MD: Brookes.

Bullock, L. M. & Gable, R. A. (Eds.) (1997). *Making collaboration work for children, youth, families, schools, and communities.* Reston, VA: Council for Exceptional Children.

Carlsen, B. & Aadvik, A. (2006). Patient involvement in clinical decision-making: the effect of GP attitude on patient satisfaction. *Health Expectations, 9*, 148–157.

Carney, M. M. & Buttell, F. (2003). Reducing juvenile recidivism: Evaluating the wraparound services model. *Research on Social Work Practice, 13*, 551–568.

Castro, F. G., Barrera, M. & Martinez, C. R. (2004). The cultural adaptation of prevention interventions: Resolving tensions between fidelity and fit. *Prevention Science*, *5*(1), 41–45.

Christenson, S. L., Godber, Y. & Anderson, A. R. (2003). Critical issues facing families and schools. *LSS Review*, *2*(1), 8–9.

Christenson, S. L. & Havsy, L. H. (2004). Family–school–peer relationships: Significance for social, emotional, and academic learning. In J. E. Zins, R. P. Weissberg, M. C. Wang & H. J. Walberg (Eds.), *Building academic success on social and emotional learning* (pp. 59–75). New York: Teachers College Press.

Christenson, S. L., Rounds, T. & Gorney, D. (1992). Family factors and student achievement: An avenue to increase students' success. *School Psychology Quarterly*, *7*, 178–206.

Clark, H. B., Lee, B., Prange, M. E. & McDonald, B. A. (1996). Children lost within the foster care system: Can wraparound service strategies improve placement outcomes? *Journal of Child and Family Studies*, *5*, 39–54.

Clark, H. B., Prange, M. E., Lee, B., Stewart, E. S., McDonald, B. B. & Boyd, L. A. (1998). An individualized wraparound process for children in foster care with emotional/behavioral disturbances: Follow-up findings and implications from a controlled study. In M. H. Epstein, K. Kutash & A. Duchnowski (Eds.), *Outcomes for children and youth with emotional and behavioral disorders and their families: Programs and evaluation best practices* (pp. 513–542). Austin, TX: Pro-ED, Inc.

Dumka, L. E., Garza, C. A., Roosa, M. W. & Stoerzinger, H. D. (1997). Recruitment and retention of high risk families into a preventive parent training intervention. *Journal of Primary Prevention*, *18*, 25–39.

Dunst, C. J. (1997). Conceptual and empirical foundations of family-centered practice In R. Illback, C. Cobb & H. Joseph, Jr. (Eds.), *Integrated services for children and families: Opportunities for psychological practice* (pp. 75–91). Washington, DC: American Psychological Association.

Dunst, C. J. & Trivette, C. M. (1994). Empowering case management practices: A family-centered centered perspective. In C. J. Dust, C. M. Trivete & A. G. Deal (Eds.), *Supporting and strengthening families* (pp. 187–196). Cambridge, MA: Brookline Books.

Eccles, J. S. & Harold, R. D. (1996). Family involvement in children's and adolescent's schooling. In A. Booth & J. F. Dunn (Eds.), Family-school links: How do they affect educational outcomes? (pp. 3–34). Mahway, NJ: Lawrence Erlbaum Associates.

Freire, P. (1985). *The politics of education: Culture, power and liberation* (translated by Donaldo Macedo). South Hadley, MA: Bergin & Garvey.

Furstenberg, F. F. Jr., Cook, T. D., Eccles, J., Elder, G. H. Jr. & Sameroff, S. (1999). *Managing to make it: Urban families and adolescent success*. Chicago: University of Chicago Press.

Garcia, J. A. & Weisz, J. R. (2002). When youth mental health care stops: Therapeutic relationship problems and other reasons for ending youth outpatient treatment. *Journal of Consulting and Clinical Psychology*, *70*, 439–443.

Glisson, C. (2002). The organizational context of children's mental health services. *Clinical Child and Family Psychology Review*, *5*(4), 233–253.

Griffin, J. A., Cicchetti, D. & Leaf, P. J. (1993). Characteristics of youths identified from a psychiatric case register as first-time users of services. *Hospital & Community Psychiatry, 44*(1), 62–65.

Griffith, J. (1998). The relation of school structure and social environment to parent involvement in elementary schools. *Elementary School Journal, 99*(1), 53–80.

Harden, J. (2005). "Unchartered waters": The experience of parents of young people with mental health problems. *Qualitative Health Research, 15*(2), 207–223.

Harrington, J., Noble, L. M. & Newman, S. P. (2004). Improving patients' communication with doctors: A systematic review of intervention studies. *Patient Education and Counseling, 52*(1), 7–16.

Harry, B., Klingner, J. K. & Hart, J. (2005). African American families under fire: Ethnographic views of family strengths. *Remedial and Special Education, 26*(2), 101–112.

Hawley, K. M. & Weisz, J. R. (2003). Child, parent and therapist (dis)agreement on target problems in outpatient therapy: The therapist's dilemma and its implications. *Journal of Consulting and Clinical Psychology, 71*(1), 62–70.

Henderson, A. T. & Mapp, K. L. (2002). *A new wave of evidence: The impact of school, family, and community connections on student achievement.* Austin, TX: Southwest Educational Development Laboratory.

Hill, N. E., Castellino, D. R., Lansford, J. E., Nowlin, P., Dodge, K. A., Bates, J., et al. (2004). Parent academic involvement as related to school behavior, achievement, and aspirations: Demographic variations across adolescence. *Child Development, 75*(5), 1491–1509.

Hoagwood, K. E. (2005). Family-based services in children's mental health: A research review and synthesis. *Journal of Child Psychology and Psychiatry, 46*(7), 690–713.

Hoover-Dempsey, K. V., Bassler, O. C. & Brissie, J. S. (1992). Explorations in parent-school relations. *Journal of Educational Research, 85*(5), 287–294.

Hoover-Dempsey, K. V., Walker, J. M. T. & Sandler, H. M. (2005). Implications. *Elementary School Journal, 106*(2), 105–130.

Huey, S. J., Henggeler, S. W, Brondino, M. J. & Pickrel, S. G. (2000). Mechanisms of change in multisystemic therapy: Reducing delinquent behavior through therapist adherence and improved family and peer functioning. *Journal of Consulting & Clinical Psychology, 68*, 451–467.

Jensen, P. S., Hoagwood, K. & Trickett, E. J. (1999). Ivory tower or earthen trenches? Community collaborations to foster real-world research. *Applied Developmental Science, 3*, 206–212.

Kazdin, A. E. (1996). Dropping out of child psychotherapy: Issues for research and implications for practice. *Clinical Child Psychology and Psychiatry, 1*, 133–156.

Kazdin, A. E., Holland, L. & Crowley, M. (1997). Family experience of barriers to treatment and premature termination from child therapy. *Journal of Consulting and Clinical Psychology 65*, 453–463.

Kazdin, A. E. & Mazurick, J. L. (1994). Dropping out of child psychotherapy: Distinguishing early and late dropouts over the course of treatment. *Journal of Consulting and Clinical Psychology, 62*, 1069–1074.

Kazdin A. E., Mazurick, J. L. & Bass, D. (1993). Risk for attrition in treatment of antisocial children and families. *Journal of Clinical Child Psychology, 22,* 2–16.

Kazdin, A. E. & Wassell, G. (1999). Barriers to treatment participation and therapeutic change among children referred for conduct disorder. *Journal of Clinical and Child Psychology, 28,* 160–172.

Kendziora, K. T., Bruns, E., Osher, D., Pacchiano, D. & Mejia, B. (2001). *Wraparound: Stories from the field.* Washington, DC: Center for Effective Collaboration and Practice, American Institutes for Research.

Kendziora, K. Spier, E., Helsel, F., Albright, L., Navojosky, B. & Joseph, N. (2005, June). *Research and practice: A family-focused early childhood center and its long-term impact on children with serious behavioral and developmental concerns.* Symposium presented at the 12th Annual Building on Family Strengths Conference, Portland, OR.

Lynn, C. J., McKay, M. M., Hibbert, R., Carrera, S., Lawrence, R., Miranda, A., Jarvis, A. Gamble, D. & Palacios, J. et al. (2001). Developing collaborations with parents and schools to promote urban-child mental health. *Emotional & Behavioral Disorders in Youth, 1*(2), 31–32, 45.

Maddux, J. E. (2002). Self-efficacy. In C. R. Snyder & S. J. Lopez (Eds.), *Handbook of positive psychology* (pp. 277–287). New York: Oxford University Press.

McDonald, L. (1998). Systematically building multiple protective factors to increase Head Start children's mental health: The evaluated and replicated multifamily FAST program. In F. Lamb-Parker, J. Hagen, R. Robinson & C. Clark (Eds.), *Children and families in an era of rapid change: Creating a shared agenda for researchers, practitioners and policy makers* (pp. 274-275). Washington, DC: U.S. Department of Health and Human Services, Administration for Children, Youth and Families.

McKay, M. M., Gonzales, J. J., Quintana, E., Kim, L. & Abdul-Adil, J. (1999). Multiple family groups: An alternative for reducing disruptive behavioral difficulties of urban children. *Research on Social Work Practice, 9,* 593–607.

McKay, M. M., Pennington, J., Lynn, C. & McCadam, K. (2007). Treatment engagement with caregivers of at-risk children: Gaps in research and conceptualization. *Journal of Child and Family Studies, 16*(2), 183–196.

McKnight, J. L. (1985). *The careless society: Community and its counterfeits.* New York: Basic Books.

Merton, R. K. (1957). *Social theory and social structure,* rev. and ex. ed. Glencoe, IL: Free Press.

Morrissey-Kane, E. & Prinz, R. J. (1999). Engagement in child and adolescent treatment: The role of parental cognitions. *Clinical Child and Family Review, 2,* 183–198.

Miller, G. E. & Prinz, R. J. (1990). Enhancements of social learning family interventions for childhood conduct disorder. *Psychological Bulletin, 108,* 291–307.

National Council on Disability (2004). *Consumer-directed health care: How well does it work?* Washington, DC: National Council on Disability.

New Freedom Commission on Mental Health (2003) *Achieving the promise: Transforming mental health care in America, final report* (DHHS Pub. SMA-03-3832). Rockville, MD.

Osher, D. (2000). Breaking the cultural disconnect: Working with families to improve outcomes for students placed at risk of school failure. In I. Ira Goldenberg (Ed.), *Urban education: Possibilities and challenges confronting colleges of education* (pp. 4–11). Miami: Florida International University.

Osher, D. (2002). Creating comprehensive and collaborative systems. *Journal of Child and Family Studies, 11*(1), 91–101.

Osher, D. & Hanley, T. V. (1997). Implications of the national agenda to improve results for children and youth with or at risk of serious emotional disturbance. In R. J. Illback and C. M. Nelson (Eds.), *Emerging school-based approaches for children with emotional and behavioral problems: Research and practice in service integration* (pp. 7–36). Binghamton, NY: Haworth Press.

Osher, D. & Hanley, T. V. (2001). Implementing the SED national agenda: Promising programs and policies for children and youth with emotional and behavioral problems. *Education and Treatment of Children, 24*(2), 1–29.

Osher, T. W., Blau, G. & Osher, D. (2006, December) *Family driven practice: How families can collaborate with professionals and youth to promote and influence it.* Workshop at Federation of Families for Children's Mental Health (FFCMH) Conference, St, Louis, MO.

Osher, T. W. & Osher, D. (2002). The paradigm shift to true collaboration with families. *Journal of Child and Family Studies, 11*(1), 47–60.

Owens, P. L., Hoagwood, K., Horwitz, S. M., Leaf, P. J., Poduska, J. M., Kellam, S. G. et al. (2002). Barriers to children's mental health services. *Journal American Academy of Child and Adolescent Psychiatry, 41*(6), 731–738.

Paulus, P. B., Larey, T. S. & Dzindolet, M. T. (2001). Creativity in groups and teams. In M. E. Turner (Ed.), *Groups at work: Theory and research* (pp. 319–338). Mahwah, NJ: Lawrence Erlbaum Associates.

Prinz, R. J. & Miller, G. E. (1994). Family-based treatment for childhood antisocial behavior: Experimental influences on dropout and engagement. *Journal of Consulting and Clinical Psychology, 62*, 645–650.

Prinz, R. J. & Miller, G. E. (1996). Parental engagement in interventions for children at risk for conduct disorder. In: R. D. Peters & R. J. McMahon (Eds.), *Preventing childhood disorders, substance abuse and delinquency* (pp. 161–183). Thousand Oaks, CA: Sage.

Prinz, R. J., Smith, E. P., Dumas, J., Laughlin, J. E., White, D. W. & Barron, R. (2001). Recruitment and retention of participants in prevention trials involving family-based interventions. *American Journal of Preventive Medicine, 20*(1S), 31–37.

Rast, J., Bruns, E. J., Brown, E. C., Peterson, C. R. & Mears, S. L. (working paper). Impact of the wraparound process in a child welfare system: Results of a matched comparison study.

Resendez, M.G., Quist, R.M. & Matshazi, D. G. M. (2000). A longitudinal analysis of family empowerment and client outcomes. *Journal of Child and Family Studies, 9*, 449–460.

Richard, C. & Lussier, M. (2007). Measuring patient and physician participation in exchanges on medications: Dialogue ratio, preponderance of initiative, and dialogical roles. *Patient Education and Counseling, 65*(3), 329–341.

Ross, K. B. & McLaughlin, K. A. (2006). Collaborative Intervention in Clinical Settings. *Journal of Medical Speech-Language Pathology, 14*(1), xi–xiv.

Rzepnicki, T. L. (1987). Recidivism of foster children returned to their own homes: A review and new directions for research. *Social Service Review, 61*, 56–70.

Schaeffer, C. M. (2001). Moderators and mediators of therapeutic change in multisystemic treatment of serious juvenile offenders. *Dissertation Abstracts International: Section B: The Sciences and Engineering, 61*(12-B), 6720.

Snell-Johns, J., Mendez, J. L. & Smith, B. H. (2004). Evidence-based solutions for overcoming access barriers, decreasing attrition, and promoting change with underserved families. *Journal of Family Psychology, 18*(1), 19–35.

Spoth, R. & Redmond, C. (1993). Study of participation barriers in family-focused prevention: Research issues and preliminary results. *International Quarterly of Community Health Education, 13*, 365–388.

Spoth, R. & Redmond, C. (1995). Parent motivation to enroll in parenting skills programs: A model of family context and health belief predictors. *Journal of Family Psychology, 9*, 294–310.

Spoth, R., Redmond, C. & Shin, C. (2000) Modeling factors influencing enrollment in family-focused preventive intervention research. *Prevention Science, 1*, 213–225.

Strain, P. S. & Timm, M. A. (2001). Remediation and prevention of aggression: An evaluation of the regional intervention program over a quarter century. *Behavioral Disorders, 26*(4), 297–313.

Suter, J. C. (2007). *A critical review of the evidence base for wraparound.* Paper presented at the Building on Family Strengths: Research and Services in Support of Children and their Families Conference, Portland, OR. Retrieved 16 August, 2007, from http://www.rtc.pdx.edu/conference/Presentations/pdf90bSuter.pdf.

Szapocznik, J., Perez-Vidal, A., Brickman, A., Foote, F. H., Santisteban, D. A., Hervis, O., et al. (1988). Engaging adolescent drug abusers and their families into treatment: A strategic structural systems approach. *Journal of Consulting and Clinical Psychology, 56*, 552–557.

Taub, J., Tighe, T. A. & Burchard, J. (2001). The effects of parent empowerment on adjustment for children receiving comprehensive mental health services. *Children's Services: Social Policy, Research & Practice, 4*(3), 103–122.

U.S. Department of Education, Office of Elementary and Secondary Education (2002). *No child left behind: A desktop reference.* Washington, DC: Author.

U.S. Public Health Service (1999). *Mental health: A report of the surgeon general.* Washington, DC: Author.

U.S. Public Health Service (2000). *Report on the surgeon general's conference on children's mental health.* Washington, DC: Author.

Webster-Stratton, C. (1994). Advancing videotape parent training: A comparison study. *Journal of Consulting and Clinical Psychology, 62*, 583–593.

Weisz, J. R. & Hawley, K. M. (1998). Finding, evaluating, refining, and applying empirically supported treatments for children and adolescents. *Journal of Clinical Child Psychology, 27*, 206–216.

Weisz, J. R. & Jensen, P. S. (1999). Efficacy and effectiveness of child and adolescent psychotherapy and pharmacotherapy. *Mental Health Services Research, 1,* 125–157.

Williams, B. E. (1988). Parents and patients: Members of an interdisciplinary team on an adolescent inpatient unit. *Clinical Social Work Journal, 20,* 78–91.

# 4

# Cultural Influences on Child Development: *The Middle Years*

TAWARA D. GOODE AND WENDY A. JONES

## INTRODUCTION

Culture influences every aspect of life. It defines who we are as human beings. Culture has multiple dimensions that intersect in time and space with common and distinct manifestations for individuals, groups and societies. Culture is a paradox—as its many dimensions remain constant yet others evolve and change—and it is both learned and unlearned. This chapter explores the cultural influences on child development during the middle years from ages 5 to 13. It is hypothesized that providers of behavioral health services must have a solid understanding of the multiple dimensions and dynamics of culture for this age group and that the efficacy of any evidence-based approaches to prevention and treatment must be implemented within the cultural contexts of children, their families and communities.

This hypothesis is used to examine the literature and organize the chapter in the following the sections:

- Cultural and linguistic diversity in the United States: A demographic context
- Defining culture
- Cultural contexts of the child and family dyad
- Cultural contexts of middle childhood
- Culture and the developmental tasks of middle childhood

## SIGNIFICANT INCREASES IN CULTURALLY AND LINGUISTICALLY DIVERSE POPULATIONS: A DEMOGRAPHIC CONTEXT

Demographic data indicate that in 2000 almost one third of the U.S. population was from racially and ethnically diverse groups other than White, representing an increase from one fourth of the population in 1990 (U.S. Census Bureau, 2000). According to the American Community Survey conducted by the U.S. Census Bureau in 2004, an estimated 14.3% of the U.S. population is

**Table 4.1**  Children Age 5 Through 17 Who Speak a Language Other Than English

| Language Spoken | Number of Children |
|---|---|
| Spanish | 6,830,090 |
| Chinese | 237,620 |
| French | 229, 270 |
| Vietnamese | 205,060 |
| German | 164,855 |
| Korean | 156,080 |
| Tagalog | 127,790 |
| Arabic | 124,220 |
| Russian | 117,520 |
| French Creole | 112,620 |
| Miao, Hmong | 82,655 |

between 5 and 14 years of age, or approximately 37,112,474 children and youth. A significant percentage of this population of children and youth is members of diverse racial and ethnic groups. This is largely attributed to higher birth rates among these groups and immigration patterns. The census bureau predicts that this trend will continue and that by the year 2030, 60% of the U.S. population will self-identify as White, Non-Hispanic and 40% will self-identify as members of other diverse racial and ethnic groups.

Census data also indicate that more than 47 million persons speak a language other than English at home, and of these more than 21 million speak English less than very well. Additionally, the Modern Language Association (2000) reported that 9,779,088 children and youth between the ages of 5 and 17 years speak a language other than English. Table 4.1 provides a listing of the top 10 languages spoken by these youth. An estimated 25.3% of the foreign-born population, or 11,893,572 people, lives in linguistic isolation, a term coined by the census bureau describing households where no person over the age of 14 speaks English very well (U.S. Census Bureau, 2000).

These demographic trends have significant implications not only for the population of children, youth and their families seeking and receiving behavioral health services but also for the nation's health and mental health care workforce (Bennett et al., 2003; Guhde, 2003; Martin-Holland, Bello-Jones, Shuman, Rutledge & Sechrist, 2003). Given this contextual reality, behavioral health-care systems need to undergo fundamental change to embrace and to respond effectively to the diversity within U.S. society. Of particular relevance to providers of child and adolescent behavioral health services is the need for cultural and linguistic competence: the capacity to acquire values, knowledge and skill sets to work effectively cross-culturally. This includes providers' capacity to translate evidenced-based practices into the cultural, linguistic and social contexts of the families and communities they serve. A growing body of evidence documents cultural competence and linguistic competence as essential skill sets for providers of both health and behavioral health services, as necessary for the provision of quality care and as effective approaches to address disparities in access to and use of care and in outcomes for racial and ethnic communities.

**Table 4.2**   Selected Definitions of Culture

| Definition or Framework | Author |
|---|---|
| "Culture is a set of meanings, behavioral norms, and values used by members of a particular society, as they construct their unique view of the world." | Alarcon, Foulks & Vakkur (1998) p. 6 |
| "Culture is conceived as a set of denotative (what is or beliefs), connotative (what should be, or attitudes, norms and values), and pragmatic (how things are done or procedural roles) knowledge, shared by a group of individuals who have a common history and who participate in a social structure." | Basabe, Paez, Valencia, González, Rime & Diener (2002) p. 104 |
| "The term culture refers to social reality. It can be defined as a complex collection of components that a group of people share to help them adapt to their social and physical world." | Yamamoto, Silva, Ferrari & Nukariya (1997) p. 34 |
| "Culture is a shared pattern of belief, feeling, and knowledge that ultimately guide everyone's conduct and definition of reality." | Griffith & Gonzalez (1994) p. 1379 |
| "Culture is a shared organization of ideas that includes the intellectual, moral and aesthetic standards prevalent in a community and the meanings of communicative actions." | LeVine (1984) p. 66 |
| "Culture is as an integrated pattern of human behavior which includes but is not limited to thought, communication, languages, beliefs, practices, customs, rituals, manners of interacting, roles, relationships and expected behaviors of a racial, ethnic, religious, social, or political group. Culture is transmitted to succeeding generations, is dynamic in nature, and changes over time." | National Center for Cultural Competence (2001) p. 1 |
| "Culture is a person's/group's beliefs, their interactions with the world, and how they are affected by the environment in which they exist." | Gaetano Lotrecchiano (2005) p. 3 |
| "The shared values, traditions, norms, customs, arts, history, folklore, and institutions of a group of people that are unified by race, ethnicity, language, nationality, or religion." | Welch, M. (2003) p. 1 |
| "Culture is a system of collectively held values, beliefs, and practices of a group which guides decisions and actions in patterned and recurrent ways. It encompasses the organization of thinking, feeling, believing, valuing and behaving collectively that differentiates one group from another. Values and beliefs often function on an unconscious level." | Suganya Sockalingam (2004) p. 4 |

## DEFINING CULTURE

### Definitions of Culture and Common Elements

The literature defines culture in myriad ways. Use of the term *culture* spans a wide spectrum that ranges from the culture of a group of people or society to pop culture; youth culture; urban, rural or frontier culture; organizational culture and the cultures associated with specific disciplines or fields of study to name a few. The definitions listed in Table 4.2 were selected because of their relevance to conceptualizing and understanding the impact of culture on child development for children 5 to 13 years of age.

A close examination of these definitions and frameworks reveals greater similarities than differences. This chapter provides a summary of the common elements most important to understanding culture:

- It is applicable to all peoples.
- It is value laden and tells group members how to behave and provides their identity.
- It structures perceptions and shapes behaviors.

- It is based on values and belief systems.
- It is multifactorial, multilayered and multidimensional.
- It exists at conscious and unconscious levels.
- It is active, dynamic and malleable over time.
- It varies in expression both among and between individual group members.
- It permeates every aspect of life.

These common elements indicate the complexity of culture. Culture is almost always defined within the context of a group—providing the code of behavior and the identity of a group and its members. The focus on the group within these definitions and frameworks may inadvertently obscure the individual as an active participant in the dynamics of culture. Harkness and Super (1996) developed "The Developmental Niche," a model that explores the impact of culture on child development. This model espouses that the child is not a passive recipient of culture and that his or her unique characteristics and temperament influence the transmission of culture from caretakers, community and society as a whole. This underscores the principle that aspects of culture are manifested differently within each individual. A member of a cultural group may not necessarily embrace all of the beliefs, values, practices and modes of communication that are attributed to the group. For example, the code of behavior demonstrated by an individual may be somewhat or distinctly different from that of the group to which he or she is a member. This view of culture acknowledges the many within-group differences and the inherent diversity among each individual or group member. It is particularly relevant to children in middle childhood as peer group membership, social competence and burgeoning self-identity rank among the primary developmental tasks during this period.

## Cultural Factors That Influence Diversity Among Individuals and Groups

Many perceive diversity as limited to race and ethnicity. Although race and ethnicity are important social constructs among people in the United States, they are only two of the numerous cultural factors that influence diversity among individuals and groups. The framework (Figures 4.1 and 4.2) adapted from Mason (1998) is offered here as a useful tool to examine diversity in a broader context that explores the multiple facets and dimensions of culture in greater depth. One example is family constellation. The concept of family and the definition of the family unit are culture bound. Culture defines who is embraced as family such as nuclear, extended and fictive kin (familiar bonds with individuals who are not related by blood). It defines the expected roles for males, females, adults and children. Last, culture determines the relationships and manners of interacting between family members and those external to the family unit.

Though not intended to be all inclusive, the factors presented in the framework have a significant influence on children in middle childhood, families and the communities in which they live. Providers of child and adolescent behavioral health services must have an understanding of these factors and their relevance to evidence-based practices.

**Figure 4.1** Internal factors.

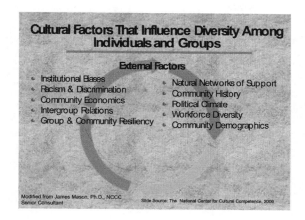

**Figure 4.2** External factors.

## Views and Perceptions of Cultural Identity

In a review of selected studies and articles, it is noted that this literature primarily focuses on the concept of ethnic and racial identity rather than cultural identity (Ancis, 2004; Dosamantes-Beaudry, 1997; Johnson-Powell & Yamamoto, 1997; Nagel, 1994; Phinney, 1990; Roberts et al., 1999; Taylor-Gibbs & Nahme-Huang, 2003). A contextual reality of the United States is that historically racial and ethnic group identification has been based on skin color and notions of superiority and inferiority. As a result, self-identity has and continues to be disproportionately influenced by concepts of race and ethnicity as opposed to culture in the United States. A discussion of this literature follows.

Many researchers conclude that racism has a deleterious effect on the development of self-identity and self-image in children. Children express an understanding of both their own and others' racial identity as early as 3 years of age. They describe cultural group attributes of others (usually modeled after their parent's description) at 3, 4 or 5 years of age (Banks & McGee-Banks,

1997). Children generally limit their expression of cultural attributes to physical descriptors and learn the values associated with these—either negative or positive—from the adults in their environment. For example, Dosamantes-Beaudry (1997, p. 132) stated, "Each culture determines the kind of body-image its children will construct because each culture has its own standards of beauty and these influence and mold what children learn to exalt or denigrate about their bodies." Moreover, Yamamoto, Silva, Ferrari, and Nukariya (in Johnson-Powell and Yamamoto, 1997, p. 45) stated, "Racism is linked to racial awareness, the latter phenomenon beginning during early childhood. Therefore, minority children learn early that their ethnic identity may not be a source of self-respect." Based on this literature it is abundantly clear that self-identity during the middle years is critically impacted by the magnitude of racism, discrimination and bias in U.S. society.

There are several different constructs and theories that explore the developmental nature of ethnic identity. Smith, Walker, Fields, Brookins & Seay (1999, p. 868) put forth two constructs related to ethnic identity in children: compartmentalization and developmental. The first construct states that children are able to extract or compartmentalize their perception of themselves from the perceptions of their racial or ethnic group, "enabling them to develop a positive self-esteem in the face of negative pejorative information about one's racial-ethnic group." In the second construct, the researchers posit that ethnic identity follows a developmental path and that children at the lower end of the middle-years spectrum lack sufficient cognitive development to integrate their understanding of ethnic identity and self-esteem. However, as children's cognitive capacity grows with age, they become more conscious of social perceptions of their ethnic group. They then begin to link their ethnic group membership with their self-identity, and self-esteem can be positively or negatively impacted.

Comprehensive literature reviews and studies conducted by Roberts et al. (1999) and Phinney (1990) reported social identity theory, acculturation theory and identity formation theory as the three theories most often used to explain cultural identity. Social identity theory emphasizes the positive nature of belonging to an ethnic group and that the positive attributes of the group are internalized and bolster self-esteem among its members. The implications of this theory for children in the middle years are that the stronger the positive experiences within their group, the greater sense of ethnic pride, affiliation and self-identification. Acculturation theory addresses how immigrant groups relate to the new societies in which they live and how they identify with their own ethnic group. There are two schools of thought in acculturation theory. The first describes ethnic identity as occurring along a continuum "ranging from strong ethnic ties at one extreme to strong mainstream ties at the other" (Phinney, 1990, p. 501). This theory espouses that acculturation requires the weakening of ethnic identity. The second school of thought delineates acculturation as a two-dimensional process in which the individual develops a relationship with the new culture while simultaneously maintaining his or her ethnic identity. Researchers and leaders in the field have applied acculturation theory not only to immigrant groups but also to racial and ethnic groups with long-standing histories in the United States. For example, Table 4.3 cites two major principles that the National Center for Cultural Competence (2001)

**Table 4.3**   Major Values and Principles Integral to Cultural Competence in Systems of Care

| Values and Principles |
| --- |
| Providers must recognize that racial and ethnic populations have to be at least bicultural and that this status may create a unique set of issues to which they must have the capacity to respond effectively. |
| Providers must have the capacity to inquire about and understand an individual's or family's cultural identity and levels of acculturation to apply the helping principle of "starting where the client is." |

adapted from Cross, Bazron, Dennis, and Isaacs (1989) that give credence to this worldview.

Acculturation theory emphasizes the significance of the psychosocial processes required of children in the middle years to navigate multiple cultural contexts and their dynamic relationships to ethnic self-identity. Last, identity formation theory frames ethnic identity as a developmental process that involves exploring and learning about one's ethnic group and culminates with an understanding, acceptance and conscious choice to commit to being a member of that group. Identity formation theory, when applied to children in the middle years, suggests that ethnic identity is diffuse and does not completely occur until later in adolescence.

This chapter's discussion of the definitions, theoretical frameworks and constructs presented in the literature underscores the importance of understanding the impact of culture on child development for children 5 to 13 years of age. We would be remiss, however, if we did not address an essential element of cultural competence: the capacity for self-assessment. The process of cultural competence self-assessment can benefit practitioners by heightening awareness, influencing attitudes toward practice and motivating the development of knowledge and skills (National Center for Cultural Competence, 2004). A self-assessment checklist for providers of child and adolescent behavioral health services is provided in the Appendix.

Lynch and Hanson (1992, p. 35) provided an insightful and eloquent analogy of culture including the need for self-reflection: "Culture is akin to being the person observed through a one-way mirror; everything we see is from our own perspective. It is only when we join the observed on the other side that is possible to see ourselves and others clearly—but getting to the other side of the glass presents many challenges." Providers should routinely self-reflect and keep in mind the following:

- They view the world through their own cultural lens.
- Their world view impacts approaches to delivering behavioral health services to children, adolescents and their families.
- Evidence-based practices for prevention and treatment must be developed for or adapted to the culture of the populations that they are serving.

Table 4.4 provides a listing of thoughts about culture that aid providers to reflect on their interactions with children in middle childhood, their families and communities.

**Table 4.4**  Thoughts About Culture: Considerations for Providers

Understanding another culture is a continuous and not a discreet process.

It requires experience as well as study to understand the many subtleties of another culture.

Stereotyping is probably inevitable in the absence of frequent contact with or study of other cultures.

What seems to be logical, sensible, important and reasonable in one culture may seem illogical, irrational and unimportant to an outsider.

When people talk about other cultures, they tend to describe the differences rather than the similarities.

Differences between cultures are often seen as threatening and are often described in negative terms.

It is probably necessary to know the language of another culture to understand that culture in depth.

## CULTURAL CONTEXTS OF THE CHILD AND FAMILY DYAD

As previously stated, the definition, meaning and composition of family are culture bound. Though many definitions for the term *family* were reviewed for this study, the following definition, developed by United Advocates for Children of California (2005), was selected for use because of its rich and inclusive conceptualization of family that integrates culture:

> Family is an enduring relationship, whether biological or non-biological, chosen or circumstantial, connecting a child/youth and parent/caregiver through culture, tradition, shared experiences, emotional commitment and mutual support.

Just as the concept of family is culturally determined, so too are the significance, roles and expectations of children. The chapter next explores the influence of culture on the child and family dyad during the middle years.

### Values and Belief Systems

Values are one of the common threads in the definitions of culture reviewed for this chapter. Values form the basis for beliefs, norms, behaviors and practices for any cultural group. Values (1) develop early in life; (2) are imparted by direct experiences with others, particularly parents, caregivers and other family members; and (3) define what is right or wrong and good or bad based on norms internal to the group. Beliefs are ideas or convictions perceived to be true, by individuals or groups, often without evidence to support their veracity.

These constructs are particularly important for the middle years because children in this age group are in the formative stages of development. Children are gaining an understanding of their identity and culture based on family and community values. At the lower range of this age spectrum, children integrate the values, beliefs and practices of their parents and caregivers into their behaviors and attitudes. As children grow older and as their cognitive abilities advance, they learn the values and beliefs of others, distinguish differences between values that are internal and external to their family and culture and make conscious decisions to accept or reject them. Children during this stage of development become increasingly capable of regulating their behavior based on cultural values, beliefs and norms.

## Child-Rearing Beliefs and Practices

Kitayama and Rose-Markus (1994) suggested that a cultural group's perceptions are shaped by the habitual and normative aspects of social behavior. Culture plays a significant role in the formation of parental beliefs and practices related to child rearing: "Parent's understanding of the nature of children, the structure of their development, and the meaning of behavior are to a large extent shared by members of a cultural group" (Harkness & Super, 1996, p. 2). Adults assimilate their key cultural understandings and beliefs about the nature and meaning of parenthood, child development and desired behaviors and use these values to select child-rearing practices. In *From Neurons to Neighborhood,* a landmark study published by the National Research Council and the Institute of Medicine in 2000 (p. 239), the authors observed, "Even within relatively homogenous groups, parents deploy their childrearing responsibilities in widely different ways. Confronted with this task, researchers have continued to pursue the dimensions of control and warmth but they have also extended their reach to capture the ways in which parents support learning and make investments and choices that affect the well-being and future prospects of their children." This research offers evidence that an understanding of child-rearing beliefs and practices, from a cultural perspective, is indeed essential to any meaningful engagement of parents or caregivers in prevention and intervention efforts for children in the middle years.

## Parental Expectations for Child Development

There is a wide variation in the growth and development of children during the middle years: height or physical stature, physical strength and endurance and onset of puberty. Researchers document that there also is wide variation in parental expectations of their children; however, the preponderance of these studies addresses early childhood. Nonetheless, their implications span the boundary of early childhood to the middle years. Pachter and Dworkin (1997) and Goodnow and Collins (1990) found that the underlying expectations for the attainment of developmental skills differ across ethnocultural groups. This research found concordance in expectations for gross motor and language development but vast differences in parental expectations for social and personal competency (e.g., activities of daily living, self-help skills, and comportment). Carlson and Harwood (2000) examined differences in parental expectations for attainment of milestones and found a high degree of variance between racial and ethnic groups (e.g., Anglo, Filipino, and Puerto Rican mothers).

This chapter explores the childhood years from 5 to 13 years of age. This is a highly value-laden transitional period. At age 5, children typically enter kindergarten and may leave early-child-care or early-education settings behind. This transition raises issues of increased demands on social-emotional, cognitive and self-help skills. It may be a time of particular stress for parents and for their children. Thirteen years of age marks entry into the beginning phases of adolescence. There are many cultural rituals to celebrate this stage of development. In some communities this age is associated with rites of passage, a tradition that asks the ancestors' guidance into young adulthood. In other cultural traditions Bat Mitzvah and Bar Mitzvah not only mark entering adolescence; they also declare a commitment and acceptance of religious faith and teachings. Confirmation is yet another religious milestone that honors acceptance of the church at an individual level that confirms a youth's commitment to his or her faith. Many families look to religious and spiritual doctrine to guide their children's moral development.

## Gender Roles

Transference of codes of behavior and norms for male and female children occur early in development and are steeped in culture. These behavioral norms generally differ for male and female children and are typically linked to such factors as birth order and age. For example, what it is to be a "good boy" or "good girl" may involve athleticism, modesty, being responsible for siblings, doing household chores, performing well in school, participating in religious and spiritual services, and being respectful to adults or elders. Each of these is expressed differently based on gender and culture. This stage of development is characterized by children forming same-sex friendships and moves toward peer-group membership with opposite sex.

## Interactions Outside the Family Unit

There are differential expectations for behaviors inside and outside the family unit. These codes of behavior govern such dynamics as communication, interactions with adults (both those who are known to the family and strangers), peer relationships and deference paid to authority figures. Among many cultures, parents and caregivers often exercise more caution with children at the lower end of this age spectrum (protectiveness) and become increasingly lenient as the children grow older. The opposite may be true in other cultures. Some parents may hold a closer rein on children when physical maturity begins—again exercising a sense of caution and protection from individuals and situations that are out of the immediate control of the family unit. This period may be marked with conflict as children have a growing sense of independence and need to explore the world outside of the family.

In summary, the cultural influences on the child and family dyad during the middle years are dynamic and multidimensional. Families are the children's first teachers. They pass down values, beliefs, traditions and norms that are held in high esteem within the cultural contexts of the family and community: "Every culture must devise the ways of passing on the wisdom and skills of past generations to its young" (Newman & Newman, 1991, p. 356). The child and family dyad is the medium through which this torch is passed.

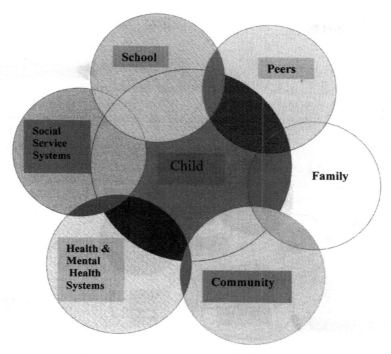

**Figure 4.3** Graphic depiction of some cultural contexts that influence child development during the middle years.

## CONVERGENCE OF CULTURAL CONTEXTS DURING MIDDLE CHILDHOOD

Numerous cultural contexts converge and influence child development during the middle years. Figure 4.3 is a graphic representation of many, but not all, of these contexts. A discussion of each follows.

### The Child

Harkness and Super (1996) developed a theoretical framework for conceptualizing the cultural structuring of a child's daily environment known as the development niche. The niche is composed of three components: (1) the physical and social settings of everyday life; (2) the routine customs of care; and (3) the psychology of the child's caregivers, including cultural practices, beliefs and expectations of the child's parent and other caregivers. Harkness and Super asserted that the child is highly influenced by caregivers' belief systems and the environment. The child, however, is not a sponge that simply absorbs these cultural influences within their environment. The child is indeed an active participant and shapes the niche through individual characteristics such as temperament, age, gender, birth order, sexual identity and orientation, health status, mental health status and physical ability or disability. This model of understanding cultural influences is of particular importance given the major developmental tasks of middle childhood—such as early moral development, sex-role identification, social competence—that are delineated in the next section of the chapter.

## Family

Throughout the chapter, an emphasis is placed on viewing children within the cultural contexts of their families. Within the family unit, the literature recognizes parents as being the most powerful models, guides and designers of children's social and cultural experiences. Cross et al. (1989) stated that the family, as defined by each culture, is the primary system of support and preferred intervention. This has two significant implications. First, evidence-based prevention and intervention practices are not culturally devoid—they must address the cultural beliefs and practices of families to be effective. Second, providers of child and adolescent behavioral health services must use a practice model that incorporates cultural contexts of children, families and communities in the delivery of care.

## Peers

Peer relationships provide another cultural context for children in the middle years: "To be healthy, children must form relationships not only with their parents, but also with siblings, and with peers" (U.S. Department of Health and Human Services, 1999, p. 126). Through peers children learn a range of cultural values, norms and perspectives that may differ from those of their family and community. The peer group affords the opportunity to explore these differences in a nonthreatening manner. It also fosters an acceptance of difference based on affinity and common interests. Peer-group approaches should be an integral component of evidence-based prevention and intervention as it is one of the most important contexts for shaping and influencing behavior during the middle years.

## Community

Several definitions of community are applicable to the concepts of culture addressed in this chapter. Warren (1978) (as cited in Goode, 2001, p. 2) defined community as "a framework for living—a complex network of people, institutions, shared interests, locality and sense of psychological belonging." Merriam-Webster's Dictionary (1994) (as cited in ibid., p. 2) defined community as "an interacting population of various kinds of individuals in a common location; a body of persons with common interest scattered through a larger society; and joint ownership or participation." These definitions offer different perspectives yet share a commonality that is applicable to concepts of culture addressed in this chapter. LeVine (1984, p. 67) stated, "Culture is a shared organization of ideas that includes the intellectual, moral and aesthetic standards prevalent in a community." These definitions underscore the need for evidence-based prevention and intervention practices to address children and families within the cultural contexts of their communities. Spurlock and Norris (in Johnson-Powell &Yamamoto, 1997, p. 46) upheld this assertion and suggested, "Children who learn that their community is undesirable and unsafe develop a high level of mistrust toward their social environment, which leads to a worldview marked with suspicion."

## School

School is one of the most prominent social environments for children during the middle years. It a forum in which multiple cultural contexts intersect and may affirm or conflict with cultural values, beliefs and norms of children, their families and the communities in which they live. Several theories describe one aspect of culture as the capacity to compartmentalize—meaning that the environment dictates how culture is conveyed. These theories posit that culture is expressed differently in different settings such as home and school. Fordham and Ogbu (1986, p. 179) suggested, "Maintaining a strong ethnic identity may present problems in negotiating schooling in the USA." Fordham (1988, p. 60) asserted, that "the ethos of schools in the U.S. might necessitate compromising one's ethnic identity" to be accepted within this environment.

In contrast, the school can provide a rich environment to implement evidence-based prevention and intervention practices and is a natural setting to foster respect for and appreciation of the many cultural differences among children, families and communities.

## Social Service Systems

Unfortunately, during the middle years many children come in contact with their local social service systems, and a disproportionate percentage of these children are from racially and ethnically diverse groups. Although some progress has been made in addressing cultural and linguistic differences in these systems, numerous challenges remain: "Culturally responsive approaches incorporate the individual client or clients' biography, style, social networks, and special techniques and strategies appropriate to the client's culture, customs, and life habits" (Ancis, 2004, p. 13).

Social service systems need to integrate evidence-based prevention and intervention practices that are adapted to the cultural and linguistic contexts of the communities they serve and that are tailored to children in middle childhood.

## Mental Health and Health Systems

Nationally, systems that provide behavioral health and health-care services are struggling to respond effectively to the preferences and needs of children and families from diverse cultural groups. Cultural and linguistic competence is recognized by many experts as a fundamental aspect of quality health and mental health care. Both are essential approaches to reducing disparities by improving access to and use of care and health and mental health outcomes. Ancis (2004, p. 13) stated, "Clinicians employing culturally responsive approaches either integrate culture-specific theories and interventions with contemporary Western approaches, reconfigure traditional Western approaches, or implement novel strategies in assisting clients." There is an emerging body of evidence to support the efficacy of cultural and linguistic competence. This evidence must be drawn upon and integrated into prevention and intervention approaches for children in middle childhood and their families.

Although each of these cultural contexts are presented separately, they are integrally linked, are interdependent and do not exist in isolation of one another. This suggests that evidence-based approaches must be multidimensional and will require continual adaptation to respond to the convergence of cultural contexts during the middle years.

## CONVERGENCE OF CULTURAL CONTEXTS DURING MIDDLE CHILDHOOD AND THE EVIDENCE

There is an array of definitions and standards of what constitutes "evidence-based" practice. Hoagwood, Burns, Kiser, Ringeisen & Schoenwald (2001, p. 1180) stated, "The term evidence-based has been used to refer to analytic reviews of bodies of studies on a target problem or group." These researchers further indicate that in child and adolescent mental health "the term evidence-based is most often used to differentiate therapies—generally psychosocial—that have been studied with varying degrees of rigor from therapies that are used but have not been studied or have not been studied well" (ibid.). There are differing criteria for evidence-based practices espoused by researchers, professional societies, community providers and ethnic-specific mental health associations and alliances. The field of child and adolescent mental health has yet to reach consensus on what constitutes an evidence-based practice.

The following criteria were used to search for efficacious evidence-based practices that are designed for the cultural contexts as described in this chapter: "Two or more studies that show the intervention to be superior to a wait-list control condition, or one experiment meeting the American Psychological Association criteria for 'well established' treatment, or three single-case studies must be conducted" (Hoagwood et al., 2001).

There are few studies on evidence-based practices for children in the middle years focusing on the cultural contexts, as defined in this chapter, that simultaneously address culture, language and cultural and linguistic competence. Further, most of the literature reviewed addressed evidence-based practices for children 12 years and older.

Table 4.5 examines one evidence-based practice for each of the cultural contexts including family, school, social service system and mental health and health systems. The table provides a synopsis of the evidence-based practice, its history and the populations served. A critical analysis also is provided of the extent to which the specific practices incorporate cultural and linguistic competence as defined in the following section.

### Cultural Competence

The National Center for Cultural Competence embraces a conceptual framework and model for achieving cultural competence adapted from the work of Cross et al. (1989). The National Center for Cultural Competence uses this framework and model to underpin all of its activities. Cultural competence requires that organizations do the following:

- Have a congruent, defined set of values and principles and demonstrate behaviors, attitudes, policies and structures that enable them to work effectively cross-culturally
- Have the capacity to (1) value diversity; (2) conduct self-assessment; (3) manage the dynamics of difference; (4) acquire and institutionalize cultural knowledge; and (5) adapt to the diversity and cultural contexts of communities they serve
- Incorporate the first two points into all aspects of policymaking, administration, practice and service delivery and to systematically involve consumers, key stakeholders and communities

Cultural competence is a developmental process that evolves over an extended period of time. Individuals, organizations and systems are at various levels of awareness, knowledge and skills along the cultural competence continuum.

## Linguistic Competence

Linguistic competence (Goade, T. and James, W., 2006) is the ability of an organization and its personnel to communicate effectively and to convey information in a manner that is easily understood by diverse audiences including persons of limited English proficiency, those who have low literacy skills or are not literate and individuals with disabilities. Linguistic competency requires organizational and provider capacity to respond effectively to the health literacy needs of populations served. The organization must have policy, structures, practices, procedures and dedicated resources to support this capacity. This may include, but is not limited to, the use of the following:

- Bilingual and bicultural or multilingual and multicultural staff
- Cross-cultural communication approaches
- Cultural brokers
- Foreign language interpretation services including distance technologies
- Sign language interpretation services
- Multilingual telecommunication systems
- Videoconferencing and telehealth technologies
- Teletype or text telephone (TTY) and other assistive technology devices
- Computer-assisted real-time translation (CART) or viable real-time transcriptions (VRT)
- Print materials in easy-to-read, low-literacy, picture and symbol formats
- Materials in alternative formats (e.g., audiotape, Braille, enlarged print)
- Varied approaches to share information with individuals who experience cognitive disabilities
- Materials developed and tested for specific cultural, ethnic and linguistic groups
- Translation services including the following:
  - Legally binding documents (e.g., consent forms, confidentiality and patient rights statements, release of information, applications)
  - Signage
  - Health education materials
  - Public awareness materials and campaigns
- Ethnic media in languages other than English (e.g., television, radio, Internet, newspapers, periodicals)

Although Table 4.5 reports on only one evidence-based practice per cultural context, other practices merit mentioning and should be critically examined for their efficacy with diverse cultural groups and for cultural and linguistic competence as articulated in Table 4.5.

- "Incredible Years Series" is a set of training curricula for parents, teachers and children designed to support social competence and to prevent, to reduce and to treat conduct problems in young children (3 to 8 years of age). Trained facilitators use video vignettes to encourage problem solving and group discussion. The parent training component is the core of

**Table 4.5**  Evidence-Based Practices for Cultural Contexts

| Cultural Context | Description | Intended Population | Critical Reflections on Cultural and Linguistic Competence |
|---|---|---|---|
| **Family**<br><br>Functional Family Therapy (FFT) (Elliott, 2002a) | FFT is a well-documented prevention and intervention practice that has been in existence since 1969, with 25 successful replications and citations in 13 journals. FFT is a three-phase program that uses assessment and intervention as key components to help families achieve obtainable change and to become more productive.<br><br>The program consists of the following:<br><br>(1) Engagement and motivation: Uses reframing and related techniques to impact maladaptive beliefs, perceptions and emotional responses.<br><br>(2) Behavior change: Highlights individualized and developmentally appropriate techniques through the use of training on communication, interpersonal relationships, parenting skills, discipline, problem solving and conflict management.<br><br>(3) Generalization: Families are supported to generalize and apply new skills to other situations through case management based on individualized family functional needs and their interface with community and environmental resources. | FFT is designed for youth ages 11 to 18 who are in or at risk for out-of-home placement in residential or juvenile detention settings due to delinquency, violence, substance use, conduct disorder, oppositional defiant disorder and disruptive behavior disorder.<br><br>FFT has been applied to diverse population groups including White, African American, Hispanic/Latino, Asian American, Native American and combined heritage in a range of settings including rural, suburban and urban and reportedly with same degree of efficacy. | Although FFT has been widely used for culturally and linguistically diverse families, the studies fail to document critical elements of cultural and linguistic competence as applied to this evidence-based practice. Replications indicate adaptations were made to address issues of culture and ethnicity; however, they were limited to the following:<br><br>(1) Ethnic concordance with families and therapists<br>(2) Provision of home-based services<br>(3) Extending hours of service delivery<br><br>The literature does not provide clear evidence of how culture and language are consistently addressed in adaptations to the FFT model. Noticeably absent were references to the following:<br><br>• Therapist–family language concordance<br>• Interpretation and translation services<br>• Cross-cultural communication skills<br>• Professional development and in-service training to support therapists to acquire knowledge of the cultural beliefs and practices of diverse families and communities<br><br>There is no reference to the intersection of primary care and mental health in this treatment model. |

**School**

Life Skills Training (LST) (Elliott, 2002b)

LST is a three-year intervention that is implemented in classroom settings by teachers and is designed to prevent or reduce gateway drug use (i.e., tobacco, alcohol and marijuana). There have been 19 major short- and long-term evaluation studies to test the effectiveness of LST. LST provides general life skills training and social resistance skills training to sixth and seventh graders. The curriculum includes 15 sessions taught in school settings by regular classroom teachers in the first year, 10 booster sessions in the second year, and 5 sessions in the third year.

Three components of the program are as follows:

(1) Personal self-management skill: Decision making, problem solving, self-control skills for with anxiety and self-improvement skills
(2) Social skills: Communication and general social skills
(3) Drug-related information and skill development: Knowledge and information concerning drugs, skills for resisting influence from media and peers and life skills training

LST is designed for use with middle school or junior high students. It has been implemented with White populations in urban, suburban and rural settings and with African American, Hispanic and Asian American populations in urban settings.

LST reflects values, principles and practices of cultural and linguistic competence.

LST supports modification to address the following:

Demographic factors (e.g., age, gender, and social class)

Cultural factors (e.g., ethnic and cultural identity)

Community factors (e.g., resources, neighborhood organizations and availability of drugs)

School factors (e.g., school bonding, size, climate)

Family factors (e.g., communication, discipline, monitoring, parental drug use, parental attitudes toward drug use)

Peer influence factors (e.g., friends' drug use or pro-drug attitudes)

LST replication models employed the following sequence:

1. Exploratory/qualitative research consisting of focus-group testing and key informant interviews
2. Expert review of intervention methods and materials
3. Consumer-based review of intervention materials and methods
4. Small-scale pilot studies
5. Large-scale randomized field trials

LST exemplifies values, principles and practices of culture competence:

• The unique needs and preferences of individuals, children, families, organizations and communities served are tailored (e.g., changed graphics and language to reflect the diversity of the community).
• Practice is driven by culturally preferred choices, not by culturally blind or culturally free interventions.
• The concept of self-determination is extended to the community.

The literature does not provide clear evidence of that LST has been implemented in languages other than English, including sign language.

There is no reference to the intersection of primary care and mental health in this treatment model.

(continued)

**Table 4.5 (Continued)**

| Context | Description | Intended Population | Critical Reflections on Cultural and Linguistic Competence |
|---|---|---|---|
| **Social Service System** | | | |
| Multisystemic Therapy (MST) (Elliott, 2002c) | MST is an intensive family- and community-based treatment addressing the multiple determinants of serious antisocial behavior in juvenile offenders. This approach views individuals as embedded in a network of systems that are complex and interconnected. MST has been in existence since the 1970s, was evaluated in eight published random trials beginning in 1986, and is currently undergoing 14 randomized trials in North America and Norway. The goal of MST is to promote behavior change within the youth's natural environment using the strengths of each system, including family, peers, school, neighborhood and indigenous support network to facilitate change. MST is a home-based model that employs strategic family therapy, structural family therapy, behavioral parent training and cognitive behavior therapy. | MST focuses on chronic, violent or substance-abusing male or female juvenile offenders between the ages of 12 and 17 years who are at risk for out-of-home placement and their families. MST has been implemented with White and African American youth—predominantly males. | MST reflects a number of the values, principles and practices of cultural competence: Families are full collaborators and guide treatment planning. This is commensurate with a key value of cultural competence: Families are ultimate decision-makers for services and supports for their children or themselves. Extended family and informal support networks reflect the culture of the youth and family. This is consistent with a value of cultural competence: Involves working in conjunction with natural, informal support and helping networks within culturally diverse communities. Treatment teams reflect the ethnic make-up of the population being served. Multicultural teams provide a framework in which culturally appropriate and inappropriate practices can be identified and discussed. This is consistent with practices: recruitment, hiring and retention of a diverse and culturally competent workforces and uses a practice model that incorporates culture in the delivery of services and supports. There is no reference to the intersection of primary care and mental health in this treatment model. |

## Mental Health and Health Systems

Cognitive Behavioral Therapy (CBT) (Miranda et al., 2005; National Association of Cognitive-Behavioral Therapists, 2006)

CBT is a form of psychotherapy based on a scientific framework that thoughts cause feelings and behaviors in people, rather than external forces (e.g., things, people, situations, events). CBT promotes that changing the way a person thinks has a positive impact on the way he or she feels and ultimately behaves. The goal of the therapy is to assist the person to (1) identify feelings, thoughts and behaviors, before and after a condition related emotional response or behavior; and (2) unlearn unwanted reactions and learn new ways of reacting. There are five approaches to CBT:

Rational emotive behavior therapy
Rational behavior therapy
Rational living therapy
Cognitive therapy
Dialectic behavior therapy

CBT is appropriate for school-age children (6–12 year olds) and adolescents. Specific age ranges vary by the condition treated. For example, when used to treat depression and anxiety CBT is appropriate for school-age and preadolescent populations. CBT has been implemented with children and youth across socioeconomic levels and for White, African American, Asian and Latino population groups.

Although CBT has been used to treat White, African American and Latino youth and their families, much of the literature does not address the values, principles and essential elements of cultural and linguistic competence. The majority of this literature does not provide clear evidence of how culture and language are consistently addressed in the CBT model. Noticeably absent were the following:

Acknowledgement and understanding of cultural variations in the expression of feelings, thought and behaviors and their implications for this intervention and family constellation (e.g., stepparents).

No data about gender differences in the effectiveness of CBT, although the majority of studies document more sample grouping with males. This is probably reflective of the representation of children and youth being referred to or receiving treatment.

In 2005 there were no studies documenting the efficacy of CBT with Native American or Alaska Native populations. Of the groups studied for depression and anxiety there were no significant difference in outcomes in the use of CBT by race and ethnicity.

There was no reference to the intersection of primary care and mental health in this treatment model.

the program, strengthening parental competencies including monitoring, confidence and positive discipline, and encourages parent involvement in academic and social experiences (Elliott, 2002e).

- Multidimensional treatment foster care (MTFC) is an alternative to placement in residential treatment facilities for adolescents who experience problems with chronic delinquency and antisocial behavior. Community families are recruited and trained to provide placements, treatment and supervision to adolescents participating in the program. MTFC parents are trained in behavior management methods to provide a structured, therapeutic living environment. Family therapy is provided to the youth's biologic or adoptive families to assist them in using the structured system used within the MTFC home (Elliott, 2002d).

- Parent management training interventions use parent training on behavioral techniques to reduce behaviors such as temper tantrums, non-compliance, aggression, defiance, stealing and destruction of property (Miranda et al., 2005).

- Cuento therapy uses oral and written stories, folk tales or biographies to improve self-concept in 5- to 9-year-old Hispanic and Latino children at risk for emotional and behavioral problems (ibid.).

In summary, there are few evidence-based prevention and intervention approaches that have been developed for children in middle childhood. The evidence-based practices reviewed for this chapter do not consistently (1) identify and isolate culture and language as independent variables; (2) specify the components or elements of the intervention that address the cultural contexts of the child, family, community or system; or (3) delineate the adaptations necessary to ensure efficacious implementation for diverse cultural and linguistic groups. Our observations have been substantiated in the literature by researchers including Weisz, Huey & Weersing (1998, p. 70): "EBT's [evidence-based therapies] based on work with mainstream samples may not take into account the language, values, customs, child-rearing traditions, expectancies for child and parent behavior, and distinctive stressors and resources associated with different cultural groups." Moreover, Lau (2006, p. 296) stated, "It is plausible that certain EBTs with established efficacy will not generalize to improve certain presenting problems in certain ethnic communities." The prevailing attitude of evidence-based practices being the intervention of choice for any population is being questioned. A vocal segment exists within the field of child and adolescent mental health that is advocating for and presenting compelling evidence that many evidence-based practices require cultural adaptations (Barrera & Gonzalez Castro, 2006; Bernal & Saez-Santiago, 2006; Hogg Foundation for Mental Health, 2006; Miranda, Nakamura & Bernal, 2003; Nagayama Hall, 2001). Providers of child and adolescent mental health services must have processes to determine the efficacy and appropriateness of all evidence-based practices within the cultural contexts of the populations and communities served. Such processes need to be legitimized by organizational policy and practice guidelines to achieve equity in outcomes and reduction of disparities.

# CULTURE AND THE DEVELOPMENTAL TASKS OF MIDDLE CHILDHOOD

Children in middle childhood experience striking physical, cognitive and socioemotional changes. During this period, it is anticipated that children will achieve cognitive, emotional and social milestones such as maintaining secure attachments, satisfying social relationships and effective coping skills. Growth and development across the cognitive, social and emotional domains do not occur within a vacuum; children are impacted and influenced by their cultural environment consisting of their family, peer-group and social contexts. This section examines the culturally influenced developmental, cognitive and psychosocial processes of children and youth during middle childhood. It also explores the influence of culture on the developmental tasks of middle childhood (from the age range of 5 to 13 years).

Psychosocial theory describes human development as resulting from the interactions between the individual's needs and abilities and the demands and expectations of society at specific stages of development across the lifespan. Each developmental stage is characterized by sequential completion of developmental tasks that define healthy, normal development at each age, in a particular society or culture.

## Developmental Tasks

### Early Moral Development

Early moral development in children involves the process of integrating parental values, standards and limits into a child's worldview. During this internalization process, a child learns the moral code of the family and community and is able to guide his or her behavior using the moral code. Families have their individual moral code based on their unique cultural values and experiences. It is important to note that a family or community's moral code may vary from that of school or society.

### Sex-Role Identification

Sex-role identification takes place prior to the middle childhood period. Children in this age range demonstrate an awareness of their own gender and its implications for social relationships and behavior. Cultural groups have their own perceptions and norms for individuals based on concepts of masculinity and femininity and male and female identities. Children understand these cultural norms: If one is in a certain role, one is expected to act in a certain way.

### Self-Esteem

Concepts of self-esteem emerge from children's understanding of themselves, their cultural environments, the interactions between the two and the consequences of these transactions. Children become much attuned to the slightest implication that they are not meeting the expectations of what or how a boy or girl in their cultural group should do or be. This attunement can give way to feelings of guilt and failure and to issues with self-doubt, self-comparison with peers, self-evaluation and self-criticism. Problems with self-esteem may arise when cultural beliefs dictate superiority of one group over another based on class, nationality, immigration status, race, ethnicity or religion.

### Group Play

Group play provides a bridge between the fantasy play of the toddler and pre-schooler and the emergence of the more structured team sports and games of the child and adolescent in the middle years. The emphasis of group play is on peer collaboration and cooperation. From the family perspective, some cultural groups place restrictions on their children's ability to participate in group play situations due to factors such as gender, class, perceived social status and racial, ethnic or religious affiliation.

### Friendships

In the middle years, friendships provide developmental and social benefits. Children choose close friends based on common interests and activities, enjoyment of each other's company and willingness to help or support. Friendships afford the opportunity for close bonds of companionship, loyalty, mutual reinforcement for good or ill, reliance and a sense of belonging. Children in the middle years who participate in positive peer friendships share perspectives, experiences and knowledge within the contexts of social interactions. Some children's ability to form close friendships is influenced by cultural perspectives that may limit or hinder associations with peers that are nonfamily members or are from cultural backgrounds different from their own.

### Social Competence

Some children during the middle years lack social competence. Newman and Newman (1991, p. 666) defined social competence as "the skills involved in making friends, maintaining friendships and enjoying the benefits of close peer relationships." Children develop social competence from the practices and messages observed, experienced and received within their family environment via parental or caretaker behaviors, discipline techniques and child-rearing styles used by parents and caretakers. These behaviors and practices are imitated and, for better or worse, are integrated into the child's social repertoire, positively or adversely affecting opportunities for close friendships. Children may experience caretaking or parenting styles and discipline techniques that vary significantly from mainstream convention.

### Concrete Operational Thought

Children in the middle years experience changes in their cognitive development. Jean Piaget's theory of cognitive development labels this phase as concrete operational thought and defines it as "a stage in cognitive development in which rules of logic are applied to things that are observable or manipulatable physical relations" (Newman and Newman, 1991, p. 650). In concrete operations, children recognize and exercise their ability to perform actions on objects mentally instead of just physically. The skills of this stage of intellectual development enable children to (1) understand that an object does not stop existing because it changes form or container (conservation); (2) group objects by a shared common feature (classification), as well as grouping objects hierarchically, so that new groupings include previous subgroups; and

(3) mentally combine the concepts and skills of conservation and classification to learn to add, subtract, multiply and divide. In concrete operations, children learn to think logically and to understand the predictability of events. With these new skills, they are better able to problem solve and to apply this new reasoning to peer relationships, games, team play and their own self-evaluation. At this time, children also begin to seek logic and order in their personal and social worlds. It is important to note that concepts of logic and order may have varied meanings and significance for different cultural groups. Some families experience many transitions of a planned and unplanned nature. For children in this stage of cognitive development, unpredictability, instability and chaotic situations can cause frustration. This is particularly evident for children and youth who are homeless and experience transience and major instability and disruptions in living situations.

## Self-Evaluation

During the middle years there is an emphasis on skill building and a focus on self-evaluation. As children strive to attain internal and external standards of achievement, they simultaneously attempt to manage feedback from others regarding their performance. Within the school environment children are often grouped for subjects by ability and receive recognition for academic triumphs and challenges. In this age group, children are able to incorporate outside evaluation of the quality of their performance with their own self-appraisal. Newman and Newman (1991 p. 345) stated that by age 11, "children differentiate specific areas of competence that contribute to overall self-evaluation; particularly cognitive/academic, social and physical competence."

Families have differential expectations and understandings of success and failure. Some families view achievement from a collective or group perspective rather than from an individual one. In this light, a child's successes or failures can be seen as bringing honor or shame to the family or as having a positive or negative effect on how the family is viewed within their cultural or ethnic community. In other instances families may place a high value on comportment. When their child receives a report card with A's in all areas except citizenship, because of "talking back to adults," the child is punished for a significant amount of time because he or she violated the family value, grades not withstanding.

## Team Play

Children in middle childhood are able to make significant contributions to the social groups to which they belong. Children participate in teams within the school environment and may also participate in team sports within their communities.

Through team play children begin to develop an understanding of group and personal success. Team membership assists children in developing a sense of (1) relinquishing personal goals for team goals; (2) the interdependence of each team member—that completion of individual tasks contribute to the overall success or failure of the group; (3) the importance of working together to achieve a common goal; and (4) competition. Team play teaches children that the result of competition is a win-or-lose situation that can be a source of satisfaction and success or of frustration and failure. Newman and Newman (1991, p.355) noted, "Social environments do not reinforce success in all areas equally…. It is extremely difficult for the child that does not perform well in the culturally valued skill or area to compensate through mastery of another." In some families a high value is placed on athleticism. Think for a moment of the father who has always excelled in sports and expects that his child will do the same. The child lacks athleticism but excels academically. The father loves his child but admonishes the child to do better in sports—the area the father highly values.

### Peer-Group Membership

Peer-group membership is of particular significance during the middle years. Toward the latter stages of the middle years (roughly ages 10–11) children become more concerned with the opinions, expectations and approval of their peer group. Children are more sensitive to other's appraisal of their performance. Evaluations of this sort can assist children in assessing their own behavior and in identifying personal goals. For the early adolescent, peer-group friendships represent more complex social relationships and offer companionship, fun, understanding, support and emotional intimacy. At this time youth spend increasing amounts of time away from home, with friends as the dominant focus of their existence. Peer groups tend to develop standards such as inclusion or exclusion of individuals based on physical or intellectual abilities, race, ethnicity or cultural background and physical characteristics. Although this is a time when children become increasingly more independent from their families, they maintain an attachment to the values, expectations and orientation of their families. Many families perceive this period of independence as a semiseparation or perceive the family and its values as diminishing in importance. This is often the beginning of a critical period for many families.

### Physical Maturation

There is variability as to when physical maturation begins. Some children experience physical changes early on, whereas others experience changes during early adolescence. Differences in individual maturation suggest that during early adolescence the peer group is more diverse than in other periods. Puberty can influence psychological and social development in a number of ways. First, during this period of growth children get taller and stronger and experience increased endurance and coordination as a byproduct of physical development. Second, changes in outward appearance may affect the way early adolescents are perceived by others (e.g., appearing less cuddly or huggable; appearing threatening). Last, physical development can impact the way that early adolescents view themselves (e.g., more or less adult-like depending on their expectations and cultural and social norms related to body types).

Culturally ascribed values related to body build will influence social acceptance by peers and adults. Researchers (Mendelson and White, 1985 and Martin et al., 1988 [as cited in Newman & Newman, 1991]) indicate that there is little relationship between being overweight and self-esteem during the middle years. This changes significantly in early adolescence, when being overweight and obese are associated with negative perceptions of one's body and appearance and lower self-esteem. This, too, is culturally influenced as what constitutes being overweight varies significantly from culture to culture.

## *Formal Operations*

In early adolescence, children begin to think of the world in new ways as their skills of abstract thinking develop. Piaget described these new, more complex capacities of thought as formal operations, or "the final stage of cognitive development, characterized by reasoning, hypothesis generating and hypothesis testing" (Newman & Newman, 1991, p. 654). Formal operational thought allows children to develop hypothesis as a way of explaining events and to follow the implied logic of a specific hypothesis. During this period of intellectual development, early adolescents are able to (1) mentally manipulate multiple categories and variables simultaneously, such as "the relationship between speed, distance and time in order to plan a trip" (Acredolo, Adams & Schmid, 1984, as cited in Newman & Newman, 1991, pp. 376–377); (2) think about the future; (3) make hypotheses about a possible logical sequence of events (e.g., college or job possibilities based on academic outcomes of high school); (4) anticipate the consequences of their actions; (5) test the truth of statements by finding evidence that supports or disputes the statement; and (6) think realistically about others, themselves and the world. Early adolescents are also aware of family, cultural and community norms and expectations for their behavior. They know that different norms may govern the same behavior in other families, cultural groups and communities. Deciding to act in a culturally acceptable manner demonstrates a commitment to that culture or society.

## CONCLUSION

We believe that providers of behavioral health services must have a solid understanding of the multiple dimensions and dynamics of culture for children in middle childhood and that the efficacy of any evidence-based approaches to prevention and treatment must be implemented within the cultural contexts of children, their families and communities. Thus, the service provider needs to recognize the following:

- Culture influences every aspect of life.
- The child is not a passive recipient of culture, and his or her unique characteristics and temperament influence how culture is transmitted from parents and caretakers, community and society as a whole.
- Families are the cultural guides for their children and transmit complex patterns of values, belief systems, codes of behaviors, norms and the path toward cultural identity.
- Communities provide a framework for living and are the environmental and cultural contexts in which children and their families live, learn, work, play, worship and thrive.

## REFERENCES

Alarcon, R. D., Foulks, E. F. & Vakkur, M. (1998). *Personality disorders and culture: Clinical and conceptual interactions.* New York: Wiley.

Ancis, J. (Ed.). (2004). *Culturally responsive interventions: Innovative approaches to working with diverse populations.* New York: Brunner-Routledge.

Banks, J. A. & McGee-Banks, C. A. (Eds.) (1997). *Multicultural education: Issues and perspectives,* 3d ed. Needham Heights, MA: Allyn & Bacon.

Barrera, M. & Gonzalez Castro, F. (2006, Winter). A heuristic framework for the cultural adaptation of interventions. *Clinical Psychology: Science and Practice, 13*(4), 311–316.

Basabe N., Paez, D., Valencia, J., González, J., Rime, B. & Diener, E. (2002). Cultural dimensions, socioeconomic development, climate and emotional hedonic level. *Cognition and Emotion, 16*(1), 103–125.

Bennett J. A., Fleming, M. L., Mackin, L., Hughes, A., Wallhagen, M. & Kayser-Jones, J. (2003, March). Recruiting ethnically diverse nurses to graduate education in gerontological nursing: Lessons from a successful program. *Journal of Gerontology Nursing, 29*(3), 17–22.

Bernal, G. & Saez-Santiago, E. (2006). Culturally centered psychosocial interventions. *Journal of Community Psychology, 34*(2), 121–132.

Carlson, V. J. & Harwood, R. L. (2000). Understanding and negotiating cultural differences concerning early developmental competence: The six raisin solution. *ZERO TO THREE Bulletin of the National Center for Infants, Toddlers, and Families, 20*(3), 19–24.

Cross, T., Bazron, B., Dennis, K. & Isaacs, M. (1989). *Towards a culturally competent system of care: A monograph on effective services for minority children who are severely emotionally disturbed,* vol. 1. Washington, DC: Georgetown University Child Development Center.

Dosamantes-Beaudry, I. (1997). Embodying a cultural identity. *Arts in Psychotherapy, 24*(2), 129–135.

Elliott, D. (Ed.) (2002a). *Blue prints for violence prevention: Functional family therapy.* Denver, CO: Kendall Printing Company.

Elliott, D. (Ed.) (2002b). *Blue prints for violence prevention: Life skills training.* Denver, CO: Kendall Printing Company.

Elliott, D. (Ed.) (2002c). *Blue prints for violence prevention: Multisystemic therapy.* Denver, CO: Kendall Printing Company.

Elliott, D. (Ed.) (2002d). *Blue prints for violence prevention: Multidimensional treatment foster care.* Denver, CO: Kendall Printing Company.

Elliott, D. (Ed.) (2002e). *Blue prints for violence prevention: The incredible years: Parent, teacher and child training series.* Denver, CO: Kendall Printing Company.

Fordham, S. (1988). Racelessness as a factor in Black student's school success: pragmatic strategy or pyrrhic victory? *Harvard Educational Review, 58,* 54–84.

Fordham, S. & Ogbu, J. U. (1986). Black student's school success: Coping with the burden of "acting White." *Urban Review, 18,* 176–206.

Ginsburg, G. S. & Drake, K. L. (2002). School-based treatment for anxious African American adolescents: A controlled pilot study. *Journal of the American Academy of Child & Adolescent Psychiatry 41*(7), 768–775.

Goode, T. D. (2001). *Policy Brief 4—Engaging Communities to Realize the Vision of One Hundred Percent Access and Zero Health Disparities: A Culturally Competent Approach.* Washington, DC: Georgetown University Center for Child & Human Development.

Goode, T. D. (2006). *Promoting Cultural Competence and Cultural Diversity in Early Intervention and Early Childhood Settings.* Washington, DC: Georgetown University Center for Child & Human Development. (Original work published June 1989).

Goode, T. & Jones, W. (2006). *Definition of Linguistic Competence. National Center for Cultural Competence.* Washington, DC: Georgetown University Center for Child and Human Development. Retrieved on 10 April, 2006 from http://gucchd.georgetown.edu/nccc. (Original work published 2000).

Goodnow, J. J. & Collins, W. A. (1990). *Development according to parents: The nature, sources and consequences of parents' ideas.* Hillsdale, NJ: Erlbaum.

Griffith, E. E. H. & Gonzalez, C. A. (1994). Essentials of cultural psychiatry. In C. Yudofsky, R. Hales & J. Talbott (Eds.), *The American Psychiatric Press textbook of psychiatry*, 2d ed. Arlington, VA: American Psychiatric Press (pp. 1379–1404).

Guhde, J. A. (2003, Winter). English-as-a-second language (ESL) nursing students: Strategies for building verbal and written language skills. *Journal of Cultural Diversity, 10*(4), 113–117.

Harkness, S. & Super, C. (1996). *Parents cultural belief systems: Their origins, expressions and consequences.* New York: Gilford Press.

Hoagwood, K., Burns, B., Kiser, L., Ringeisen, H. & Schoenwald, S. (2001). Evidence-based practice in child and adolescent mental health services. *Psychiatric Services, 52*(9), 1179–1189.

Hogg Foundation for Mental Health (2006). *Cultural adaptation: Providing evidence-based practices to populations of color.* Retrieved 2 November 2006 from http://www.hogg.utexas.edu/programs_cc.html.

Johnson-Powell, G. & Yamamoto, J. (Eds.) (1997). *Transcultural Child Development: Psychological Assessment and Treatment.* New York: John Wiley & Son Publishing.

Kitayama, S. & Rose-Markus, H. (Eds.) (1994). *Emotion and culture: Empirical studies of mutual influence.* Washington, DC: American Psychological Association.

Lau, A. (2006). Making the case for selective and directed cultural adaptations of evidence-based treatments: Examples from parent training. *Clinical Psychology: Science and Practice, 13*(4), 295–310.

LeVine, R. (1984). Properties of culture: An ethnographic view. In R. A. Schweder and R. A. LeVine (Eds.) *Culture theory: Essays on mind, self and emotion.* New York: Cambridge University Press. pp. 67–87.

Lotrecchiano, G. (2005, September 28). *Methods for Cultural Understanding: Assumptions and Definitions of Culture.* Paper presented at Leadership Education in Neurodevelopmental Disability Course Children's Hospital National Medical Center, Washington, DC.

Lynch, E. W. & Hanson, M. J. (1992). *Developing cross-cultural competence: A guide for working with children and their families.* Baltimore, MD: Paul H. Brookes Publishing Company.

Martin-Holland, J., Bello-Jones, T., Shuman, A., Rutledge, D. N. & Sechrist, K.R. (2003). Ensuring cultural diversity among California nurses. *Journal of Nursing Education 42*(6), 245–248.

Mason, J. (1998). *Internal and External Cultural Factors Influencing Diversity.* Paper presented at National Center for Cultural Competence, National Advisory Committee Meeting. Washington, DC.

Miranda, J., Bernal, G., Lau, A., Kohn, L., Hwang, W. C. & LaFromboise, T. (2005). State of the science on psychosocial interventions for ethnic minorities. *Annual Review of Clinical Psychology, 1,* 113–142. Retrieved 10 August, 2006 from http://www.arjournals.annualreviews.org.

Miranda, J., Nakamura, R. & Bernal, G. (2003). Including ethnic minorities in mental health intervention research: A practical approach to a long-standing problem. *Culture, Medicine and Psychiatry, 27,* 467–486.

Modern Language Association (MLA) (2000). *Most spoken languages in the entire United States.* Retrieved 27 June 2002 from http://www.mla.org/map_data_results&state_id.

Nagayama Hall, G. (2001). Psychotherapy research with ethnic minorities: Empirical, ethical, and conceptual issues. *Journal of Consulting and Clinical Psychology, 69*(3), 502–510.

Nagel, J. (1994). Constructing ethnicity: Creating and recreating ethnic identity and culture. *Social Problems, 41*(1), 152–176.

National Association of Cognitive-Behavioral Therapists (2006). Cognitive-behavioral therapy. Retrieved 17 November 2006 from http://www.nacbt.org/whatiscbt.htm.

National Center for Cultural Competence (2001). *Definitions of culture.* Washington, DC: Georgetown University Child Development Center.

National Center for Cultural Competence (2004). *Cultural competence health practitioner assessment.* Retrieved 15 June 2006 from http://www11.georgetown.edu/research/gucchd/nccc/features/CCHPA.html.

National Research Council and Institute of Medicine (2000). From neurons to neighborhoods: The science of early childhood development. Committee on Integrating the Science of Early Childhood Development. In Jack P. Shonkoff and Deborah A. Phillips (Eds.), *Board on Children, Youth, and Families, Commission on Behavioral and Social Sciences and Education* (p. 239). Washington, DC: National Academy Press.

Newman, B. & Newman, P. (1991). *Development through life: A psychosocial approach,* 5th ed. Pacific Grove, CA: Brookes/Cole Publishing Company, 329–365; 367–413; 647–668.

Pachter, L. M. & Dworkin, P. H. (1997). Maternal expectations about normal child development in 4 cultural groups. *Archives of Pediatrics & Adolescent Medicine, 151*(11), 1144–1150.

Phinney, J. (1990). Ethnic identity in adolescents and adults: Review of research. *Psychological Bulletin, 108*(3), 499–514.

Roberts, R., Phinney, J. Masse, L., Chen, Y., Roberts, C. & Romero, A. (1999). The structure of ethnic identity of young adolescents from diverse ethnocultural groups. *Journal of Early Adolescence, 19*(3), 301–322.

Smith, E., Walker, K., Fields, L., Brookins, C. & Seay, R. (1999). Ethnic identity and its relationship to self-esteem, perceived efficacy and prosocial attitudes in early adolescence. *Journal of Adolescence, 22,* 867–880.

Sockalingam, S. (2004, September 10). *Diversity and Culture.* Paper presented at System of Care Symposium Bethesda, MD.

Taylor-Gibbs, J. & Nahme-Huang, L (2003). *Children of color: Psychosocial interventions with culturally diverse youth.* San Francisco: Jossey-Bass.

The American Institute for Cognitive Therapy (2006). *Child and adolescent treatment.* Retrieved 17 November 2006 from http://www.cognitivethera-pynyc.com/child.asp.

United Advocates for Children of California (2005). *Definition of family,* Retrieved 22 May 2006 from http://www.uacc4families.org.

U.S. Census Bureau (2000). *Census of Population, Summary File 1-Count of Persons Under Age 25 by Single Year of Age, Matrix: PCT12.* Retrieved 5 March 2006 from http://factfinder.census.gov/servlet/DCSubjectShowTablesServlet?_ts=199132104280.

U.S. Census Bureau, American Community Survey (2004). *Table S0101 U.S. Population by Age & Sex.* Retrieved 22 May 2006 from http://factfinder.census.gov/servlet/STTable?_bm=y&-geo_id=01000US&-qr_name=ACS_2005_EST_G00_S0101&-ds_name=ACS_2005_EST_G00_&-_lang=en&-_caller=geoselect&-state=st&-format=.

U.S. Department of Health and Human Services (1999). *Mental Health: A Report of the Surgeon General—Executive Summary.* Rockville, MD: U.S. Department of Health and Human Services, Substance Abuse and Mental Health Services Administration, Center for Mental Health Services, National Institutes of Health, National Institute of Mental Health.

Weisz, J. R., Huey, S. & Weersing, V. R. (1998). Psychotherapy outcome research with children and adolescents: The state of the art. *Advances in Clinical Child Psychology, 20,* 49–91.

Welch, M. (2003). Teaching diversity and cross-cultural competence in health care: A trainers guide (3rd ed.). Perspectives of Differences, Diversity Training and Consultation Services for Health Professionals. San Francisco, CA: Perspective of Differences, Diversity Training and Consultation Services for Health Professionals.

## APPENDIX 1. PROMOTING CULTURAL DIVERSITY AND CULTURAL COMPETENCY

### Self-Assessment Checklist for Personnel Providing Behavioral Health Services and Supports to Children, Youth and their Families*
Children with Disabilities & Special Health Needs and their Families

**Directions:**      Please select A, B, or C for each item listed below.

A = Things I do frequently
B = Things I do occasionally
C = Things I do rarely or never

---

* Adapted from: *Promoting Cultural Competence and Cultural Diversity in Early Intervention and Early Childhood Settings,* June 1989. Revised 2006.

## Physical Environment, Materials and Resources

_____ 1. I display pictures, posters and other materials that reflect the cultures and ethnic backgrounds of children, youth, and families served by my program or agency.

_____ 2. I insure that magazines, brochures, and other printed materials in reception areas are of interest to and reflect the different cultures of children, youth and families served by my program or agency.

_____ 3. When using videos, films, CDs, DVDS, or other media resources for mental health prevention, treatment or other interventions, I insure that they reflect the cultures of children, youth and families served by my program or agency.

_____ 4. When using food during an assessment, I insure that meals provided include foods that are unique to the cultural and ethnic backgrounds of children, youth and families served by my program or agency.

_____ 5. I insure that toys and other play accessories in reception areas and those, which are used during assessment, are representative of the various cultural and ethnic groups within the local community and the society in general.

## Communication Styles

_____ 6. For children and youth who speak languages or dialects other than English, I attempt to learn and use key words in their language so that I am better able to communicate with them during assessment, treatment or other interventions.

_____ 7. I attempt to determine any familial colloquialisms used by children, youth and families that may impact on assessment, treatment or other interventions.

_____ 8. I use visual aids, gestures, and physical prompts in my interactions with children and youth who have limited English proficiency.

_____ 9. I use bilingual or multilingual staff or trained/certified interpreters for assessment, treatment and other interventions with children and youth who have limited English Proficiency.

_____ 10. I use bilingual staff or multilingual trained/certified interpreters during assessments, treatment sessions, meetings, and for other events for families who would require this level of assistance.

_____ 11. When interacting with parents who have limited English proficiency I always keep in mind that:

_____ * limitations in English proficiency is in no way a reflection of their level of intellectual functioning.

_____ * their limited ability to speak the language of the dominant culture has no bearing on their ability to communicate effectively in their language of origin.

_____ * they may or may not be literate in their language of origin or English.

_____ 12. When possible, I insure that all notices and communiqués to parents, families and caregivers are written in their language of origin.

_____ 13. I understand that it may be necessary to use alternatives to written communications for some families, as word of mouth may be a preferred method of receiving information.

_____ 14. I understand the principles and practices of linguistic competency and:

_____ * apply them within my program or agency.

_____ * advocate for them within my program or agency.

_____ 15. I understand the implications of health/mental health literacy within the context of my roles and responsibilities.

_____ 16. I use alternative formats and varied approaches to communicate and share information with children, youth and/or their family members who experience disability.

## Values and Attitudes

_____ 17. I avoid imposing values that may conflict or be inconsistent with those of cultures or ethnic groups other than my own.

_____ 18. In group therapy or treatment situations, I discourage children and youth from using racial and ethnic slurs by helping them understand that certain words can hurt others.

_____ 19. I screen books, movies, and other media resources for negative cultural, ethnic, or racial stereotypes before sharing them with children, youth and their parents served by my program or agency.

_____ 20. I intervene in an appropriate manner when I observe other staff or parents within my program or agency engaging in behaviors that show cultural insensitivity, bias or prejudice.

_____ 21. I understand and accept that family is defined differently by different cultures (e.g. extended family members, fictive kin, godparents).

_____ 22. I recognize and accept that individuals from culturally diverse backgrounds may desire varying degrees of acculturation into the dominant or mainstream culture.

_____ 23. I accept and respect that male-female roles in families may vary significantly among different cultures (e.g. who makes major decisions for the family, play and social interactions expected of male and female children).

_____ 24. I understand that age and life cycle factors must be considered in interactions with individuals and families (e.g. high value placed on the decisions of elders or the role of the eldest male in families).

_____ 25. Even though my professional or moral viewpoints may differ, I accept the family/parents as the ultimate decision makers for services and supports for their children.

_____ 26. I recognize that the meaning or value of behavioral health prevention, intervention and treatment may vary greatly among cultures.

_____ 27. I recognize and understand that beliefs and concepts of emotional well-being vary significantly from culture to culture.

_____ 28. I understand that beliefs about mental illness and emotional disability are culturally-based. I accept that responses to these conditions and related treatment/interventions are heavily influenced by culture.

_____ 29. I understand the impact of stigma associated with mental illness and behavioral health services within culturally diverse communities.

_____ 30. I accept that religion, spirituality and other beliefs may influence how families respond to mental or physical illnesses, disease, disability and death.

_____ 31. I recognize and accept that folk and religious beliefs may influence a family's reaction and approach to a child born with a disability or later diagnosed with a physical/emotional disability or special health care needs.

_____ 32. I understand that traditional approaches to disciplining children are influenced by culture.

_____ 33. I understand that families from different cultures will have different expectations of their children for acquiring self-help, social, emotional, cognitive, and communication skills.

_____ 34. I accept and respect that customs and beliefs about food, its value, preparation, and use are different from culture to culture.

_____ 35. Before visiting or providing services in the home setting, I seek information on acceptable behaviors, courtesies, customs and expectations that are unique to families of specific cultures and ethnic groups served by my program or agency.

_____ 36. I seek information from family members or other key community informants that will assist in service adaptation to respond to the needs and preferences of culturally and ethnically diverse children, youth, and families served by my program or agency.

_____ 37. I advocate for the review of my program's or agency's mission statement, goals, policies, and procedures to insure that they incorporate principles and practices that promote cultural diversity and cultural and linguistic competence.

_____ 38. I keep abreast of new developments in pharmacology particularly as they relate to racially and ethnically diverse groups.

_____ 39. I either contribute to and/or examine current research related to ethnic and racial disparities in mental health and health care and quality improvement.

_____ 40. I accept that many evidence-based prevention and intervention approaches will require adaptation to be effective with children, youth and their families from culturally and linguistically diverse groups.

## HOW TO USE THIS CHECKLIST

This checklist is intended to heighten the awareness and sensitivity of personnel to the importance of cultural diversity and cultural competence in human service settings. It provides concrete examples of the kinds of values and practices that foster such an environment. There is no answer key with correct responses. However, if you frequently responded "C," you may not necessarily demonstrate values and engage in practices that promote a culturally diverse and culturally competent service delivery system for children and youth who require behavioral health services and their families.

# 5

# Public Health Principles and Approaches to Systems Interventions to Support Children's Emotional and Behavioral Health

SUSAN G. KEYS AND PHILIP J. LEAF

## INTRODUCTION

Mental health problems[1] in children present a national public health crisis (U.S. Public Health Service, 2000). Data from the National Health Interview Surveys indicate that approximately 5% of U.S. children ages 4 to 17 had emotional or behavioral problems, and for approximately 80% of these children there was an impact on their family life, friendships, learning or leisure activities (Simpson, Bloom, Cohen, Blumber & Bourdon, 2005). Studies of the prevalence of psychiatric disorders during childhood and adolescence suggest even higher rates (Kessler et al., 1994, 2005; Shaffer et al., 1996). Costello, Egger and Angold (2005) estimated that 3% to 18% of children in the United States have a psychiatric disorder that causes significant functional impairment (Federal Definition of Serious Emotional Disturbance, 1993), with the median estimate of 12% being twice the estimate produced by the National Health Interview Surveys.

Research has long demonstrated that for most people who experience an emotional or behavioral problem as adults, the onset of problems occurred during childhood or adolescence (Burke, Burke, Regier & Rae, 1990). The National Comorbidity Survey Replication study concluded recently that half of all life-time cases of mental illness began by age 14 (Kessler et al., 2005). Not only do emotional and behavioral problems disrupt the functioning of children and their families, but these problems are also often precursors to delinquency, substance abuse, health-risking sexual behaviors and school failure (Capaldi, Stoolmiller, Clark & Owen, 2002; Costello, Foley & Angold, 2006; Mrazek, Biglan & Hawkins 2004; Tolan & Dodge, 2005). Specifically, children in first grade who have problem behaviors are at increased risk for drug and alcohol use as early adolescents (Kaplow, Curran & Dodge, 2002); children who have poor social skills are at later risk for substance abuse disorders (Green et al. 1999); and children who lack prosocial skills are likely to be rejected by peers and tend to gravitate toward other rejected children, which in turn influences involvement in antisocial activities (Keenan, Loeber, Zhang, Stouthamer-Loeber & Van Kammen, 1995). If we are to reduce the overall burden presented by emotional and behavioral problems, it is critical that efforts begin long before individuals need to have specialty mental health services.

## Insufficient Services

Unfortunately, the majority of children and adolescents who need mental health services fail to receive any services, and for those who do receive services, many are not getting adequate or appropriate services (Leaf et al., 1996; Olfson, Gameroff, Marcus & Waslick, 2003; Angold, Erkanli, Egger & Costello, 2002). Professionals tends to focus on children with the most serious disorders, with limited or no attention given to those who may have emotional or behavioral problems but who do not have such significant impairment that they would be diagnosed as having a disorder; many conditions may persist and get worse because so little attention is paid to prevention and early detection and treatment. It is important to explore whether options other than those that focus only on children with the most severe problems might be more effective in reducing the overall dysfunction associated with emotional and behavioral problems.

Approximately 10% of children designated as having definite or severe difficulties are not able to afford mental health services, and only about 45% of those with problems have any contact with a mental health professional (Simpson et al., 2005). The authors caution that the 45% contact rate could be an inflated estimate of services given that contact does not equate to actual services delivered or frequency of interaction. Even if full knowledge of the extent to which children with mental disorders fail to receive adequate treatment and support does not exist, there is ample evidence indicating that the availability of services remains insufficient for the degree of need. Although there is an increasing emphasis on evidence-based treatments and we have several treatments that have proven effective in tightly controlled clinical studies (Burns & Hoagwood, 2002), there is considerable evidence suggesting many if not most children receive treatment that is of dubious value or of inadequate intensity or duration (Jenson, Weersing, Hoagwood & Goldman, 2005; Weisz, McCarty & Valeri, 2006).

Given the large number of America's children experiencing emotional and behavioral health problems and the small number receiving effective services, it is clear that there needs to be a significant change in the way these problems are approached by clinicians, families and policy makers. Rather than emphasizing efforts to reduce the serious consequences of childhood emotional and behavioral problems, federal, state and local governments need to pay greater attention to understanding how public policy, health-care financing, and community promotive and preventive supports and services could reduce the incidence and prevalence of emotional and behavioral problems and the concomitant social and economic costs.

Many countries in Europe are organizing efforts to promote positive mental health and to prevent emotional problems and behaviors because they recognize that "a lack of positive mental health is a threat to public health, the quality of life and the economy of Europe" (Jane-Llopis & Anderson, 2005, p. 4) and that the "social and economic costs of mental ill-health for societies are wide ranging, long lasting and enormous" (ibid., p. 5). These countries have recognized that "positive mental health cannot be gained by treating mental disorders alone" (ibid., p. 6).

## Data Support Positive Outcomes for Mental Health Promotion and Prevention

The positive news is that interventions exist that promote children's social and emotional competence and prevent or effectively treat childhood emotional and behavioral problems (DiGuiseppi, Gough, Taylor & Logan, 2006; Kellam & Langevin, 2003; Pumariega & Winters, 2003; Weisz, Sandler, Durlak & Anton, 2005; Gullotta & Bloom, 2003). For example, Weisz et al. (2005) summarized finding from several prevention programs suggesting that children who participated in prevention programs continued to demonstrate positive behaviors years after program participation. Higher achievement, less sexual activity, delinquency, conduct disorder, drug use and antisocial behavior were reported for children who received the interventions than for those who did not. Other studies have identified benefits to children whose families participate in family skills training (Kumpfer & Alvarado, 2003), including reductions in aggression, conduct disorder, attention deficit and hyperactivity and oppositional defiant disorder (Kazdin, 1995; Sanders, 1996; Taylor & Biglan, 1998), as well as later drug abuse (Dishion & Andrews, 1995) and delinquency (Alvarado & Kumpfer, 2000).

Research has shown support for universal, whole-school and multiyear social-emotional or social skills instructional programs designed to enhance children's social-emotional competence, such as Second Step (Grossman et al., 1997), Positive Youth Development Program (Weissberg, Bartoon & Shriver, 1997; Caplan et al., 1992), Interpersonal Cognitive Problem Solving (Shure & Spivack, 1988) and Promoting Alternative Thinking Strategies (Greenberg, Kusche, Cook & Quamma, 1995; Grossman et al., 1997). Other programs aimed at reducing disruptive behavior in schools have focused on changing the school's ecology by addressing contextual variables in the school, such as the Child Development Project (Battistich, Schaps, Watson & Solomon, 1996), the Bullying Prevention Program (Olweus, 1993) and Positive Behavioral Interventions and Supports (PBIS) (Sugai & Horner, 2002). Although the specific elements and foci of these programs may differ program to program, all build on earlier research demonstrating multiple, interdependent and mutually reinforcing pathways to healthy development (CASEL, 2003; Gottfredson, 2001).

Besides reducing the disability associated with emotional and behavioral problems, many interventions have been shown to be cost-effective through reduction in school absences, reduced need for special education programs, reduced costs for incarceration and reduction in expenditures for out-of-home placements and residential treatment, as well as increased numbers of children who are gainfully employed, contributing members of society as adults (Aos, Lieb, Mayfield, Miller & Punnuci, 2004).

## Too Few Communities Implement Interventions Known To Be Effective

The sad news is that despite the availability of these effective promotive and preventive interventions, too few communities have access to these practices. In many instances communities have neither mechanisms to identify which

interventions would best serve their community nor implementation procedures in place that would be consistent with those identified as critical to
an intervention's success. These shortcomings are further compounded by
community leaders, a clinical workforce and family members with limited
understanding of mental health promotion and prevention, how these types
of interventions are vital components of a comprehensive, population-based
system of care and how they might intervene to create supportive policies and
practices.

## Purpose

This chapter proposes that communities, including mental health professionals, consumer advocates and policy makers, expand their focus and activities beyond a concern with a treatment-based system of care to encompass a
broader perspective that focuses on positive development, mental health promotion and prevention and addresses individual, family and community promotive, risk and protective factors. This cannot be accomplished by focusing
on children alone but requires adopting a public health or population-based
approach that engages multiple systems—individual, family, school, neighborhood and community—and recognizes that these systems exist within
specific cultural, historical, sociopolitical and economic settings (Herrman,
Saxena & Moodie, 2005). Such actions and solutions need to include a full continuum of complementary interventions—from mental health promotion and
youth development to prevention and treatment to maximize and support
emotional and behavioral health and positive development for all children
and youth. As George Albee (1998, p. 373) said, "No mass disorder afflicting
humankind has ever been eliminated or brought under control by attempts
at treating the affected individual." The chapter identifies the activities of
a public health approach and the multiple system interventions that need
to occur if communities are to achieve a comprehensive, population-based
system of care.

## A PUBLIC HEALTH APPROACH

A public health approach focuses on the health (inclusive of mental health)
of an identified population. This approach, also referred to as a population-
based approach, focuses not only on traditional areas of medicine—diagnosis, treatment, and etiology—but also on health promotion, disease prevention
and access to and evaluation of interventions (U.S. Department of Health and
Human Services, 1999). A public health approach supports a broad spectrum
of interventions that include the promotion of mental health, the prevention
of illness and disability and the treatment and rehabilitation of those affected
(Herrman, Saxena, Moodie & Walker 2005). These may be related and may
overlap, but each needs to exist as part of a public health framework (ibid.).

Efforts to improve the emotional and behavioral health of children through
a public health approach consist of a number of discrete activities (Figure 5.1).
These activities include the following:

- Detecting and defining the problem through surveillance
- Identifying promotive, risk and protective factors

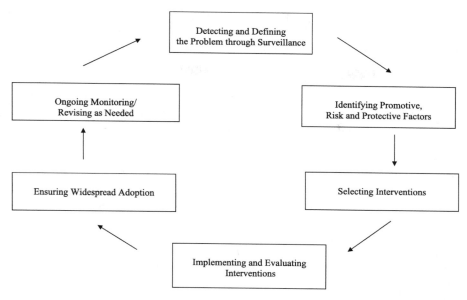

**Figure 5.1**   Public health activities.

- Selecting interventions aimed at promoting strengths, reducing risk and enhancing protective factors
- Implementing and evaluating interventions to see if they have an impact on the incidence and prevalence of the targeted problem—and to see if they promote social and emotional competence
- Ensuring the widespread adoption of the selected interventions and practices
- Ongoing monitoring to determine processes and procedures to continue and where to revise

## Detecting and Defining the Problem Through Surveillance

One of the greatest impediments to effective action is that many have opinions concerning the extent of problems, but few have data on which to base firmly held convictions. If a community is to create effective and efficient programs and campaigns that actually result in changing the prevalence of emotional and behavioral problems, it is critical that planning and policy efforts begin with data based on surveillance of strengths and weaknesses in the community or communities of interest. In addition to actual surveys, communities detect problems by using data often readily available through established data collection systems, such as juvenile justice referrals, school discipline records, police reports, hospital admissions, referrals to helping agencies and poverty indicators such as number of children participating in free and reduced school lunch programs. Positive indicators are also important, although may be a missing part of a community's data collection infrastructure. Positive indicators may include numbers of student entering school ready to learn, numbers of student graduating to a successful next step in their career path, numbers of student demonstrating social and emotional competence and numbers of parents employed. In addition, communities need to have an established mechanism or organizing body to review, to integrate across different databases and to use surveillance data to select interventions, to monitor progress and to evaluate outcomes. The Communities That Care (CTC) intervention (Hawkins, Catalano & Arthur, 2002) provides an example of how communities can be guided and mobilized to address these shortcomings. CTC provides a structure through which community members are able to learn about promotive, risk and protective factors in their community, to develop skills for helping diverse groups work together to assess and prioritize risk and protective factors and to match these priorities with effective prevention strategies. The CTC process also helps community members evaluate the impact of their efforts. Without collaborative relationships among varied community leaders, service providers, helping institutions, family members and individuals and without ongoing mechanisms to support communication, problem solving, decision making and strategic planning, a community will have difficulty marshalling the across-system efforts needed to move toward a goal of children living, playing and learning successfully.

Once a community has established that a problem does indeed exist (and for our purposes a problem could mean behaviors and emotional states the community wishes to prevent or to diminish, as well as behaviors or emotional states the community wishes to promote), the community should further define the problem. The community does this by identifying the needs and strengths of the population of concern, as well as the needs and strengths of the various systems that will interact to support change, improvement or positive development in the target population.

At this first stage of problem solving, a community considers appropriate goals or outcomes for the both the population of interest and the related supporting systems. Surveillance data can also help a community pinpoint specific types of problems and neighborhoods where problems are more prevalent (Hawkins et al., 2002).

Recent work by Aos et al. (2004) documented the cost-effectiveness of a number of preventive interventions. Because communities have numerous policies and programs that contribute to the high rates of mental disorders, actions might be prioritized in terms of costs and the magnitude of the benefits likely to accrue (Biglan, Foster, Holder & Brennan, 2005; Biglan, Mrazek, Carnine & Flay, 2003).

## Identifying Promotive, Risk and Protective Factors

Efforts to prevent or reduce the impact of emotional or behavioral problems should focus on both promoting assets and remediating problems and risks. A promotive factor is any characteristic or behavior that strengthens the likelihood of positive development. A risk factor is any characteristic or behavior associated with an increased chance that a young person will engage in high-risk behaviors or will develop a mental illness. Protective factors are any characteristics or behaviors that reduce the chance of a young person engaging in high-risk behavior or developing a mental illness. Neither promotive, risk nor protective factors are necessarily causal for a given individual. However, for those who have these factors as part of their life experience, the likelihood of a positive course of development increases for those who have promotive factors; the likelihood of engaging in high-risk behaviors or developing a mental illness increases for those who have multiple risk factors; and for those who

**Table 5.1**   Definitions of Promotive, Risk, and Protective Factors

| | |
|---|---|
| Promotive Factor | Any characteristic or behavior that strengthens the likelihood of a youth's positive development |
| Risk Factor | Any characteristic or behavior that increases the chance that a young person will engage in risky behaviors or develop a mental illness |
| Protective Factor | Any characteristic or behavior that reduces the chance of a young person's engaging in risky behavior or developing a mental illness |

have protective factors, it is less likely that the individual will engage in high-risk behaviors or develop a mental illness (Table 5.1).

Theory and research support several observations about risk factors:

1.  Most risk factors are not problem specific but may relate to many problems.
2.  A single risk factor generally does not substantially increase the likelihood that a problem may occur; however, greater numbers of factors do correlate with a higher prevalence and incidence of problems.
3.  Mental health problems, substance abuse and various high-risk behaviors often co-occur, interact and are related to the same types of risk factors (Hawkins, Catalano & Arthur, 2002).

Identifying promotive, risk and protective factors is central to implementing a population-based approach. It is promotive, risk and protective factors that should be the primary targets of interventions, and it is well documented that a "risk reduction/protection enhancement model is the best available framework" for preventing health and behavior problems (Hawkins et al., 2002, p. 953). If interventions are successful, positive development proceeds, risk decreases, protective factors increase and prevalence rates decrease.

**Selecting Interventions**

Optimally, a community should select interventions according to which interventions have demonstrated effectiveness in addressing the promotive, risk and protective factors prioritized as most important by the community. Many communities continue to implement interventions for which there is no evidence of effectiveness or for which there is evidence that suggests the intervention is not effective. Too few communities have developed a process for systematically assessing risk, promotive and protective factors and using this assessment to drive the selection of interventions (Hawkins et al., 2002). There are aids for communities, such as the Web-based community guide developed recently as part of First Lady Laura Bush's Helping America's Youth initiative. This guide is a useful tool for communities seeking to link risk and protective factors with evidence-based interventions (see http://guide.helpingamericasyouth.gov/ for more information).

When selecting interventions it is important to understand that different types of interventions may be more effective for specific groups of children or for different community circumstances. Originally proposed by Gordon (1983), more widely promulgated by the Institute of Medicine (IOM) (Mrazek &

Haggerty, 1994) and adapted for education by Sugai, Sprague, Horner & Walker (2000), interventions have been categorized according to levels of risk.

- A universal intervention is for all individuals in the general population or a whole population group that has not been identified on the basis of individual risk. Interventions at the universal level may promote positive development or may prevent problems from occurring. Many do both. A school-based social competency program such as Promoting Alternative Thinking Strategies (Greenberg et al., 1995) offered to all students in a school is an example of a universal intervention. PBIS also targets all students through interventions that impact the school and classroom environment. PBIS also has components aimed at youth at risk or those exhibiting problem behaviors. The High/Scope Perry Preschool Program (Schweinhart et al., 2005) offers another example of a universal intervention promoting the positive development of young children. Longitudinal data from this intervention also support the longer-term promotion and prevention benefits, indicating fewer habitual criminals, adult welfare recipients, fewer arrests, a higher rate of home ownership and a higher earning rate of those who participated in the program when compared with controls.
- A selective intervention targets individuals or subgroups whose risk of developing emotional or behavioral problems is significantly higher than average. Examples of selective interventions include home visitation programs for low-birth-weight infants, preschool programs for children from impoverished neighborhoods and support groups for children who have suffered a loss or trauma.
- An indicated intervention is intended for individual who have some symptoms of an emotional or behavioral problem but whose symptoms are not severe or prolonged enough to meet diagnostic criteria. Examples of indicated interventions for children with early emotional or behavioral problems are intensive parent–child programs, mentoring programs and social-emotional skill building.
- A treatment intervention is intended for those who have a diagnosed emotional or behavioral health problem. Multisystemic family therapy (Henggeler & Lee, 2003) is an example of a treatment intervention. This intervention is home based and targets individual juveniles, ages 12–17, who are chronically violent and abuse substances. The approach is multisystemic in that it often includes interventions in more than one of the systems (i.e., individual, family, peer, school, and neighborhood) that compose the social ecology of the targeted youth.

As currently operationalized in most communities, system of care efforts are directed almost exclusively toward a specific child whose needs would require more intensive services. In contrast, a population-based approach focuses on the needs of an identified population of children with interventions occurring across all four levels of intervention. From a population perspective, interventions target the promotive, risk and protective factors that have the greatest potential to affect large numbers of children. Communities that wish to apply a public health or population-based approach need to develop a full continuum of services and programs that include all levels of intervention: universal, selective, indicated and treatment.

## Implementing and Evaluating Interventions

The failure of many well-intentioned programs cautions that careful monitoring is required to assure interventions are implemented with fidelity and to produce the intended results. Evidence-based interventions have been developed using carefully tuned implementation methodologies. If communities implement an intervention without regard to the established methodology, it is unclear if the intervention will yield the same results. Implementing an intervention with fidelity refers to the degree to which a program is implemented as it was originally designed and tested.

Communities need to determine results outcomes and indicators of these outcomes to monitor progress (or lack of progress). It is important to differentiate between a lack of expected outcomes because of poor implementation and a lack of improvement despite the implementation of an intervention as intended.

## Ensuring the Widespread Adoption of the Interventions and Practices

Often programs start with subsets of a community and need to be expanded once success is documented. In addition to testimonials, policy makers and funders increasingly require data that support positive outcomes before increasing or continuing funding. It is important that selected programs have the capacity for expansion if expansion to other groups is a need of the community. Taking an intervention from a few groups to many requires the political will of those in decision-making positions as well as a sufficient infrastructure. Without these two components, communities will not have the fiscal and political base or structures to sustain programs and practices.

Programs that need to engage youth, family members, service providers and policy makers benefit from the inclusion of all stakeholders, including families and youth, in planning and oversight groups. Successful projects frequently have both an implementation committee monitoring the day-to-day activities and a multiagency and family advisory group to aid in social marketing, resource development and policy making.

Data collection, information management and communication systems are other necessary infrastructure ingredients. These are the grease that keep the day-to-day operations moving and the leadership and management teams and broader community well informed. Decision making should be based on data. Sharing information across agencies and partners requires tools for managing and communicating information in a way that facilitates access to the information, data-based decision making and procedures for monitoring quality of implementation.

Training, technical assistance, coaching and monitoring all need to be provided. All are linked to the interventions and practices selected for implementation by the community—and need to assure that those who implement the interventions are culturally competent, qualified and adequately trained. This requires planning, resources and management oversight. Training without follow-up coaching and supervision is less likely to yield consistent, effective implementation. Recently the State of Maryland has undertaken the task of implementing across the state a school-wide evidence-based approach to discipline and violence prevention. The training, technical assistance and coaching infrastructure includes state-supported large-group training events, school-based site visits for technical assistance and monitoring from members of a state leadership team and school-system supported coaches who provide direct, ongoing support to school implementation teams. Larger school systems have established supervision systems for coaches by designating lead coaches.

Last, to operate optimally, technological tools need to be developed and used to support the data, information, communication, training, monitoring and technical assistance systems.

## Ongoing Monitoring and Revising

Monitoring needs to focus not only on whether programs are being implemented as planned but also whether the health of the population is improving. Too many programs monitor only the amount of services provided without determining whether the results are as expected. Service providers frequently are not equipped to monitor outcomes because they have little relationship with youth or families once services are ended or the families and youth disengage. Also, not all interventions result in positive outcomes. If change occurs in a negative direction, or little or no change in outcomes occurs, it is important to make adjustments in the interventions.

## Integrating a Public Health Framework with Systems Interventions

All individuals within a community (whether that community is a school, a neighborhood, or a nation) are affected by the health of its individual members. It is important to recognize that emotional and behavioral health does not reside solely within the child. Intervention activities cannot occur in isolation from the family, social, political and cultural systems that exist in all communities. Gordon and Yowell (1999) posited that being at risk for problems refers not simply to the characteristics of the person but more importantly to the interaction of personal characteristics and the context in which the person grows and develops. Hernandez and Hodges (2003) discussed a strategy that aids communities in the identification of needed programs and the creation of community-wide infrastructures for supporting these programs. Consistent with this chapter's presentation, Hernandez & Hodges discuss the need to monitor multiple levels in order to obtain positive results. Thus program development needs to be concerned with issues at the level of society, such as fiscal policies and stigma; issues at the level of the organization, such as staff capacity and training and case load; and issues at the level of the provider youth interaction, such as the ability to deliver an intervention with high fidelity. All three levels exist together and compose a system of care.

Bronfenbrenner (1979, p. 3) described this system of care as a "set of nested structures, each inside the next, like a set of Russian dolls" (Figure 5.2). The individual exists as a system at the core of this structure, surrounded by four concentric levels:

1.  The microsystem, which focuses on relationships with persons within the day-to-day environment such as family, school, classroom and peer group

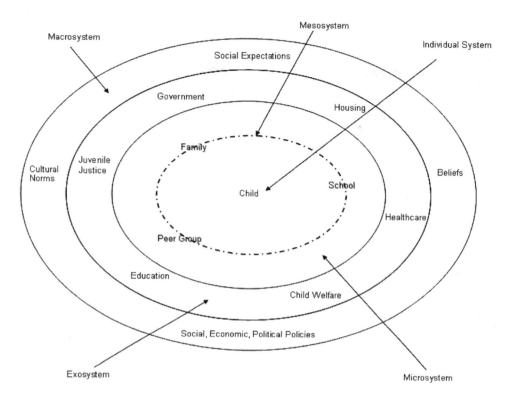

**Figure 5.2**   Levels of a public health framework's levels represented structures nested inside each other.

2.  The mesosystem or the interrelationship among the various microsystems (e.g., the relationship between the family and the school)
3.  The exosystem, which emphasizes the linkages to the larger core social institutions of society such as government, education, child welfare, housing, juvenile justice and health-care systems. Services and policies that emanate from these institutions have an impact on the lives of children and families—protection, education, rehabilitation, shelter, promotion of health and prevention and treatment of disease. In most communities these institutions function independently with little coordination or integration of programs, services and data at either the institutional or child level.
4.  The macrosystem, which attends to the cultural system or norms, common beliefs, social expectations and economic, social and political policies

In the State of Illinois' recently unveiled statewide strategic plan for building a comprehensive children's mental health system, the state demonstrates how activities at the macrosystem can affect children's social and emotional development. Goal 1 of the plan mandates that the state develop and strengthen prevention, early intervention and treatment policies, programs and services. As part of this goal, the plan recommends that local school systems incorporate social and emotional development as an integral component of a school's mission and a necessary feature of academic readiness and school success (Blagojevich & Shaw, 2005). The plan further asks that the Illinois State Board of Education work to ensure that all school districts develop a policy that incorporates social and emotional development into each district's education program, that learning standards are incorporated within the Illinois Learning Standards and that collaboration be increased among schools, school-based mental health, community mental health, health-care, juvenile justice, substance abuse and developmental disability agencies.

Promotive, risk and protective factors exist within the microsystem, mesosystem, exosystem and macrosystem—or individuals, families, peer groups, schools, the core social institutions of the community and cultural systems, norms and policies of society and social groups. Positive development and emotional and behavioral health requires action across of all of these systems.

Drawing on the work of others (Health Education Authority, 1997; Lehtinen, Riikonen & Lahtinen, 1997), Herrman, Saxena & Moodie (2005) suggested that promotion interventions cluster around three distinct environmental, social and individual objectives that overlap with the contextual systems suggested by Bronfrenbrenner (1979):

- The development and maintenance of healthy communities, which provide a safe and secure environment, including a child's caretaking environment, suitable housing, positive educational experiences, employment with good working conditions and a supportive political infrastructure
- The individual's ability to interact with the social world through skills like participating, tolerating diversity and mutual responsibility. Positive experiences of early bonding, attachment, relationships, communication and feelings of acceptance are associated with positive social connectedness. For children, the ability to form close relationships with other children and adults is important and highly dependent on a variety of social skills.
- The individual's ability to deal with personal thoughts and feelings, the management of life and emotional resilience

From all of these perspectives, health, as well as problems, is closely connected to actions and activities within the interconnected systems that form the social-ecological environment within which children grow and develop. Communities that want to effect positive development and positive mental health through a comprehensive system of services and supports will need to consider interventions across multiple systems—however these systems are described.

## Family and School

To achieve maximum outcomes, systems need to interact to support children and families. As an example, this section describes interventions for two critical microsystems.

## Family

Responsibility for emotional and behavioral health of children is shared by many systems, yet the family exerts the earliest and most direct influence. Research demonstrates that parenting effectiveness efforts that target family communication styles, behavior management and problem-solving skills, goal setting and how to monitor an older child's social activities are effective in preventing behavioral problems (Johnson, 2004). Some interventions might target all families within an identified population (universal), such as providing parenting skills training for first-time parents, or others might target those families most at risk because of economic or social disadvantage, mental disorders or substance use (selective, indicated). Functional family therapy, multisystemic therapy, and the nurse family partnership are examples of three evidence-based interventions specifically for families with identified risk factors (Alexander & Parsons, 1982; Henggeler & Lee, 2003; Olds, 2002).

Other examples of family-focused interventions that are health promoting for children are those cited by the Implementing Mental Health Promotion Action (IMPHA) network (Jane-Llopis & Anderson, 2005):

- Home-based visits for pregnant women and those with new babies that include education about healthy development, parenting skills and mother–baby interaction
- Screening and brief intervention programs for pregnant women to reduce or stop the use of addictive substances
- Early detection and treatment of postpartum depression
- Education for first-time parents, including the parent–child relationship, the importance of reading to children and other preschool preparation

Families must be recognized and valued as critical partners in helping. Family members and other caregivers should be meaningful involved in planning, implementing and evaluating interventions. Decision-making mechanisms that include family members as equal participants with those in other systems need to be strengthened or created. Such mechanisms need to be accessible to family members in terms of location, time and language and need to include norms that convey parity in decision making and respect for the knowledge and experience that family members contribute to the program planning process. Making interventions accessible and culturally acceptable are important considerations.

## School

It is well recognized that schools have a significant influence on the development of children and adolescents and are an important settings for interventions that promote health and reduce the risk for social and emotional problems. Yet schools vary to the extent to which their climate and practices promote learning and social development. Some of the best researched mental health promotion and prevention programs—those with consistently positive outcomes—were developed for use in schools. In a recent national survey of school-based mental health services, 59% of the schools surveyed indicate that they implement curriculum-based prevention programs, with 78% indicating they have implemented school-wide strategies to promote safe and drug-free schools (Foster et al., 2005). Promotion and prevention intervention for school settings include such things as the following:

- Whole-school curriculum-based social competency programs (universal)
- Interventions that target school and classroom climate such as PBIS (universal)
- Screening and early identification practices for those at risk of school failure or emotional and behavioral problems and for those already experiencing a problem (selective)
- Individual or small-group evidence-based interventions (e.g., anger management, impulse control, communication skills, problem-solving skills) for those identified with emotional and behavioral problems (selective and targeted)
- Teacher programs that focus on classroom management (universal and selective)
- High-quality academic curricula supported by effective pedagogy (universal)
- Preschool education programs that support cognitive, language and social-emotional development and overall school readiness (universal, selective)

It is well documented that schools are a major provider of mental health services (Rones and Hoagwood, 2000). A common model of practice is to locate clinicians in the school building. Clinicians in this case may be employed directly by the school system or may be employed by a community mental health agency under contract by the school system to provide these services.

Schools provide a single point of contact for services for students and families and often allow easier access than community-based clinics. Stigma can be minimized when services are provided as part of the normal ebb and flow of the school day.

Although schools offer enormous potential for implementing a full continuum of universal, selective, indicated and treatment interventions, not all schools welcome what some perceive as activities that take time away from academic instruction. Schools today are under considerable pressure to demonstrate yearly progress on academic goals for all students. Demonstrating the connection between mental health and academic achievement is imperative for the community seeking to use the educational system as a vehicle to promote children's positive development and emotional and behavioral health.

## CONCLUSION

This chapter has emphasized that a comprehensive children's mental health system requires interventions across multiple systems, including individuals, families, schools, communities and government, and that communities should adopt a public health framework—including activities that promote mental health and positive development and prevent emotional and behavioral problems—to guide their efforts. Although the United States is a leader in the development and testing of discrete interventions and programs, it lags behind many countries in terms of developing and implementing public policies and practices that promote mental health and development. A number of

European countries have undertaken systematic efforts to reduce emotional and behavioral problems and to promote positive mental health. They have done so because "providing the most evidence based treatment for one half of all people with depression would only reduce the current burden of depression by less than one quarter. On the other hand, evidence demonstrates that mental health promotion and mental disorder prevention can lead to health, social and economic gain, increases in social inclusion and economic productivity, reductions in the risks for mental and behavioral disorders, and decreased social welfare and health costs" (Jane-Llopis & Anderson, 2005, p. 6). Understanding that emotional and behavioral problems are largely preventable or can be minimized with prevention and early intervention efforts, the State of Illinois' recently presented strategic plan to support children's mental health (Blagojevich & Shaw, 2005) is a model other states might want to follow.

## ENDNOTE

1. This chapter uses emotional and behavioral problems to describe all mental and behavioral health difficulties experienced by children. Mental health and emotional health are used interchangeably. Disorder as defined by the American Psychiatric Association's Diagnostic and Statistical Manual of Mental Disorders (DSM-IV) refers to a "clinically significant behavioral or psychological syndrome or pattern that occurs in an individual and that is associated with present distress (e.g., a painful symptom) or disability (i.e., impairment in one or more important areas of functioning) or with a significantly increased risk of suffering death, pain, disability, or an important loss of freedom" (American Psychiatric Association, 2000, p. xxxi). Use of the term problem acknowledges that not every child with a need for mental health care has such significant impairment that it qualifies as a disorder.

## REFERENCES

Albee, G. W. (1998). No more rockscrubbing. *Journal of Community and Applied Social Psychology, 8*, 373–375.

Alexander, J. F. & Parsons, B. V. (1982). *Functional family therapy: Principles and procedures.* Carmel, CA: Brooks/Cole.

Alvarado, R. & Kumpfer, K. L. (2000). Strengthening America's families. *Juvenile Justice, 7*(2), 8–18.

American Psychiatric (2000). *Diagnostic and Statistical Manual of Mental Disorders,* 4th ed. Washington, DC: author.

Angold, A., Erkanli, A., Egger, H. L. & Costello, E. J. (2002). Stimulant treatment for children: A community perspective. *Journal of the American Academy of Child and Adolescent Psychiatry, 39*, 975–984.

Aos, D., Lieb, R., Mayfield, J., Miller, M. & Punnuci, A. (2004). *Benefits and costs of prevention and early intervention programs for youth.* Olympia: Washington State Institute for Public Policy.

Battistich, V., Schaps, E., Watson, E. & Solomon, D. (1996). Prevention effects of the Child Development Project: Early finding from an ongoing multisite demonstration trial. *Journal of Adolescent Research, 11*, 12–35.

Biglan, A., Foster, S. L., Holder, H. D. & Brennan, P. A. (2005). *The prevention of multiple problems of youth.* New York: Guilford Press.

Biglan, A., Mrazek, R. J., Carnine, D. & Flay, B. R. (2003). The integration of research and practice in the prevention of youth problem behaviors. *American Psychologist, 58,* 433–440.

Blagojevich, R. R. & Shaw, B., (2005). *Strategic plan for building a comprehensive children's mental health system in Illinois: Executive summary.* Chicago: Illinois Children's Mental Health Partnership.

Bronfenbrenner, U. (1979). *The ecology of human development.* Cambridge, MA: Harvard University Press.

Burke, K. C., Burke, J. D., Regier, D. A. & Rae, D. S. (1990). Age at onset of selected mental disorders in five community populations. *Archives General Psychiatry, 47,* 511–518.

Burns, B. J. & Hoagwood, K. (Eds.) (2002). *Community Treatment for youth: Evidence-based interventions for severe emotional and behavioral disorders.* New York: Oxford Press.

Capaldi, D. M., Stoolmiller, M., Clark, S. & Owen, L. D. (2002). Heterosexual risk behaviors in at-risk young men from early adolescence to young adulthood. Prevalence, prediction, and STD contraction. *Developmental Psychology, 38,* 394–406.

Caplan, M., Weissberg, R. P., Grober, J. S., Sivo, T. J., Gradly, K. & Jacoby, C. (1992). Social competence promotion with inner-city and suburban young adolescents: Effects on school adjustment and alcohol use. *Journal of Consulting and Clinical Psychology, 60,* 56–63.

Collaborative for Academic, Social, and Emotional Learning (CASEL) (2003). *Safe and sound: An educational leader's guide to evidence-based social and emotional learning programs.* Chicago: CASEL.

Costello, E. H., Egger, H. & Angold, A. (2005). 10-Year research update review: The epidemiology of child and adolescent psychiatric disorders: I: Methods and public health burden. *Journal of the American Academy of Child and Adolescent Psychiatry, 44*(10), 972–986.

Costello, E. J., Foley, D. & Angold, A. (2006). 10-Year research update review: The epidemiology of child and adolescent psychiatric disorders: II: Developmental epidemiology. *Journal of the American Academy of Child and Adolescent Psychiatry, 45*(1), 8–25.

DiGuiseppi, M J., Gough, E., Taylor, R. & Logan, S. (2006). *School-based secondary prevention programs for preventing violence* (Cochrane Database of Systematic Reviews, issue 3, art. CD004606. DO1: 10.1002/14651858. DC004606.pub2).

Dishion, T. J. & Andrews, D. W. (1995). Preventing escalation in problem behaviors with high-risk young adolescents: Immediate and 1-year outcomes. *Journal of Consulting and Clinical Psychology, 63,* 538–548.

Federal Definition of Serious Emotional Disturbance (1993). 58 Fed. Reg. 29425.

Foster, S., Rollefson, M., Doksum, T., Noonan, D., Robinson, G. & Teich, J. (2005). *School mental health services in the United States, 2002–2003* (DHHS Pub. [SMA] 05-4068). Rockville, MD: Center for Mental Health Services, Substance Abuse and Mental Health Services Administration.

Gordon Jr., R. S. (1983). An operational classification of disease prevention. *Public Health Reports, 98,* 107–109.

Gordon, E. & Yowell, C. (1999). Cultural dissonance as a risk factor in the development of students. In E. Gordon (Ed.), *Education and justice: A view from the back of the bus* (pp. 34–51). New York: Teachers College Press.

Gottfredson, D. (2001). *Schools and delinquency.* New York: Cambridge University Press.

Greene, R. W., Biederman, J., Faraone, S. B., Wilens, T. E., Mick, E. & Blier, H. K. (1999). Further validation of social impairment as a predictor of substance use disorders: Finding from a sample of boys with and without ADHD. *Journal of Clinical Child Psychology, 28,* 349–354.

Greenberg, M. T., Kusche, C., Cook, E. & Quamma, J. (1995). Promoting emotional competence in school-aged children: The effects of the PATHS curriculum. *Developmental Psychopathology, 7,* 117–136.

Grossman, D. D., Neckerman, H. J., Koepsell, T. D., Liu, P., Asher, K., Beland, K. et al. (1997). Effectiveness of a violence prevention curriculum among children in elementary school. *Journal of the American Medical Association, 277,* 1605–1611.

Gullotta, T. P. & Bloom, M. (2003) (Eds.). *The encyclopedia of primary prevention and health promotion.* New York: Kluwer/Academic.

Hawkins, J. D., Catalano, R. F. & Arthur, M. W. (2002). Promoting science-based prevention in communities, *Addictive Behaviors, 27,* 951–976.

Health Education Authority (1997). *Mental health promotion: A quality framework.* London: Author.

Henggeler, S. W. & Lee, T. (2003). Multisystemic treatment of serious clinical problems. In A. E. Kazdin and J. R. Weisz (Eds.), Evidence-based psychotherapies for children and adolescents (pp. 301–322). New York: Guilford Press.

Hernandez, M. & Hodges, S. (2003). *Crafting logic models for systems of care: Ideas into action.* [Making children's mental health services successful series, vol. 1]. Tampa: University of South Florida, The Louis de la Parte Florida Mental health Institute, Department of Child and Family Studies.

Herrman, H., Saxena, S. & Moodie, R. (Eds.) (2005). *Promoting mental health: Concepts, emerging evidence, practice. Report of the World Health Organization, Department of Mental Health and Substance Abuse in collaboration with the Victorian Health Promotion Foundation and the University of Melbourne.* Geneva: World Health Organization.

Herrman, H., Saxena, S., Moodie, R. & Walker, L. (2005). Introduction: Promoting mental health as a public health priority. In H. Herrman, S. Saxena & R. Moodie (Eds.), *Promoting mental health: Concepts, emerging evidence, practice. Report of the World Health Organization, Department of Mental Health and Substance Abuse in collaboration with the Victorian Health Promotion Foundation and the University of Melbourne* (pp. 2–17). Geneva: World Health Organization.

Jane-Llopis, E. & Anderson, P. (2005). *Mental health promotion and mental disorder prevention. A policy for Europe.* Nijmergen, Netherlands: Radboud University Nijmegen.

Jenson, P. S., Weersing, R., Hoagwood, K E. & Goldman, E. (2005). What is the evidence for evidence-based treatments? A hard look at our soft underbelly. *Mental Health Services Research, 7,* 53–74.

Johnson, R. L. (2004). *The National Institutes of Health (NIH) state-of-the-science conference on preventing violence and related health-risking social behaviors in adolescents.* Retrieved 8 July 2006 from http://www.consensus.nih.gov/.

Kaplow, J. B., Curran, P. J. & Dodge, K. (2002). The Conduct Problems Prevention Research Group: Child, parent, and peer predictors of early-onset substance use: A multi-site longitudinal study. *Journal of Abnormal child Psychology, 30,* 199–216.

Kazdin, A. E. (1995). *Conduct disorders in childhood and adolescence,* 2d ed. Thousand Oaks, CA: Sage.

Kellam, S. G. & Langevin, D. J. (2003). A framework for understanding "evidence" in prevention research and programs. *Prevention Science, 4,* 137–153.

Keenan, K., Loeber, R., Zhang, Q., Stouthamer-Loeber, M. & Van Kammen, W. B. (1995). The influence of deviant peers on the development of boys' disruptive and delinquent behavior: A temporal analysis. *Development and Psychopathology, 7,* 715–726.

Kessler, R. C., Berglund, P., Demler, O., Jin, R., Merikangas, K. R. & Walters, E. E. (2005). Lifetime prevalence and age-of-onset distributions of DSM-IV disorders in the national comorbidity survey replication. *Archives of General Psychiatry, 62,* 593–602.

Kessler, R. C., McGonagle, K. A., Zhao, S., Nelson, C. G., Hughes, M., Eshleman, S. et al. (1994). Lifetime and 12 month-prevalence of DSM-III psychiatric disorders in the United States. Results from the National Comorbidity Study. *Archives of General Psychiatry, 51,* 8–19.

Kumpfer, K. L. & Alvarado, R. (2003). Family-strengthening approaches for the prevention of youth problem behaviors. *American Psychologist, 58,* 457–465.

Lehtinen, V., Riikonen, E. & Lahtinen, E. (1997). *Promotion of mental health on the European agenda.* Helsinki: National Research and Development Centre for Welfare and Health (STAKES).

Leaf, P. J., Alegria, M., Cohen, P., Goodman, S., Horwitz, S., Hoven, C. et al. (1996). Mental health service use in the community and schools: Results from the Four-Community MECA Study. *Journal of the American Academy of Child & Adolescent Psychiatry, 35*(7), 889–897.

Mrazek, P. J., Biglan, P. J. & Hawkins, J. D. (2004). *Community monitoring systems: Tracking and improving the well-being of America's children and adolescents.* Falls Church, VA: Society for Prevention Research.

Mrazek, P. J. & Haggerty, R. J. (Eds.) (1994). *Reducing risks for mental disorders: Frontiers for preventive intervention research.* Washington, DC: National Academy Press.

Olds, D. L. (2002). Prenatal and infancy home visiting by nurses: From randomized trials to community replication. *Prevention Science, 3,* 153–72.

Olfson, M., Gameroff, M. J., Marcus, S. C. & Waslick, B. D. (2003). Outpatient treatment of child and adolescent depression in the United States. *Archives of General Psychiatry, 60,* 1236–1242.

Olweus, D. (1993). *Bullying at school: What we know and what we can do.* Oxford: Basil Blackwell.

Pumariega, A. J. & Winters, N. C. (Eds.) (2003). *The handbook of child and adolescent systems of care.* San Francisco: Jossey-Bass.

Rones, M. & Hoagwood, K. (2000). School-based mental health services: A research review. *Clinical Child and Family Psychology Review, 3,* 223–241.

Sanders, M. R. (1996). New directions in behavioral family intervention with children. In T. H. Ollendick & R. J. Prinz (Eds.), *Advances in clinical child psychology,* vol. 18 (pp. 283–330). New York: Plenum Press.

Shaffer, D., Fisher, P., Dulcan, M. K., Davies, M., Piacentini, J., Schwab-Stone, M. E. et al. (1996). The NIMH Diagnostic Interview Schedule for children Version 2.3 (DISC-2.3): Description, acceptability, prevalence rates, and performance in the MECA Study. Methods for the epidemiology of child and adolescent mental disorders study. *Journal of the American Academy of Child and Adolescent Psychiatry, 35,* 865–877.

Schweinhart, L. H., Montie, J., Xiang, Z., Barnett, W.S., Belfield, C. R. & Nores, M. (2005). *Lifetime effects: The High/Scope Perry Preschool Study Through Age 40.* (Monograph of the High/Scope Educational Research Foundation, 14). Ypsilanti, MI: High Scope Press.

Shure, M. B. & Spivack, G. (1988). Interpersonal cognitive problem solving. In R. H. Price, E. L. Cowen, R. P. Lorion & J. Ramos-McKay (Eds.), *Fourteen ounces of prevention: A casebook for practitioners* (pp. 69–82). Washington, DC: American Psychological Association.

Simpson, G. A., Bloom, B., Cohen, R. A., Blumberg, S. & Bourdon, K. H. (2005). *Children with emotional and behavioral difficulties: Data from the 2001, 2002, and 2003 National Health Interview Surveys. Advance data from vital and health statistics; no 360.* Hyattsville, MD: National Center for Health Statistics.

Sugai, G. & Horner, R., (2002). The evolution of discipline practices: School-wide positive behavior support. *Child and Family Therapy, 24,* 23–50.

Sugai, G., Sprague, J. R., Horner, R. H. & Walker, H. M. (2000). Preventing school violence: The use of office discipline referrals to assess and monitor school-wide discipline interventions. *Journal of Emotional and Behavioral Disorders, 8,* 94–101.

Taylor, T. K. & Biglan, A. (1998). Behavioral family interventions for improving child rearing: A review for clinicians and policy makers. *Clinical Child and Family Psychological Review, 1,* 41–60.

Tolan, P. H. & Dodge, K. A. (2005). Children's mental health as a primary care and concern: A system for comprehensive support and services. *American Psychologist, 60,* 601–614.

U.S. Department of Health and Human Service (1999). *Mental health: A report of the surgeon general.* Rockville, MD: Author.

U.S. Public Health Service (2000). *Report of the surgeon general's conference on children's mental health: A national action agenda.* Washington, DC: U.S. Department of Health and Human Services.

Weissberg, R. P., Bartoon, H. A. & Shriver, T. P. (1997). The social competence promotion program for young adolescents. In G. W. Albee & T. P. Gullotta (Eds.), *Primary prevention works* (pp. 268–290). Thousand Oaks, CA: Sage.

Weisz, J. R., McCarty, C. A. & Valeri, S. M. (2006). Effects of psychotherapy for depression in children and adolescents: A meta-analysis. *Psychological Bulletin, 132,* 132–140.

Weisz, J. R., Sandler, I. N., Durlak, J. A. & Anton, S. A. (2005). Promoting and protecting youth mental health through evidence-based prevention and treatment. *American Psychologist, 60*, 628–648.

# 6

# Childhood Risks Associated with Adoption

**DOREEN ARCUS AND PATRICK CHAMBERS**

## INTRODUCTION

School-age children who are adopted are a diverse group. They include children who were adopted as infants and whose birth parents and adoptive parents have a positive, ongoing relationship. They include children adopted long after infancy due to abuse or neglect in the biological family and whose birth parents are prohibited from contact with them, and they include children who are adopted after lengthy stays in institutional settings about whose birth parents little is known.

Children are considered adopted when individuals other than their biological parents assume legal parental responsibilities for them. Adoptions may be domestic or international and conducted through private or public agencies. Adoptions vary in their degree of openness with respect to contact between the birth parents and adoptive family. Children in open adoptions have information about their birth family and may continue to have contact, whereas children in closed adoptions do not have continuing contact although they may have information. Special needs adoptions involve children in categories that are associated with lower probabilities of finding a permanent home: sibling groups, older child, minority-group status or medical or psychological challenges.

## PREVALENCE AND DEMOGRAPHICS

In 2000 the U.S. Census gathered information on the relationship of children to the householder. The distribution of children biologically related to parents was more or less evenly divided by age as a function of the number of children born each year. Among the 1.6 million children who were adopted, however, school-age children and adolescents are overrepresented. The dramatic increase in number of adopted children, as seen in Figure 6.1, represents the multiple paths by which children come into adoption and the diversity of older adopted children.

Data on the type of adoptions that take place each year in the United States are sparse, as only four states (Connecticut, Delaware, Massachusetts, and Minnesota) require that adoption agencies be licensed to place children in

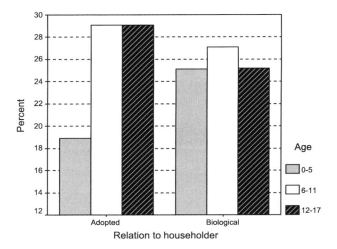

**Figure 6.1**   Distribution of children by relationship to householder and age of child (Kreider, 2003).

adoptive homes. Policy and practice with respect to who is allowed to adopt varies across the states. One third of the adoptions finalized in Massachusetts in 2004 were of children from foster care; the remaining two thirds were from private agencies (57% international and 9% domestic) (Center for Adoption Research, 2006). Adoption by gay and lesbian couples is prohibited by some states, including Florida and Mississippi (Families Like Ours, 2006). Despite the increase in adoptions by nontraditional families, Massachusetts data indicate that the vast majority of private adoptions continue to be to two-parent families, with 11% to single persons and only 3% to gay or lesbian couples (Center for Adoption Research, 2006).

Of adopted children identified in the 2000 U.S. Census, 13% were born in other countries, 48% from Asia, 33% from Latin America, and 16% from Europe (Kreider, 2003). Some variation in place of origin by age of child reflects changing sociopolitical conditions, most notably the dissolution of the Soviet Union in 1991, which resulted in large numbers of children available for adoption around that time. Although the one-child family policy in China also resulted in a marked increase in international adoptions of Chinese infants over the 1990s, China accounted for only 3% of all foreign-born adopted children in the United States in 2000 compared with Korea at 22%.

Census data reveal the socioeconomic status of households of adopted children in the United States to be higher than the norm. Their annual income was 17% higher than households of biological children on average, and the parents of adopted children were less likely to have dropped out of high school and more likely to have attained advanced college degrees (Kreider, 2003).

Children who are adopted are more likely to be girls than boys. This represents a shift from the well-established sex ratio among the general population in favor of boys. Census data show 106 males for every 100 females among biological children under age 18 but only 90 males for every 100 females among adopted children, with fewer in the preschool years and a narrowing of the gap at later ages (Kreider, 2003). Most infants placed for adoption internationally are girls due to cultural preferences to retain boys in the birth family; 93% of the children adopted from China at the time of the 2000 census were girls.

Women who adopt also prefer to adopt girls, especially when they are single women (Chandra, Abma, Maza & Bachrach, 1999; Groze, 1991). Despite these preferences, the gap does decrease across middle childhood, which probably reflects the fact that abuse and neglect do not occur with such strong gender bias, yielding a more evenly divided group of older children who are in need of adoption.

## MAJOR THEORETICAL PERSPECTIVES

Several theoretical perspectives have special relevance to conceptualizing risk and resiliency among children who are adopted. According to attachment theory the child forms a secure base for exploring the world in his or her relationship with a consistent, sensitive and responsive caregiver during infancy and early childhood. This early attachment further forms the basis for other relationships to follow (Bowlby, 1969, 1973). Because adopted children are not likely to have had noninterrupted relationships from the earliest days, attachments—and by this theory, development—may be at risk. However, the system is not without plasticity, and children may develop new attachments with their adoptive family members just as children display different attachment patterns across different relationships outside adoption (Main & Weston, 1981).

The school-age child capable of concrete operational thought—the Piagetian stage of development in which children can consider multiple aspects of a problem simultaneously—is able to process that being adopted by one set of parents also means being "given up" by another. Hence, the very nature of the child's adoptive attachments is complex, as one set of emotional attachments is so intimately tied to another set of emotional losses. The subjective experience of such losses may display in other domains if the child's contemplations or musings interfere with sustained focused attention on the tasks of daily life such as school work and may help to explain the modest gap between school achievement and intelligence quotient (IQ) attainment that emerges across studies of children who are adopted (Main, 1999; van IJzendoorn & Juffer, 2005).

The web of interconnected relationships in adoption may best be conceptualized through a systems or ecological lens. Family systems may be viewed as bounded sets of interrelated parts that exhibit coherent behavior. Although there are several family systems theories, they hold several tenets in common (Walsh, 2003):

1. All parts of the system are interrelated and interdependent.
2. The system has boundaries that may be relatively open and fluid or closed and inflexible.
3. The whole of the family is more than the sum of its parts.
4. There are rules and beliefs that are shared within the system.
5. There may be subsystems or alliances between certain members of the family.
6. Members interact in relatively predictable patterns.

Although services to adoptive families are generally considered desirable supports, Groze (1994) pointed out that the relation of the child welfare system to children and parents is both a resource and stress to the adoptive family system, as it brings a whole new set of relationships and alliances into the family dynamic.

Bronfenbrenner's (1989) systems theory of development places the child at the center of an active ecology that includes contexts in which the child plays both direct (e.g., family, school) and indirect (e.g., parent's job) roles, as well as the interrelations among members of these contexts and the cultural envelope in which the child and system evolve. Unlike older socialization models, an ecological view sees effects across the ecology as bidirectional. That is, the child is as likely to influence the parent as the parent is to influence the child. Clearly, correlational studies leave the direction of effect open to interpretation, as in Judge's (2003) finding that stress levels among parents of adopted children varied with the extent of behavior problems in their children.

This theory also holds that ecological transitions, or changes in some aspect of the ecology, mark times during which change rather than stability is likely to be seen in the child. Ecological transitions occur with the entry of a child into a family, the exit of a parent or even a change in job or school. Arcus and McCartney (1989) found more variability in young single children's social behavior over a 14-month period among those whose family constellation changed with the addition of a younger sibling compared with those who remained singletons. Similar behavior likely is displayed in the biological children of families who adopt as well as the adoptive children of families who add another child through birth or subsequent adoption. Changes in family structure have been found to vary with behavioral problems among older adopted chidren. O'Connor, Caspi, DeFries and Plomin (2003) reported a correlation of biological risk to psychopathology among adopted 12-year-olds, but only for children whose parents had divorced and not for children in intact families.

## WHAT ARE THE RISKS?

In considering the risks associated with adoption in children of school age, it is critical to consider the variety of circumstances tied to adoption. For example, children adopted from child welfare agencies with a history of abuse, neglect and multiple foster placements bring these histories into their adoptive experience. In fact, for these children such experiences are integral parts of their adoption, since without such negative circumstances there would be no need for adoption in the first place.

Children who are adopted appear to be at heightened relative risk for problems across many domains, often beginning with the cognitive advances of middle childhood that permit children to process the salience of their adopted status and the complexity of their losses in the broader social milieu (Brodzinsky, 1993). Among girls adopted from China living in the United States and Canada, for example, scores on the Child Behavior Checklist (CBCL) (Achenbach, 1991) were not elevated for preschoolers. However, depression and anxiety scores were elevated among school-age girls, and more school-age girls than preschoolers (16% v. 5%) scored above normal range for total problems (Tan & Marfo, 2006).

However, as Brodzinsky (1993) was among the first to note, most adopted children appear to do quite well—this despite the fact that he and his colleagues found that school-age children who had been adopted were rated as having more behavior problems, less social competence and lower school achievement than nonadopted children. Just as Tan and Marfo (2006) found two decades later, most of the adopted children scored in the normal range (Brodzinsky, Schecter, Braff & Singer, 1984).

Risk, on average, is probably not as telling for children who are adopted as the increased risk at the extremes. A nationally representative school survey of 10- to 13-year-old children found moderately increased risk for substance use, skipping school, emotional distress, diminished hope for the future, health and physical problems, fighting and lying to parents among children who had been adopted, especially boys. Moreover, among those children who did evidence problems, significantly more adopted youth were among those with the most severe problems (Miller et al., 2000). Similar patterns were observed in a study following children who had been adopted internationally and a comparison group of nonadopted children in the Netherlands over a three-year period into early adolescence (Verhulst, 2000). Adopted youth reported more of an increase in problems over time, and, although the majority were doing well, more adopted males' ratings fell in the clinical range for delinquency (6.5% v. 1%) and more adopted females' in the clinical range for aggressive behavior (7.3% v. 1.4%).

Not only may risk may be related to adoption per se, but also the heightened sensitivity of adopted parents may be related to potential problems and access to treatments (Miller et al., 2000; Warren, 1992). In fact, in a meta-analysis of 62 adoption studies involving more than 17,000 children, van IJzendoorn and Juffer (2005) found consistent evidence of cognitive catch-up among adopted children compared with children who remained in the original environments such that they concluded that adoption acted as a natural intervention in cognitive development. Of particular interest was a subset of studies indicating that adopted children were referred for special education services at twice the rate of the general population, a finding that may be interpreted as the proverbial glass that is either half empty or half full. Although the need for such services might put children at risk for poor academic outcomes, obtaining appropriate services when needed enhances the probability of academic success.

## Biological and Genetic Factors

Adoption has been a paradigm used to examine the relative contribution of genetic and environmental factors to development by comparing the degree to which children resemble their biological and their adoptive parents, but the role of genetics in adoption need not be limited to biology. The emergence of behavioral problems that have a genetic component might represent a challenge to the adoptive family both in terms of fit and experience as well as the standard features of the disorder. For example, parents whose children are diagnosed with dyslexia or other learning disabilities frequently can associate that diagnosis with the profile of someone else in the family when the child is biologically theirs. For children by adoption, however, parents may not have a familiar referent for the same issues. There may be challenges in accepting the child's need for special education, and the child's learning difference may become symbolic of other differences associated with adoptive status (e.g., infertility or loss). Still, for other families adoption might provide just enough psychological distance to permit parents to acknowledge evidence of problems requiring attention, as suggested by the rates of referrals for help among adopted children. The literature has not come close to explaining these potentially very complicated interactions.

There is a growing body of evidence that suggests a continuing role of genetics and biological factors in the development of children who are adopted. The degree to which children adopted from adverse circumstance show recovery in traits clearly genetically influenced (e.g., height, IQ) has been viewed as a hallmark of the power of the environment (Dennis, 1973; Golden, 1994; Scarr & Weinberg, 1976; Winick, Meyer & Harris, 1975). Even from the extreme deprivation of Romanian orphanages, Rutter, O'Connor and the ERA Study Team (2004) found substantial catch-up in weight by age 6 years among children adopted into British families in the United Kingdom. Unlike gains in body weight, however, head circumference failed to demonstrate significant catch-up by age 6 and remained 1.5 standard deviations below norms. Furthermore, the degree of cognitive impairment was correlated with head circumference but not with adoptive parents' level of education, regardless of whether or not the children showed extreme malnourishment at time of entry to the United Kingdom. McGuinness, Ryan, and Robinson (2005) also found overall competence as measured on the CBCL at 11 years predicted by birth weight in children adopted from the former USSR and living in the United States. These data suggest a biologically driven contribution to cognitive levels in the absence of a nurturing early environment and differ from other findings of strong linkages between adopted children's cognitive functioning and adoptive parents' levels of education (Dumye, Dumaret & Tomkiewicz, 1999).

To oversimplify the discussion as one of genetics versus environment, however, is to ignore the pathways by which these two powerful forces likely interact in all children, including those who are adopted. Genetics may mediate environmental effects as with language abilities, achievement and social adjustment (Gilger, Ho, Whipple & Spitz, 2001; O'Connor, Caspi, DeFries & Plomin, 2000). Genetic effects may change with development as do the effects on reading, which amplify during later childhood and into adolescence (Wadsworth, Corley, Hewitt & DeFries, 2001). They may depend on gender as is seen in the risk for conduct disorder, which shows greater genetic effects for boys compared with girls (Braungart-Rieker, Rende, Plomin, DeFries & Fulker, 1995). Genes may have evocative effects that alter aspects of the environment itself. For example, scores of adoptive sibling pairs were found to be significantly less similar when compared with those of biologically related siblings using Home Observation and Measurement of the Environment (HOME) assessments (Braungart, Plomin & Fulker, 1992), and adopted children who were at genetic risk for antisocial behavior were found to experience negative parenting more often than their peers at low genetic risk (O'Connor, Deater-Deckard, Fulker, Rutter & Plomin, 1998).

The complexity of genetic influence is apparent in considering the overrepresentation of attention deficit hyperactivity disorder (ADHD) among adopted children (Deutsch, Swanson & Bruell, 1982). Although this finding has been interpreted as evidence of the genetic transmission of impulsive behavioral profiles that resulted in an unplanned or unwanted pregnancy in the biological parents, a host of environmental and other biological influences may be contributing factors. These include the stresses of an unwanted pregnancy and the potential for uterine effects, as well as the risks in abusive environments that promote hypervigilance and threaten developing attentional regulation.

## Individual Factors Influencing Risk and Resiliency

Juffer, Stams and van IJzendoorn (2004) studied 176 7-year-old children adopted from Sri Lanka, Korea, or Colombia into Dutch families living in the Netherlands using Block's (1971) formulation of ego functioning. According to Block, ego control is the ability to regulate impulse by inhibiting or expressing it, and ego resiliency is the capacity to accommodate the degree of ego control in response to contextual demands. In a replication of findings among adolescents by Robins, John, Caspi, Moffitt and Stouthamer-Loeber (1996), Juffer and colleagues found the fewest problems overall among ego-resilient children, more internalizing problems among overcontrolling children and more externalizing behavior problems among undercontrolling children.

The gender of the child is likely to interact with other cultural factors. A nationwide study in China, for example, revealed that adopted children in one-child families were less likely to be enrolled in school compared with biological children, especially when they were girls (Liu, Wyshak & Larsen, 2004). Gender is also likely to relate to aspects of development in adopted children in much the same way it does in children who are not adopted, although evidence is sparse. Dutch studies of 7-year-olds adopted internationally as infants revealed effects of gender. Compared with boys, girls displayed higher social development and more ego control (but not resiliency) and were rated as popular by their peers more often than typical for the general population (30% v. 13%). Boys, on the other hand, were more likely to display externalizing behavior problems (Stams, Juffer, Rispens & Hoksbergen, 2000; Stams, Juffer & van IJzendoorn, 2002). In adolescence, adoption has been associated with higher risk across domains, with effect sizes larger for males (Miller et al., 2000).

## Family Factors Influencing Risk & Resiliency

Children appear at most risk when they enter adoption with a history of early family experience that is either absent or aversive for a prolonged period. Because the child's age at adoption frequently is confounded with time spent in an institutional setting or the duration of abuse or neglect, it is often used as a proxy for the extent of early deprivation.

Hoksbergen, Rijk, Van Dijkum and Laak (2004) found heightened externalizing and total problem scores among 8-year-old children adopted from Romania and living in the Netherlands, with 30% of the adopted group scoring in the clinical range, in a replication of Ames's (1997) findings with children from Romanian orphanages adopted into Canadian families. Of the children in Hocksbergen's group, 72% arrived in the Netherlands with medical problems at an average age of 34 months. Later arrival (after age 2) was associated with parents' assessments of problems encountered in upbringing and the total problem score on the CBCL.

Similar though attenuated effects are found beyond the extreme circumstances of Romanian adoptees. Howard, Smith and Ryan (2004) examined reports of behavior problems among 11- to 13-year-old children who were living with their biological families or who had been adopted domestically (all before 6 months), internationally (average age at adoption 1.5 years) or from the child welfare system (average age of adoption 3.6 years). Only the last two groups were overrepresented in the top quartile of scores on the Behavior Problem Index.

Although children adopted in infancy are as likely to form secure attachments with their adoptive parents as biologically related children, children adopted at later ages with a history of physical or sexual abuse show compromised attachment patterns across a variety of indicators (Groze, 1996; Singer, Brodzinsky, Ramsay, Steir & Waters, 1985). More 6-year-old children who spent 24 to 42 months in the extreme privation of Romanian orphanages before being adopted into the United Kingdom evidenced disinhibited attachment patterns compared with their peers who had spent less than 18 months in the institutions before adoption (33% v. 6%; Rutter et al., 2004).

Similar patterns emerge in domestic adoptions associated with early aversive family circumstance. Reilly and Platz (2003) studied 249 families of children in special needs adoptions with placements when the child was 3 years on average. More than one third of the children were reported to have severe or profound problems with anger, impulsivity, defiance, tantrums and hyperactivity—all behaviors that can be associated with a history of trauma. The incidence of reported disabilities was also higher than in the general population, exceeding 40% for behavioral, emotional and learning disabilities and developmental delay, and parents reported more problems with sibling groups than with children adopted singly. Curiously, the severity of problems reported correlated with the amount of time the child had lived in the adoptive home. It is critical to recall, however, that age of the child and duration of the parenting effort are confounded with time in the home. Hence, the correlation evident in parental report is more likely a reflection of the developmental emergence of these types of problems over the course of childhood (e.g., learning disabilities become apparent with increased school demands; the sequelae of sexual abuse is triggered by the onset of puberty) or the toll of child behavior problems on parents over time (Hoksbergen et al., 2004) than it is a product of the adoptive family environment.

There is little evidence that adoptive families provide different ongoing environments than nonadoptive families. Deater-Deckard, Fulker and Plomin (1999) found a single difference—higher parent-rated negativity—in annual assessments of the family environments of adoptive and nonadoptive families when their children were between 10 and 12 years of age. In contrast, cohesion and functioning among families of African American 11- to 14-year-old children adopted transracially was rated higher than the norm. As with families in general, adoptive families are a heterogeneous group. Individual differences in their ongoing dynamic are likely to outweigh commonalities due to adoption.

These differences have been associated with children's social competence and academic performance. Even though Family Environment Scale (FES) cohesion levels declined from age 7.7 to 11 years, higher FES cohesion, along with higher birth weight, was moderately predictive of more total competence on the CBCL in a sample of children adopted from Russia and living in the United States (McGuinness et al., 2005; McGuinness & Pallansch, 2000; Moos & Moos, 1986). In a sample of Dutch children adopted as infants, mother–infant secure attachment and maternal sensitivity predicted positive social and cognitive development at age 7 (Stams et al., 2002).

Attachments in adoption involve more than one set of parents. As children are able to process that their adoption in one family is the loss of another, thoughts about their birth parents are to be expected. Smith and Brodzinsky (2002) studied 8- to 12-year-old children and their coping styles for the loss of birth parent. Not surprisingly, they found that children who were placed at later ages into adoptive homes were less curious about their birth families because they had more firsthand knowledge. In general, however, curiosity and preoccupation were associated with positive coping strategies, but avoidant coping was correlated with anxiety and depression. Negative affect about birth-parent loss was linked to depression and low self-worth. These results are consistent with the work of collaborative studies from Minnesota and Texas. In a large sample of children aged 4 to 12 and their adoptive families, no differences in children's self-esteem or multiple indices of socioemotional functioning were found to vary with the degree of openness in the adoptive family–birth-parent relationship. However, adoptive parents in more open arrangements showed higher degrees of empathy about adoption, talked about adoption more freely and showed less fear that the birth parent would reclaim the child (Grotevant & McRoy, 1997). When a small subset of these children were studied—all of whom were at high risk for poor outcomes due to birth family, prenatal or perinatal factors or preplacement circumstance—children whose families demonstrated more collaboration in relationships across the kinship network were found to have lower levels of socioemotional problems than those whose relationships were less collaborative (Grotevant, Ross, Marchel & McRoy, 1999). It may be that openness enhanced parental self-efficacy, which allowed adoptive parents to support the child's resiliency in the face of risk.

Fathers emerged as significant factors in discriminating Canadian couples who were able to sustain their special needs adoptions and those whose adoptions disrupted within a year of placement (Westhues & Cohen, 1990). Compared with families that disrupted, families that sustained were likely to have husbands who were rated positively by their wives and who themselves rated the family's affective involvement and expression positively. These were also couples who had been married longer, were employed in high-status jobs and were unlikely to have considered adoption due to a history of miscarriage.

Family factors may also correlate with child cognitive abilities. Petrill, Deater-Deckard, Schatschneider and Davis (2005) studied 262 children who had been adopted at about 1 year of age and found that reading abilities correlated with family factors such as parents' level of education, parents' attitudes toward education, the number of books read and parental involvement with homework. Similarly, Dumye et al. (1999) found a strong association between adopted children's levels of cognitive functioning and adoptive parents' levels of educational achievement.

In contrast, cognitive levels were not associated with characteristics of the adoptive family at ages 6 or 11 years among Romanian adoptees whose early years were marked by extreme institutional deprivation (Beckett et al., 2006; Rutter et al., 2004). Hence, the links between family factors and cognition might be limited to children whose experiences are within some normal expectable range and may not extend to children whose early experiences are exceptionally neglectful or abusive, which might result in neurological compromise.

There is no evidence that sexual orientation of the adoptive parents is related to child outcomes (American Academy of Pediatrics, 2002; Paige, 2005). A longitudinal study of the children of lesbian families failed to find that parents influenced the sexual orientation of their children (Golombok & Fisher, 1996). A comprehensive review of the literature provided "no support for the belief that lesbians or gay men are less suitable than heterosexuals to serve as adoptive or foster parents" (Patterson, 1996, p. 270). Of course, families in the gay and lesbian community are not a homogeneous lot. Some data suggest that children—not limited to children by adoption—are better adjusted when lesbian mothers are more egalitarian with respect to child care and when families have a supportive social network (Patterson, 1995, 1996).

The role of siblings in the families of children who are adopted is not well understood. Although child welfare agencies have traditionally attempted to keep siblings together through foster care and adoption, the data are not conclusive. Several studies examined the link between sibling placement and risk for disruption or dissolution. In his review, Rosenthal (1993) found that sibling placements might increase risk for termination, especially when there are children already in the home, and found evidence that sibling placements may be beneficial. Higher levels of anxiety and depression, more social problems and more total problems have been reported among children placed separately from biological siblings compared with those placed with siblings (Erich & Leung, 2002; Groze, 1996). On the other hand, parents who have adopted sibling groups report lower expectations, more child behavior problems and lower family functioning compared with parents who adopt individual children in special needs adoptions (Leung & Erich, 2002; Reilly & Platz, 2003).

As Festinger (1984) noted, these data cannot be evaluated meaningfully without understanding the reasons for sibling or separate adoptions in the first place. Children placed with siblings may show fewer problems than those placed together because their manageable profile permitted social workers to find a single home that could manage multiple children. On the other hand, when children bring an excessive array of problems into foster care and adoption, the placement of several siblings in the same home may simply overwhelm the adoptive family, thus making separate placements the most likely way to ensure permanency.

## Social and Community Factors Influencing Risk and Resiliency

Children do not only enter families through adoption; they enter the larger communities in which their families live, communities that present potential challenges as well as resources for the child. Compared with parents of biological children, a higher proportion of parents of children adopted from the child welfare system (mean age 12 years) reported problems with their children's abilities to make friends, to choose appropriate friends and to make good decisions in their community. Along with parents of children adopted as infants, they rated their children as more likely to have problems getting along well with others in the neighborhood and fitting into organized groups (Howard et al., 2004). Problems maintaining friends may cost the child in other domains since close friendships during middle childhood appear to have a buffering effect against the development of externalizing behavior problems in the face of family adversity (Criss, Pettit, Bates, Dodge & Lapp, 2002).

The community can also be a source of support. When 12- to 14-year-olds who had been adopted from the child welfare system were asked to whom they turned to for help when needed, they described an informal network of supportive others including school and friends, family and trustworthy people. Friends and siblings were identified as the most effective sources of support, and adoption professionals were not mentioned. The contention that others did not fully understand the adoption experience was identified as one of the most significant barriers for children seeking advice or other assistance (Ryan & Nalavany, 2003).

Arcus, Milewski, Brown and Merrill's (2002) study of foster care may lend some experimental support concerning the contention that others may not fully appreciate the experience of adoption. When adults were asked to rate the psychological characteristics evidenced in children's drawings that they believed to be created by children in foster care and children living with their biological families, a significant difference emerged in the ratings of participants who had personal experience with someone who had been in care compared with those who never had known anyone in foster care. The experienced group rated the drawings of children purportedly in care as evidencing less happiness and more social and maturational problems than those of children in intact families. However, despite the elevated prevalence of problems with children in foster care, the naïve group simply rated them as less happy.

Although culture can clearly be a central issue in many adoptive families, especially those whose children are internationally and transracially adopted, there is little empirical attention to the link between ethnic identification and outcomes for children. There is evidence that the larger context in which cultural origins of parents and child match or do not match is itself changing. Thirty years ago, Kim (1977) found that only a minority of U.S. parents who had adopted children from Korea emphasized the child's ethnic identity. Twenty years later, 90% of U.S. adoptive parents engaged in a study of international adoptions thought it was important to expose their child to his or her birth culture (Trolley, Wallin & Hansen, 1995). When parents of young children adopted from China were recently asked about the importance of their children's cultural heritage, they consistently agreed that exposure to Chinese culture was beneficial to their children's personal adjustment and identity (Rojewski, 2005).

To explore the link of such exposure to child adjustment, Yoon (2001, 2004) asked children adopted from Korea and living in the United States (mean age 14 years) to rate their parent's warmth, communication and support of ethnic socialization as correlates of the child's self-reports of collective self-esteem, well-being, and distress. Both living in an ethnically diverse neighborhood and parental support for exploring the child's ethnic identity correlated with higher collective self-esteem, which, in combination with parental warmth and communication, was related to more well-being and less distress. Additionally, the presence of a sibling also from Korea—but not siblings in general—was correlated with less self-reported distress.

Deeper questions about culture and adoption challenge the pathways by which some children are considered for adoption in the first place. In a critical ethnographic analysis, Hand (2006) suggested that the overrepresentation of communities of indigenous people in foster care and adoption is, at least in part, the result of a cultural mismatch. She argued that child welfare institutions and policies fail to attend to the strengths, values and meanings of families such as those in the Ojibwe tribe and therefore foster the movement of children rather than the nurturance of the family of origin through a blend of the best of indigenous and majority cultures.

## EVIDENCE-BASED TREATMENTS AND INTERVENTIONS

In this section we examine evidence to support treatment practices to improve the functioning of children and families in need of help.

### What Works

No interventions specifically targeting adoptive families that demonstrated success with multiple replications were uncovered in our review of the literature.

### What Might Work

Although there are few empirical studies, there is support for interventions to enhance the development of children who are adopted that are based on attachment and family systems theory and that focus on the expanding social world of the child across the school years.

The most common basis for traditional approaches to adoption interventions and supports has been attachment theory (Barth & Miller, 2000; Smith & Howard, 1999). Despite this, there has been only one series of studies examining attachment intervention with adopted children and their parents. Juffer, Rosenboom, Hoksbergen, Riksen-Walraven and Kohnstamm (1997) studied efforts to enhance attachments in adoptive families who either had biological children at the time of adoption (the mixed group, both biological and adoptive children) or who did not (the adoption-only group). The intervention broadly consisted of providing information on sensitive parenting to mothers at 6 and 9 months. Significant intervention effects were observed at 12 months for maternal sensitive responsiveness, infant–mother attachment and infant exploratory competence for the adoption-only group but not for the smaller, mixed sample. The follow-up study at age 7 revealed a different story (Stams, Juffer, van IJzendoorn & Hoksbergen, 2001). There were no effects of intervention evident in the adoption-only group, but there appeared to be delayed effects for children in the mixed group, increased ego resiliency and ego control for girls and decreased internalizing problems for both boys and girls.

Several explanations are possible for these trends, including the confounding differences in the parity and experience of mothers. None of the infants who were adopted into mixed families were the first child in their new family; about half were the second, and the rest were third to fifth. In the adoption-only families the adopted infant was the first child in each case, confounding family type with experience of the parents. New parents, therefore, may have had more room for improvement in their attachment behaviors in infancy. As infants grew into children, experienced parents continued to have models of child development to foreshadow what was to come with the adopted child. Although many of the known effects of parity occur most often in the first postpartum weeks, significant main and moderating effects of parity on mother–infant interaction have been found with 5-month old infants in nonadoptive families (Corter & Fleming, 2002; Fish & Stifter, 1993). Obviously, parity findings have been generated with biological offspring and may not generalize to adoption of infants or to adoption of older children. Nonetheless, it is possible that attachment-based interventions have limited applications that are appropriate for some of the children some of the time.

Few postadoption services have included evaluations of their success in preventing disruption or dissolution. In reviewing those that have, Barth and Miller (2000) noted general agreement about their effectiveness with particularly high regard for services that connect parents to groups or other adoptive parents that can offer respite and support. The authors argue that the availability of only four projects with small sample sizes and methodological idiosyncrasies require other sources of data to inform postadoption service planning. To that end they summarize findings from studies that reported parents' opinions about the types of services they would find helpful, opinions that fell into three major categories.

Information and educational services began with complete disclosure about the child's medical, social and genetic history. Other services in this category included written materials or presentations relevant to the particular child or to adoption in general. Clinical services included counseling, which was often named as useful but seldom used, and respite, again seldom used but highly praised when it was. Finally, material services included monetary subsidies, medical care and special education. These requests appear to reflect the complicated circumstances of older child adoptions. Barth and Miller (2000) suggested that the traditional attachment model be replaced—or at least supplemented—with multisystemic sources of support that target complex needs, such as those due to abuse or neglect, and do so in a way that adapt as these needs change with development and across social contexts.

These recommendations are in line with findings from Illinois postadoption services for children placed at older ages. Smith and Howard (1999) reported findings with more than 400 families who sought out services. These were not new adoptions. The children had been with their adoptive families almost nine years on average. More than 90% scored in the clinical range on the CBCL, and, especially among children with evidence of posttraumatic stress, problems appeared greatest around age 12. Hence, it is unlikely that attachment work alone would meet the needs of these families. Indeed, Smith and Howard reported that many families had previously sought assistance from a variety of providers without effect.

The central effort of the Illinois program was to teach parents to interpret problem behavior in the context of the child's history and development through individual meetings and participation in support groups. Smith and Howard (1999) reported five cornerstone practices of their adoption preservation services:

1. Workers are flexible and available, able to come to the home and provide 24-hour on-call service.
2. Workers integrate information from a variety of sources during assessments to develop a comprehensive view of the child, family and problem.

3.  Workers provide a variety of types of interventions, including support groups, participating in special education team meetings at the child's school and offering counseling services to all members of the family.
4.  Adoption issues continue to be raised throughout the service period.
5.  Workers encourage parents to care for themselves as well as their children and to depersonalize problem behavior.

Of these, parents were most enthusiastic about support groups. Presumably these groups struck such a responsive chord because other parents struggling with children's problem behavior would "get it," an antidote to the major barrier Ryan and Nalavany (2003) found to children's help-seeking behavior—that others could not really appreciate the experience of adoption.

When participating Illinois parents were asked open-ended questions about the benefits of the program, they praised the nontraditional delivery of services and availability and flexibility of workers. Areas in which they felt most challenged centered around dealing with anger, antisocial and attachment problems, as well as issues involving the family system. For example, "We had been in family therapy before but we were still struggling, in fact, my husband and I were barely keeping our marriage together. The AP was the first agency that informed us of the kinds of challenges that many adoptive children and families face. We just had no idea. I just thought I was doing everything incorrectly" (Zosky, Howard, Smith, Howard & Shelvin, 2005, p. 11). Areas parents identified as being those in which services had the most positive impact were understanding their child's behavior and feelings (most commonly cited), learning advocacy to access necessary resources, improving communication, dealing with the child's anger, understanding and working with attachment issues and understanding the unique grief and identity issues that arise in adoption. In line with Barth and Miller's (2000) suggestion, attachment-based work is a small portion of the types of support work that parents found helpful.

There is considerable convergence with the findings of a survey of 873 adoptive parents eight years after their adoption from public, private or independent agencies in California as part of a larger longitudinal study (Brooks, Allen & Barth, 2002). Although most parents did not use postadoption services, many read books or articles on adoption. Parents who adopted through public agencies used counseling services for child and family more often than other parents. It is important to note that the children adopted through public agencies were adopted later (mean age = 31 months), were slightly older at the time of the survey (mean age = 12 years) and were very likely to have special needs (72% medical or learning; 52% history of abuse or neglect) compared with the two other groups who were adopted during infancy: about 8 years old at the time of the study and much less likely to have special needs. Generally, about two thirds of each group found services to be helpful when used, with public adoption parents somewhat less likely to find services—with the exception of support groups for adopted children—helpful.

Brooks et al. (2002) also asked parents what types of services they would put in place if designing postadoption supports. Information on the child's medical, social and genetic history was identified as important by 85% of respondents. Additional information resources on adoption, including legal and financial aspects, were endorsed by a majority of parents. Single parents and parents of children who had a history of abuse or neglect or who presented behavioral or emotional problems were likely to endorse clinical services as well, including support groups for parents and children.

Finally, ecocultural theory suggests that interventions not be limited to the family, especially since school is one of the most salient social contexts of middle childhood. In addition to the special education planning and advocacy that Smith and Howard (1999) described, children who are adopted might be particularly sensitive to traditional curricular units. Our review of the literature revealed no empirical studies of the efficacy of curricular or instructional interventions with children who are adopted.

In summary, what might work appears to depend on the parent, the child and the child's history and place in developmental and social contexts. Special needs adoptions require specialized supports and are likely to be enhanced by the social and emotional support of a group of peers with shared experiences and perspectives.

## What Does Not Work

When formal sources of support and intervention become necessary, it is unlikely that traditional providers, such as the pediatrician, will be well prepared for some of the complex types of problems that some adoptive families face. Many medical and even psychological training and residency programs fail to provide an adequate curriculum on the topic of adoption as a long-term life process. A nationwide survey of fellows in general pediatrics asked these physicians to rate the quality of their residency training, tapping into areas relevant to adoptive families (American Academy of Pediatrics, 1998). Although many aspects of training were rated as very good, only 31% gave high ratings to their training in developmental and behavioral issues. Moreover, training was rated as poor by significant numbers of physicians in the areas of international health (58%), violence prevention and management (44%), substance abuse (34%) and learning disabilities (37%). Hence, parents are likely to have to search for providers who have specific expertise in the areas in which their child or family is experiencing problems. There are indicators that relevant training opportunities may be improving. As Pavao (1998) observed, the literature on adoption tripled in volume across the 1990s.

Children's needs change with development. Family decisions at the time of adoption should anticipate the needs of the eventual adolescent as well as those of the presenting infant, toddler or child, as there is evidence that the rules of engagement agreed to at adoption placement are not likely to change. Frasch, Brooks and Barth (2000) conducted a longitudinal study of families adopting from foster care and found that mothers tended to be the decision makers with respect to contact between birth and adoptive family. When they had made the decision at the outset not to have any contact with birth families, the decision was likely to stand. Mothers who were open at first—even with hesitation—to contact with birth-family members were likely to continue the relationships across the eight years of the study.

One important lesson from this study is that contact per se can be with any member of the birth family, and, since these were adoptions from foster care in which birth parents were likely to have been abusive or neglectful to their children, most contacts were through related persons other than parents. Relatives such as siblings, aunts or grandparents may be valuable connections as the child struggles with the complexity of attachment and loss over the course of middle childhood. However, it might be more difficult to initiate contact after it had been terminated than if some relationship had been carved out from the outset.

Adoption is a lifelong relationship. Intervention services that are intensive but brief have generally not been found to be effective in supporting or sustaining that relationship (Smith & Howard, 1999).

## Overall Comments on Good Interventions

It is important to recognize the divergence of needs among children who are adopted—from none at all to multiple and severe. Although adoption may be a central issue for some children's problems, it may not be for others. Although attachment-focused interventions may be useful with some children, they will not be for all. There are also differences across development and across contexts. Although children may not display problems at younger ages, they may emerge with development, particularly around the transition to adolescence.

Attachment may be the basis for many intervention programs, but traditional approaches to attachment in mother–infant pairs probably have limited applications to older children. Children adopted as infants and children adopted at later ages likely evoke and tolerate attachment behaviors quite differently from each other. Consider the infant whose immaturity results in total dependence on the caregiver for basic sustenance compared with the 6-year-old capable of independent movement, of getting a jacket when he or she is cold and of making a peanut butter sandwich when he or she is hungry. The infant begins to trust caregivers who respond to his or her needs by holding, feeding, clothing and comforting. Clearly, the new parents of older children will have to search for alternative or additional ways of building mutual attachments, and times during which the child is more vulnerable (e.g., sickness) might become more salient. Moreover, the child who comes into an adoptive home from an aversive history may finally have a safe place to release years of rage and anger, as in one newly placed 6-year-old child's proclamation from his time-out seat, "I hate you! I hate this whole family! And I ain't never talking to you. Did you hear me, Mom? I ain't never talking to you again—not till you're dead!" This example illustrates the importance of helping parents to understand their child's behavior in the context of his or her history, to depersonalize the anger or rage that may find itself expressed and to identify elements of emergent attachment ("Did you hear me, Mom?"). At the same time, it is important for the child to understand his or her anger and to learn appropriate ways to deal with it.

Many families who are not in need of intervention when their child is younger may find that the situation changes dramatically around the transition to adolescence. The psychosocial tasks of adolescence that center on identity development bring adoption issues to the forefront, and especially for children adopted through child welfare, problems tended to peak around 12 years (Smith & Howard, 1999). Although parents who adopted infants outside the child welfare system may not generally use, or endorse the value of, clinical services when their children were younger as Brooks et al. (2002) found, they may do so later. Hence, middle childhood might function as a sort of calm before the storm, a time to ensure that adoption is an open topic in the relationship and to connect with other parents who have adopted as a source of information and support.

The importance of parent and child support groups in intervention is clear from the results of both Barth and Miller (2000) and Smith and Howard (1999). A group of individuals with shared experience and meaning is a fundamental source of support in daily life and in interventions for a variety of issues from weight loss to dissertation writing to addiction recovery. Technology provides avenues via Web sites and discussion groups for support to individuals living in isolated communities without sufficient diversity to build a personal network.

It is important that individuals with the appropriate expertise and training guide interventions. The degree to which others understand the experience of adoption and the failure of many training programs to include adoption related curricula are barriers to obtaining effective services and supports. The experience of obtaining professional help but finding it not to be helpful, as many of the parents reported to Smith and Howard (1999), may indicate to the parent that the presenting problems are hopeless and may contribute to a declining sense of parental agency and reluctance to seek help when needed. Although parents with more education are likely to seek additional opinions, parents with less may be more likely to view the professional as absolute authority and less likely to have the resources to continue to invest in services that haven't shown benefit. Adoption agencies would do well to clarify the limitations of general practitioners and to provide referrals to appropriate resources.

As Smith and Howard (1999) recommended, interventions for children who have been adopted and their families should possess the characteristics of any good intervention program. They should be guided by an understanding of each family system and the environments in which that system operates. They should be supportive and respectful, should be focused on individual needs and should help families to find whatever resources will help them to function well. Because the challenges of parenting children who have been hurt are not confined to office hours, they should be flexible and creative in designing a system that can be available to families without overburdening caseworkers.

## PSYCHOPHARMACOLOGY AND ADOPTED CHILDREN

No studies specifically examining the role of psychopharmacological treatments with children who are adopted were found in our review of the literature.

That said, overreliance on psychopharmacology to the exclusion of cognitive behavioral interventions is one of the risks of the culture of managed medical care. When children move from foster care to adoptive homes, there is likely to be a period of transition to the new family, school and social milieu exacerbating any attentional or behavioral problems the child might have. Hence, it is critical that medications, if prescribed, be reevaluated after the child, family and school have had opportunities to adjust.

Additionally, child posttraumatic stress disorder symptoms frequently present as ADHD, learning or behavioral problems. Although the child with ADHD might benefit from a psychostimulant regime, he or she might also benefit from pharmacologic or other management of conduct problems, depression or anxiety that may be trauma related.

## PREVENTION

This section considers practices that work to minimize the problems associated with adoption and to enhance functioning and well-being for the child and adoptive family. Approaches to child welfare that emphasize family preservation and the employment of support services are attempts to prevent the need for adoption in the first place and are addressed elsewhere (see Chapter 10, this volume).

### What Works

No interventions specifically targeting adoptive families that demonstrated success with multiple replications were uncovered in our review of the literature.

### What Might Work

Providing complete information to parents at the outset is one potentially powerful method of preventing problems from emerging. Repeatedly, parents have identified this as one of the most commonly requested forms of support in the adoption process (Barth & Miller, 2000; Brooks et al., 2002). Still, significant numbers of adoptive parents report that they had received inadequate information from the agency (58%) or that their child's problems were more extensive than the agency reported (37%) (Reilly & Platz, 2003). As Zosky et al. (2005) noted, this is a grave concern in light of the observation that unrealistic parental expectations are a significant predictor of disruption (Groze, 1994, 1995).

When parents adopt children from cultural backgrounds different from their own, they may be at a loss for how to affirm the child's cultural identity. Vonk and Angaran (2001) sampled adoptive parents who participated in cultural competency training sessions in preparation for, or following, transracial adoptions to assess the effectiveness of such a program in three areas:

1. Increasing racial awareness
2. Increasing awareness of coping skills for dealing with racism or prejudice
3. Increasing awareness of the importance of multicultural planning

Their pilot results with a small group ($n = 20$) indicated positive changes in all areas, and anecdotal reports indicated that a documentary film titled *Struggle for Identity,* which features young adults who have been adopted transracially, discussing their own experiences (New York State Citizen's Coalition for Children, 1998) was a powerful vehicle for discussion and awareness. The support group was a central component of this intervention as parents met regularly with other parents similarly engaged in transracial adoptions. Follow-up studies, more methodologically rigorous, will be informative about long-term effects. Following Yoon (2001, 2004), such programming has the potential to enhance collective self-esteem and well-being and to lessen distress for the transracially adopted child.

Potential school problems may be prevented with communication and creativity. Pavao (1998) recommended assigning a "family orchard" rather than "family tree" in elementary genetics units. The orchard acknowledges the complexity of genes and environments and the contributions of more than one set of parents to the child's life. Moreover, it is applicable to children in a variety of nontraditional family structures. Not all academic units are so obvious for their potential salience to adoption. When one child was discussing a geography assignment on the city of Seoul (his birthplace) and country of Korea with his mother, he remarked, "I understand how you told me that my birth mother could not take care of me, but what was wrong with all those other billions of people" (Pavao, 1998, p. 48)? This example illustrates the importance of communication not only between parent and child but also between parent and teachers to ensure that the classroom environment is sensitive to, and respectful of, adoption-related issues that might be painful or confusing for some children.

In addition to academic considerations, school brings a host of social relationships into the child's life. The degree to which the child's adoption status interacts with those relationships will vary depending on the social milieu and a host of individual factors. Yoon (2001, 2004) found more positive adjustment indices among children adopted from Korea who lived in ethnically diverse neighborhoods, and Patterson (1995, 1996) reported children of gay and lesbian parents to be better adjusted in neighborhoods presenting a supportive social network including other similar families. Hence, it may be that choice of residence in a diverse environment would contribute to preventing problems in children's social relationships. When that is not possible, efforts to celebrate diversity and to find opportunities for children to connect with others like themselves (e.g., special camps) might be helpful.

Adoption, however, need not rule every relationship the child has, and it is not appropriate for children to feel the need to explain intimate details of their lives to any and all interested parties. Fahlberg (1991) recommended developing a cover story, a response to inquiries that is honest but protective of boundaries. Brief explanations of why a child is not living with birth parents (e.g., "My parents couldn't take care of me so I got a new family who could"; "That's private and I'd rather not talk about it.") offer the child a script for handling interactions that might evoke confusion, conflict or emotional arousal and thereby have the capacity to contribute to the child's sense of agency and social competency.

Authoritative parenting styles—a combination of warmth and limit setting that leaves room for negotiation when appropriate—has been repeatedly linked to positive outcomes for children, from preschool through adolescence and with diverse families, though not necessarily adoptive families. It has been associated with secure attachment as reported by children and adolescents from grades 4 through 11 (Karavasilis, Doyle & Markiewitz, 2003). Authoritative parenting has been associated with adolescents' academic success via development of autonomy and a healthy orientation toward work (Steinberg, Elman & Mounts, 1989). Authoritative parenting has been linked with decreased risk in the presence of drug-using peers during adolescence (Mounts & Steinberg, 1995). It has been found to be effective not only at the level of the individual parent and child but also for the presence of authoritative parenting among the members of the child's social network. Lower delinquency and substance abuse rates for 14- to 18-year-olds, lower school misconduct and peer conformity for boys and lower distress and higher psychosocial competence for girls were found when authoritative parenting was prevalent among the parents of adolescent's friends (Fletcher, Darling, Steinberg & Dornbusch, 1995). Moreover, these positive associations have been found in a variety of ecological niches across ethnicity, socioeconomic class and parent marital status (Steinberg, Darling & Fletcher, 1995; Steinberg, Mounts, Lamborn & Dornbusch, 1991). Hence, the adoptive family may also benefit from authoritative parenting, especially in preparation for the challenges of adolescence.

## What Does Not Work

We found no clear empirical evidence of prevention efforts that failed to work in our review of the literature.

## RECOMMENDED BEST PRACTICES

Interventions for the families of adoption should be responsive to the individual needs of those families—needs that may change over time and vary across contexts. The literature suggests that best intervention practices include the following:

- Those that offer information about adoption in general and the child specifically
- Those that provide support groups for parents as well as children
- Those that focus on attachment issues in the context of the child's age and history
- Those that include multisystemic approaches to family support
- Those that are guided by individuals with appropriate training and expertise

Psychopharmacological practices with children who are adopted should ensure that the child's history is fully considered and should be based on careful differential diagnosis and reevaluated as adjustments occur.

Although prevention research is thin, best practices appear to be the following:

- Those that provide complete information from the outset to encourage realistic expectations
- Those that support an appreciation of issues related to ethnic identity, especially when parents and children do not share the same ethnic heritage
- Those that promote communication between parent and child and parent and school
- Those that offer strategies to accommodate to adoption-related issues in school and social contexts
- Those that promote authoritative parenting that is warm, democratic and firm and capable of adapting to the emergent needs and challenges of adolescence

# REFERENCES

Achenbach, T. M. (1991). *Manual for the youth self-report and 1991 profile.* Burlington: University of Vermont, Department of Psychiatry.

American Academy of Pediatrics (1998). *Continuing medical education and graduate medical education experiences of pediatric generalists* (Periodic Survey 40, Executive Summary). Retrieved 10 October 2005 from http://www.aap.org/research/periodicsurvey/ps40exs.htm.

American Academy of Pediatrics (2002). Technical report: Co-parent or second-parent adoption by same-sex parents. *Pediatrics, 109,* 341–344.

Ames, E. (1997) *The development of Romanian children adopted into Canada: Final report.* Burnaby: Simon Fraser University (funded by National Welfare Grants).

Arcus, D. & McCartney, K. (1989). When baby makes four: Family influences on the stability of behavioral inhibition. In J. S. Reznick (Ed.), *Perspectives in behavioral inhibition* (pp. 197–218). Chicago: University of Chicago Press.

Arcus, D., Milewski, T., Brown, K. & Merrill, J. (2002). *Children in foster care and the eye of the beholder.* Poster presented at the annual convention of the American Psychological Association, Chicago, August 22–25.

Barth, R. P. & Miller, J. M. (2000). Building effective post-adoption services: What is the empirical foundation? *Family Relations: Interdisciplinary Journal of Applied Family Studies, 49,* 447–455.

Beckett, C., Maughan, B., Rutter, M., Castle, J., Colvert, E., Groothues, C. et al. (2006). Do the effects of early severe deprivation on cognition persist into early adolescence? Findings from the English and Romanian adoptees study. *Child Development, 77,* 696–711.

Block, J. (1971). *Lives through time.* Berkeley, CA: Bancroft Books.

Bowlby, J. (1969). *Attachment and loss: Volume 1: Attachment.* New York: Basic Books.

Bowlby, J. (1973). *Attachment and loss: Volume 2: Separation.* New York: Basic Books.

Braungart, J. M., Plomin, R. & Fulker, D. W. (1992). Genetic influence on the home environment during infancy: A sibling adoption study of the HOME. *Developmental Psychology, 28,* 1048–1055.

Braungart-Rieker, J., Rende, R. D., Plomin, R., DeFries, J. C. & Fulker, D. W. (1995). Genetic mediation of longitudinal associations between family environment and childhood behavior problems. *Development and Psychopathology, 7,* 233–245.

Brodzinsky, D. M. (1993). Long term outcomes in adoption. *Future of Children, 3,* 153–166.

Brodzinsky, D. M., Schecter, D. E. Braff, A. M. & Singer, L. M. (1984). Psychological and academic adjustment in adopted children. *Journal of Consulting and Clinical Psychology, 52,* 582–590.

Bronfenbrenner, U. (1989). *The ecology of human development.* Cambridge, MA: Harvard University Press.

Brooks, D., Allen, J. & Barth, R. P. (2002). Adoption services use, helpfulness, and need: A comparison of public and private agency and independent adoptive families. *Children and Youth Services Review, 24,* 213–238.

Center for Adoption Research (2006). *Adoption in Massachusetts: Private and public agency placements and practices in 2004* (Worcester, MA: University of Massachusetts Medical School). Retrieved 10 June 2006 from http://www.umassmed.edu/adoption/reports.cfm.

Chandra, A., Abma, J., Maza, P. & Bachrach, C. (1999). *Adoption, adoption seeking, and relinquishment for adoption in the United States* (Vital and Health Statistics, 306). Hyattsville, MD: National Center for Health Statistics.

Corter, C. & Fleming, A. (2002). Psychobiology of maternal behavior in human beings. In M. H. Bornstein (Ed.) *Handbook of parenting: Vol. 2: Biology and ecology of parenting,* 2d ed. (pp. 141–181). Mahwah, NJ: Erlbaum.

Criss, M. M., Pettit, G. S., Bates, J. E., Dodge, K. A. & Lapp, A. L. (2002). Family adversity, positive peer relationships, and children's externalizing behavior: A longitudinal perspective on risk and resilience. *Child Development, 73,* 1220–1237.

Deater-Deckard, K., Fulker, D. W. & Plomin, R. (1999). A genetic study of the family environment in the transition to early adolescence. *Journal of Child Psychology and Psychiatry, 40*(5), 769–775.

Deutsch, C. K., Swanson, J. M. & Bruell, J. H. (1982). Overrepresentation of adoptees in children with attention deficit disorder. *Behavior Genetics, 12,* 231–237.

Dennis, W. (1973). *Children of the creche.* New York: Appleton-Century-Crofts

Dumye, M., Dumaret, A. C. & Tomkiewicz, S. (1999). How can we boost IQ's of "dull children"?: A late adoption study. *Proceedings of the National Academy of Sciences, 95,* 8790–8794.

Erich, S. & Leung, P. (2002). The impact of previous type of abuse and sibling adoption upon adoptive families. *Child Abuse & Neglect, 26*(10), 1045–1058.

Fahlberg, V. I. (1991). *A child's journey through placement.* Indianapolis: Perspectives Press.

Families Like Ours (2006). *Adoptions options index.* Retrieved 1 June 2006 from http://www.familieslikeours.org/modules/icontent/index.php?page=62.

Festinger, T. (1984). *No one ever asked us: A postscript to the foster care system.* New York: Columbia University Press.

Fish, M. & Stifter, C. (1993). Mother parity as a main and moderating influence on early mother infant interaction. *Journal of Applied Developmental Psychology, 14*(4), 557–572.

Fletcher, A., Darling, N., Steinberg, L. & Dornbusch, S. (1995). The company they keep: Relation of adolescents' adjustment and behavior to their friends' perceptions of authoritative parenting in the social network. *Developmental Psychology, 31*(2), 300–310.

Frasch, K. M., Brooks, D. & Barth, R. P. (2000). Openness and contact in foster care adoptions: An eight-year follow-up. *Family Relations: Interdisciplinary Journal of Applied Family Studies, 49,* 435–446.

Gilger, J. G., Ho, H.-Z., Whipple, A. D. & Spitz, R. (2001). Genotype–environment correlations for language-related abilities: Implications for typical and atypical learners. *Journal of Learning Disabilities, 34,* 492–502.

Golden, M. H. (1994). Is complete catch-up possible for stunted malnourished children? *European Journal of Clinical Nurtition, 48* (supplement 1), 58–70. Retrieved 1 June 2006 from http://www.unu.edu/Unupress/food2/UID06E/uid06e00.htm.

Golombok, S. & Fisher, F. (1996). Do parents influence the sexual orientation of their children? Findings from a longitudinal study of lesbian families, *Developmental Psychology, 32,* 3–11.

Grotevant, H. D. & McRoy, R. G. (1997). The Minnesota/Texas Openness in Adoption Research Project: Evolving policies and practices and their implications for development and relationships. *Applied Developmental Science, 1,* 166–184.

Grotevant, H. D., Ross, N. M., Marchel, M. A. & McRoy, R. G. (1999). Adaptive behavior in adopted children: Predictors from early risk, collaboration in relationships within the adoptive kinship network, and openness arrangements. *Journal of Adolescent Research, 14,* 231–247.

Groze, V. (1991). Adoption and single parents: A review. *Child Welfare, 70,* 321–332.

Groze, V. (1994). Clinical and non-clinical adoptive families of special needs children. *Families in Society, 75,* 90–104.

Groze, V. (1996). *Successful adoptive families.* Westport, CT: Praeger.

Groze, V. K. (1995). A 1- and 2-year follow-up study of adoptive families and special needs children. *Children and Youth Services Review, 18,* 57–82.

Hand, C. A. (2006). An Ojibwe perspective on the welfare of children: Lessons of the past and visions for the future. *Children and Youth Services Review, 28,* 20–46.

Hoksbergen, R., Rijk, K., Van Dijkum, C. & Laak, J. T. (2004). Adoption of Romanian children in the Netherlands: Behavior problems and parenting burden of upbringing for adoptive parents. *Journal of Developmental & Behavioral Pediatrics, 25*(3), 175–180.

Howard, J. A., Smith, S. L. & Ryan, S. D. (2004). A comparative study of child welfare adoptions with other types of adopted children and birth children. *Adoption Quarterly, 7*(3), 1–30.

Judge, S. (2003). Determinants of parental stress in families adopting children from Eastern Europe. *Family Relations: Interdisciplinary Journal of Applied Family Studies, 52*(3), 241–248.

Juffer, F., Rosenboom, L. G., Hoksbergen, R. A. C., Riksen-Walraven, J. M. A. & Kohnstamm, G. A. (1997). Attachment and intervention in adoptive families with and without biological children. In W. Koops, J. B. Hoeksma & D. C. Van den Boom (Eds.), *Development of interaction and attachment: Traditional and non-traditional approaches* (pp. 93–108). Amsterdam: North Holland.

Juffer, F., Stams, G. J. M. & van IJzendoorn, M. H. (2004). Adopted children's problem behavior is significantly related to their ego resiliency, ego control, and sociometric status. *Journal of Child Psychology and Psychiatry, 45*(4), 697–706.

Karavasilis, L., Doyle, A. & Markiewicz, D. (2003). Associations between parenting style and attachment to mother in middle childhood and adolescence. *International Journal of Behavioral Development, 27*(2), 153–164.

Kim, D. S. (1977, March–April). How they fared in American homes: A followup study of adopted Korean children. *Children Today, 6,* 2–6, 31.

Kreider, R. M. (2003). *Adopted children and stepchildren*. Washington, DC: US Bureau of the Census. Retrieved 1 June 2006 from http://www.census. gov/prod/2003pubs/censr-6.pdf.

Leung, P. & Erich, S. (2002). Family functioning of adoptive children with special needs: Implications of familial supports and child characteristics. *Children and Youth Services Review, 24*(11), 799–816.

Liu, J., Wyshak, G. & Larsen, U. (2004). Physical well-being and school enrollment: A comparison of adopted and biological children in one-child families in China. *Social Science and Medicine, 59*(3), 609–623.

Main, M. (1999). Epilogue. Attachment theory: Eighteen points with suggestions for future studies. In J. Cassidy & P. R. Shaver (Eds.), *Handbook of attachment: Theory, research, and clinical applications* (pp. 845–887). New York: Guilford.

Main, M. & Weston, D. (1981). The quality of the toddler's relationship to mother and to father: Related to conflict behavior and the readiness to establish new relationships. *Child Development, 52,* 932–940.

McGuinness, T. & Pallansch, L. (2000). Competence of children adopted from the former Soviet Union. *Family Relations: Interdisciplinary Journal of Applied Family Studies, 49*(4), 457–464.

McGuinness, T. M., Ryan, R. & Robinson, C. B. (2005). Protective influences of families for children adopted from the former soviet union. *Journal of Nursing Scholarship, 37*(3), 216–221.

Miller, B. C., Fan, X., Grotevant, H. D. Christensen, M. Coyl, D. & van Dulman, M. (2000). Adopted adolescents' overrepresentation in mental health counseling: Adoptees' problems or parents' lower threshold for referral? *Journal of the American Academy of Child and Adolescent Psychiatry, 39,* 1504–1511.

Moos, R. H. & Moos, B. A. (1986). *The family environment scale manual*, 2d ed. Palo Alto, CA: Consulting Psychologist Press.

Mounts, N. & Steinberg, L. (1995). An ecological analysis of peer influence on adolescent grade point average and drug use. *Developmental Psychology, 31*(6), 915–922.

New York State Citizen's Coalition for Children (Producer) (1998). *Struggle for identity* (documentary videotape). Rochester, NY: PhotoSynthesis Productions.

O'Connor, T. G., Caspi, A., DeFries, J. C. & Plomin, R. P. (2000). Are associations between parental divorce and children's adjustment genetically mediated? *Developmental Psychology, 36,* 429–437.

O'Connor, T. G., Caspi, A., DeFries, J. C. & Plomin, R. (2003). Genotype–environment interaction in children's adjustment to parental separation. *Journal of Child Psychology and Psychiatry, 44*(6), 849–856.

O'Connor, T. G., Deater-Deckard, K., Fulker, D., Rutter, M. & Plomin, R. (1998). Genotype–environment correlations in late childhood and early adolescence: Antisocial behavior problems and coercive parenting. *Developmental Psychology, 34,* 970–981.

Paige, R. U. (2005). *Proceedings of the American Psychological Association, Incorporated, for the legislative year 2004* (Minutes of the meeting of the Council of Representatives July 28 and 30, 2004, Honolulu, HI). Retrieved 18 November 2004 from http://www.apa.org/governance.

Patterson, C. (1995). Families of the lesbian baby boom: Parents' division of labor and children's adjustment. *Developmental Psychology, 31,* 115–123.

Patterson, C. (1996). Lesbian and gay parenthood. M. H. Bornstein (Ed.), *Handbook of parenting, vol. 3: Status and social conditions of parenting* (pp. 255–274). Mawhaw, NJ: Erlbaum.

Pavao, J. M. (1998). *The family of adoption.* Boston: Beacon Press.

Petrill, S. A., Deater-Deckard, K., Schatschneider, C. & Davis, C. (2005). Measured environmental influences on early reading: Evidence from an adoption study. *Scientific Studies of Reading: Special Issue: Genes, Environment, and the Development of Reading Skills, 9*(3), 237–259.

Reilly, T. & Platz, L. (2003). Characteristics and challenges of families who adopt children with special needs: An empirical study. *Children and Youth Services Review, 25*(10), 781–803.

Robins, R. W., John, O. P., Caspi, A., Moffitt, T. E. & Stouthamer-Loeber, M. (1996). Resilient, overcontrolled, and undercontrolled boys: Three replicable personality types. *Journal of Personality and Social Psychology, 70,* 157–171.

Rojewski, J. W., (2005). A typical American family? How adoptive families acknowledge and incorporate Chinese cultural heritage in their lives. *Child and Adolescent Social Work Journal, 22,* 133–164.

Rosenthal, J. A. (1993). Outcomes of adoptions of children with special needs. *Future of Children, 3,* 77–88.

Rutter, M., O'Connor, T. G. & the English and Romanian Adoptees (ERA) Study Team (2004). Are there biological programming effects for psychological development? Findings from a study of Romanian adoptees. *Developmental Psychology, 40*(1), 81–94.

Ryan, S. D. & Nalavany, B. (2003). Adopted children: Who do they turn to for help and why? *Adoption Quarterly, 7*(2), 29–52.

Scarr, S. & Weinberg, R. (1976). IQ test performance of Black children adopted by White families. *American Psychologist, 31,* 726–739.

Singer, L. M., Brodzinsky, D. M., Ramsay, D., Steir, M. & Waters, E. (1985). Mother–infant attachment in adoptive families. *Child Development, 56,* 1543–1551.

Smith, D. W. & Brodzinsky, D. M. (2002). Coping with birthparent loss in adopted children. *Journal of Child Psychology and Psychiatry, 43*(2), 213–223.

Smith, S. L. & Howard, J. A. (1999). *Promoting successful adoptions: Practice with troubled families.* Thousand Oaks, CA: Sage.

Stams, G. J. M., Juffer, F., Rispens, J. & Hoksbergen, R. A. C. (2000). The development and adjustment of 7-year-old children adopted in infancy. *Journal of Child Psychology and Psychiatry, 41*(8), 1025–1037.

Stams, G. J. M., Juffer, F. & van IJzendoorn, M. H. (2002). Maternal sensitivity, infant attachment, and temperament in early childhood predict adjustment in middle childhood: The case of adopted children and their biologically unrelated parents. *Developmental Psychology, 38*(5), 806–821.

Stams, G. J. M., Juffer, F., Van IJzendoorn, M. H. & Hoksbergen, R. A. C. (2001). Attachment-based intervention in adoptive families in infancy and children's development at age seven: Two follow-up studies. British Journal of Developmental Psychology, 19, 159–180.

Steinberg, L., Darling, N. & Fletcher, A. (1995). Authoritative parenting and adolescent adjustment: An ecological journey. *Examining lives in context: Perspectives on the ecology of human development* (pp. 423–466). Washington, DC: American Psychological Association.

Steinberg, L., Elman, J. & Mounts, N. (1989). Authoritative parenting, psychosocial maturity, and academic success among adolescents. *Child Development, 60*(6), 1424–1436.

Steinberg, L., Mounts, N., Lamborn, S. & Dornbusch, S. (1991). Authoritative parenting and adolescent adjustment across varied ecological niches. *Journal of Research on Adolescence, 1*(1), 19–36.

Tan, T. X. & Marfo, K. (2006). Parental ratings of behavioral adjustment in two samples of adopted Chinese girls: Age-related versus socio-emotional correlates and predictors. *Journal of Applied Developmental Psychology, 27*(1), 14–30.

Trolley, B. C., Wallin, J. & Hansen, J. (1995). International adoption: Issues of acknowledgement of adoption and birth culture *Child and Adolescent Social Work Journal, 12*, 465–479.

van IJzendoorn, M. H. & Juffer, F. (2005). Adoption is a successful natural intervention enhancing adopted children's IQ and school performance. *Current Directions in Psychological Science, 14*(6), 326–330.

Verhulst, F. C. (2000). Internationally adopted children: The Dutch longitudinal adoption study. *Adoption Quarterly, 4*(1), 27–44.

Vonk, M. E. & Angaran, R. (2001). A pilot study of training adoptive parents for cultural competence. *Adoption Quarterly, 4*(4), 5–18.

Warren, S. B. (1992). Lower threshold for referral for psychiatric treatment for adopted adolescents. *Journal of the American Academy of Child & Adolescent Psychiatry, 31*(3), 512–517.

Wadsworth, S. J., Corley, R. P., Hewitt, J. K. & DeFries, J. C. (2001). Stability of Genetic and Environmental Influences on Reading Performance at 7.12, and 16 years of age in the Colorado Adoption Project. *Behavior Genetics, 31*, 353–359.

Walsh, F. (2003). *Normal family processes: Growing diversity and complexity.* New York: Guilford.

Westhues, A. & Cohen, J. S. (1990). Preventing disruption of special-needs adoptions. *Child Welfare, 69*, 141–155.

Winick, M., Meyer, K. K. & Harris, R. C. (1975). Malnutrition and environmental enrichment by early adoption. *Science, 190*, 1173–1175.

Yoon, D. P. (2001). Causal modeling predicting psychological adjustment of korean-born adolescent adoptees. *Journal of Human Behavior in the Social Environment, 3*(3–4), 65–82.

Yoon, D. P. (2004). Intercountry adoption: The importance of ethnic socialization and subjective well-being for Korean-born adopted children. *Journal of Ethnic and Cultural Diversity in Social Work, 13*, 71–89.

Zosky, D. L., Howard, J. A., Smith, S. L., Howard, A. M. & Shelvin, K. H. (2005). Investing in adoptive families: What adoptive families tell us regarding the benefits of adoption preservation services. *Adoption Quarterly, 8*(3), 1–23.

# 7

# Divorce and Children

**KORTET MENSAH AND MARK FINE**

## INTRODUCTION

Nearly 50% of children in the United States will experience the divorce of their parents before their 18th birthday. The adjustment for these children are somewhat poorer than their counterparts whose parents remain married. However, the adjustment differences between these two groups of children are relatively small and can be lessened by several parenting practices including cooperative parenting, effective communication between parents and minimal spousal conflict that involves their children. As such, practitioners have designed several interventions to facilitate parents' and children's successful adaptation post-divorce. This chapter describes the effects of divorce on children and effective intervention and prevention strategies aimed at improving children's well-being.

### Definitions

*Divorce* is the legal termination of a marriage and involves several legal issues affecting children. These legal issues include the determination of custody arrangements, visitation rights, child-support awards and parenting plans. Parents who are awarded legal custody have the legal authority to make decisions regarding the child's welfare. These parents can either have sole custody, meaning one parent has legal responsibility for the child (with the other parent being the noncustodial parent), or joint custody with both parents having legal responsibility for the child. Parents also have physical custody, which refers to where the child physically resides. A parent is considered a residential parent if the child lives with that parent for the majority of the time, whereas the other parent is referred to as the nonresidential parent. Nonresidential and noncustodial parents can be awarded visitation, which stipulates the amount of time these parents spend with their children. One parent (usually the nonresidential or noncustodial parent) provides child support (or financial assistance) to the other parent to aid in raising the child. Finally, parents can develop a parenting plan to outline the agreements they reach regarding child-rearing issues (e.g., custody, visitation both during the year and on special holidays, financial support for standard and special expenses like music lessons, athletic or academic camps, college, communication between parents).

## Historical Trends

Each year since the mid 1970s, more than 1 million children have experienced a parental divorce, and the proportion of children affected by divorce has increased substantially in the 21st century (Amato, 1994). Approximately 50% of current first-time marriages will end in divorce, compared with the estimated 5% divorce rate during the 18th and 19th centuries (Amato & Irving, 2006; Fine, 2003). In addition, the prevalence of divorce varies among different racial and ethnic groups, with African Americans having the highest rates followed by Latinos, European Americans, and Asian Americans (Fine, 2003).

Divorce-related experiences are connected to several legal and social conditions. With respect to the legal context, prior to the 1960s, fault-based divorces were granted when one spouse satisfactorily demonstrated to the court that the other spouse had done something wrong during the marriage, such as being cruel or adulterous (Amato & Irving, 2006). With these divorces, the allegedly guilty spouse was expected (or, based on the courts' allocation of resources, was required) to accept responsibility for violating the marriage contract and received less favorable settlements in terms of marital property, alimony (spousal maintenance), child support and child custody. However, by the mid 1980s, all 50 states had instituted no-fault divorces, beginning with the California state legislature's elimination of fault-based divorces in 1969. With no-fault divorces, divorce was granted based on irreconcilable differences, suggesting that the marriage was irretrievably broken (Amato & Irving, 2006). The notion of fault was also removed from the award of spousal support but remained to some extent for the award of child custody. Currently, the majority of divorces in the United States are no-fault divorces (ibid.).

During the 1990s, due to historically high divorce rates and the belief that divorce was becoming too easy to obtain, legislative efforts were undertaken to make it more difficult to obtain a divorce (e.g., longer waiting periods, reinstituting fault-based divorce), but most states were unsuccessful in passing such legislation. Instead, federal policies were initiated to strengthen marriages via the 1996 federal welfare reform legislation and other efforts. For example, several states have publicly funded premarital education classes, have increased the fee for a marriage license and have created educational materials about how to build strong marriages.

In addition to changing legal circumstances, there have also been changes in societal views of divorce. Prior to the 1960s, public attitudes toward divorce were negative, with many early family scholars viewing divorce as a serious social problem. These individuals believed that the family, formed by a marriage, was the primary social institution and that its deterioration posed a threat to the larger society. Moreover, some believed that marital dissolution was a selfish and unrespectable act of the spouses because they put their needs ahead of their children's needs, which was thought to lead to negative consequences for their children. However, by the late 1970s, the stigma of divorce decreased, and many Americans considered divorce as an unfortunate yet common event (Amato & Irving, 2006). Moreover, the increase in women's employment (and financial independence), rising expectations for personal satisfaction and the declining stigma of divorce were cited as reasons for the increasing divorce rate. Additionally, the increased level of support divorced spouses received from their families was thought to be another reason for the increase in the divorce rate. With their families' support, spouses tended to seek divorce when they became dissatisfied with their relationships, even if their marriage did not include serious problems.

## Theories

Researchers have used several theories or models to understand divorce and its effects on family members; here, we briefly describe four of these theories. First, the social exchange perspective suggests that individuals evaluate their relationships based on an analysis of the costs and benefits for remaining in their current relationship compared with the costs and benefits of alternate relationships. Consequently, if the costs of the relationship outweigh the benefits and exceed what individuals believe they can obtain in alternate relationships, they are more likely to terminate their current relationship. Second, the symbolic interaction perspective suggests that the meanings individuals attach to their experiences influence their behaviors. This perspective proposes that individuals actively attempt to make sense of their experiences to cope with difficult circumstances. Applying this perspective to divorce, individuals may attach very different meanings to the same divorce-related events.

Third, the social cognitive perspective emphasizes that individuals learn from observing the behaviors of important others. With respect to divorce, this perspective leads us to acknowledge that children learn about relationships from observing their parents' behaviors. Based on this assumption, researchers have explored the reasons why children of divorce are more likely to divorce than their counterparts from intact families, as well as sex differences in children's adjustment (e.g., girls seem to experience fewer negative consequences from divorce than boys). Practitioners and program developers also use this perspective as the basis for the content of parent education programs for divorcing parents that emphasize using effective communication (e.g., reduce spousal conflict or arguments, communicate directly with each other, keep children out of their disputes) and problem-solving skills in front of their children. Finally, the narrative approach suggests that individuals describe and emotionally react to major events in their lives in story-like form, which helps them deal with major life stressors. Applying this concept to divorce, spouses construct conceptually manageable accounts of how their marriage ended (Harvey & Fine, 2006). Partners may have very different accounts of the relationship deterioration process because these stories might serve different purposes for each partner and because each partner's recollections of events could possibly be distorted (Hopper, 2001). However, regardless of their accuracy, these stories clearly influence partners' behaviors postdivorce.

## Effects of Divorce on Children

Divorce and events related to divorce, including marital conflict and separation, are very stressful events in children's lives. Often, children, depending on their age, display a variety of signs of disturbance in the months following the divorce (e.g., sadness, anger, anxiety, sleep and concentration disturbance, aggression), with the effects of such distress varying among children. However, after the initial adjustment period, most children successfully adapt to their new family life with minimal long-term ill effects. Nonetheless, children who experience their parents' divorce, on average, have lower levels of academic, behavioral, emotional and psychological well-being than children from contin-uously intact two-parent families (Amato, 1994, 2005; Fine, 2003). Moreover, the differences between these two groups are small, which indicates that factors other than the divorce itself play an important role in determining children's adjustment levels (Amato, 2005). Some children from divorced families may have parents who separate amicably and can cooperatively co-parent after their divorce, which help these children cope well, whereas some children in con-tinuously intact families may experience violence, inept parenting and serious parental conflict that impede their development. Moreover, children's psycho-logical well-being tends to improve over time, partly due to the decrease in high parental conflict after the divorce (Behrman & Quinn, 1994). It must be noted that children of divorce often have problems long before their parents' divorce and that the effects of their parents' divorce and events related to the divorce simply add to their preexisting difficulties (Cherlin et al., 1991).

## DSM-IV Criteria

Divorce is a stressful event rather than a characteristic of the child who expe-riences it. Thus, whereas divorce can affect children's adjustment, it is not sufficient, by itself, to justify assigning a mental disorder diagnosis to those children who have experienced it. However, two considerations should be kept in mind. First, children from divorced families may develop adjustment problems severe enough to justify the diagnosis of a mental disorder. Such diagnoses tend to fall into two categories:

1. Internalizing disorders, consisting primarily of depression, anxiety, and low self-esteem
2. Externalizing disorders, consisting of acting-out behavior and conduct problems

Although the evidence suggests that children from divorced families are, indeed, more likely to be given these psychiatric diagnoses (Barber & Demo, 2006), divorce itself should be considered a risk factor rather than a diagnostic entity in itself.

Second, divorce is not an experience that randomly befalls children. Compared with children from first-marriage, intact families, children who experience divorce tend to be more likely to come from families with family, marital and individual psychological problems (Emery, 1999). Therefore, even if divorce had not occurred in their families, children who later experience divorce may be more likely to experience psychological problems warranting a DSM-IV diagnosis. As a result, it is important to keep in mind that children of divorce come from families with a constellation of factors that may increase their psychological risk even in addition to the divorce itself.

## BIOLOGICAL AND GENETIC FACTORS

Although divorce is a stressful event rather than a characteristic of the indi-vidual, researchers have attempted to identify biological and genetic fac-tors that increase the likelihood of later divorce. This section first reviews predictors of the likelihood of divorce, then discusses mechanisms that may explain the intergenerational transmission of divorce effect and finally discusses genetically related personality and psychiatric characteristics that make individuals so-called poor marriage material and increase their likelihood of divorce.

## Predictors of Divorce Proneness

As noted earlier, divorce is not experienced by a random segment of the general population but is more likely to occur for some segments of the population than others. A wealth of literature has identified predictors, although not necessarily causes, of divorce. For example, in terms of demographic characteristics, adults who marry when they are young, who are less religious, who cohabit before marriage, and who are from lower socioeconomic circumstances are particularly likely to divorce (Rodrigues, Hall & Fincham, 2006). As a result, children who later experience the divorce of their parents are more likely to come from these groups of parents having a higher risk of divorce. In addition, as noted further in the following section, genetically transmitted personality characteristics have also been identified that may contribute to the risk of divorce.

## Intergenerational Transmission of Divorce

Children whose parents have divorced have an elevated risk of themselves later divorcing (Amato, 1996), a phenomenon known as the intergenerational transmission of divorce. Amato (1996) found that children under age 12 at the time of their parent's divorce had a 60% higher risk of divorce, whereas those age 13 to 19 had a 23% greater likelihood of divorce than their peers who did not experience parental divorce. In an attempt to explain this intergenerational transmission of divorce, Amato found that children who experienced parental divorce were more likely to divorce as adults because they were particularly likely to engage in problematic behaviors, such as easily getting angered, jealous, irritated or becoming critical of others. Interestingly, those who were over 20 years old at the time of their parents' divorce had a 20% reduction in divorce likelihood.

Another mechanism explaining the intergenerational transmission of divorce is genetics. Because divorce is an event that people experience, and because events themselves cannot be genetically transmitted, divorce per se cannot be passed down genetically from parents to children. However, the likelihood of divorce could be genetically determined, and, in fact, there is strong evidence suggesting that genetic factors account for a large proportion of the intergenerational transmission of divorce effect. Lykken and McGue (1992) found that concordance rates (the likelihood that, if one twin divorced, the other twin would also divorce) were strongly and consistently higher for identical twins, who share virtually 100% of their genetic material, than for fraternal twins, who share approximately 50% of genetic material. Given that twins raised in the same home, whether identical or fraternal, tend to have similar environments, this evidence is suggestive of a genetic component to divorce risk.

## Personality and Psychiatric Factors That Influence the Likelihood of Divorce

How might genetic factors contribute to the chances that one will experience a divorce? The most commonly identified factor is personality characteristics. For women and men, Jockin, McGue, and Lykken (1996) found that 30% and 42%, respectively, of the heritability of divorce risk was due to personality characteristics that are genetically transmitted. In particular, high levels of neuroticism (i.e., the tendency to experience negative emotions, such as fear, guilt, sadness, anger and embarrassment) have been strongly related to divorce risk (Rodrigues et al., 2006). In addition, high levels of extraversion and low levels of agreeableness and conscientiousness predict a higher risk of divorce. Thus, there is evidence to suggest that genetic factors affect personality functioning, which, in turn, affects divorce risk.

In addition to personality factors, psychiatric problems have also been identified as contributing to divorce proneness. Most major mental disorders are associated with an increased risk of divorce, particularly bipolar disorder (manic-depressive disorder), major depression, anxiety disorders, and substance abuse disorders (Rodrigues et al., 2006), with the psychiatric predictors of divorce differing somewhat for men and women.

In sum, genetic factors are related to divorce proneness, primarily because personality characteristics and psychiatric disorders lead to difficulties in relationship functioning. In addition, it is also possible that the consequences of divorce on children are related not only to the more commonly studied environmental factors but also to genetic factors that affect their personality and psychiatric functioning.

## INDIVIDUAL FACTORS AFFECTING RISK AND RESILIENCY

A number of individual factors affect children's adjustment to divorce. Before describing these, however, it is important to note again the existence of considerable evidence that children's level of functioning before the divorce is one of the primary factors determining how well they will adjust following divorce (Cherlin et al., 1991). Thus, it is misleading to conclude that the social, academic or psychological problems that some children of divorce experience are necessarily caused by the divorce; rather, these problems may have preceded the divorce and perhaps were exacerbated by divorce-related stressors. Nevertheless, a number of factors are related to how well children manage these divorce-related stressors. To the extent that these factors are related to positive adjustment, they are considered to foster resiliency; to the extent that they detract from adjustment, they exacerbate risk.

### Temperament

Although there has been very limited research on how divorce adjustment is related to child temperament, there are compelling reasons to suggest that temperament is likely to be a very influential factor in determining children's postdivorce adjustment. Temperament, unlike personality, is considered to be genetically transmitted and to be present virtually at birth. A number of temperaments have been identified, with the basic distinction between a so-called easy and a so-called difficult temperament being the most common.

Children who have easy temperaments are open to new experiences, are generally free of extreme levels of anxiety and tension, typically comply with their parents' parenting demands and adjust well to environmental changes. By contrast, children with difficult temperaments are frightened by new experiences, experience high levels of anxiety, are less compliant with their parents' wishes and are distressed by change.

Clearly, adjustment to divorce would seem to be facilitated by an easy temperament. Hetherington and Kelly (2002, p. 148) suggested, "... The stresses of divorce magnify the effects of a difficult temperament on destructive parent-child relationships but may increase the positive effects of an easy temperament" (p. 148). They indicate that children with easy temperaments grow in resiliency as their adaptive manner leads others to respond positively to them.

## Sex of Child

The literature has typically reported that boys have a more difficult time than girls following divorce (Hetherington & Kelly, 2002). However, although this general pattern has merit, several cautions need to be kept in mind. First, the sex differences, when they are found, tend to be relatively small. Second, it is difficult to disentangle the effects of a child's sex from custodial status. Most children live with their mothers following divorce, which might indicate that girls' supposedly better postdivorce adjustment is really a function of the fact that they live with their same-sex parent, whereas boys do not. Third, the effects of divorce seem to vary depending on the adjustment dimension studied. For example, aggressive behavior (i.e., externalizing behaviors) tends to be more common in boys following divorce, whereas depression (i.e., internalizing behaviors) is more common among girls after divorce (Emery, 1999). Thus, it seems that the differences between boys and girls even before or outside of divorce (i.e., boys typically engage in more externalizing behaviors than girls; girls typically have more internalizing problems than do boys) become even more pronounced following divorce.

According to Hetherington and Kelly (2002), the reasons why boys have a more difficult time following divorce than girls is that (1) boys receive less emotional support from their overwhelmed custodial mothers, who, at least until adolescence, find it more difficult to parent a son than a daughter; and (2) boys suffer from the lack of a father or other adult male presence.

## Race

The divorce-related experiences of African American children have been studied much less frequently than those of White children. Nevertheless, unlike the pattern of negative divorce effects for White children, a number of studies have found that African American children who have experienced divorce do not fare more poorly than African American children whose parents are continuously married (Fine & Schwebel, 1991). This lack of negative effects stemming from divorce is presumed to be due to the African American community placing less of a stigma on divorce and single parenthood, having particularly close extended family ties and being characterized by high levels of social support. Unfortunately, we know very little about how children from other ethnic or racial groups (e.g., Asian Americans, Hispanic Americans) experience and adjust to divorce.

## Age

Several theories (e.g., attachment, cognitive developmental, psychodynamic) converge in suggesting that children who are relatively young (less than 5 or 6 years old) at the time of divorce would experience more negative outcomes than children who are older when their parents divorce. In addition, it would be helpful for intervention purposes if there were such clear age-related differences in children's adjustment to divorce. However, despite considerable research attention, the findings are mixed. Some studies have found that young children have more problems following divorce, some studies have found no differences, and still other investigations have indicated that older children have more difficulties following divorce (Emery, 1999). There are also no clear patterns in terms of how children's current age—which is separate from their age at the time of the divorce—is related to their adjustment to divorce. The only clear time-related effect is that studies have consistently demonstrated that children's adjustment following divorce improves over time, regardless of either their age at the time of the divorce or their current age. Given the vast number of variables that influence children's postdivorce adjustment, perhaps it should not be too surprising that children's age has no clear and unambiguous relations to their adjustment.

In sum, although the general pattern is that children with easy temperaments, those who are girls and those who are African American adjust more favorably over time to divorce, these factors are only a part of the story. Fortunately, because temperament, a child's sex and a child's race are immutable factors that are not amenable to change, other factors, particularly the family processes described following, are likely to play a greater role in determining how resilient children are to their parents' divorce. It is these other family-related processes that have received the greatest attention from practitioners.

## FAMILY FACTORS INFLUENCING RISK AND RESILIENCY

Researchers suggest that several familial factors influence children's initial reactions and later adjustment to their parents' divorce (Amato, 1994, 2005; Behrman & Quinn, 1994; Fine, 2003). First, high levels of conflict are stressful for children and can teach them ineffective ways to manage disagreements, especially if parents argue heatedly or resort to physical violence (Amato, 1994, 2005). Moreover, when parents involve their children in their fights by communicating negative messages to each other through their children or recruiting them as allies in their arguments, children tend to feel caught in the middle, experience loyalty strains and feel emotionally insecure (Amato, 1994). As such, children from divorced families who experience a decrease in parental conflict are often times better off than those children from continuously intact families with high conflict. However, children can be protected from the negative outcomes of high levels of parental conflict if they experience a close and warm relationship with at least one parent (Blaisure & Geasler, 2006).

Second, the parenting skills of both parents can influence children's adjustment. Children fare better when they have parents (residential and nonresidential) who are warm and supervise and monitor their behavior. Moreover, children's well-being is also improved when nonresidential parents (usually fathers) are closely involved in their lives (Amato, 2005). In essence, children who have a close relationship with both their parents (especially when there is limited parental conflict) are more likely to positively adjust to their parents' divorce than children who do not have a close relationship with both of their parents.

Third, experiencing stressful life events (e.g., economic hardship, moving, parental remarriage, changing schools) can lead to variations in children's reactions to divorce (Behrman & Quinn, 1994). For instance, when children experience several changes in residences and schools and have limited or reduced socioeconomic status, they tend to feel less secure and evidence more academic, emotional and conduct problems. Typically, divorced custodial parents (especially mothers) experience severe declines in their standard of living, which sometimes involves moving to poor and high-crime neighborhoods with inadequately equipped school systems. Along with the change in neighborhood characteristics, divorced custodial mothers may face difficulties in providing the basic living and academic necessities to ensure the psychological and behavioral well-being of their children.

Moreover, when parents do not cooperatively co-parent (by agreeing on their parenting rules and supporting each other's decisions), they are more likely to undermine each other's authority and to not provide effective models of interpersonal skills (e.g., showing respect, effective conflict resolution, clear communication). In turn, these children might lack the necessary skills to establish and maintain positive peer and, later, intimate relationships (Amato, 2005).

Fifth, the custodial parent's adjustment to divorce is another factor influencing children's adjustment to divorce. Following divorce, custodial parents often exhibit lower levels of emotional well-being (e.g., symptoms of depression and anxiety), which in turn are likely to impair their child-rearing behaviors (Hetherington, Cox & Cox, 1982; Fine, 2003). However, over time, many parents are able to become less depressed, to maintain a supportive social network and to establish new, mutually satisfying romantic relationships, thus improving their well-being and parenting postdivorce.

Finally, parents' understanding of the impact of divorce on their children also influences their adjustment and their parenting strategies, which in turn affects their children's adjustment. Some researchers contend that parents need to be educated about the effects of family conflict on children, about ways to deescalate conflicts, about strategies for focusing on the children's best interests and about the needs and developmentally appropriate behaviors of children during and after divorce (Blaisure & Geasler, 2006). Several intervention and prevention programs are designed based on this premise. In these programs, parents are taught about the impact of their behaviors on their children and effective parenting (and co-parenting) strategies to facilitate their children's and their own adjustment.

In short, regardless of children's family structure, children have the best chances of thriving when their families provide loving, nurturing, stable and protective environments that are free from high levels of conflict.

## SOCIAL AND COMMUNITY FACTORS
## INFLUENCING RISK AND RESILIENCY

Several specific social and community factors may promote or hinder children's adjustment to their parents' divorce. First, society's views of divorce, the level of stigma placed on divorced families and the presence of intervention programs influence these children's adjustment. For instance, during the 1970s when divorcing spouses and their children were subjected to social scrutiny and received minimal assistance in obtaining and adjusting to their divorce, researchers found that children in these divorcing families sometimes experienced clinical depression, sleep disturbances and poor academic performance (Amato & Irving, 2006). These negative outcomes were thought to be common among these children but not among their counterparts living in continually intact families. Moreover, few interventions were available to these children to aid in their adjustment. However, as society's views of divorce became less negative, and scholars started to report that the differences between children in divorced families and children in intact families were relatively small and could be positively influenced by interventions, more assistance was offered to children from divorced families to facilitate their adjustment.

Second, the nature of available community and school-based programs affects children's postdivorce adjustment. In poor communities that are mostly populated with single-parent homes and that have limited resources such as dilapidated homes and poorly equipped schools and programs, children fare worse than those living in communities with more and higher-quality resources (Duncan, 1994). More specifically, these children's outcomes are negatively impacted in neighborhoods that lack community and school-based programs that facilitate their adjustment. For instance, children who have supportive adults in the community who serve as role models and who provide additional support (support that these children may not be getting from their parents) do better in school and exhibit fewer behavioral problems (Dornbusch, Ritter & Steinberg, 1991). Furthermore, school-based programs that teach children about the effects of divorce, that normalize their feelings about their parents' divorce and that teach them effective communication and coping strategies tend to minimize the negative effects of divorce.

Third, changes in school-related policies can also serve to enhance children's well-being postdivorce (Crosbie-Burnett, 1994). For example, some school districts have adapted more inclusive views and definitions of *families* to include multiple households and an extended family network, often referred to as *binuclear families.* Such policies promote cooperative coparenting and encourage both residential and nonresidential parents to be actively involved in their children's schooling. With both parents being involved in their children's education, the schools will be better able to communicate to the parents their children's strengths, challenges and needs, which can then be handled by all necessary parties (e.g., both parents and the school staff). Moreover, schools that amend their existing policies and curricula to eliminate first-marriage family bias (i.e., only nuclear families are regarded in a positive light) and to include the needs of other types of families (e.g., single parent, binuclear, and stepparent) are normalizing and validating the experiences of their students living in different family structures (ibid.).

Similarly, school districts that provide professional development workshops for all their school personnel (especially those who directly interact with students and other family members) to sensitize their staff to the variability in students' families and to discourage their use of negative language to describe families (e.g., *broken home*) destigmatize the experiences of these families and convey more supportive messages to children about their family circumstances, which hopefully reduces peer rejection and the ridicule of children living in divorced families.

## EVIDENCE-BASED TREATMENT INTERVENTIONS

### What Works

### *Meditation*

Mediation is an alternative, lower-cost dispute resolution strategy designed to help divorcing spouses make decisions about child-related issues, including child support, custody and visitation, as well as property division and spousal support (alimony). Usually conducted by trained professionals (e.g., legal, mental health or human service professionals) who meet state requirements, mediation uses a collaborative, win–win process in which parents maintain control of decisions affecting their families (instead of relying on a judge to make such decisions). In a series of meetings, couples jointly create parenting plans that outline the couples' agreement about property, financial, residential and child-care and child-rearing issues, and they are taught communication, problem-solving and negotiation skills, which often lead to greater investment in and compliance with child-support and custody agreements outlined in the parenting plan (Blaisure & Geasler, 2006). Although the effectiveness of mediation needs to be much more thoroughly evaluated, some studies suggest that divorcing spouses who use mediation have faster resolution of issues, are less likely to return to court to contest their original divorce agreements and are more satisfied with their agreements than spouses who obtain divorces through litigation (Emery, 1999; Sbarra & Emery, 2006). Moreover, compared with couples using traditional litigation, divorcing spouses using mediation tend to spend less money and have fewer court hearings to work out the details of their divorce (Behrman & Quinn, 1994).

However, spouses with more bargaining or negotiating power or skills can fare better in these agreements than spouses without such power or skills. Hence, mediation may not work for all spouses, especially when there are large power differences between partners or when one or both partners have personality or relational problems that make them unable to engage in the necessary negotiation and compromise process.

### *Joint Physical Custody*

With the goal of granting children substantial amounts of time with each parent, joint physical and legal custody provide both parents with legal rights and responsibilities for their children. Joint physical custody is also associated with greater father involvement, child-support payments and satisfaction with this arrangement than with sole maternal custody. Moreover, some researchers suggest that children in joint physical custody are better adjusted than children in other custody arrangements (Amato, 1994), although the changes in residence might be stressful for some children. Children might also experience more stress if they encounter continual parental conflict in both homes, which can negatively affect their development. As such, joint physical custody is most beneficial for families with minimal conflict. Consequently, this custody arrangement is usually awarded to couples that request it; these couples are usually less hostile and more cooperative, and the fathers may be very committed to their children prior to divorce.

## *Programs for Children*

There are several therapeutic interventions and educational programs designed to help children adjust to their parents' divorce (Blaisure & Geasler, 2006; Fine, 2003). Therapeutic interventions involve individual and group therapy during which children learn about problem-solving strategies and are supported as they learn to cope with their parents' divorce. Researchers suggest that children who participate in these programs exhibit less psychological distress (e.g., less anxiety and depression; improved self-concept), fewer maladaptive beliefs about divorce and better classroom behaviors (Amato, 1994).

Similarly, children in educational programs report improvements in their well-being. School-, community-, or court-based programs typically involve 15 or fewer children who meet for 8 to 14 sessions (totaling approximately 5 hours) to discuss their feelings, to gain information about divorce-related issues and strategies for adjusting to changes in their families and to develop coping skills (Fine, 2003). One such program is the Children of Divorce Intervention Program (CODIP), which is a school-based, 12-session program targeting 9- to 12-year-olds (Pedro-Carroll, Sutton & Wyman, 1999). This program is believed to be effective with children of various racial and ethnic groups due to several adjustments to the program (e.g., placing greater emphasis on extended family, normalizing various types of families for children of color, namely African American and Hispanic children) (Fine, 2003). Children in this program reported favorable results such as an improved self-image and fewer worries about their families; their parents and teachers also reported better adjustment, problem-solving skills and academic performance.

## What Might Work
### *Parent Education Programs*

Parent education programs are designed to educate parents on how to help their children deal with difficult divorce-related experiences. These programs focus on normative developmental needs of children at different ages, their reactions to divorce and the benefits of cooperative co-parenting with limited interparental conflict. Participants in Children in the Middle and Children First, two divorce education programs, reported greater improvements in parental communication and reduced parental conflict than other divorcing couples that did not attend such programs (Kramer, Arbuthnot, Gordon, Rousis & Hoza, 1998). Moreover, parents in the Children First program who had high levels of parental conflict and low levels of adaptive parenting prior to beginning the program had lower relitigation rates, whereas there was no reduction in relitgation rates among participants with low levels of parental conflict and who were parenting effectively (Kramer & Kowal, 1998). Similarly, Arbuthnot, Kramer, and Gordon (1997) reported that parents in the Children in the

Middle program had lower relitigation rates when they had higher levels of skill mastery (e.g., decreased triangulation of children into parental conflicts), which indicates the importance of emphasizing skill development in parent education programs.

Consumer satisfaction evaluations of these and other parent education programs suggest positive results. For instance, parents reported positive feelings about the program even if they were initially resistant about participating in the program, reported increased parental cooperation and increased awareness of the harmful effects of coercive parental conflicts and reported that the program was very helpful to them (Blaisure & Geasler, 2006). However, these results do not definitively indicate that the programs are successful in changing behavior. Moreover, although these parents reported changes in their parenting behavior, such reports do not necessarily reflect changes in their own behavior and do not necessarily reflect improvements in their children's subsequent adjustment (Fine, 2003). Hence, more research that goes beyond consumer satisfaction evaluations is needed to determine the effects (short and long term) of these programs on both parental and children's behaviors.

## What Does Not Work

Two governmental interventions do not seem to provide definite improvements in children's well-being. More specifically, the governments' efforts to strengthen marriage by changing the tax code or making divorce legally more difficult to obtain appear to have only minor effects on divorce rates and minimal improvements in children's adjustment (Amato, 2005). For instance, if the legal system was changed to make divorce more difficult, the number of children living in separated but nondivorced families would likely increase. Moreover, the likelihood of children living in high-conflict two-parent families would also increase if divorce became more difficult to obtain, which is just as (or even more) detrimental to children's adjustment as living in single-parent families. Hence, changing the legal system to decrease the frequency of divorce is unlikely to improve children's well-being. Furthermore, tax benefits to married couples would lead to further (relative) disadvantages for single parents and their children, which might negatively affect these children's well-being (Amato, 1994).

Overall, children- and parent-focused interventions that emphasize effective communication and problem-solving skills as well as provide information about children's developmental needs and reactions to divorce seem to be most effective in helping children and their parents adjust to divorce. Parents are encouraged to cooperatively co-parent, which involves agreeing on rules and expectations and respectfully communicating with each other; effective co-parenting leads to better parental adjustment, which in turn positively affects their parenting skills and their children's adjustment. Moreover, practitioners working with children from divorced families are encouraged to teach these children about divorce-related issues and ways of dealing with such challenging issues, to provide a forum for them to discuss their feelings and to gain support from other children who are dealing with their parents' divorce, and to offer strategies for improving their self-image and problem-solving skills.

## PSYCHOPHARMACOLOGY

Because divorce is a stressor that does not necessarily cause children to have clinically significant psychological problems, there is obviously no psychopharmacological intervention that would be indicated for all children experiencing their parents' divorce. However, as noted earlier, some children do, indeed, develop internalizing (e.g., depression, anxiety, low self-esteem), externalizing (e.g., acting-out behaviors, substance abuse), and academic (e.g., lower school grades, disruptive classroom behavior) problems that fall in the clinical range. For those children, psychotropic medications may be helpful. For example, for some children whose attention deficit disorder has been exacerbated by the stress of divorce, stimulant medication may be helpful in curbing antisocial behavior. For depressed children, especially those in their teenage years, whose mood has become even more dysphoric since the divorce, a trial of antidepressant medication may be indicated. Thus, in the extreme cases in which children develop clinical problems following divorce, psychotropic medications may be an ancillary to other forms of treatment.

## PREVENTION

In this section, we consider two aspects of prevention. First, we provide information on interventions that are designed to prevent divorce itself. Second, we discuss interventions that may reduce the negative consequences of divorce on children.

### Preventing Divorce
### *What Works*

The most effective programs to prevent divorce per se are premarital education programs designed to strengthen the institution of marriage. These premarital education programs teach partners and couples the requisite skills, knowledge, attitudes and beliefs to have a mutually satisfying marriage. The best-known example of such a program is the Premarital Relationship Enhancement Program (PREP) (Markman, Floyd, Stanley & Lewis, 1986), which is designed to teach couples ways to handle differences and negative affect more constructively and to enhance positive aspects of their relationship. More specifically, interventions are both behavioral (e.g., teaching structured techniques for effective communication and problem solving) and cognitive (e.g., teaching partners the destructiveness of negative interpretations of spousal behavior, to identify and modify relationship expectations). Evaluations have suggested that PREP is effective in reducing the likelihood of divorce for as many as 12 years following the intervention as well as in enhancing the quality and satisfaction of the participants' marriages (Stanley, Markman, St. Peters & Leber, 1995).

### *What Does Not Work*

Some states have implemented (or are considering implementing) stricter laws designed to make divorce more difficult to obtain. Have such changes or might such changes be successful in reducing the divorce rate? Though it is probably too early to determine if a return to stricter divorce laws (e.g., longer waiting periods, requiring counseling before granting a divorce) will have an impact on divorce rates, we argue that such an approach is unlikely to be effective, at least on a grand scale, for the following reasons. First, even if the divorce rates are reduced, it is likely that they would only be slightly reduced and that the vast majority of divorces would still occur. Second, such a strategy does not strengthen marital relationships, so the actual rate of marital breakdown (i.e., the disintegration of the marriage) is unlikely to change even if couples have a more difficult path toward obtaining a divorce. Thus, children may not be exposed to divorce per se, but children in disintegrated marriages would still be exposed to problematic family processes, such as marital conflict, that threaten their well-being.

## Ameliorating the Negative Consequences of Divorce on Children
### *What Might Work*

The parenting education programs for divorcing parents reviewed earlier in this chapter could also be considered secondary prevention activities in that they are designed to support and enhance children's postdivorce adjustment, before problems either begin or become magnified. The theory of change underlying such programs is that children's postdivorce adjustment can most efficiently be enhanced indirectly by directly working with their parents and teaching them how to best deal with their children. When such programs are legally mandated, they are genuinely preventive in nature because all parents are required to participate regardless of how well their children are adjusting. As noted earlier, parents report that such programs are satisfying and worthwhile, although long-term impact data are sorely lacking.

Another potentially helpful approach to helping children before serious divorce-related problems emerge is support groups for children themselves. Because such groups are made available to all children who have experienced parental divorce, they can be considered preventative in nature. These groups differ from the more structured group-based programs (e.g., CODIP) discussed earlier in the chapter in that they are less structured and more open-ended. However, it should be noted that the more structured interventions discussed earlier are also available for all children who have experienced divorce, not just for children who have exhibited adjustment difficulties.

In these support groups, children are invited to attend group meetings to share their feelings and experiences and to work on ways to cope with their circumstances. These support groups are typically led by trained facilitators, but it is often helpful if, particularly for adolescents, one of the group members takes on some leadership responsibility as well. It is helpful if such groups are sponsored by or conducted within settings that children routinely frequent, such as schools or churches. Although there is no direct evidence that support groups specifically targeting children of divorce are effective, a wealth of evidence exists to suggest that such support groups are helpful for a very wide range of problems, concerns, and issues (Yalom, 1995). Support groups help participants identify their feelings, recognize that they are not alone in their experiences, strategize new and more effective ways of managing stressful circumstances and establish new supportive relationships with others with similar experiences. It seems likely that such groups for children experiencing parental divorce would yield comparable benefits.

## RECOMMENDED BEST PRACTICE

In summary, children's adjustment to divorce can be positively affected by several intervention and prevention strategies. First, research suggests that parent education programs that focus on teaching parents how to reduce interparental conflict, to enhance co-parenting and to increase their understanding of the effects of divorce on children are somewhat effective (and have promise) in reducing the negative effects of divorce on divorcing couples and their children. Second, couples and parents (married and unmarried) who are interested in enhancing their children's adjustment can learn the skills, knowledge and attitudes necessary for creating a mutually satisfying relationship or marriage. By learning about what it takes to sustain a successful relationship or marriage, in marriage-enrichment prevention programs, these couples reduce their likelihood of divorcing, thus preemptively bypassing divorce-related events that could negatively affect their children.

Hence, practitioners should encourage couples to use these intervention and prevention programs as a means of strengthening their relationship to hopefully prevent divorce. Similarly, practitioners should encourage divorcing parents to enroll their children in programs that teach them about ways to deal with challenging divorce-related issues, as well as effective communication and coping strategies. In these programs, children should be able to freely discuss and better understand their feelings and concerns about their families and to gain support from peers going through similar experiences.

Moreover, practitioners are encouraged to assess their clients (children of divorce) for signs of severe maladjustment (e.g., internalized or externalized disorders, academic problems) that may be caused or exacerbated by their parents' divorce. These professionals can then determine if these children fall within the clinical range warranting a psychiatric diagnosis or prescribed psychotropic medications; these medications should supplement other forms of treatment (e.g., individual, group or family therapy).

## REFERENCES

Amato, P. R. (1994). Life-span adjustment of children to their parents' divorce. *Future of Children, 4*, 143–164.

Amato, P. R. (1996). Explaining the intergenerational transmission of divorce. *Journal of Marriage and the Family, 58*, 628–640.

Amato, P. R. (2005). The impact of family formation change on the cognitive, social, and emotional well-being of the next generation. *Future of Children, 15*, 75–96.

Amato, P. R. & Irving, S. (2006). Historical trends in divorce in the United States. In M. A. Fine & J. H. Harvey (Eds.), *Handbook of divorce and relationship dissolution* (pp. 41–58). Mahwah, NJ: Erlbaum.

Arbuthnot, J., Kramer, K. M. & Gordon, D. A. (1997). Patterns of relitigation following divorce education. *Family and Conciliation Courts Review, 35*, 269–279.

Barber, B. L. & Demo, D. H. (2006). The kids are alright (at least, most of them): Links between divorce and dissolution and child well-being. In M. A. Fine & J. H. Harvey (Eds.), *Handbook of divorce and relationship dissolution* (pp. 289–311). Mahwah, NJ: Erlbaum.

Behrman, R. E. & Quinn, L. S. (1994). Children and divorce: Overview and analysis. *Future of Children, 4*, 4–14.

Blaisure, K. R. & Geasler, M. J. (2006). Educational interventions for separating and divorcing parents and their children. In M. A. Fine & J. H. Harvey (Eds.), *Handbook of divorce and relationship dissolution* (pp. 575–599). Mahwah, NJ: Erlbaum.

Cherlin, A. J., Furstenberg, F. F., Chase-Lansdale, P. L., Kiernan, K. E., Robins, P. K., Morrison, R. et al. (1991). Longitudinal studies of effects of divorce on children in Great Britain and the United States. *Science, 252*, 1386–1389.

Crosbie-Burnett, M. (1994). The interface between stepparent families and schools: Research, theory, policy, and practice. In K. Pasley & M. Ihinger-Tallman (Eds.), *Stepparenting: Issues in theory, research, and practice* (pp. 199–216). Westport, CT: Greenwood Press.

Dornbusch, S. M., Ritter, P. L. & Steinberg, L. (1991). Community influences on the relations of family statuses to adolescent school performance: Differences between African Americans and non-Hispanic Whites. *American Journal of Education, 99*, 543–567.

Duncan, G. J. (1994). Families and neighbors as sources of disadvantage in the schooling decisions of White and Black adolescents. *American Journal of Education, 103*, 20–53.

Emery, R. E. (1999). *Marriage, divorce, and children's adjustment*, 2d ed. Thousand Oaks, CA: Sage.

Fine, M. A. (2003). Divorce, childhood. In T. P. Gullota & M. Bloom (Eds.), *Encyclopedia of primary prevention and health promotion* (pp. 435–441). New York: Kluwer Academic/Plenum Publishers.

Fine, M. A. & Schwebel, A. I. (1991). Resiliency in black children from single-parent families. In W. A. Rhodes & W. K. Brown (Eds.), *Why some children succeed despite the odds* (pp. 23–40). New York: Praeger.

Harvey, J. H. & Fine, M. A. (2006). Social construction of accounts in the process of relationship termination. In M. A. Fine & J. H. Harvey (Eds.), *Handbook of divorce and relationship dissolution* (pp. 189–221). Mahwah, NJ: Lawrence Erlbaum Associates.

Hetherington, E. M., Cox, M. & Cox, R. (1982). Effects of divorce on parents and children. In M. Lamb (Ed.), *Nontraditional families: Parenting and children development* (pp. 233–259). Hillsdale, NJ: Lawrence Erlbaum Associates.

Hetherington, E. M. & Kelly, J. (2002). *For better or for worse: Divorce reconsidered*. New York: Norton.

Hopper, J. (2001). The symbolic origins of conflict in divorce. *Journal of Marriage and the Family, 63*, 430–445.

Jockin, V., McGue, M. & Lykken, D. T. (1996). Personality and divorce: A genetic analysis. *Journal of Personality and Social Psychology, 71*, 288–299.

Kramer, K. M., Arbuthnot, J., Gordon, D. A., Rousis, N. J. & Hoza, J. (1998). Effects of skill-based versus information-based divorce education programs on domestic violence and parental communication. *Family and Conciliation Courts Review, 36*, 9–31.

Kramer, K. M. & Kowal, A. (1998). Long-term follow-up of a court-based intervention for divorcing parents. *Family and Conciliation Courts Review, 36*, 452–465.

Lykken, D. T. & McGue, M. (1992). Genetic influence on risk of divorce. *Psychological Science, 6,* 368–373.

Markman, H. J., Floyd, F., Stanley, S. & Lewis, H. (1986). Prevention. In N. Jacobson & A. Gurman (Eds.), *Clinical handbook of marital therapy* (pp. 174–194). New York: Guilford.

Pedro-Carroll, J. L., Sutton, S. E. & Wyman, P. A. (1999). A two-year follow-up evaluation of a preventive intervention for young children of divorce. *School Psychology Review, 28,* 467–476.

Rodrigues, A. E., Hall, J. H. & Fincham, F. D. (2006). What predicts divorce and relationship dissolution? In M. A. Fine & J. H. Harvey (Eds.), *Handbook of divorce and relationship dissolution* (pp. 85–112). Mahwah, NJ: Erlbaum.

Sbarra, D. A. & Emery, R. E. (2006). In the presence of grief: The role of cognitive-emotional adaptation in contemporary divorce mediation. In M. A. Fine & J. H. Harvey (Eds.), *Handbook of divorce and relationship* (pp. 553–573). Mahwah, NJ: Erlbaum.

Stanley, S. M., Markman, H. J., St. Peters, M. & Leber, B. D. (1995). Strengthening marriages and preventing divorce: New directions in prevention research. *Family Relations, 44,* 392–401.

Yalom, I. D. (1995). *The theory and practice of group psychotherapy,* 4th ed. New York: Basic Books.

# 8

# Stepfamilies and Children*

CHARLES B. HENNON, BRUNO HILDENBRAND AND ANDREA SCHEDLE

## INTRODUCTION

The stepfamily is not a variant form of the so-called normal nuclear family but is a distinct family form.[1] Recognizing and accepting this is vital to making stepfamilies peaceful settings for children to grow up. Scholars have reached this conclusion only after a long and problematic intellectual journey (Ganong & Coleman, 2004; Levin & Sussman, 1997; Théry, 1998). The lack of recognized role models for the stepfamily is lamented in the literature. Myths about the stepfamily continue to hold sway. These myths include the following (Ganong & Coleman, 2004; Rutter, 1994):

- The stepmother is mean, manipulative and jealous.
- The stepfather is sexually suspect and a potential molester.
- The ex-wife plays the victim, is out for revenge and meddles in the affairs of the new family.
- The ex-husband is withdrawn, inept and absent.
- The children suffer from pathologies and development shortfalls and are pests who wreck their parents' lives.

### The History of a Term

The development of the terms used to describe stepfamilies reflects the societal and scholarly understanding of this family type. It is often suggested that the term *step* has negative connotations (e.g., the wicked stepmother; stepchild to refer to someone who is not appreciated) and thus should be avoided (Claxton-Oldfield, 2000; Leon & Angst, 2005; Minuchin, Nichols & Lee, 2007). The following are alternatives to the word stepfamily: remarried families, reconstituted family, patchwork family, blended family, binuclear family and continuation family (*Fortsetzungsfamilien*). Similarly, various terms have been used for stepparents: added parent, acquired parent, half-parent, nonparent, other mother, psychological parent, second or third parent, social father and sociological parent (Ganong & Coleman, 2004). In this chapter, we use the terms stepfamily, stepparent (stepmother and stepfather) and stepchild in a neutral way, without negative or positive connotations.

* The authors thank Larry Ganong and Kay Pasley for their helpful comments in preparing this chapter, and Tom Gullotta for his helpful editorial suggestions. However, all omissions or other deficiencies are the responsibility of the authors.

## History

Stepfamilies are not new. In tribal cultures, depending on whether they are patrilineal or matrilineal or feature polygamy, stepchildren are the norm, though their existence can create situations that require resolution (Lallemand, 1998).

Until recently, limited life expectancy and a high degree of maternal mortality meant that stepfamilies were common. Between the 16th and 18th century in England and France, they represented 25% to 30% of all marriages (Peuckert, 2004). Such families were also common in the United States (Goldscheider, Hogan & Bures, 2001; Levin & Sussman, 1997). In the two decades following the Second World War, the biological nuclear family was considered the normal family, and divorce was frowned on. The situation subsequently changed in different ways in different countries. In 2000, around 5% of all children in Germany were growing up in stepfamilies, and about 7% of all families were stepfamilies (Bien, Hartl & Teubner, 2002). Today, the figures for Western Germany are similar to those for Italy and Spain (Peuckert, 2004). In the United Kingdom, one in eight children lives in a stepfamily, and it is estimated that by 2010 there will be more stepfamilies than biological families (BBC, 1999). Though the stepfamily is less common than the nuclear family in Germany and Europe in general, in the United States it is expected to outnumber the nuclear family in the near future (Carter & McGoldrick, 2004). Approximately one half of marriages each year in the United States are remarriages for one or both of the partners, and about 65% of these people have children from previous relationships (Adler-Baeder & Higginbotham, 2005).

Currently, the proportion of stepfamily households (both married and unmarried partners) is about 8% to 9% percent of all U.S. households (Kreider & Fields, 2005). This figure does not include situations where stepchildren and stepparents do not co-reside. That is, the child might be living in a single-parent household and have a remarried parent and thus stepparent living elsewhere or the child might be in foster care. Estimates place the proportion of children who can be expected to be stepchildren at some point before reaching the age of 18 years at 33% of all children. Of all families, 40% will be stepfamilies before the youngest child reaches age 18 (Bumpass, Raley & Sweet, 1995; Glick, 1989). If we consider children of any age whether living with or without the stepparent, the estimate is that more than 50% of children would be stepsons or stepdaughters by the year 2000 in the United States.

In the United States, the term *stepchild* was used traditionally to refer to the child who came to be related to a person through marriage to the child's parent. The words *stepchild* and *stepfamily* now include families formed by nonmarital cohabitation (same- or opposite-sex partners). Today, unmarried people can refer to the children of their partners as their stepchildren (Bumpass et al., 1995; Kreider, 2003). Ganong and Coleman (2004, p. 2) suggested "defining who is and is not in a stepfamily can be controversial," and the definitions are not limited to marriages or to those who reside in the same households (ibid., pp. 2–3):

> A stepfamily is one in which at least one of the adults has a child (or children) from a previous relationship. A stepparent is an adult whose

partner has at least one child from a previous relationship. A stepchild is a person whose parent (or parents) is partnered with someone who is not the child's biological or adoptive parent. Notice that these definitions do not limit stepfamily status only to those who reside in the same household. A stepparent and stepchild do not have to live together all the time, or even part of the time, to have a relationship together and to share family membership.

Further, in the United States and other Western nations, many couples who remarry cohabit first. Thus, cohabitation (living together) "is a better psychological and social marker of the beginning of a stepfamily than is a definition based on legal remarriage" (ibid.).

## Research and Theory Traditions

The manner in which separation, divorce, remarriage and the establishment of stepfamilies are viewed by society has changed. This is reflected in the ways child development and the influence of children on stepfamilies have been studied (Fthenakis, Niesel & Griebel, 1997; Ganong & Coleman, 2004; Goldscheider & Sassler, 2006; Walper & Schwarz, 1999). Initially, studies of divorce and remarriage placed breakdown center stage. Nontraditional families were judged against the standard of the nuclear family. This deficit-focused research led to the listing of the negative consequences of postdivorce and stepfamilies for children (Wallerstein, Lewis & Blakeslee, 2000).

Research projects then explored models of reorganization in an attempt to grasp the circumstances in which child development takes places when family structures change (Fthenakis et al., 1997). These studies emphasized that divorce and remarriage not only involve disadvantages but also may offer children opportunities. Systemic counseling and therapy illuminated the fact that family systems persist in changed forms (see Krähenbühl, Jellouschek, Kohaus-Jellouschek & Weber, 2001). Presently, researchers no longer refer to the "poor children of divorced parents" but to complex families of importance and interest to social research because they can teach us much about marriage, gender roles, parenthood, bringing up children and the difficulties of family life (Rutter, 1994). Finally, the transitional approach addresses divorce and remarriage from a family development perspective (Fthenakis & Textor, 2000). The family development approach, especially combined with family stress perspectives, appreciates the various careers of families without the prescriptive lens of "what should be" (Crosbie-Burnett, 1989; White & Klein 2002).

Theoretical models commonly used to explain stepfamily functioning and the development of children are stress models, models of stepparent and parent involvement, stepparent and parent parenting style and the selection hypothesis (i.e., differences between step- and other children are due to factors predating the cohabitation or remarriage of parents). Evolutionary theory is also used, especially for parental investments in children and the incidences of child abuse (Adler-Baeder, 2006; Ganong & Coleman, 2004; Hofferth & Anderson, 2003).

## Typology of Stepfamilies

- What do stepfamilies have in common? If we take composition to be a criterion, then it is that the two biological parents are joined by at least one other "parent" whose status is not given by nature but requires a special social framing. A stepfamily may be established following the death of a parent, a divorce or the end of a cohabitation relationship or may bring a period of unmarried single parenthood to an end (either via marriage or cohabitation). Stepchildren may be the biological children of the partner resulting from multiple relationships (i.e., the stepchildren are half-siblings). The stepparent could be the same sex as the biological parent. Further, stepfamilies can extend across several households. Bien and colleagues (2002) make the following terminological suggestions (see Ganong & Coleman, 2004, for different typologies):
  - Primary stepfamily: is one in which the child mainly lives with one biological parent and the new partner.
  - Secondary stepfamily: the family of the parent living elsewhere (perhaps with a new partner), with whom the child sometimes stays
  - Simple stepfamily: Most common type of primary stepfamily; may come into being either as a stepmother family, in cases where the biological father brings children into the new family, or as a stepfather family, should the biological mother bring children into the new family
  - Composite stepfamily: Both partners bring children with them into the relationship but have no children together
  - Complex stepfamily: The stepchildren are joined by shared biological children
  - Repeatedly fragmented stepfamily (also termed serial marriage): The composition of the family changes more than once as a result of repeated divorce or death

Other alternatives are stepfamilies where there are adoptive children, or other children such as grandchildren, extended kin (e.g., cousins) or foster children (Bain et al., 2002). In some cases all biological siblings do not live in the same stepfamily household, a situation termed split custody (Kaplan, Hennon & Ade-Ridder, 1993).

Stepfamilies featuring the biological children of the remarried parents alongside their biological children from previous families make up more than half of such families in Germany (Peuckert, 2004). In more than 80% of these cases, simple stepfamilies are stepfather families (Krähenbühl, Schramm-Geiger & Brandes-Kessel, 2000; Ritzenfeld, 1998). In the United States approximately 5.1 million children (one in six) under the age of 18 live with a stepparent (Kreider, 2003). Of these 51.1 million children living with two parents, 4.9 million (10%) lived with a stepparent and a biological parent. Usually this was a stepfather and a biological mother (4.1 million). Adoptive fathers were often first stepfathers (Kreider & Fields, 2005).

In the 2000 U.S. Census, of all stepfathers, 91% were married and 9% not married. About 8% reported having an unmarried partner. About 1% of stepfathers reported having no partner. About 1% were formerly married. Regarding stepmothers, 64% were married and 36% not married. Of those not married, 22% had an unmarried partner. Around 12% had no current partner, and of these stepmothers, 8% had been formerly married (Kreider, 2003). Overall, 217,000 stepparents who had unmarried partners reported having stepchildren under the age of 18 years in their households. Most likely, these were the biological children of their partners. Fifty-one percent of currently unmarried stepfathers and 41% of currently unmarried stepmothers had never been married.*

## BIOLOGICAL AND GENETIC FACTORS

A review of the literature revealed few possible biological and genetic factors related to stepfamilies. One of these was earlier pubertal timing for girls (see, e.g., Comings, Muhleman, Johnson & MacMurray, 2002; Ellis & Garber, 2000).

## INDIVIDUAL FACTORS INFLUENCING RISK AND RESILIENCY

As the new family grows together, stepchildren must master several developmental tasks. These include giving up hope that their biological parents will reunite; refashioning their relationship with the parent living elsewhere; forming a relationship with the stepparent; dealing with loyalty issues; coping with how the formerly single parent is now distributing attention and affection in new ways; developing a relationship with the stepsiblings (should there be any); and coming to terms with the new routines and rituals of everyday family life. Werner (2000) cautioned against viewing individual resiliency separately from family resiliency. She described the relationship between individuals and their social environment through a "spiral staircase model." Children's individual dispositions lead them to select a favorable environment for themselves: one that protects them, nurtures their abilities and bolsters their self-confidence. In such milieus, children develop their dispositions and thus learn, step by step, to cope with life's challenges. Models of the link between individual and social environment in the development of resiliency are thus interactive models.

Other approaches have pointed to the importance of a complex range of conditions shaping how a stepchild adapts to the new family circumstances (Staub & Felder, 2003). Individual factors such as age, gender, previous experience of relationships, disabilities and behavioral or psychological disorders play important roles. Although it is possible to locate research findings on the influence of a child's gender and age in the context of the stepfamily, we lack studies on other influencing factors. Researchers mention the following factors as generally helpful to how children adapt following the transition to the stepfamily: the child's age (younger children do better) and female gender (applies only until puberty; see Ferri, 1984; Napp-Peters, 1995). In general,

---

* It is estimated that the 2000 U.S. Census identified only about two thirds of all stepchildren living with a stepparent (married or unmarried), due to how the data were collected (Kreider, 2003). For one thing, if the householder was the biological parent of the child and the householder was remarried (i.e., there was a stepparent present), the child would be counted as biological. Only if the householder were the stepparent would children be counted as stepchildren.

resilient children have the following characteristics: average to above-average intelligence; good problem solving; consistently good relations with at least one primary reference individual; a good capacity for emotional self-regulation and a facility to form emotional attachments; a school and leisure time environment that nurtures the child's social development; and a robust, active and sociable temperament with a high self-esteem and self-confidence (Rutter, 2000; Werner, 2000).

The child's development may be at risk should he or she have experienced additional family ruptures, have required special support because of disabilities or have exhibited behavioral or psychological disorders (Kasten, Kunze & Mühlfeld, 2001). It should be noted that the problems and issues identified as characteristic of stepchildren are not related to personal pathologies or addictions. Though it is likely that many stepchildren face these challenges, stepfamily living is not the cause per se. These challenges, however, often become stepfamily relationship problems. Some evidence suggests that some stepfamilies may function poorly because of personal pathologies and addictions of the adults or children rather than due to factors related to divorce, bereavement or structural characteristics (Ganong & Coleman, 2004).

No consistent findings are available on ethnic factors, although one might speculate that if a particular group identifies strongly with having biological children, there may be some tension, favoritism or other transactional issues influencing child development in stepfamilies. Some ethnic groups (e.g., African Americans) appear to operate with more flexibility regarding the parental role using a multiple-parental model and kin. In such cases, conflicted interactions among stepfamily members due to competing roles might be weaker. Development outcomes for stepchildren in these circumstances could well differ from other stepchildren. For example, one study reported that Black stepfathers spend less time in activities with children and that Hispanic stepfathers are less warm (Hofferth & Anderson, 2003). Ethnic and racial differences in stepchildren's development have been understudied (Adler-Baeder & Higginbotham, 2005).

We assume that identity issues are more important to young members of interethnic stepfamilies than those from ethnically homogenous ones. On the other hand, the distinction between biological and stepparent is more pronounced in the former than in the latter type of family. However, even here, should the stepfamily break down, this is due to several factors, and child-related risk factors are not decisive.

## FAMILY FACTORS INFLUENCING RISK AND RESILIENCY

The literature is mixed on whether living in a stepfamily places a child at risk. Some scholars find that children from stepfamilies are twice as likely to suffer psychological problems as children from nuclear families (20% as opposed to 10%) but less than children from single-parent families (Furstenberg, 1987; Hetherington & Stanley-Hagan, 2002). Stepchildren are more likely to be placed with another family because their parents cannot successfully manage the situation (Kuppinger, 1990). In the United States, stepchildren are more likely to drop out of school, to be involved in delinquency as well as to be abused, but these are not common occurrences. Long-term behavioral and emotional disorders, poor educational performance, lack of self-esteem, depression, substance abuse and various health problems are mentioned as typical problems faced by children from stepfamilies (Michaels, 2006; Napp-Peters, 1995). Some researchers state that stepchildren leave the family home, enter into relationships and have children at an earlier age than those from nuclear families (Hofferth & Anderson, 2003; McLanahan & Booth, 1989; McLanahan & Bumpass, 1988). It is also claimed that stepchildren are more likely to be admitted to care and receive therapy (Stich, 1993). In a 25-year series of studies, Wallerstein and her colleagues (2000) described the difficult lives of children in divorced households. Some scholars have, however, accused Wallerstein et al. of basing findings on an unrepresentative sample (Ahrons, 2004). Other studies (from various countries) indicated that parental remarriage when the child was young was not related to emotional problems in early or middle adulthood. In one study, differences in adjustment as adults were apparently related to conditions and individual factors present prior to the stepfamily formation or perhaps to the child's age at the time of the remarriage (Ganong & Coleman, 2004), and Ahrons (2004) reported that the majority of stepchildren coped well with divorce and their life within the stepfamily.

In comparison with younger or older children, preadolescent children are vulnerable to negative outcomes when a parent remarries (Pasley, 2000). The age of a child when the parent remarries is a factor in achieving an integrative stepparent–stepchild relationship and the degree of bonding. Stronger bonding appears to develop between stepchild and stepparent when children are younger (Adler-Baeder & Higginbotham, 2005; Fine, Coleman & Ganong, 1998; Hofferth & Anderson, 2003; Marsiglio, 2004). The literature suggests that stepfathers are more authoritarian, coercive and disengaged than biological fathers (Marsiglio, Amato, Day & Lamb, 2000). The developmental outcomes of such parenting practices can affect adversely the stepchild–stepparent relationship (Bray & Kelly, 1998; Ganong & Coleman, 2004). Likewise, the child's behavior and attitude toward the stepparent can influence the relationship in a reciprocal manner affecting the level of parental stress and parenting practices (Adler-Baeder & Higginbotham, 2005; Peterson & Hennon, 2005).

Four areas have been the focus of most of the large body of research and clinical literature on the risks for children of stepfamily living: (1) academic achievement; (2) psychological adjustment and emotional well-being (i.e., internalizing behaviors); (3) behavioral problems (i.e., externalizing behaviors); and (4) interpersonal relationships. Some recent studies investigate physiological development. Stepchildren are usually compared with children living with two biological parents or one parent (usually the mother) and occasionally with adopted or foster children. Studies of stepfamilies and stepchildren seldom focus on identifying factors, structures and processes facilitating the enhancement of resiliency and healthy stepfamily functioning (see Michaels, 2006 for exceptions). Rather, research has addressed primarily problem-focused questions providing answers on what does not work (Adler-Baeder & Higginbotham, 2005).

Ganong and Coleman (2004, p. 146) summarized this large body of literature:

> In virtually every area of assessment, stepchildren are found to fare more poorly, on average, than children living with both of their parents. Stepchildren are generally similar on outcome measures to children living

with single parents, who are usually single mothers. Sometimes, but not always, these mean differences disappear when social class, time living in the stepfamily, and other variables are added to the statistical models. The overall conclusion is that stepchildren generally are at greater risk for problems than are children living with both of their parents, and they are comparable to children living with mothers only.

Often overlooked in this literature is that the differences between stepchildren and children living in other family arrangements "are quite small" (Ganong & Coleman, 2004, p. 147). For example, meta-analytic reviews report effect sizes that are often negligible (Amato, 1994; Dunn et al., 1998; Reifman, Villa, Amans, Rethinam & Telesac, 2001). For example, Amato (1994) reported an overall effect size of −.17, meaning that on average stepchildren do exhibit more negative behaviors. However, it also means that 43% of stepchildren scored better on the outcome measures than did the average child who was living with two biological parents (see Ganong & Coleman, 2004, p. 147). Hetherington and Kelly (2002) asserted that for most outcomes measured, at least three of every four stepchildren do fine.

Ganong and Coleman (2004) stressed that the basis for many of the revealed issues of stepchildren is the inappropriate use of a first-marriage model for guiding interactions and considerations about life in a stepfamily. These mixed findings encourage us to look at the predicament of stepchildren in the stepfamily without preconceptions.

It has been argued that an important family-level variable in establishing and maintaining resiliency in stepfamilies (or postdivorce families) is communication efficacy (Afifi & Hamrick, 2006). Papernow (2001, p. 4) referred to the need for "conducting difficult conversations wisely." Visher and Visher (1990) asserted that stepfamilies can succeed if they master the challenge of moving from the previous family culture to the creation of a joint stepfamily culture. Successful stepfamilies are characterized by six factors: (1) losses have been mourned; (2) realistic expectations are held; (3) the couple is unified; (4) appropriate rituals are established; (5) step relationships are formed and satisfactory; and (6) the various households involved cooperate. Kelly (1995) reported that successful stepfamilies are flexible, have a sense of humor, show respect, are patient and communicate well. Michaels (2006) added that successful stepfamilies have informed commitment including a proactive stance to achieving strong marital and family bonds and a strong sense of family developed around the time of the remarriage.

Should stepchildren have problems, researchers identify the conditions within the stepfamily and the nature of their relationship with the biological parent living elsewhere, either alone or in a new relationship, as underlying them. In her longitudinal study, Napp-Peters (1995) established that children who have lost contact with the parent living elsewhere suffer from particularly intense loss, anxiety and behavioral problems. There is general agreement that stepchildren's age plays a role in how they cope with life in the stepfamily. Children of nursery or preschool age are thought to face the least problems (Jones, Tepperman & Wilson, 1995; Peuckert, 2004). Those between 6 and 12 years of age are claimed to suffer the most difficulties because they are particularly likely to face conflicts of loyalty. This applies especially to girls who develop a close relationship with the mother following dissolution of the biological family and see the mother's new partner as a threat. Conflicts with the stepparent then typically arise in adolescence in relation to the latter's authority (Hetherington, Cox & Cox, 1985). Establishing a stepfamily when the children are adolescents can be difficult (Hofferth & Anderson, 2003).

Regardless of whether growing up as a stepchild carries greater risk than growing up in the biological family, our overview shows that researchers are paying more attention to the family situation of stepchildren, placing it center stage when tackling the resiliency of such children and the risks they faced. Most scholars agree that certain family conditions (i.e., successful co-parenting, integration of a stepparent into the stepfamily, and being aware of their structural complexity) are particularly important to ensuring that stepchildren have a positive experience. These essential family conditions are discussed next.

## Successful Co-parenting

Successful co-parenting is key to the stepfamily's health. This means that the parents' relationship has a decisive impact on the child's psychological well-being. Co-parenting means that even though the parents may separate as a couple, they continue as parents and share responsibility for raising their child or children.

Successful co-parenting frees children from the conflict arising from the need to divide their loyalty between the parent living elsewhere and the stepfamily. Although scholars recognize that it is in the child's best interest for parents to establish a positive co-parenting system, this can make heavy demands on the parents (Adamsons & Pasley, 2006; Pasley & Minton, 1997). Positive co-parenting is the exception rather than the rule within the context of everyday life. In one German study by Bien et al. (2002), one third of the children had no access to the parent living elsewhere, another one third saw the parent sporadically, and about one fourth only once a month. Only one tenth saw the nonresident parent several times a week or every day. This means that for about one third of the children in this study, there was at least a chance that the parents would develop a co-parenting system. Co-parenting possibilities improved if the parents were well educated and shared custody.

In the United States, Furstenberg and Nord (1985) reported that less than 50% of the children between 11 and 17 years of age with divorced parents saw their father during the last year, and almost 40% had no contact with him during the past five years. Black fathers are more likely to continue the parent–child relationship following a divorce than others (Furstenberg, Nord, Peterson & Zill, 1983). Stephens (1996) reported that about 33% of children lose contact with their fathers after the remarriage of either parent. Seltzer and Brandreth (1994) reported that about 25% see their fathers at least weekly, and Seltzer (1991) indicated that almost 50% of divorced fathers see their children one to three times per month. Divorced fathers tend to be less involved with their children over time, due, in part, to their children's maturation (Lamb, 2000; Pasley & Braver, 2004). The quality of the contact could be more important in maintaining a relationship and healthy child outcomes than either the frequency or duration of the contact (Buchanan, Maccoby & Dornbusch, 1996). Mothers' interference with visitation and a continuing conflictual interparental relationship encourages fathers' distancing. However, geographic distance also explains some of the decline in father involvement (Henley & Pasley, 2005).

Identity investment, the value of being a father and identity satisfaction in that role, are related to a father's postdivorce involvement with their children (Stone & McKenry, 1998). Fathers in cooperative interparental relationships remain involved with their children, regardless of satisfaction or investment in their identities as fathers (Henley & Pasley, 2005). This research draws attention to the importance of positive co-parental relationships for nonresident fathers and ultimately for their children.

## Integration of Stepparent

Researchers suggest that stepparents can help children by supporting the biological parents as they fulfill child-rearing tasks. Expert opinion does not necessarily expect the stepparent to assume the role of social parents. Stepmothers, however, are susceptible to social expectations that it is the women who are responsible for the expressive aspects of social relations—that is, for making sure that children in the stepfamily receive care and affection (Visher & Visher, 1991). Thus, they can be seen in competition with the biological mother (Walper, 1993). On the other hand, stepfathers generally refrain from participating in child rearing and tend to play a mostly economic supporting role (Hetherington & Stanley-Hagan, 2002; Jones et al., 1995).

Researchers generally emphasize that the integration of a stepparent into a stepfamily is a lengthy process of several years (Hetherington & Stanley-Hagan, 2002), which may or may not culminate in the stepparent assuming the responsibility of social parenthood (Carter & McGoldrick, 2004). Carter and McGoldrick regard the position within the life course and family career of the partners who found a stepfamily as especially significant: The greater the difference between the couple's experience of the life course, the more difficult the transition becomes and the longer it takes for the new family to integrate. The relationship between stepparents and their stepchildren may be typed in various ways. They may be called aunt or uncle (Rutter, 1994) or referred to as a friend (Théry & Dhavernas, 1998). Though the terms of address used (e.g., father, mother) imply the structure of the nuclear family, it can deny the characteristic features of the stepfamily (Bray & Kelly, 1998). Buehler and Pasley (2000) saw no connection between ambiguous paternal physical and psychological presence, a more common characteristic of stepfamilies than first families, and greater adjustment problems among preadolescents and adolescents.

## Structural Complexity

It is apparent that stepfamilies do better if they are aware of their structural complexity rather than if they use a first-marriage model indicating a "retreat from complexity" (Goldner, 1982, p. 205; Peuckert, 2004; Visher, Visher & Pasley, 2003). This includes not only the coexistence of biological and other forms of parenthood (from relatives through friendship to social parenthood) but also the fact that the stepfamily has to add to a preexisting family history. It also includes the fact that family membership may take a different form (Visher et al., 2003).

Studies have shown that parents and children may perceive things quite differently in this respect. Whereas children between 7 and 11 years of age in one study counted their out-of-home biological father as a member of the family, the parents did not (Ritzenfeld, 1998). Other studies show that 15% of stepparents do not consider their stepchild a member of the family, even if the child lives with them (Bernstein, 1989). In another study, 31% of stepchildren excluded their stepparents from the family (Furstenberg & Cherlin, 1991). On the other hand, it has emerged that a good relationship between children and their biological out-of-home father does not put their relationship with their stepfather at risk (Walper & Schwarz, 1999). In fact, a good relationship with the biological parents makes it more likely that the child will have a good relationship with the stepparent. Should the child have a stable relationship with his father, for example, there is less risk that rivalry will emerge (Staub & Felder, 2003).

The boundaries within stepfamilies differ from those in nuclear families. The kinship system may play a supportive role within nuclear families, particularly at times of crisis (Rutter, 1994). However, the reincorporation of the kinship system into the sphere of child rearing following divorce and remarriage or the founding of a stepfamily without marriage (cohabitation) may put at risk the development of the stepfamily as a family with an identity of its own (Carter & McGoldrick, 2004). Another issue is the incorporation of various sets of grandparents and stepgrandparents. For example, the parents of the nonresidential parent might be "eliminated" from the "family." To date, there has been relatively little research on the role of grandparents in childhood development in stepfamilies (see Ganong & Coleman, 2004, for an overview).

Our review shows that the stepfamily is not condemned to be a deviant family form whose salvation lies in approximating the "normal model." Stepfamilies can confront successfully their complexity and can develop effective solutions. Our review of the literature also lends support to the concept of positive co-parenting.

## Being at Risk

However valid we may consider stepfamilies to be as a distinct family form, we should recognize the risks they entail. It is true that most stepfamilies are neither violent nor the setting for physical or sexual abuse. Still, findings of Jones et al. (1995) are of interest. They stated that the presence of a stepparent is one of the best epidemiological predictors for child abuse. A study by Russell (1999) reported that a stepdaughter has a 1 in 6 chance of sexual abuse by a stepfather compared with a 1 in 50 chance by her biological father. Parker and Parker (1986) found that girls with a stepfather are twice as likely to be abused as those with just a biological father. The research generally supports that children living with a nonbiological adult are more at risk for abuse (Daly & Wilson, 1998; Giles-Sims, 1997).

Some scholars explain these differences by claiming that the incest taboo is less effective in complex family forms (Giles-Sims, 1997; Messer, 1969; Théry, 1998). Others explain that stepparents are more likely to be abusers with reference to sociobiology and evolutionary theory (Giles-Sims, 1997; Hofferth & Anderson, 2003; Jones et al., 1995). These parents often spare their biological children from abuse, providing an argument against the claim that violence in stepfamilies is due to an overrepresentation of violent individuals among the remarried. Moreover, according to Canadian studies, stepchildren are assaulted and killed more often than biological children. Stepchildren below the age of 3 years are seven times more likely to suffer nonlethal physical injury than children growing up with both biological parents. They are 100 times more likely to suffer fatal abuse. Other Canadian studies have shown that infants in stepfamily households are 40 times more likely to be registered with the authorities as victims of physical violence than children with their biological parents. They are twice as likely to be murdered (Jones et al., 1995). British data support this finding (Daly & Wilson, 1994).

Though the previously given estimates are based on small cell sizes, the Danish child database covers every child in Denmark. For the cohort born in 1981, the fatalities (due to abuse and otherwise) among children from 1 to 3 years of age are distributed among the various family forms as follows: 92.1% of children grew up with their biological parents yet make up only 82.3% of children who died between 1 and 3 years of age; 7.0% of children were with their mothers in single-parent families, but such children were 10.6% of those who died; and 0.4% of children had mothers who lived with a new partner (i.e., stepfamilies), yet 5.4% of all fatalities among children ages 1 to 3 years occurred in this type of family (Dencik & Lauterbach, 2002).

A critical analysis of published studies on the incidence of physical abuse of children in families (Adler-Baeder, 2006) suggests that because of methodological shortcomings (i.e., analysis of households rather than perpetrator–victim relations, unclear definition of physical abuse particularly the failure to distinguish between physical and sexual violence, insufficiently large sample sizes, failure to factor in class affiliation) it is impossible to state with confidence whether stepfamilies are overrepresented with respect to the incidence of physical abuse of children. Adler-Baeder points to the urgent need for further studies both comparing first families and stepfamilies and comparing different groups within the stepfamily population, and especially the need to focus on patterns of family functioning that place children more at risk for abuse.

## SOCIAL AND COMMUNITY FACTORS INFLUENCING RISK AND RESILIENCY

A stepfamily's prospect of developing into an independent family form offering children a positive milieu in which to grow depends on the social attitudes toward the family (Gerlach, 2001). In grappling with their new family status, they lack almost any generally recognized behavioral models (Ganong & Coleman, 2004; Hofferth & Anderson, 2003). The stepfamily's effort to achieve societal acceptance as a family form can cause challenges. That said, Hetherington and Stanley-Hagan (2002) noted that as stepfamilies become more common, the number of children with behavioral problems from stepfamilies is falling. It is thought that the growth of joint custody arrangements has contributed to this in the United States (Ahrons & Rodgers, 1987); the same is true for Germany (Bien et al., 2002).

# EVIDENCE-BASED TREATMENT INTERVENTIONS FOR CHILDREN LIVING IN STEPFAMILIES

## What Works

A search of the literature did not uncover interventions that met the criteria of three successful trials.

## What Might Work

The self-help movement is a strength-based effort that understands the member to be simultaneously both a caregiver and care receiver (Gullotta & Bloom, 2003a). Self-help can be as informal as reading a book or discussing the issue with a friend in a similar situation, or as formal as belonging to an organized self-help group (Ganong & Coleman, 2004). Self-help groups have potential for offering their members support and information. For example, Stepfamilies International (http://www.stepfamilies-international.org) and the National Stepfamily Resource Center (http://www.stepfamilies.info) offer information (e.g., books, magazines, games) and sites for stepfamilies.

About 20% of children raised in stepfamilies develop behavioral problems, requiring treatment or placement with another family. It is above all the stepchildren rather than the biological children that are affected when their parent remarries. For example, of 111 identified patients in 94 stepfamilies, a stepchild was the problem child in 90 cases (Krähenbühl et al., 2001). According to Rutter (1994), the figure of around 20% of children with serious problems in stepfamilies could be reduced to 10% and thus brought into line with the number of children who grow up in so-called normal families whose development is marked by "pathological disorders," if professionals worked with stepfamilies earlier. Rutter suggested that stepfamilies should be provided with information about the developmental tasks facing them right from the outset. Efforts should be made to improve the family's communication skills and to accept the uniqueness of the stepfamily whose differences from the nuclear family are entirely legitimate (Carter & McGoldrick, 2004; Ganong & Coleman, 2000; Kaplan & Hennon, 1992).

A model that might work is based in systemic family therapy and Gestalt psychology (Papernow, 1993). It describes seven stages in the development of stepfamilies, unfolding in three phases and featuring developmental tasks for the stepfamily. The first three stages (fantasy, immersion, awareness) occur during the initial phase. They relate to the tasks of giving up unrealistic expectations, of a child's hopes that his or her biological parents will reunite and of acknowledging these feelings in oneself and others and finding new ways to respond.

In the second phase (mobilization, action), the task is confronting the differences between family members and establishing new rituals, routines and behavioral patterns in the stepfamily and establishing appropriate familial boundaries. In the final phase (contact, resolution) the focus is on developing meaningful relationships within the stepfamily and establishing the stepparent's role. Though issues relating to grief and loyalty may still occur, children should be better able to cope with them. Readers can also consult Hetherington and Kelly (2002), who proposed an empirically grounded three-stage model of the development of stepfamilies.

One specialized field within the sphere of therapy is sexual abuse treatment. As noted earlier, stepchildren are at higher risk of sexual abuse. In the treatment of abused youth, Finkelhor and Daro (1997) recommended a parent-focused approach. The treatment goal is to remind the parents of their duty of care, while assisting them in helping their children cope with the abuse they have experienced.

Scholars agree that should stepchildren do poorly at school, experience behavioral problems or lack of self-esteem, the helping process should be family focused. Children are at risk for difficulties if the biological parents do not co-parent successfully and if the stepfamily functions poorly. Thus, therapists should pay attention to family structure issues (Krähenbühl et al., 2001).

Beside family therapy, clinicians should assist the child in coping and adapting with the challenges of school and family life. This approach often leads to greater acceptance and motivation among the divorced parents experiencing feelings of exhaustion and failure. There is support for the value of family therapy, both generally (Pinsof & Wynne, 1995) and specifically with the issues stepfamilies experience (Carter & McGoldrick, 2004; Klann & Hahlweg, 1994; Krähenbühl et al., 2001; Minuchin et al., 2007).

One goal of therapy with remarried families is to establish an open family system with manageable boundaries and revised gender roles (Carter & McGoldrick, 2004). This process involves establishing a functioning and open co-parental system involving both former partners. The former partners need to come to terms with the emotional separation, particularly should they have failed to talk about it or should they be in a state of constant conflict with one another. They should establish an approach to the children that emphasizes the autonomy of the married couple's relationship and that leaves decisions on custody and visiting rights to parents. Finally, parents should accept their child's possible mixed emotions and divided parental loyalty.

Visher, Visher and Pasley (1997) studied couples with stepchildren who had therapy on one or more occasions to understand what helps. The couples were from the White American upper- middle class and members of the Stepfamily Association of America. The couples studied recommend that therapists validate the stepfamily as such, normalize its situation, work toward reducing feelings of helplessness and, above all, strengthen the couple's relationship. The authors concluded that family therapy should be preceded by relationship counseling for the couple. Rhoden and Pasley (2000) suggested that the theoretical orientation of the therapist might interact with gender-related characteristics and might influence the effectiveness of therapy. Family structure can also interact with gender characteristics, leading women in simple stepfamily structures perceiving the helpfulness of therapy differently from women in complex stepfamilies. Bray (1994) recommended using genograms for gaining understanding of complex relationships and structures as well as for presenting problems. Genograms also helps families appreciate the complexity of challenges faced (see Magnuson & Shaw, 2003 for an overview of genogram use in therapy with stepfamilies).

## What Does Not Work

A review of the literature did not uncover an intervention that should not be used at the present time. However, if children do experience problems, family therapy appears to be a better option that individual therapy.

## PSYCHOPHARMACOLOGY

Not surprisingly, there is no drug to treat the stepfamily and its members. Issues such as depression that may accompany the formation of a new stepfamily can be responsive to pharmacological interventions and are discussed elsewhere in this volume.

## THE PROMOTION OF THE HEALTHY DEVELOPMENT OF CHILDREN IN STEPFAMILIES

Some studies find no differences between children in stepfamilies and those in biological families, whereas others reveal an inconsistent picture (Coleman, Ganong & Fine, 2000). Many, if not most, stepchildren do not have behavioral, emotional or social problems and do well academically. Hetherington and Kelly (2002) asserted that for most outcomes measured, at least three of every four stepchildren do fine. However, given the concern about stepchildren and their developmental outcomes, it is suggested that awareness of the complexities of stepfamily living be heightened and that educational programs be initiated to help promote healthy development of children. Most stepfamily problems are preventable. However, most people do little to prepare themselves for stepfamily life (Ganong, Coleman & Hans, 2006; Michaels, 2006).

### What Works

The review of the literature did not reveal preventive measures that stand the test of three successful trials.

### What Might Work

Attempts have been made to educate stepfamilies to prevent possible problems. Stepfamilies who do not avail themselves of educational (or good self-help) preventive measures are at higher risk for family and childhood problems related to poor stepfamily functioning (Adler-Baeder & Higginbotham, 2005; Ganong et al., 2006).

In the case of stepfamilies in the initial stages of their establishment, preventive measures should be geared toward informing them about the distinctive structural features of stepfamilies, about the range of feasible family constructions and about predictable crises. Attention to resiliency strategies should be reinforced. Intentionality and redefinitions of what it means to be a family should be stressed (Ganong et al., 2006; Michaels, 2006). Helping children recognize the issues particular to stepfamily living, as well as more general relationship and developmental tasks, is important. Self-help groups that facilitate the transition to the stepfamily, as a unique type of family characterized by two cores, appear helpful. These inform participants about the specific structural traits of stepfamilies, common challenges and potential resolutions, and foster communication skills.

Many different types of content are appropriate for family life education, but understanding the complexity of stepfamilies, communication, problem solving, parenting (including parental stress that influences childhood development and behaviors), money management and financial support of children, conflict de-escalation strategies, anger management and dealing with feelings (including loyalty issues) appear especially warranted (Adler-Baeder

& Higginbotham, 2005; Hughes & Schroeder, 1997; Kaplan & Hennon, 1992; Lawton & Sanders, 1994). The challenge is raising awareness among potential and existing stepfamilies to the potentialities of preventive measures and to make these educational efforts available, timely and relevant. The World Wide Web might facilitate these efforts (Ganong et al., 2006). However, as the Web serves increasingly as self-help and as a source for education, the quality of the information available must continue to be scrutinized and critiqued (Hennon, Peterson, Polzin & Radina, 2006; Hughes & Hans, 2004).

## What Does Not Work

Although a review of the literature did not uncover any intervention that should not be used at the present time, the prevention literature suggests that educational interventions alone are often unsuccessful. Educational interventions are likely to succeed when new skills are repeatedly practiced, when social support is nurtured, when competencies are enhanced and when system change occurs (Gullotta & Bloom, 2003b).

## RECOMMENDED BEST PRACTICE

An educational approach that promotes social competency and encourages natural caregiving is central to both preventive and therapeutic measures (Adler-Baeder & Higginbotham, 2005; Blaisure & Geasler, 2006; Gullotta & Bloom, 2003a; Hennon & Arcus, 1993; Hughes & Schroeder, 1997; Kaplan & Hennon, 1992; Radina, Wilson & Hennon, in press; Visher & Visher, 1996).

## Prevention

Professionals such as nursery, primary and secondary school teachers (Crosbie-Burnett, 1995; Pasley & Ihinger-Tallman, 1997), religious officiaries and family-life educators should do the following:

- Promote the acceptance of stepfamilies as a legitimate family form.
- Encourage the biological parents to share custody as the legal foundation of the co-parenting system, when appropriate. That is, the biological parents should continue to exercise parental responsibility while stepparents take on supportive roles.
- Establish comprehensive educational interventions that promote social competency and nurture natural caregiving for stepfamilies. Programs should be culturally relevant and specific, empirically grounded and theoretical informed (see Adler-Baeder & Higginbotham, 2005).
- Support self-help groups that facilitate the transition to the stepfamily, as a unique type of family. These inform participants about structural traits of stepfamilies and foster communication skills.

## Treatment

Visher and Visher (1996) believed that education is the greatest need for stepfamilies and that many stepfamilies would not have clinical need if preventive education on stepfamily dynamics and development were provided and better accessed. Only around 20% of children from stepfamilies develop behavioral problems and require therapy or are placed with another family. This figure could be halved if stepfamilies embraced support measures at an early stage. Therapists explain a stepfamily's need for therapy to unsuitable family circumstances rather than personal pathology. They identify the biological and stepparents' inability to cope with the structural features of a binuclear family and their tendency to model themselves on the nuclear family as the underlying dilemma requiring treatment. Understanding the stepfamily as a binuclear family means the children are members of two family systems and ensuring that both biological parents accept responsibility for child rearing. A positive co-parenting system is seen as the best way of ensuring that children in stepfamilies develop in a healthy manner.

Effective therapeutic approaches are family focused (Ganong & Coleman, 2004), though children may receive individual treatment:

- Focus on the family history, life course and family career of the individuals and subsystems involved: By scrutinizing family history, the therapist is able to make use of the clients' experience of separation, stepfamily life and family of origin. The greater the partners' differences in terms of their position in the life course and family career, the greater the challenges they face in establishing a stepfamily.
- Accept that establishing a stepfamily is a long process with no certain outcome: As the process unfolds, clinicians need to help their clients find solutions anchored in models other than the so-called normal nuclear family and to encourage stepfamilies to develop their own unique structures. Here, there is a particular need to bear in mind the internal and external boundaries of the family, which may differ in form from those of normal families, individuals' differing status within the family as well as varying loyalties.
- Involve the parent living elsewhere: A parent should not be allowed to quit parenthood. It is desirable to include the parent living elsewhere and his or her partner in the therapy. The goal is to construct a positive co-parenting system in which the parents' partners play a supportive role. Such a system presents challenges, and failure is a distinct possibility. Yet, should they succeed, the stepchildren are more likely to have a fitting positive environment in which to grow.
- Pay attention to gender role stereotypes: Stepmothers risk fulfilling expectations that they bear responsibility for the child's social and emotional life and thus compete with the biological mother in a problematic way. In contrast, biological fathers frequently are marginalized. The goal is to encourage both to value the contribution they can make to the child's healthy development.
- Enable parents and stepparents to accept the range of emotions felt by their stepchildren, whose situation is characterized by loss, ambivalence and an uncertain future: This is an appropriate alternative to a belief that regards the stepfamily as a flawed nuclear rather than binuclear family and demands that the children deny their feelings for the sake of this myth.
- Clarify the position of stepsiblings within the stepfamily's sibling system: This is the issue of *hers*, *his* and *ours*. It is important to consider the change of position as oldest, middle or youngest child created by the

establishment of a stepfamily. Despite the challenges, stepfamilies can and do succeed.

## ENDNOTE

1. In this chapter the term nuclear family refers to the biological, often the first-marriage, family.

## REFERENCES

Adamsons, K. & Pasley, K. (2006). Coparenting following divorce and relationship dissolution. In M. A. Fine & J. H. Harvey (Eds.), *Handbook of divorce and relationship dissolution* (pp. 241–262). Mahwah, NJ: Lawrence Erlbaum.

Adler-Baeder, F. (2006). What do we know about the physical abuse of stepchildren? A review of the literature. *Journal of Divorce & Remarriage, 44*(3–4), 67–81.

Adler-Baeder, F. & Higginbotham, B. (2005). Implications of remarriage and stepfamily formation for marriage education. *Family Relations, 53*, 448–458.

Afifi, T. D. & Hamrick, K. (2006). Communication processes that promote risk and resiliency in postdivorce families. In M. A. Fine & J. H. Harvey (Eds.), *Handbook of divorce and relationship dissolution* (pp. 435–456). Mahwah, NJ: Lawrence Erlbaum.

Ahrons, C. (2004). *We're still family. What grown children have to say about their parents' divorce.* New York: HarperCollins.

Ahrons, C. & Rodgers, R. H. (1987). *Divorced families: A multidisciplinary developmental view.* New York: Norton.

Amato, P. R. (1994). The implications of research findings on children in stepfamilies. In A. Booth & J. Dunn (Eds.), *Stepfamilies: Who benefits? Who does not?* (pp. 81–87). Hillsdale, NJ: Erlbaum.

BBC (1999, June 24). *Life in a stepfamily.* Retrieved 26 August 2006 from http://news.bbc.co.uk/2/hi/uk_news/377214.stm.

Bernstein, A. C. (1989). *Yours, mine, and ours: How families change when remarried parents have a child together.* New York: Norton.

Bien, W., Hartl, A. & Teubner, M. (Eds.) (2002). *Stieffamilien in Deutschland: Eltern und Kinder zwischen Normalität und Konflikt* [Stepfamilies in Germany: Parents and children between normality and conflict]. Opladen, Germany: Leske & Budrich.

Blaisure, K. R. & Geasler, M. J. (2006). Educational interventions for separating and divorcing parents and their children. In M. A. Fine & J. H. Harvey (Eds.), *Handbook of divorce and relationship dissolution* (pp. 575–604). Mahwah, NJ: Lawrence Erlbaum.

Bray, J. H. (1994). Assessment issues with stepfamilies. *Family Journal, 2*, 163–166.

Bray, J. H. & Kelly, J. (1998). *Stepfamilies: Love, marriage, and parenting in the first decade.* New York: Broadway Books.

Buchanan, C. M., Maccoby, E. E. & Dornbusch, S. M. (1996). *Adolescents after divorce.* Cambridge, MA: Harvard University Press.

Buehler, C. & Pasley, K. (2000). Family boundary ambiguity, marital status, and child adjustment. *Journal of Early Adolescence, 20,* 281–308.

Bumpass, L. L., Raley, R. K. & Sweet, J. A. (1995). The changing character of stepfamilies: Nonmarital childbearing. *Demography, 32,* 425–436.

Carter, B. & McGoldrick, M. (Eds.) (2004). *The expanded family life cycle: Individual, family and social perspectives,* 3d ed. Boston: Allyn & Bacon.

Claxton-Oldfield, S. (2000). Deconstructing the myth of the wicked stepmother. *Marriage and Family Review, 30,* 51–58.

Coleman, M., Ganong, L. & Fine, M. (2000). Reinvestigating remarriage: Another decade of progress. *Journal of Marriage and the Family, 62,* 1288–1307.

Comings, D. E., Muhleman, D., Johnson, J. P. & MacMurray, J. P. (2002). Parent-daughter transmission of the androgen receptor gene as an explanation of the effect of father absence on age at menarche. *Child Development, 73,* 1046–1051.

Crosbie-Burnett, M. (1989). Application of family stress theory to remarriage: A model for assessing and helping stepfamilies. *Family Relations, 38,* 323–331.

Crosbie-Burnett, M. (1995). The interface between stepparent families and schools: Research, theory, policy, and practice. In K. Pasley & M. Ihinger-Tallman (Eds.), *Remarriage and stepparenting: Current research and theory* (pp. 199–216). New York: Guilford.

Daly, M. & Wilson, M. (1994). Stepparenthood and the evolved psychology of discriminative parental solicitude. In S. Parmigiami & F. S. vom Saal (Eds.), *Infanticide and parental care* (pp. 121–134). Chur, Switzerland: Harwood Academic Publishers.

Daly, M. & Wilson, M. (1998). *The truth about Cinderella: A Darwinian view.* New Haven, CT: Yale University Press.

Dencik, L. & Lauterbach, J. (2002). Mor og Far or Mor og hendes nye partner. Om børns familier og familieskift gennem opvæksten I senmoderniteten [Mom and dad and mom and her new partner. About families of children and change of family by growing up in late modernity]. In M. Hermansen & A. Poulsen (Eds.), *Samfundets børn* [The children of the society] (pp. 75–126). Århus, Denmark: Klim.

Dunn, J., Deater-Deckard, K., Pickering, K. I., O'Connor, T., Golding, J. & the Avon Longitudinal Study of Parents and Children (ALSPAC) Team (1998). Children's adjustment and pro-social behaviour in step-, single-parent, and non-step family settings: Findings from a community study. *Journal of Child Psychology and Psychiatry, 39,* 1083–1095.

Ellis, B. J. & Garber, J. (2000). Psychosocial antecedents of variation in girls' pubertal timing: Maternal depression, stepfather presence, and marital and family stress. *Child Development, 71,* 485–501.

Ferri, E. (1984). *Stepchildren: A national study. A report from the National Child Development Study.* Windsor, England: NFER-Nelson.

Fine, M. A., Coleman, M. & Ganong, L. (1998). Consistency in perceptions of the stepparent role among stepparents, parents, and stepchildren. *Journal of Social and Personal Relationships, 15,* 810–828.

Finkelhor, D. & Daro, D. (1997). Prevention of child sexual abuse. In M. E. Helfer & R. S. Kempe (Eds.), *The battered child,* 5th ed., rev. and exp. (pp. 615–626). Chicago: University of Chicago Press.

Fthenakis, W. E., Niesel, R. & Griebel, W. (1997). Scheidung als Reorganisation-sprozess: Interventionsansätze für Kinder und Eltern [Divorce as reorganization process: Intervention approaches for children and parents]. In K. Menne, H. Schilling & M. Weber (Eds.), *Kinder im Scheidungskonflikt: Beratung von Kindern und Eltern bei Trennung und Scheidung* [Children in the divorce conflict: Consultation of children and parents when parents separate or divorce], 2d ed. (pp. 261–289). Weinheim, Germany: Juventa.

Fthenakis, W. E. & Textor, M. R. (Eds.) (2000). *Pädagogische Ansätze im Kindergarten* [Educational approaches in the kindergarten]. Weinheim, Germany: Beltz.

Furstenberg, F. Jr. (1987). The new extended family: The experience of parents and children after remarriage. In K. Pasley & M. Ihinger-Tallman (Eds.), *Remarriage and stepparenting: Current research and theory* (pp. 42–61). New York: Guilford.

Furstenberg, F. Jr. & Cherlin, A. (1991). *Divided families: What happens to children when parents part.* Cambridge, MA: Harvard University Press.

Furstenberg, F. Jr. & Nord, C. W. (1985). Parenting apart: Patterns of childrearing after marital disruption. *Journal of Marriage and the Family, 47,* 893–900.

Furstenberg, F. Jr., Nord, C. W., Peterson, J. L. & Zill, N. (1983). The life course of children of divorce: Marital disruption and parental contact. *American Sociological Review, 48,* 656–668.

Ganong, L. & Coleman, M. (2000). Close relationships in remarried families. In C. Hendrick & S. Hendrick (Eds.), *Handbook on close relationships* (pp. 155–168). Newbury Park, CA: Sage.

Ganong, L. H. & Coleman, M. (2004). *Stepfamily relationships: Development, dynamics, and interventions.* New York: Kluwer Academic.

Ganong, L. H., Coleman, M. & Hans, J. (2006). Divorce as prelude to stepfamily living and the consequences of redivorce. In M. A. Fine & J. H. Harvey (Eds.), *Handbook of divorce and relationship dissolution* (pp. 409–434). Mahwah, NJ: Lawrence Erlbaum.

Gerlach, P. (2001). *Building a high-nurturance stepfamily.* Philadelphia: Hibris.

Giles-Sims, J. (1997). Current knowledge about child abuse in stepfamilies. In I. Levin & M. Sussman (Eds.), *Stepfamilies: History, research, and policy* (pp. 215–230). New York: Haworth.

Glick, P. (1989). Remarried families, stepfamilies, and stepchildren: A brief demographic profile. *Family Relations, 38,* 24–27.

Goldner, V. (1982). Remarriage family: Structure, system, future. In J. C. Hansen & L. Messenger (Eds.), *Therapy with remarried families* (pp. 187–206). Rockville, MD: Aspen.

Goldscheider, F. K., Hogan, D. & Bures, R. (2001). A century (plus) of parenthood: Changes in living with children, 1880–1990. *History of the Family, 6,* 477–494.

Goldscheider, F. K. & Sassler, S. (2006). Creating stepfamilies: Integrating children into the study of union formation. *Journal of Marriage and Family, 68,* 275–291.

Gullotta, T. P. & Bloom, M. (2003a). Primary prevention at the beginning of the 21st century. In T. P. Gullotta & M. Bloom (Eds.), *The encyclopedia of primary prevention and health promotion* (pp. 116–120). New York: Kluwer/Academic.

Gullotta, T. P. & Bloom, M. (Eds.) (2003b). *The encyclopedia of primary prevention and health promotion.* New York: Kluwer/Academic.

Henley, K. & Pasley, K. (2005). Conditions affecting the association between father identity and father involvement. *Fathering, 3*, 59–80.

Hennon, C. B. & Arcus, M. (1993). Life-span family life education. In T. H. Brubaker (Ed.), *Family relations: Challenges for the future* (pp. 181–210). Newbury Park, CA: Sage.

Hennon, C. B., Peterson, G. W., Polzin, L. & Radina, M. E. (2006). Familias de ascendencia mexicana residentes en Estados Unidos: Recursos para el manejo del estrés parental [Resident families of Mexican ancestry in the United States: Resources for the handling of parental stress]. In R. Esteinou (Ed.), *Fortalezas y desafíos de las familias en dos contextos: Estados Unidos de America y México* [Strengths and challenges of families in two contexts: The United States of America and Mexico] (pp. 225–282). México, D. F.: Centro de Investigaciones y Estudios Superiores en Antropología Social (CIESAS) y Sistema Nacional para el Desarrollo Integral de la Familia (DIF).

Hetherington, E. M., Cox, M. & Cox, R. (1985). Long-term effects of divorce and remarriage on the adjustment of children. *Journal of the American Academy of Child Psychiatry, 24*, 518–530.

Hetherington, E. M. & Kelly, J. (2002). *For better or worse: Divorce reconsidered.* New York: Norton.

Hetherington, E. M. & Stanley-Hagan, M. (2002). Parenting in divorced and remarried families. In M. H. Bornstein (Ed.), *Handbook of parenting: Being and becoming a parent.*, 2nd ed. (pp. 287–316). Mahwah, NJ: Erlbaum.

Hofferth, S. L. & Anderson, K. G. (2003). Are all dads equal? Biology versus marriage as a basis for paternal investment. *Journal of Marriage and Family, 65*, 213–232.

Hughes, R. Jr. & Hans, J. (2004). Understanding the effects of the Internet. In M. Coleman & L. H. Ganong (Eds.), *Handbook of contemporary families: Considering the past, contemplating the future* (pp. 506–520). Thousand Oaks: CA: Sage.

Hughes, R. Jr. & Schroeder, J. D. (1997). Family life education for stepfamilies. In I. Levin & M. Sussman (Eds.), *Stepfamilies: History, research, and policy* (pp. 281–300). New York: Haworth.

Jones, C. L., Tepperman, L. & Wilson, S. J. (1995). *The futures of the family.* Englewood Cliffs, NJ: Prentice-Hall.

Kaplan, L. & Hennon, C. B. (1992). Remarriage education: The Personal Reflections Program. *Family Relations, 41*, 127–134.

Kaplan, L., Hennon, C. B. & Ade-Ridder, L. (1993). Splitting custody of children between parents: Impact on the sibling system. *Families in Society: The Journal of Contemporary Human Services, 74*, 131–144.

Kasten, H., Kunze, H.-R. & Mühlfeld, C. (2001). *Pflege- und Adoptivkinder in Heimen* [Maintaining foster and adopted children in homes]. Bamberg, Germany: IFB.

Kelly, P. (1995). *Developing healthy stepfamilies: Twenty families tell their stories.* New York: Haworth.

Klann, N. & Hahlweg, K. (1994). *Bestandsaufnahme in der institutionellen Ehe-, Familien- und Lebensberatung* [Stocktaking in the institutional marriage—family and life consultation]. (Schriftenreihe des Bundesministeriums für Familie, Senioren, Frauen und Jugend; Bd. 48, 2). Bundesministerium für Familie, Senioren, Frauen und Jugend, Referat Öffentlichkeitsarbeit. Stuttgart; Berlin; Köln: Kohlhammer.

Krähenbühl, V., Jellouschek, H., Kohaus-Jellouschek, M. & Weber, R. (2001). *Stieffamilien. Struktur–Entwicklung–Therapie* [Stepfamilies: Structure–development–therapy]. Freiburg, Germany: Lambertus.

Krähenbühl, V., Schramm-Geiger, A. & Brandes-Kessel, J. (2000). *Meine Kinder, deine Kinder, unsere Kinder: Wie Stieffamilien zusammenfinden* [My children, your children, our children: How stepfamilies form]. Reinbek bei Hamburg, Germany: Rowohlt.

Kreider, R. M. (2003, October). *Adopted children and stepchildren: 2000* (Census 2000 Special Reports). Washington, DC: U.S. Census Bureau.

Kreider, R. M. & Fields, J. (2005, July). *Living arrangements of children: 2001* (Current Population Reports, P70-104). Washington, DC: U.S. Census Bureau.

Kuppinger, L. (1990). Zur Situation der Herkunftsfamilie vor und nach der Inpflegegabe [To the situation of the origin family before and after their children are given away]. In *Hamburger Pflegekinderkongreß "Mut zur Vielfalt"* [Hamburg congress of care child "Courage to Variety"] (pp. 134–139). Münster, Germany: Votum.

Lallemand, S. (1998). Sozialanthropologie und die Fortsetzungsfamilie [Social anthropology and the continuation family]. In M.-T. Meulders-Klein & I. Théry (Eds.), *Fortsetzungsfamilien: Neue familiale Lebensformen in plurisdisziplinärer Betrachtung* [Continuation families: New familial ways of life in multidisciplinary perspective] (pp. 59–80). Konstanz, Germany: UVK.

Lamb, M. E. (2000). The history of research on father involvement: An overview. *Marriage and Family Review, 29,* 23–42.

Lawton, J. M. & Sanders, M. R. (1994). Designing effective behavioral family interventions for stepfamilies. *Clinical Psychology Review, 14,* 463–496.

Leon, K. & Angst, E. (2005). Portrayals of stepfamilies in film: Using media images in remarriage education. *Family Relations, 54,* 3–23.

Levin, I. & Sussman, M. (Eds.) (1997). *Stepfamilies: History, research, and policy.* New York: Haworth.

Magnuson, S. & Shaw, H. E. (2003). Adaptation of the multifaceted genogram in counseling, training, and supervision. *Family Journal, 11,* 45–54.

Marsiglio, W. (2004). When stepfathers claim stepchildren: A conceptual analysis. *Journal of Marriage and Family, 66,* 22–39.

Marsiglio, W., Amato, P., Day, R. & Lamb, M. E. (2000). Scholarship on fatherhood in the 1990s and beyond. *Journal of Marriage and the Family, 62,* 1173–1191.

McLanahan, S. & Booth, K. (1989). Mother-only families: Problems, prospects and politics. *Journal of Marriage and the Family, 51,* 557–580.

McLanahan, S. & Bumpass, L. (1988). Intergenerational consequences of family disruption. *American Journal of Sociology, 94,* 130–137.

Messer, A. A. (1969). The "Phaedra Complex." *Archives of General Psychiatry, 21*, 213–218.

Michaels, M. L. (2006). Factors that contribute to stepfamily success: A qualitative analysis. *Journal of Divorce and Remarriage, 44*(3–4), 53–66.

Minuchin, S., Nichols, M. P. & Lee, W.-Y. (2007). *Assessing families and couples: From symptom to system.* Boston: Allyn & Bacon.

Napp-Peters, A. (1995). *Familien nach der Scheidung* [Families after divorce]. München, Germany: Kunstmann.

Papernow, P. L. (1993). *Becoming a stepfamily: Patterns of development in remarried families.* San Francisco: Jossey-Bass.

Papernow, P. L. (2001, February 23–24). *Working with stepfamilies.* Paper presented at the National Conference on Stepfamilies, New Orleans, LA.

Parker, H. & Parker, S. (1986). Father-daughter sexual abuse: An emergent perspective. *American Journal of Orthopsychiatry, 56*, 531–541.

Pasley, K. (2000). *Does living in a stepfamily increase the risk of delinquency in children?* Retrieved 14 July 2006 from http://www.saafamilies.org/faqs/findings/3.htm.

Pasley, K. & Braver, S. L. (2004). Measuring father involvement in divorced, non-resident fathers. In R. Day & M. Lamb (Eds.), *Conceptualizing and measuring father involvement* (pp. 217–240). Mahwah, NJ: Lawrence Erlbaum.

Pasley, K. & Ihinger-Tallman, M. (1997). Stepfamilies: Continuing challenges for the schools. In T. N. Fairchild (Ed.), *Crisis intervention strategies for school-based helpers* (pp. 60–100). Springfield, IL: Charles C. Thomas.

Pasley, K. & Minton, C. (1997). Generative fathering after divorce and remarriage: Beyond the "disappearing dad." In A. J. Hawkins & D. C. Dollahite (Eds.), *Generative fathering: Beyond deficit perspectives* (pp. 118–133). Thousand Oaks, CA: Sage.

Peterson, G. W. & Hennon, C. B. (2005). Conceptualizing parental stress with family stress theory. In P. C. McKenry & S. J. Price (Eds.), *Families and change: Coping with stressful events and transitions,* 3d ed. (pp. 25–48). Thousand Oaks, CA: Sage.

Peuckert, R. (2004). Familienformen im sozialen Wandel (5., überarbeitete und erweiterte Auflage) [Family forms in social change (5th extended edition revised)]. Stuttgart, Germany: UTB.

Pinsof, W. M. & Wynne, L. (1995). The efficacy of marital and family therapy: An empirical overview, conclusions, and recommendations. *Journal of Marital and Family Therapy, 21*, 585–613.

Radina, M. E., Wilson, S. M. & Hennon, C. B. (in press). Parental stress among U.S. Mexican heritage parents: Implications for culturally relevant family life education. In R. L. Dalla, J. Defrain, J. Johnson & D. Abbott (Eds.), *Strengths and challenges of new immigrant families: Implications for research, policy, education, and service.* Lanham, MD: Lexington Books.

Reifman, A., Villa, L. C., Amans, J. A., Rethinam, V. & Telesac, T. Y. (2001). Children of divorce in the 1990s: A meta-analysis. *Journal of Divorce & Remarriage, 36*, 27–36.

Rhoden, J. L. & Pasley, K. (2000). Factors affecting the perceived helpfulness of therapy with stepfamilies: A closer look at gender issues. *Journal of Divorce & Remarriage, 34*(1–2), 77–93.

Ritzenfeld, S. (1998). *Familienbeziehungen in Stiefvaterfamilien. Ein Vergleich der Beziehungen in Stief- und Kernfamilien unter besonderer Berücksichtigung von Stiefvater und Stiefkind* [Family relations in stepfather families: A comparison of the relations in step- and core families with special consideration of stepfather and stepchild]. Weinheim, Germany: Juventa.

Russell, D. E. H. (1999). *The secret trauma: Incest in the lives of girls and women*. New York: Basic Books.

Rutter, M. (2000). Resilience reconsidered: Conceptual considerations, empirical findings, and policy implications. In J. P. Sonkoff & S. J. Meisels (Eds.), *Handbook of early childhood intervention*, 2d ed. (pp. 205–220). Cambridge, England: Cambridge University Press.

Rutter, V. (1994, May–June). Lessons from stepfamilies. *Psychology Today, 27*(3), 30–39.

Seltzer, J. A. (1991). Relationships between fathers and children who live apart: The father's role after separation. *Journal of Marriage and the Family, 53,* 79–101.

Seltzer, J. A. & Brandreth, Y. (1994). What fathers say about involvement with children after separation. *Journal of Family Issues, 15,* 49–77.

Staub, L. & Felder, W. (2003). *Scheidung und Kindeswohl* [Divorce and child well-being]. Bern, Switzerland: Huber.

Stephens, L. S. (1996). Will Johnny see Daddy this week? An empirical test of three theoretical perspectives of postdivorce contact. *Journal of Family Issues, 17,* 466–494.

Stich, J. (1993). Stieffamilien. Beziehungen, die ganz normal anders sind [Stepfamilies. Relations which are different in a normal way]. In Deutsches Jugendinstitut (Ed.), Was für Kinder. Aufwachsen in Deutschland—ein Handbuch [Something for children. To grow up in Germany—a manual] (pp. 149–157). München, Germany: Kösel.

Stone, G. & McKenry, P. (1998). Nonresidential father involvement: A test of a mid-range theory. *Journal of Genetic Psychology, 159,* 313–336.

Théry, I. (1998). Einführung: Die Zeit der Fortsetzungsfamilien [Introduction: The time of the continuation families]. In M.-T. Meulders-Klein & I. Théry (Eds.), *Fortsetzungsfamilien: Neue familiale Lebensformen in plurisdisziplinärer Betrachtung* [Continuation families: New familial ways of life in multidisciplinary perspective] (pp. 19-43). Konstanz, Germany: UVK.

Théry, I. & Dhavernas, M. J. (1998). Elternschaft an den Grenzen zur Freundschaft: Stellung und Rolle des Stiefelternteils in Fortsetzungsfamilien [Parenting bordering on friendship: Position and role of the stepparents part in continuation families]. In M.-T. Meulders-Klein & I. Théry (Eds.), *Fortsetzungsfamilien: Neue familiale Lebensformen in plurisdisziplinärer Betrachtung* [Continuation families: New familial ways of life in multidisciplinary perspective] (pp. 163–204). Konstanz, Germany: UVK.

Visher, E. B. & Visher, J. S. (1990). Dynamics of successful stepfamilies. *Journal of Divorce and Remarriage, 14,* 3–12.

Visher, E. B. & Visher, J. S. (1991). *How to win as a stepfamily,* 2d ed. New York: Brunner/Mazel.

Visher, E. B. & Visher, J. S. (1996). *Therapy with stepfamilies*. New York: Brunner/Mazel.

Visher, E. B., Visher, J. S. & Pasley, K. (1997). Stepfamily therapy from the client's perspective: A qualitative analysis. *Marriage and Family Review,* *26*(1–2), 191–213.

Visher, E. B., Visher, J. S. & Pasley, K. (2003). Remarriage families and stepparenting. In F. Walsh (Ed.), *Normal family process: Growing diversity and complexity,* 3d ed. (pp. 153–175). New York: Guilford.

Wallerstein, J. S., Lewis, J. M. & Blakeslee, S. (2000). *The unexpected legacy of divorce: The 25 year landmark study.* New York: Hyperion.

Walper, S. (1993). Stiefkinder [stepchildren]. In M. Markefka & B. Nauck (Eds), *Handbuch der Kindheitsforschung* [Handbook of research in childhood] (pp. 429–438). Neuwied, Germany: Luchterhand.

Walper, S. & Schwarz, B. (Eds.) (1999). *Was wird aus den Kindern? Chancen und Risiken für die Entwicklung von Kindern aus Trennungs- und Stieffamilien* [What becomes from the children? Chances and risks for the development of children from separation and stepfamilies]. Weinheim, Germany: Juventa.

Werner, E. E. (2000). Protective factors and individual resilience. In J. P. Sonkoff & S. J. Meisels (Eds.), *Handbook of early childhood intervention,* 2d ed. (pp. 115–132). Cambridge, England: Cambridge University Press.

White, J. M. & Klein, D. M. (2002). *Family theories: An introduction,* 2d ed. Thousand Oaks, CA: Sage.

# 9

# Lesbian, Gay, Bisexual and Transgender Families and Their Children

SYLVIA KAY FISHER, SUSAN EASTERLY AND KATHERINE J. LAZEAR

## INTRODUCTION

Families headed by at least one gay, lesbian, bisexual or transgendered (LGBT) parent have become increasingly common in today's society. LGBT families present an additional family structure in society, and although there always have been same-sex parents, estimates suggest that as many 6 million children are being raised by LGBT parents (BNA, 1987; AAP, 2002). Accordingly, these estimates represent a large population of families with specialized and idiosyncratic family structures and concomitant issues that sometimes necessitate clinical interventions from culturally and linguistically competent professionals who are knowledgeable about the needs and concerns of LGBT families.

This chapter provides an overview of some of the issues associated with LGBT-headed families, including those that may lead to seeking professional services and support such as promising practices in clinical interventions. Providing services for LGBT families requires that the helping person educate himself or herself about the needs and concerns that LGBT families are likely to present during the clinical hour (Coates & Sullivan, 2006; Israel, 2006). Because much of the limited literature available about LGBT families is focused on gays and lesbians rather than on bisexual and transgendered persons, many of the studies and associated statements included in this chapter address families headed by gays and lesbians rather than by bisexual or transgendered persons.

The family structure and the nature of biological, nonbiological, legal and filial relationships between the LGBT adults and the children in LGBT-headed families have substantive consequences for how the family functions and navigates in a frequently hostile societal and legal climate. LGBT families can experience stigma, prejudice and discrimination (Patterson, 2005) and may struggle with how they should function in a predominately heterosexual society rampant with images that do not include them (Coates & Sullivan, 2006). Given the lack of recognition and the sociocultural vacuum in which many LGBT families find themselves, even identifying as an LGBT family is potentially a socio-psychological-political act that can both empower and actualize

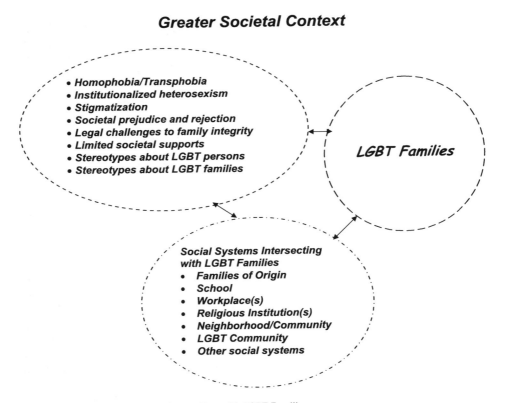

**Figure 9.1**   Societal Factors Interacting with LGBT Families.

and disempower and stigmatize LGBT families. Because many of the challenges LGBT-headed families experience stem from societal and sociological rather than from psychological factors (Brill, 2001; Hammersmith, 1987), this chapter is predicated on the understanding that stigma, homophobia (both societal and internalized) and discrimination are responsible for many stressors and aspects of problematic functioning that may result in LGBT-headed families seeking services.

Figure 9.1 provides a graphic illustration depicting the societal factors that interact regularly with LGBT families. These include the varied social systems that LGBT families live within and interface with as well as the larger societal perceptions of LGBT families, many of which are negative, stigmatizing and stereotypic. These generally negative societal attitudes can exist within the social systems that LGBT families exist in and interface with, emerging in unanticipated, yet pervasive, ways that affect LGBT families interactions with social systems.

## BIOLOGICAL AND GENETIC FACTORS

Several studies have examined why some individuals are gay or lesbian rather than heterosexual and have attempted to describe the phenomenon of being gay or lesbian (Bailey & Pillard, 1991, 1993; Hall & Kimura, 1994). Study results and their conclusions range from the perception that being homosexual is completely a personal decision or choice made by the individual to the belief that homosexuality is a biologically determined attribute in which the individual has little or no choice regarding their sexual orientation. Some studies point to mixed causality in which biological, social and psychological factors result in an individual's having a homosexual orientation. The degree of immutability of homosexuality has also been examined in these and other studies and has been theorized about in the literature. Some theories hold that homosexual orientation is relatively immutable and virtually impossible to alter, despite extensive efforts to do so, without extreme difficulty and possible harm to the psyche of the person attempting to become heterosexual (even if he or she chooses to do so willingly). Other researchers view homosexuality as a relatively flexible attribute that can be moderated or completely abandoned through personal decision or through a mix of other difficult interventions (Bailey, Bobrow, Wolfe & Mikach, 1995; Exodus International, 2005; Falk, 1989; Forstein, 2001; Golombok & Tasker, 1996; Hall & Kimura, 1994; Hamer & Copeland, 1994).

There has been empirical research to suggest that homosexuality may be genetically based (Bailey & Pillard, 1991, 1993; Hall & Kimura, 1994). Several studies of identical twins examining the issue of the genetic basis for homosexuality have generated statistically significant results (Hamer & Copeland, 1994; Hamer, Hu, Magnuson, Hu & Pattatucci, 1993). For example, in one study of identical twins, a finding was obtained in which as many as 50% of identical twin pairs had both members identify as homosexual. This remarkably high proportion suggests that there may be a genetic basis for homosexual orientation.

The American Psychological Association (APA, 2004) has developed a position statement on the issue of homosexuality:

> There are numerous theories about the origins of a person's sexual orientation; most scientists today agree that sexual orientation is most likely the result of a complex interaction of environmental, cognitive and biological factors. In most people, sexual orientation is shaped at an early age. There is also considerable recent evidence to suggest that biology, including genetic or inborn hormonal factors, play a significant role in a person's sexuality. In summary, it is important to recognize that there are probably many reasons for a person's sexual orientation and the reasons may be different for different people.

This statement is in keeping with the ideas of many professional associations and LGBT organizations that a homosexual orientation is biologically based and is relatively immutable and that relative proportions of persons with homosexual orientations in most societies are about the same, regardless of cultural differences in attitudes toward homosexuality (APA, 1994). Many of these professional associations have stated that attempts to alter sexual orientation are very difficult and may lead to unwarranted degrees of stress and possible damage to the individual seeking to become heterosexual (AAMFT, 1991; ACA, 1996; APA, 1992; American Psychiatric Association, 2007; National Association of Social Workers, 1996).

The assumption that a child is more likely to become LGBT if the child is raised by the LGBT parent (Golombok, Spencer & Rutter, 1983; Kirkpatrick, Smith & Roy, 1981) does not find support in the literature. For example,

Green (1978) reported that the sexual identity of the 37 children in participating families were affected by several factors including their LGBT parents, schooling, reading, television and interactions with peers and other family members. Green noted that 36 of 37 children appeared to have typical psychosexual development, and Green tentatively concluded that children raised in LGBT families did not appear to differ appreciably from those raised in heterosexual families with respect to psychosexual development. This finding, first reported in 1978, has been reported in subsequent studies by other researchers (Patterson, 2000, 2004; Perrin and the Committee on Psychosocial Aspects of Child and Family Health, 2002; Tasker, 1999).

Several studies have examined the issue of heritability of sexual orientation. A review of these studies generally supports the notion that sexual orientation is no more likely to be found commonly in families with same-sex or bisexual parents as in families with heterosexual parents (Bailey, Bobrow, Wolfe & Mikach, 1995; Golombok & Tasker, 1994). Estimates of the prevalence of a homosexual orientation in the general population vary demonstrably, ranging from 1.5% to nearly 10%, depending on the study (Bagley & Tremblay, 1998; Laumann, Gagnon, Michael & Michaels, 1994; McWhirter, Sanders & Reinisch, 1990). However, there appears to be virtually no empirical evidence to indicate that the rate at which children of gay, lesbian or bisexual parents are homosexual, bisexual or transgendered is any higher than the rate for heterosexual parents.

The theory that LGBT parents transmit their homosexuality or bisexuality to their children, either biologically or socially (Haynes, 1995), does not appear to be empirically valid, at least relative to the existence of any disproportionality in the frequency of children of LGBT parents who have a homosexual or bisexual orientation relative to the frequency of LGBT children of heterosexual parents. Gartrell, Deck, Rodas, Peyser & Banks (2005) found that children raised by LGBT parents are likely to exhibit greater degrees of tolerance toward LGBT persons and their orientation than other children. But again, these studies do not indicate there is any more prevalence of homosexual or bisexual behavior than in all families within the general population. Patterson's (2006) extensive review of research on the children of gay and lesbian parents suggests that the most important element of parenting by gays and lesbians that affect child outcomes appears to be the qualities of family relationships rather than parental sexual orientation, which has been supported by other findings (Cramer, 1986; Dingfelder, 2005a).

## INDIVIDUAL FACTORS INFLUENCING RISK AND RESILIENCY

There are individual factors that influence risk and resiliency in LGBT families, including the decision to be open about one's status as an LGBT person and dealing with the consequences associated with being LGBT in a fundamentally heterosexual society. *Coming out* as LGBT is defined here as being open and public about self-disclosing one's identity as an LGBT person or a member of an LGBT family (Berzon, 1988). The degree of being *out* usually occurs within boundaries or degrees of self-disclosure, ranging from coming out to oneself to being out to a small number of persons, being out to the majority of persons in one's life or being open and out to everyone in one's life, regardless of social system or how that social system intersects with the

LGBT person (Gershon, Tschann & Jemerin, 1999; Savin-Williams, 1990). The coming-out process is usually a significant process for the individual and has the potential to put the individual at risk and to provide the individual with needed supports that enhance resilience (Berzon, 1988; Green, 2000; Green & Mitchell, 2002; Savin-Williams, 1990).

Coming out is also a process in that LGBT individuals continually must come out throughout their lives (Coates & Sullivan, 2006; Cohler, 2006). Although some LGBT individuals may consider the most important coming-out event in their lives to be the personal revelation, self-discovery and ultimate understanding and acceptance that many LGBT persons experience when they make the determination that they are indeed LGBT, the reality is that even self-acceptance can be a gradual and difficult process (Kurdek, 1988, 1991). In addition, coming out to others poses risks of rejection and negative consequences to the individual, while also increasing opportunities to find social supports that contribute to the individual's well-being and cultivation of resilience (Bepko & Johnson, 2000; Savin-Williams, 1990).

A number of studies and reviews have examined the mental health status of LGBT individuals. Hart et al. (1978) reviewed research comparing adjustment levels of gays and lesbians with heterosexual and concluded that gays and lesbians did not differ from heterosexuals in their degree of psychological adjustment on a wide variety of factors. Since then, Cochran (2001) identified several emerging issues in lesbian and gay mental health, including a tendency for some gays and lesbians to manifest elevated risk levels for stress-sensitive disorders. Cochran attributed this tendency for elevated risk to stigma and discrimination that lesbians and gays experience in their daily lives and advised professionals that culturally competent care is necessary for gays and lesbians seeking mental health services. Cochran also pointed out that although affirmative therapies appear to hold promise as interventions, their efficacy has not yet been empirically investigated sufficiently to make a recommendation about their efficacy with gays and lesbians suffering the effects of stress-related disorders.

Meyer's (2003) meta-analytic review of the research evidence on the prevalence of mental disorders in lesbians, gays and bisexuals found that LGB persons had a higher prevalence of mental disorders than heterosexuals. Meyer attributed this finding to a conceptual framework of minority stress, which incorporates factors such as experienced prejudice, expectations of rejection, internalized homophobia and stigma associated with being LGB. These factors interact to create a stressful and hostile social environment that was the cause of mental health problems in LGB persons. Meyer posited that ameliorative coping processes can be implemented with LGB persons undergoing stress to help these individuals more effectively address environmental and internal stressors associated with being LGB.

An additional set of individual factors stems from the perceived role of parenting and the decision to parent by LGBT persons. Increasing numbers of studies are focusing on the reasons why LGBT persons decide to become parents, their perceptions of their own roles and how they choose to parent their children (Flaks, Ficher, Masterpasqua & Joseph, 1995; Golombok, Tasker & Murray, 1997; Patterson, 1994, 2000, 2005; Siegenthaler & Bigner, 2000). These studies generally have found that LGBT persons decide to become a parent after a relatively long decision-making process. They prefer nonphysical approaches to discipline. They are willing to go to extensive lengths to become parents and are willing to share child-care responsibilities with their partners when present. Coates & Sullivan (2006) believed that because LGBT persons must often go through a lengthy and complicated process to become parents, LGBT individuals who pursue this process may be particularly committed to the goal of becoming parents and may have extensively considered the consequences of taking on the roles and responsibilities associated with parenthood.

## FAMILY FACTORS INFLUENCING RISK AND RESILIENCY

### LGBT Families and Coming Out

Deciding whether to come out is a decision LGBT families must address on an almost daily basis as family members interface within numerous social systems, given that many of these interactions can potentially result in stigmatization and discrimination for some or all family members (Green, 2000; Green & Mitchell, 2002; Rohrbaugh, 1992; Savin-Williams, 1990). Children in LGBT families that are not out to persons in their lives may have to behave as though they themselves are closeted, operating within constraints that can impair the child's ability to make friends, to interact with others and to speak openly about their family in school, religious institutions and other venues (Coates & Sullivan, 2006; McCandlish, 1987). Although there is little research about this issue, we hypothesize that children in this situation may experience anxiety, stress and depression due to their need to keep family secrets (Lewis, 1980; Rohrbaugh, 1992). Relationships with peers and significant adults are likely to be affected, and the child may not feel comfortable seeking external support from teachers, counselors, peers and others because of the fear of stigmatization and social censure (Gershon et al., 1999).

### Variations in Family Structure and Composition

LGBT families exhibit considerable variation in family structure and composition. LGBT family structures include donor insemination, co-parent adoption of a biological child of a second parent, stepparent arrangements, foster parenting, adoptive families (in which sometimes only one same-sex parent is allowed to adopt the minor children), hetero-gay families (in which one parent is gay and the other heterosexual, which may have been purposefully designed or which can occur when one parent comes out as LGBT) and families with more than two adults functioning in the role of parents (e.g., when a lesbian couple and a male donor whose sperm donation results in the birth of a child share parenting arrangements among all three parties). Other familial configurations include having one legally recognized parent (often the biological parent) and a second parent with no legal recognition of his or her parental role in the child's life as well as lesbian families where each lesbian mother has birthed one or more children. The nonbiological parent may or may not be a legally recognized parent of the children they did not birth themselves (Brill, 2001; Patterson, 1996a, 2000, 2005; Segal-Engelchin, Erera & Cwikel, 2004; Stacey & Biblarz, 2001).

LGBT families may have either one or two parents. LGBT single parents experience parental concerns analogous to those of heterosexual single parents regarding caring for children alone, child care, dating and relationships, limited personal time and economic and work pressures (Chan, Brooks, Raboy & Patterson, 1998; Coates & Sullivan, 2006). Openly LGBT single parents may encounter difficulties in securing support from other adults to ease the burden of parenting children alone (Carroll & Gilroy, 2002; Cramer, 1986). In some case, a third individual, perhaps the donor in a case-donor insemination, may have another parental role in the family; however, there is some evidence to suggest that these individuals sometimes choose to play a nominal, if any, role in the parenting process once they have donated their sperm to assist in the conception of a child (Segal-Engelchin et al., 2004).

Children of divorce in heterosexual relationships and marriages have been documented in the literature as having issues of separation, loss and custody-related issues (American Academy of Child & Adolescent Psychiatry, 2004). There is limited evidence to indicate whether children in LGBT families have similar responses to a parental breakup. A partner or spouse who comes out as LGBT after being in a heterosexual relationship or marriage may fear possible threats to custody or visitation of the minor children because of his or her LGBT status. In some states, LGBT parents can sometimes have their custody and visitation rights severely restricted or revoked altogether (Arnup, 1999; Buell, 2001; Falk, 1989).

## Social Supports Available to the LGBT Family Unit

Although all families generally benefit from supports received from extended family and other sources, supports may be more limited for LGBT-headed families resulting in the potential impoverishment of social and other opportunities for children in the LGBT family (Brill, 2001; Coates & Sullivan, 2006; Patterson, 2005; Slater & Mencher, 1991). The needs of LGBT families can be confounded with multiple concerns, including not being open about their LGBT status and withdrawing from opportunities to seek supports because of a fear of disclosure (Coates & Sullivan, 2006; McCandlish, 1987). However, Patterson (2000) pointed out that despite challenges and stigma, lesbians and gay men appear to be succeeding in creating and sustaining effective family relationships. This finding of successful family functioning is reported also by Flaks et al. (1995), Tasker (1999), and Stacey and Biblarz (2001). Several of these researchers found in their studies that there were no statistically significant differences on a number of psychological factors between children raised in LGBT-headed and those raised in heterosexual families. These studies were undertaken with a small number of participants and thus are limited in their generalizability.

## Family of Origin and the LGBT Family

Patterson (1998) conducted an exploratory study of 37 lesbian-mother families and the frequency of their young children's contacts with extended family members. They found that these children were in more contact with the grandparents and other adult relatives of the biological mother than with the nonbiological mother. This finding was replicated in another study of 80 families (55 headed by lesbian parents and 25 headed by heterosexual parents) that reported that children in heterosexual families had more contact with the parents of the biological mother than with the parents of the father (Fulcher, Chan, Raboy & Patterson, 2002). Muzio (1996) reported that having a child can significantly alter the attitudes of the family of origin toward their lesbian members, such that previously estranged relationships with the lesbian daughter improve greatly after she becomes a parent. The new grandparents appear to have more contact with their lesbian daughter and their grandchildren and to provide additional support to the family.

## Family of Choice

Kurdek (1988) reported that LGB persons tend to socialize more with friends than with members of their family of origin. Family of choice describes the family created by LGBT families to provide social and other support (Weston, 1992). In contrast to families of origin, families of choice are composed of individuals who comprise socially formed networks of close friends who form familial bonds that can change and develop over time. These families of choice often provide extensive social support and may serve as an important factor in promoting resilience within LGBT families.

## SOCIAL AND COMMUNITY FACTORS INFLUENCING RISK AND RESILIENCY

Slater (1995) rated social oppression associated with homophobia and heterosexism as the primary stressor in lesbian family life. Similarly, Israel (2006) pointed out the detrimental effects of societal transphobia. Couples (and their children) who are out may be criticized, marginalized and even physically assaulted, whereas couples and children who are not out of the closet run the risk of being ignored or not recognized (American Academy of Child & Adolescent Psychiatry, 2006; Nelson, 1996; Sullivan & Baques, 1999). This balancing act can sometimes result in having LGBT families be out in some contexts but not in others, which can be confusing to all members of the LGBT family, but most especially children, who have to somehow remember who is supposed to know (or not know) about their family structure.

### Legal Challenges to the Integrity of the LGBT Family Unit

Custody issues can be complicated and detrimental to the well-being of affected children. Although there has been some improvement in terms of how LGBT parents are viewed with respect to the custody of their children (Falk, 1989; Kraft, 1983), there are jurisdictions in which the sexual orientation of the parents can be an impediment to custody and visitation rights as well as to the right to foster or adopt children. Legal issues affecting LGBT families are frequently preeminent in LGBT families seeking support or clinical assistance; helpers can isolate these issues for LGBT families, can assist them in prioritizing their legal needs and can help identify means of addressing them so that they can legalize their relationships and families to the fullest extent possible (Buell, 2001).

Arguments made in courts against custody of children with lesbian (and GBT) parents have revolved around issues including (1) the best interests of the child standard; (2) the lifestyle of the parent; and (3) the effect of the parent's lifestyle on the child. Moses & Hawkins (1982) reported that some courts have decided that lesbian mothers are less maternal than heterosexual mothers, a perception that plays a role in their custody determinations and an argument that appears to be gradually losing credence (Falk, 1989). The issue of the parent's lifestyle is often couched as a court concern that the gender role development of the child will be affected negatively if custody is granted to the LGBT parent (ibid.). A second flawed assumption is that the child is more likely to become LGBT if the child is raised by a LGBT parent (Golombok et al., 1983; Kirkpatrick et al., 1981). A number of studies have investigated these claims, and the evidence does not support these presumptions (Golombok & Tasker, 1996; Golombok et al., 1983; Kraft, 1983; Moses & Hawkins, 1982). A final claim is that children of LGBT parents will encounter trauma or stigma as a result of living with the LGBT parent. The argument here is that the negative societal ostracism on the LGBT parent will extend to the child and do irreparable harm. Falk (1989) reported that this assumption has resulted in the denial of custody to LGBT parents in some jurisdictions, whereas the perceived effects of stigma has not been recognized as an acceptable reason for denial of custody and visitation privileges to LGBT parents in others.

Because in many areas same-sex couples do not have the same protections afforded heterosexual married couples, same-sex families need to take special precautions to protect the rights and integrity of their family, including domestic partnership arrangements, drawing up of custody agreements and making arrangements to provide health-care services for minor children (Brill, 2001; Buell, 2001; Dingfelder, 2005b). If the nonlegally recognized same-sex partner is the only partner who is employed and the employer does not insure children who have no legal relationship to the children, then these children may be uninsured (Crespi, 2001).

Crespi (2001) reported that same-sex couples lack social constructions to guide them in family formation and in identifying significant familial milestones, which brings an added challenge to the survival and satisfactory functioning of the LGB families. He wrote that LGB families often develop their own rituals and familial paths that may only be observed by affected family members. Navigating social conventions without social signposts that address the needs of LGB families can be complicated. As the numbers and visibility of LGBT families increase, these families may develop their own social constructions that will guide other LGBT families as they develop and nurture their own families.

The availability and type of support the LGBT family receives from the extended family are important questions that helping professionals should ask to determine whether an individual or family's social support system is complicated by immediate and extended families that do not accept them (Crespi, 2001). One limitation for family development and healthy functioning stems from the lack of legal and sometimes social recognition of the nonbiological parent in same-sex couples. Several studies report that visitation with the extended family of nonbiologically related co-parents is less frequent than with that of extended families of biologically related parents (Fulcher et al., 2002; Patterson, 1996b; Vanfraussen, Ponjaert-Kristoffersen & Brewaeys 2003).

Planck (2006) reported that as more LGBT people are choosing to become parents, many are developing connections and social networks through organizations like the Family Pride Coalition and other LGBT parenting groups. These parenting groups provide social support where everyone involved can feel safe and can be open about their family status and where children can experience families similar to their own. LGBT families located in communities with more limited resources can still struggle to find other LGBT families;

on-line communities and resources are available to all LGBT families with Internet access.

## EVIDENCE-BASED TREATMENT INTERVENTIONS FOR LGBT FAMILIES

### What Works

A review of the literature did not uncover any intervention that met the criteria of three successful trials.

### What Might Work

Our search of the literature yielded several promising theoretical constructs worth further exploration. Among these, Long and Bonomo (2002) advised professionals working with LGBT families to understand the significance that class, race, ethnicity, religion and spirituality play in LGBT families. They remark that many LGBT families are White and middle class and believe that professionals working with LGBT families need to achieve cultural and linguistic competence, including experience regarding the ways that culture, language, race, ethnicity and other variables affect the functioning of LGBT families in the larger societal context.

Long, Bonomo, Andrews & Brown (2003) recommended family therapy approaches as a means of intervening with LGBT families to address some of the challenges LGBT families face. They and others encouraged clinicians to stretch the boundaries of existing family therapies to accommodate the specialized needs of LGBT families (Coates & Sullivan, 2006; LaSala, 2007). That said, specific recommendations about how family therapy should be adapted to serve the needs of LGBT families are limited, requiring the clinician to make these clinical determinations of his or her own accord and to research to assess whether family therapy is helpful is needed.

For example, LaSala (2007) reported that family therapy models often do not reflect the realities and desires of many gay and lesbian couples and stated that therapists working with this population are left to decide whether to apply these models as they are, to discard them or to attempt to modify them as they assist their clients. Although writing about couples therapy with lesbians and gays, which include issues such as intergenerational boundaries for gay and lesbian couples and the nonmonogamous relationships of gay men, LaSala's observations about how therapists can adapt family therapy models to suit the needs and preferences of lesbian and gay couples might be extrapolated to the use of family therapy models with LGBT families. Given that these adaptations are implemented effectively, LaSala's reconceptualization of family therapies augers well as a potential intervention for use with LGBT families.

Lynch and McMahon-Klosterman (2006) recommended that it is appropriate for therapists who work with LGBT stepfamilies to adopt an ally identity. Specifically, by functioning in the role of ally, the therapist can provide nonjudgmental support to members of this marginalized group, can promote trust with clients and can identify ways the stepfamily can address issues of stigma, discrimination and homophobia and can improve family functioning. Although the authors do not specifically make this recommendation, we suspect that the ally identity might be a useful model for any individual seeking to provide support to all LGBT families.

Many issues associated with LGB clients are replicated with transgendered clients, including coming out to minor and adult children, coping with prejudice and role definition problems, confronting social consternation and helping minor children address issues of stigma associated with being in a family that has a transgendered parent. Although there is little literature on transgender persons and their families available, studies generally emphasize the hostility and social censure encountered by transgendered persons (Cohler, 2006). Israel (2006) reported that transgender persons cope best with the hostile climate around them when they receive family and social support. She recommended that professionals work on facilitating even a limited support system for transgendered men and women, stating that even seemingly minimal interventions can have a positive impact on the transgendered client and can yield positive benefits that may extend to the greater family.

Coates and Sullivan (2006) offered a theoretical framework that combines complementary concepts from different theories to analyze family structures and functions in the social context of heterosexism. Elements of family systems theory, structural social work, ecological systems theory and queer theory are used to work with same-sex parents. Specific aspects of family functioning such as maintenance of boundaries around and within families, and role differentiation between parents are then explored using this theoretical framework. Coates and Sullivan projected that the gradual change in social mores will make LGBT families increasingly visible and, ultimately, that family systems approaches will be developed with the needs of LGBT families at the forefront and as the focus of the intervention.

## What Does Not Work

A review of the literature did not uncover any intervention that should not be used at the present time. Despite the paucity of clinical research in the area of LGBT family therapy and interventions, a number of proscriptions are most likely to be beneficial for clinicians to consider when working with LGBT families. Therapists are advised not to apply heterosexual role models to LGBT families (Blumstein & Schwartz, 1990). Role definitions are fluid and not as clearly delineated along the lines of gender in LGBT families, and the application of heterosexual family structures and constellations is unlikely to be on target as an approach to working with LGBT families (Peplau, 1991; Peplau, Venigas & Campbell, 1996).

The same proscription applies to an understanding of the family constellation, which might include significant adults who play parenting roles (or who may have a biological relationship to the child) but who are not full-time parents. These somewhat different conceptions of the parenting role may be new to some therapists who are used to seeing more clearly defined roles for parents and parental figures in heterosexual families. These emotional and relational bonds need to be respected fully by the therapist, and these individuals should be integrated into clinical interventions as appropriate (Coates & Sullivan, 2006; Meyer, 2003; Nelson, 1996). Negating the importance of these individuals may engender suspicion and mistrust in LGBT clients and may impair the success of clinical interventions.

Another approach that is inadequate in addressing the needs of LGBT families is a minimization of the effect of societal influences on the children and the adults within the family system. The intersections (or lack of intersections) between the family system and other social systems are integral to understanding what LGBT families experience. Specifically, the sustained effects of being closeted, ostracized or having family members who function in significant roles in the family's structure not have their role recognized legally or socially by the larger society can have long-term detrimental effects on the well-being of the LGBT family and should not be ignored in therapeutic contexts (Cohler, 2006; Nelson, 1996).

Professionals working with LGBT families may be aware that therapeutic approaches exist with the purpose of converting LGB persons to a heterosexual orientation. The term *conversion therapy* is used here as an inclusive term that includes reparative therapy (Nicolosi, 1991) and a number of interventions developed by some conservative Christian groups to dissuade LGB persons from their same-sex attraction using religiously based arguments as the foundation for these interventions. Joseph Nicolosi, founder of the National Association for Research and Therapy of Homosexuality (NARTH), has conducted several studies and has written several articles that he reports provide support for the effectiveness of his reparative therapy approach to curing homosexuality (Nicolosi, 1991; Nicolosi, Byrd & Potts, 2000). The tag line for NARTH is "Helping clients bring their desires and behaviors into harmony with their values." NARTH holds an annual conference and regularly publishes newsletters and pieces in support of the use of reparative therapy to cure homosexual behavior, if not a homosexual orientation. Reparative therapy has been interpreted as counter to the ethical recommendations regarding the appropriate interventions and care of LGBT persons specified by the American Psychological Association, the National Association of Social Workers and the Child Welfare League of America, among other professional groups (Forstein, 2001; Shroeder & Shidlo, 2001).

There is also an entire so-called ex-gay movement (Exodus International, 2005) that makes the claim that individuals have been able to alter their homosexual or bisexual orientation to adopt an exclusively heterosexual orientation. The claims made by members of the ex-gay movement are based largely on anecdotal information provided by individuals who claim to have exchanged their homosexual orientation for a heterosexual orientation. The ex-gay movement, however, differs from reparative therapy. Reparative therapy emphasizes the use of secular approaches to bring about change in homosexual orientation or homosexual behavior. The ex-gay movement does not oppose the use of reparative therapy but emphasizes religiously based approaches to bring about change in homosexual behavior or orientation. This controversial model of conversion therapy has yielded claims in both directions regarding its effectiveness: It has been an effective approach for some individuals seeking to alter their sexual orientation; other individuals report that this approach may have temporarily resulted in behavioral changes in sexual behaviors but that it was not an effective approach to change their sexual orientation over the long term (Shroeder & Shidlo, 2001).

There are several arguments in favor of the use of conversion therapy, including the following: (1) Homosexuality is a sickness or deviance from which the individual can be cured, particularly if the individual chooses to do so; (2) homosexuality is a sin according to certain religious faiths and therefore should be turned away from as the individual should do with all sin; (3) adopting certain religious beliefs and practices will allegedly heal the individual from homosexuality or bisexuality; and (4) the heterosexual life is socially accepted, is appropriate for all persons and should be the preferred way of life, so homosexual and bisexual persons should try to adopt a heterosexual lifestyle (Exodus International, 2005; Nicolosi, 1991; Nicolosi et al., 2000).

Some of the arguments raised against the use of conversion therapy include the following: (1) Individuals may spend considerable time struggling with their sexuality and then choose to pursue conversion therapy because of a fundamental lack of acceptance of who they are; (2) individuals are pressured by others in their environment to feel shame about their homosexual or bisexual orientation and to seek conversion therapy because of these external pressures rather than for any true personal reason or desire to do so; (3) attempting to change sexual orientation is like attempting to change a person's handedness, which is fundamentally inherent in the individual and is relatively or completely immutable, and the conversion therapy process is likely to result in untold stress for the individual; and (4) forcing under-age or young persons who identify as gay, lesbian or bisexual to undergo conversion therapy against their will may be abusive and potentially harmful to these youth (APA, 1998; American Psychiatric Association, 2007).

Professionals are advised not to encourage LGB parents to pursue conversion therapy to encourage them to change their sexual orientation, which has been shown to have inadequate and potentially harmful results (DeLeon, 1998). Reparative therapy, in particular, has been repudiated by many therapists and others who work with gay and lesbian clients, as well as several professional organizations (ACA, 1996; DeLeon, 1998; National Association of Social Workers, 1996). If an LGB individual seeks to pursue interventions to change his or her sexual orientation, it would be useful for professionals to help clarify the LGB individual's reasons for pursuing this course, which might entail necessitate value clarification. In addition, LGB individuals seeking reparative therapy would benefit from being informed about reparative therapy success rates and the variable effectiveness of conversion therapies in eliminating a homosexual orientation. It is unclear whether or how the children of LGB parents are likely to respond if their parent changes their sexual orientation. The consequences of LGB parents completing conversion therapy on their children are also unknown; therefore, this approach is not recommended (Forstein, 2001; Shroeder & Shidlo, 2001).

## PSYCHOPHARMACOLOGY AND LGBT FAMILIES

A review of the literature did not uncover any intervention that should be used.

## THE PREVENTION OF STIGMA AND DISCRIMINATION IN LGBT FAMILIES

### What Works

Prevention in this context is synonymous with health promotion, and this chapter emphasizes ameliorating the negative effects of stigma and discrimination toward LGBT families and nurturing coping strategies that LGBT families can use as needed. A review of the literature did not uncover any intervention that met the criteria of three successful trials.

### What Might Work

The prevention of negative societal influences associated with homophobia is difficult to achieve and requires multisystemic interventions at the individual, family and societal level using prevention's available technology (Gullotta & Bloom, 2003). Education, community organization and systems intervention efforts have been successful in some states in making others aware that LGBT families exist and want to be considered families in every sense of that word. In other states, these efforts have encountered significant resistance and the struggle for recognition continues (Arnup, 1999; Buell, 2001; Falk, 1989).

At the microlevel, using the prevention tool of education, interventions with schools, religious institutions and workplaces can be undertaken to raise the visibility of LGBT families and their needs. Educational activities include in-house training sessions, meet-and-greet events with LGBT family members and traveling photographic displays of LGBT families that provide an honest portrayal of life in LGBT families.

Also at the microlevel, the U.S. court system has not yet fully developed a body of law applicable to the LGBT family. As such, the LGBT family needs to take the necessary legal steps to ensure that their wishes are fulfilled. This educational action is referred to as *anticipatory guidance* in the prevention literature. We make specific note of this as there is anecdotal evidence to support the damage done to LGBT families who did not take the appropriate legal steps to reinforce the sustainability and efficacy of their families (Cohler, 2006; Sullivan & Baques, 1999). Many of the negative outcomes that can result from threats to the LGBT family can be prevented if thoughtful planning and foresight are pursued by the LGBT family to ensure the protection of its members.

At the macrolevel is Children of Lesbians and Gays Everywhere (COLAGE), a national, nonprofit organization run by and for children who have one or more LGBT parents (Kuvalanka, Teper, and Morrison, 2004). The mission of COLAGE is to use the prevention tool of community organization to engage, to connect and to empower people to make the world a better place for children of LGBT parents and families. COLAGE has chapters in many large urban areas across the United States, maintains a Web site of activities and topics of interest to the children of LGBT parents and conducts several retreats and family events throughout the year.

COLAGE maintains that children of LGBT parents love their parents and are happy being in their families. COLAGE acknowledges the complex and sometimes difficult emotional and sociopolitical challenges and unique experiences that children of LGBT parents face and encourages multiple opportunities for peer support, interactions and networking. Accordingly, COLAGE uses prevention's technology of natural caregiving, of competency promotion, of community organization and of systems change to build networks, to empower youth and to promote societal recognition and validation of all families.

## What Does Not Work

A review of the literature did not uncover any prevention or health-promotion intervention that should not be used at the present time.

## RECOMMENDED BEST PRACTICE

When working with LGBT families, it is advisable to consider the following issues. First, LGBT families are likely to manifest concerns about the opinions, attitudes and clinical judgments of prospective helpers when seeking counsel. LGBT families seek acceptance of their lifestyle choices and family arrangements and do not want their family structure to be viewed in a prejudicial manner or as inherently in need of clinical intervention because of the presence of one or more LGBT parents. LGBT families are likely to seek assistance from helpers who understand that their family structure is unique and can present unique challenges. Individuals seeking to assist LGBT families are advised to consider their own long-held beliefs, attitudes and subconscious assumptions about LGBT individuals and LGBT families before working with LGBT families (Ariel & McPherson, 2000; Laird & Green, 1996; Turner, Scadden & Harris, 2004).

Second, therapists are encouraged to identify external supports available to the LGBT family. For example, is there an extended family that the family can rely on for needed assistance and encouragement? Does the immediate and extended family accept the family and integrate them into the larger family's culture? Early evidence suggests that this is an important source of support for the LGBT family. When grandparents, other relatives and families of choice (frequently composed of friends and extended family members) are available, accessible and able to be relied on for supports, the to-be-expected stresses are reduced substantially, and the LGBT family is less likely to be isolated (Fulcher et al., 2002; Kurdek, 1988, 1991). It is very likely that these additional supports can serve as protective factors to bolster the effective functioning and satisfaction of the LGBT family (Brill, 2001; Coates & Sullivan, 2006).

Third, same-sex couples do lack social constructs to guide them in family formation (Ariel & McPherson, 2000; Coates & Sullivan, 2006; Crespi, 2001). This challenge does put additional burden on the LGBT family seeking to delineate and to recognize pivotal milestones in the life of the family. Accordingly, professionals working with LGBT families can help promote the development of satisfactory social networks that encourage their clients to network socially with other LGBT families who also must deal with stigma and societal prejudice. This is often easier to do in large metropolitan areas where social and networking organizations exist that are designed to encourage positive and supportive interaction between LGBT families, whereas these outlets may be comparatively limited in more rural and isolated areas (Cramer, 1986; Long et al., 2003). As a general rule, broadening the social networks for LGBT families, as with all families, is a fruitful approach that is likely to increase the social capital available to all members within an LGBT family (Coates &

Sullivan, 2006). However, when encouraging LGBT families to pursue broadening of their social networks, it is advisable that each potential interaction be evaluated on the basis of potential gain and potential risk to the LGBT family to ensure that the safety and integrity of the family is protected (Green, 2000; Green & Mitchell, 2002). Groups such as COLAGE offer children of LGBT families a safe community-based venue in which to socialize and share issues and concerns, providing them with peer support.

Fourth, professionals working with LGBT families should explore the appropriateness of encouraging LGBT families to pursue legal and social family protections as early as possible in LGBT family formation. The availability and use of legal safeguards (e.g., wills, contracts, binding agreements, powers of attorney, co-parent adoptions by nonbiological parents) can help prevent difficult crises and threats to the integrity of the LGBT family. By specifying and codifying the intentions and legal obligations of adult family members to the child and to the family's overall functioning, this form of assistance can assist the LGBT family in navigating complex legal and financial systems, can enhance family bonds and can strengthen the overall protection of the LGBT family (Arnup, 1999; Cohler, 2006).

Coates and Sullivan (2006) held that the well-intentioned therapist who generally accepts diversity is not sufficiently prepared to work with LGBT families. Instead, they advised that clinical competence rests on experience working with lesbian and gay clients and acknowledging the impact of societal factors, such as heterosexism, on parenting in the context of same-sex relationships. A challenge to the helping person working with LGBT families is to identify additional supports and interventions that facilitate the growth and development of the LGBT family, within a culturally and linguistically competent approach that honors the integrity of the family being served (Janson, 2002). Although Coates and Sullivan's observations refer to gay and lesbian parents, they may also be applicable to bisexual and transgendered parents.

Theoretical interventions have not been developed specifically to address the needs of LGBT families, but some practitioners and researchers have made recommendations about approaches that can be adapted to LGBT families. Family therapy, structural social work, queer theory and ecological systems theory have been adapted by Coates and Sullivan (2006) to address the needs of LGBT families. The adaptation of family therapy and other theoretical and clinical practices for LGBT families is in its infancy, and considerable work remains to be undertaken to have a full complement of useful practices and interventions for LGBT families.

## REFERENCES

American Academy of Child & Adolescent Psychiatry (2004, July). *Facts for families #1: Children and divorce.* Retrieved 15 May 2007 from http://aacap.org/cs/root/facts_for_families/children_and_divorce.

American Academy of Child & Adolescent Psychiatry (2006, August). *Facts for families #92: Children with lesbian, gay, bisexual and transgender parents.* Retrieved from 15 May 2007 from http://aacap.org/cs/root/facts_for_families/children_with_lesbian_gay_bisexual_and_transgender_parents.

American Academy of Pediatrics (AAP) (2002, February). Technical report: Co-parent or second-parent adoption by same-sex parents. *Pediatrics, 109,* 341.

American Association for Marriage and Family Therapy (AAMFT) (1991). *AAMFT code of ethics.* Washington, DC: Author.

American Counseling Association (ACA) (1996). ACA code of ethics and standards of practice. In B. Herlihy & G. Corey (Eds.), *ACA ethical standards casebook,* 5th ed. (pp. 26–59). Alexandria, VA: Author.

American Psychiatric Association (2007, May). Therapies focused on attempts to change sexual orientation (reparative or conversion therapies): Position statement. Retrieved 28 June 2007 from http://www.psych.org/psych_pract/copptherapyaddendum83100.cfm.

American Psychological Association (APA) (1992). Ethical principles and code of conduct. *American Psychologist, 48*(12), 1597–1611.

American Psychological Association (APA). (1998). Appropriate therapeutic responses to sexual orientation in the proceedings of the American Psychological Association, Incorporated, for the legislative year 1997. *American Psychologist, 53*(8), 882–939.

American Psychological Association (APA) (2004). *Answers to your questions about sexual orientation and homosexuality, American Psychological Association.* Retrieved 29 May 2007 from http://www.apa.org/topics/orientation.html.

Ariel, J. & McPherson, D. (2000). Therapy with lesbian and gay families and their children. Journal of Marital and Family Therapy, *26,* 421–432.

Arnup, K. (1999). Out in this world: The social and legal context of gay and lesbian families. *Journal of Gay and Lesbian Social Services, 10*(1), 1–25.

Bagley, C. & Tremblay, P. (1998). On the prevalence of homosexuality and bisexuality in a random community survey of 750 men aged 18 to 27. *Journal of Homosexuality, 36*(2), 1–18.

Bailey, J., Bobrow, D., Wolfe, M. & Mikach, S. (1995). Sexual orientation of adult sons of gay fathers. Special Issue: Sexual orientation and human development. *Developmental Psychology, 31*(1), 124–129.

Bailey, J. M. & Pillard, R. C. (1991). A genetic study of male sexual orientation. *Archives of General Psychiatry, 48,* 1089-1096.

Bailey, J. M. & Pillard, R. C. (1993). Heritable factors influence sexual orientation in women. *Archives of General Psychiatry, 50,* 217–223.

Bepko, C. & Johnson, T. (2000). Gay and lesbian couples in therapy: Perspectives for the contemporary family therapist. *Journal of Marital and Family Therapy, 26*(4), 409–419.

Berzon, B. (1988). *Permanent partners: Building gay and lesbian relationships that last.* New York: E. P. Dutton.

Blumstein, P. & Schwartz, P. (1990). Intimate relationships and the creation of sexuality. In D. P. McWhirter, S. A. Sanders & J. M. Reinisch (Eds.), *Homosexuality/heterosexuality: Concepts of sexual orientation* (pp. 307–320). New York: Oxford University Press.

Brill, S. A. (2001). *The queer parent's primer: A lesbian and gay families' guide to navigating the straight world.* Oakland, CA: New Harbinger Publications.

Buell, L. (2001). Legal issues affecting alternative families: A therapist's primer. *Journal of Gay and Lesbian Psychotherapy, 4*(3–4), 75–90.

Bureau of National Affairs (BNA) (1987, August 25). ABA Annual Forum Provides Forum for Family Law Experts. *Family Law Reporter, 13,* 1512.

Carroll, L. & Gilroy, P. J. (2002). Transgender issues in counselor preparation. *Counselor Education & Supervision, 41*(3), 233–242.

Chan, R. W., Brooks, R. C., Raboy, B. & Patterson, C. J. (1998). Division of labor among lesbian and heterosexual parents: Associations with children's adjustment. *Journal of Family Psychology, 12*(3), 402–419.

Coates, J. & Sullivan, R. (2006). Achieving competent family practice with same-sex parents: Some promising directions. In J. J. Bigner (Ed.), *An introduction to GLBT family studies* (pp. 245–270). Binghamton, NY: Haworth Press.

Cochran, S. D. (2001). Emerging issues in research on lesbians' and gay men's mental health: Does sexual orientation really matter? *American Psychologist, 56,* 931–947.

Cohler, B. J. (2006). Life-course social science perspectives on the GLBT family. In J. J. Bigner (Ed.), *An introduction to GLBT family studies* (pp. 23–49.). Binghamton, NY: Haworth Press.

Cramer, D. (1986). Gay parents and their children: A review of research and practical implications. *Journal of Counseling and Development, 64,* 504–507.

Crespi, L. (2001). And baby makes three: A dynamic look at development and conflict in lesbian families. *Journal of Gay and Lesbian Psychotherapy, 4*(3–4), 7–29.

DeLeon, P. H. (1998). Proceedings of the American Psychological Association, Incorporated, for the legislative year 1997: Minutes of the Annual Meeting of the Council of Representatives, August 14 and 17, Chicago, Illinois; and June, August and December 1997 meetings of the Board of Directors. *American Psychologist, 53,* 882–939.

Dingfelder, S. F. (2005a, December). The kids are all right. *APA Monitor on Psychology, 36*(11), 66.

Dingfelder, S. F. (2005b, December). Navigating same-sex parenting: Psychologists' roles. *APA Monitor on Psychology, 36*(11), 67.

Exodus International (2005). Exodus International Policy Statements on Homosexuality. Retrieved 13 May 2007 from http://exodus.to/content/view/34/117/.

Falk, P. J. (1989). Lesbian mothers: Psychosocial assumptions in family law. *American Psychologist, 44,* 941–947.

Flaks, D., Ficher, I., Masterpasqua, F. & Joseph, G. (1995). Lesbians choosing motherhood: A comparative study of lesbian and heterosexual parents and their children. *Developmental Psychology, 31,* 105–14.

Forstein, M. (2001). Overview of ethical and research issues in sexual orientation therapy. *Journal of Gay and Lesbian Psychotherapy, 5*(3–4), 167–179.

Fulcher, M., Chan, R. W., Raboy, B. & Patterson, C. J. (2002). Contact with grandparents among children conceived via donor insemination by lesbian and heterosexual mothers. *Parenting: Science and Practice, 2,* 61–76.

Gartrell, N., Deck, A., Rodas, C., Peyser, H. & Banks, A. (2005). The National Lesbian Family Study: 4. Interviews with the 10-year-old children. *American Journal of Orthopsychiatry, 75*(4), 518–524.

Gershon, T. D., Tschann, J. M. & Jemerin, J. M. (1999). Stigmatization, self-esteem, and coping among the adolescent children of lesbian mothers. *Journal of Adolescent Health, 24*, 437–445.

Golombok, S., Spencer, A. & Rutter, M. (1983). Children in lesbian and single-parent households: Psychosexual and psychiatric appraisal. *Journal of Child Psychology and Psychiatry, 24*, 551–572.

Golombok, S. & Tasker, F. (1994). Children in lesbian and gay families: Theories and evidence. *Annual Review of Sex Research, 5*, 73–100.

Golombok, S. & Tasker, F. (1996). Do parents influence the sexual orientation of their children? Findings from a longitudinal study of lesbian families. *Developmental Psychology, 32*, 3–11.

Golombok, S., Tasker, F. L. & Murray, C. (1997). Children raised in fatherless families from infancy: Family relationships and the socioemotional development of children of lesbian and single heterosexual mothers. *Journal of Child Psychology and Psychiatry, 38*, 783–791.

Green, R. (1978). Sexual identity of 37 children raised by homosexual or transsexual parents. *American Journal of Psychiatry, 135*, 692–697.

Green, R.-J. (2000). Coming out to family … in context. In E. Davis-Russell (Ed.), *The California School of Professional Psychology handbook of multicultural education, research, intervention, and training* (pp. 277–284). San Francisco: Jossey-Bass.

Green, R.-J. & Mitchell, V. (2002). Gay and lesbian couples in therapy: Homophobia, relationship ambiguity, and social support. In A. S. Gurman & N. S. Jacobson (Eds.), *Clinical handbook of couple therapy* (pp. 536–568). New York: Guilford Press.

Gullotta, T. P. & Bloom, M. (Eds.), (2003) Primary prevention at the beginning of the 21st century. In T. P. Gullotta & M. Bloom (Eds.), *Encyclopedia of primary prevention and health promotion* (pp. 116–122). New York: Kluwer Academic/Plenum Publishers.

Hall, J. A. Y. & Kimura, D. (1994). Dermatoglyphic asymmetry and sexual orientation in men. *Behavioral Neuroscience, 108*, 1203–1206.

Hamer, D. & Copeland, P. (1994). *The science of desire: The search for the gay gene and the biology of behavior.* New York: Simon and Schuster.

Hamer, D. H., Hu, S., Magnuson, V. L., Hu, N. & Pattatucci, A. M. L. (1993, July 16). A linkage between DNA markers on the X chromosome and male sexual orientation. *Science, 261*, 321–327.

Hammersmith, S. K. (1987). A sociological approach to counseling homosexual clients and their families. *Journal of Homosexuality, 14*(1–2) 173.

Hart, M., Roback, H., Tittler, B., Weitz, L., Walston, B. & McKee, E. (1978). Psychological adjustment of nonpatient homosexuals: Critical review of the research literature. *Journal of Clinical Psychiatry, 39*, 604–608.

Haynes, J. D. (1995). A critique of the possibility of genetic inheritance of homosexual orientation. *Journal of Homosexuality, 28*, 91–113.

Israel, G. E. (2006). Translove: Transgender persons and their families. In J. C. Bigner (Ed.), *An introduction to GLBT family studies* (pp. 51–65). New York: Haworth Press.

Janson, G. R. (2002). Family counseling and referral with gay, lesbian, bisexual, and transgendered clients: Ethical considerations. *Family Journal, 10*, 328–333.

Kirkpatrick, M., Smith, C. & Roy, R. (1981). Lesbian mothers and their children: A comparative survey. *American Journal of Orthopsychiatry, 51,* 545–551.

Kraft, P. (1983). Recent developments: Lesbian child custody. *Harvard Women's Law Journal, 6,* 183–192.

Kurdek, L. (1988). Perceived social support in gays and lesbians in cohabiting relationships. *Journal of Personality and Social Psychology, 54,* 504–509.

Kurdek, L. (1991). Correlates of relationship satisfaction in cohabiting gay and lesbian couples: Integration of contextual, investment, and problem-solving models. *Journal of Personality and Social Psychology, 61,* 910–922.

Kuvalanka, K. A., Teper, B. & Morrison, O. A. (2004). COLAGE: Providing community, education, leadership, and advocacy by and for children of GLBT parents. *Journal of GLBT Family Studies, 2*(3), 71–92.

Laird, J. & Green, R. J. (1996). Lesbians and gays in couples and families: Central issues. In J. Laird & R. J. Green (Eds.), *Lesbians and gays in couples and families* (pp. 1–12). San Francisco: Jossey-Bass.

LaSala, M. C. (2007). Old maps, new territory: Family therapy theory and gay and lesbian couples. *Journal of GLBT Family Studies, 3*(1), 1–14.

Laumann, E. O., Gagnon, J. H., Michael, R. T. & Michaels, S. (1994). *The social organization of sexuality in the United States.* Chicago: University of Chicago Press.

Lewis, K. G. (1980). Children of lesbians: Their point of view. *Social Work, 25,* 198–203.

Long, J. K. & Bonomo, J. (2002). Revisiting the sexual orientation matrix for supervision: Working with GLBTQ families. *Journal of GLBT Family Studies, 2*(3), 151–166.

Long, J. K., Bonomo, J., Andrews, B. V. & Brown, J. M. (2003). Systems therapeutic approaches with sexual minorities and their families. *Journal of GLBT Family Studies, 2*(3), 7–37.

Lynch, J. M. & McMahon-Klosterman, K. (2006). Guiding the acquisition of therapist ally identity: Research on the GLBT stepfamily as resource. *Journal of GLBT Family Studies, 2*(3), 123–150.

McCandlish, B. (1987). Against all odds: Lesbian mother family dynamics. In F. W. Bozett (Ed.), *Gay and lesbian parents* (pp. 23–38). New York: Praeger.

McWhirter, D. P., Sanders, S. A. & Reinisch, J. M. (Eds.) (1990). *Homosexuality/heterosexuality: Concepts of sexual orientation* (The Kinsey Institute Series). New York: Oxford University Press.

Meyer, I. H. (2003). Prejudice, social stress, and mental health in lesbian, gay, and bisexual populations: Conceptual issues and research evidence. *Psychological Bulletin, 129*(5), 674–697.

Moses, A. E. & Hawkins, R. O. Jr. (1982). *Counseling lesbian women and gay men: A life-issues approach.* St. Louis: CV Mosby.

Muzio, C. (1996). Lesbian co-parenting: On being/being with the invisible (m)other. In J. Laird (Ed.), *Lesbians and lesbian families: Reflections on theory and practice* (pp. 197–211). New York: Columbia University Press.

National Association of Social Workers (1996). *Code of ethics of the National Association of Social Workers.* Retrieved 23 June 2007 from http://www.ss.msu.edu/~sw/nasweth.html.

Nelson, F. (1996). *Lesbian motherhood: An exploration of Canadian lesbian families.* Toronto: University of Toronto Press.

Nicolosi, J. (1991). *Reparative Therapy of Male Homosexuality: A New Clinical Approach.* Northvale, NJ: Aronson.

Nicolosi, J., Byrd, A. D. & Potts, R. W. (2000). Retrospective self-reports of changes in homosexual orientation: A consumer survey of conversion therapy clients. *Psychological Reports, 86,* 1071–1088.

Patterson, C. J. (1994). Lesbian and gay couples considering parenthood: An agenda for research, service, and advocacy. *Journal of Gay and Lesbian Social Services, 1,* 33–55.

Patterson, C. J. (1996a). Lesbian and gay parenthood. In M. Bornstein (Ed.), *Handbook of parenting* (pp. 255–274). Hillsdale, NJ: Lawrence Erlbaum Associates.

Patterson, C. J. (1996b). Lesbian and gay parents and their children. In R. Savin-Williams & K. Cohen (Eds.), *The lives of lesbians, gays, and bisexuals: Children to adults* (pp.274–304). Fort Worth: Harcourt Brace.

Patterson, C. J. (1998). Family lives of children with lesbian mothers. In C. J. Patterson & A. R. D'Augelli (Eds.), *Lesbian, gay, and bisexual identities in families: Psychological perspectives* (pp. 154–176). New York: Oxford University Press.

Patterson, C. J. (2000). Family relationships of lesbians and gay men. *Journal of Marriage and the Family, 62,* 1052–1069.

Patterson, C. J. (2005). Lesbian and gay parents and their children: Summary of research findings. In *Lesbian and gay parenting: A resource for psychologists.* Washington, DC: American Psychological Association.

Patterson, C. J. (2005). Lesbian and gay parents and their children: Summary of research findings. (pp. 5–22). Washington, DC: American Psychological Association.

Patterson, C. J. (2006). Children of lesbian and gay parents. *Current Directions in Psychological Science, 15*(5), 241–244.

Peplau, L. A. (1991). Lesbian and gay relationships. In J. C. Gonsiorek & J. D. Weinrich (Eds.), *Homosexuality: Research implications for public policy* (pp. 177–196). Thousand Oaks, CA: Sage Publications.

Peplau, L. A., Venigas, R. C. & Campbell, S. M. (1996). Gay and lesbian relationships. In R. C. Savin-Williams & K. M. Cohen (Eds.), *The lives of lesbians, gays, and bisexuals* (pp. 250–273). Fort Worth: Harcourt Brace.

Perrin, E. C. & the Committee on Psychosocial Aspects of Child and Family Health (2002). Technical Report: Coparent or second-parent adoption by same-sex parents. *Pediatrics, 109,* 341–344.

Planck, C. (2006). Connection and community: How the Family Pride Coalition supports parents and children of GLBT families. *Journal of GLBT Family Studies, 2*(3), 39–48.

Rohrbaugh, J. B. (1992). Lesbian families: Clinical issues and theoretical implications. *Professional Psychology: Research and Practice, 23*(8), 467–473.

Savin-Williams, R. (1990). *Gay and lesbian youth: Expression of identity.* Washington, DC: Hemisphere Publications.

Shroeder, M. & Shidlo, A. (2001). Ethical issues in sexual orientation conversion therapies: An empirical study of consumers. *Journal of Gay and Lesbian Psychotherapy, 5*(3–4), 131–166.

Segal-Engelchin, D., Erera, P. I. & Cwikel, J. (2004). The hetero-gay family: An emergent family configuration. *Journal of GBLT Family Studies, 1*(3), 85–104.

Siegenthaler, A. L. & Bigner, J. J. (2000). The value of children to lesbian and nonlesbian mothers. *Journal of Homosexuality, 39,* 73–311.

Slater, S. (1995). The lesbian family life cycle. New York: Free Press.

Slater, S. & Mencher, J. (1991, July). The lesbian family life cycle: A contextual approach. *American Journal of Orthopsychiatry, 61*(3), 372–382.

Stacey, J. & Biblarz, T. J. (2001). (How) Does sexual orientation of parents matter? *American Sociological Review, 65,* 159–183.

Sullivan, T. R. & Baques, A. (1999). Familism and the adoption option for gay and lesbian parents. In T. R. Sullivan (Ed.), *Queer families, common agendas: Gay people, lesbians and family values* (pp. 79–94). Binghamton, NY: Harrington Park Press.

Tasker, F. (1999). Children in lesbian-led families—A review. *Clinical Child Psychology and Psychiatry, 4,* 153–166.

Turner, P. H, Scadden, L. & Harris, M. B. (2004). Parenting in gay and lesbian families. *Journal of Gay and Lesbian Psychotherapy, 1*(3), 55–66.

Vanfraussen, K., Ponjaert-Kristoffersen, I. & Brewaeys, A. (2003). Family functioning in lesbian families created by donor insemination. *American Journal of Orthopsychiatry, 73,* 78–90.

Weston, K. (1992). *Families we choose: Lesbians, gays, kinship.* New York: Columbia University Press.

# 10

# Children in Foster Care:
## *Prevention and Treatment of Mental Health Problems*

ROBERT W. PLANT AND LESLEY SIEGEL

## INTRODUCTION

Recent estimates indicate that there are between 500,000 and 750,000 children in foster care in the United States (Leslie et al., 2003; Rubin, Alessandrini, Feudtner & Localio, 2004; Simms, Dubowitz & Szilagyi, 2000). According to Fisher, Burraston and Pears (2005) there has been significant growth in the number of children placed in foster care with numbers more than doubling between the early 1980s and mid 1990s. During this period, the fastest growing portion of the foster care population was children under 6 years of age (GAO, 1994). Simms et al. (2000) also noted a significant increase in African American children entering foster care during this time period.

The prevalence of mental health problems in children entering foster care is significantly higher than would be expected when compared with normative groups and to other similarly disadvantaged populations (Simms et al., 2000). According to Farmer et al. (2001), serious emotional disturbance, as defined by the presence of a diagnosable psychiatric condition and significant functional impairment, was present in 78% of the children in foster care. The authors also noted rates of behavior problems, developmental delays and the need for mental health treatment of between 39% and 80% of the foster care population. Pilowsky (1995) found that a sample of children in foster care demonstrated higher rates of psychopathology in general, with a trend toward significantly higher rates of externalizing disorders (e.g., oppositional defiant disorder, conduct disorder). Similarly, the most common diagnoses of children served in child welfare systems, including foster care, are disruptive behavior disorders that include attention deficit hyperactivity disorder (ADHD), oppositional defiant disorder, and conduct disorder (Garland et al., 2001). On the Child Behavior Checklist, 75% to 80% of school-age children in foster care score in either the clinical or borderline range on one or more measures of social competence and behavior problems (Clausen, Landsverk, Ganger, Chadwick & Litrownik, 1998). Similarly, 15% of children entering foster care reported suicidal ideation (Simms et al., 2000).

The high rate of psychiatric and behavior problems in the population of children in foster care is costly, both in human and financial terms. Foster children in California make up 4% of the Medicaid population but account for more than 40% of child mental health expenditures (Rosenfeld et al., 1997).

Children in foster care are also more likely to have poor educational outcomes that include higher rates of absenteeism, disciplinary referrals, grade retention, special education status and lower academic performance (Zeitlin, Weinberg & Shea, 2006). According to one study, school failure, academic skill delays and behavioral problems were present in 69% of a sample of foster care children (Zima et al., 2000).

The population of children in foster care also shows lower levels of adaptive functioning than the general population (Clausen et al., 1998). These children demonstrate higher rates of developmental delay than the norm (Halfon, Mendonca & Berkowitz, 1995; Simms et al., 2000; Zimmer & Panko, 2006). Despite high rates of developmental delay, young children in the child welfare system are unlikely to receive developmental early childhood services (Simms et al., 2000).

The physical health-care status of children entering the foster care system is poor (Simms et. al., 2000), and most foster children do not receive adequate preventive health care. Rosenfeld et al. (1997) reported that children in foster care present with three to seven times as many medical, developmental or emotional problems as other poor children. DiGiuseppe & Christakis (2003) argued that the frequent changes in placement, typical of children in foster care, disrupt the continuity of medical care and contribute to poor health outcomes for this vulnerable population. They also note how neglect, poverty and intrauterine exposure to drugs and alcohol contribute to poor health in infancy and childhood.

Separation from family, even in the wake of years of abuse or neglect, is stressful and often traumatizing for children (Clausen et al., 1998). Placement in kinship care versus foster care appears to be associated with fewer and less severe behavioral problems (Farmer et al., 2001).

Compounding these multiple risk factors is the effect of placement instability on multiple health and developmental outcomes. On a national level, children entering foster care experience an average of three or more changes in placement before attaining permanency. Several studies have demonstrated the impact of multiple placements on the severity of behavioral health problems (Zima et al., 2000). Significant positive correlations between the number of placements and number and severity of mental health disorders have been well documented. However, James (2004) found that only placement changes due to child behavioral issues were related to poorer mental health outcomes. Routine changes in placement do not seem to be as highly correlated with psychiatric distress.

One positive finding is that placement in foster care may increase the likelihood that a child with a behavioral health problem will receive care from a mental health specialist. Farmer et al. (2001) evaluated a population of children with a mental health disorder and determined the percentage that received care from a specialty mental health provider. They found that children in foster care (84%) and those involved with social services (73%) were much more likely to receive mental health care from a specialty mental health provider than other children living in poverty (37%).

Longitudinal studies on risk and resiliency have shown that two thirds of children with four or more risk factors at age 2 demonstrated significant educational, behavioral or psychiatric difficulties. In comparison, the average foster child carries 14 risk factors that place them at extremely high risk for multiple negative outcomes (Rosenfeld et al., 1997).

It is clear that children enter foster care with significantly higher rates of psychiatric disorder, developmental delay, behavioral problems, academic and learning difficulties and health issues than the norm and even more than similarly economically disadvantaged children. In addition, the separation from family and multiple placement disruptions typically experienced by children in foster care often compound their problems. The one piece of encouraging news is that entry into the system may increase the likelihood of receiving specialized psychiatric care. Although much of the mental health care available to children and youth either lacks empirical evidence of its effectiveness or has not been demonstrated effective with children in foster care, a number of effective and emerging best practices promise hope for these children and the adults who care for them.

The population of children in foster care overlaps considerably with the population of children who have been victims of abuse and neglect (Figure 10.1). For example, the vast majority of children placed in foster care have been placed due to abuse or neglect. Although relocation and separation from family are believed to contribute to the problems encountered by children and youth placed in foster care, the abuse and neglect that necessitated placement is arguably responsible for most of the negative outcomes that have been observed. Given this, and the relative paucity in some areas of research with a foster care population, this chapter draws heavily on the abuse and neglect literature.

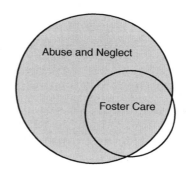

**Figure 10.1** Venn Diagram of Child Abuse/Neglect and Foster Care Populations.

## BIOLOGICAL AND GENETIC FACTORS

Children in foster care are more likely to have grown up with parents who are psychotic, alcoholic or drug addicted. The impact of these family backgrounds is likely mediated by a combination of genetic, biological and psychological processes.

The partial heritability of most major psychiatric disorders and alcoholism has been documented (Kendler, 2001). In addition, the presence of major depression, psychotic disorders and alcohol and drug abuse during pregnancy or postpartum can contribute to harmful biological processes resulting from a lack of adequate pre- and postnatal care, malnutrition or intrauterine exposure to drugs or alcohol (Pilowsky, 1995). More recent research has documented the neurodevelopmental effects of abuse and neglect (Perry, 2002) for children placed in foster care.

Physical abuse has both direct and indirect effects on brain development. Direct effects include damage to the brain caused by shaking or hitting

(Duhaime, Christian, Rorke & Zimmerman, 1998) as well as exposure to drugs or alcohol prior to birth (Mick, *Biederman, Faraone, Sayer* & Kleinman, 2002). Indirect effects include the negative impact of chronic stress associated with abusive environments on brain development (Perry, 2002). These effects contribute to deficits in multiple domains including cognitive functioning and academic performance, capacity for empathy and regulation of emotion, impulse control, attachment and social relations and physical health.

Beginning with Spitz's (1945, 1946) groundbreaking research demonstrating the poor mortality and development of children raised in the deprivation of the foundling home environment, the powerful and pervasive negative effects of severe neglect have been well documented (Perry, 2002). Neglect is particularly harmful during early childhood. The younger the age at which neglect occurs, the more harmful its impact on development due to critical periods of development that occur during infancy and early childhood. Infants and toddlers are most at risk. Severity and duration of neglect are also critical factors. Children, particularly young children, who remain in environments characterized by a profound loss of human contact and the absence of cognitive and sensory stimulation are at risk for severe and pervasive developmental delays (ibid.). The encouraging news is that the removal from a neglectful environment and the provision of appropriate human contact and stimulation through placement in foster care can reverse these delays. Many of the interventions described in this chapter are built on the recognition that, in many cases, the impact of abuse and neglect can be reduced with proper care.

## INDIVIDUAL FACTORS INFLUENCING RISK AND RESILIENCY

Relatively little is known about the individual factors that contribute to risk and resiliency of children in foster care, although there is a growing literature regarding children involved with the child welfare system (Kaplan, Pelcovitz & Labruna, 1999; McGloin & Widom, 2001). In regards to the foster care population, individual risk and resiliency can be conceptualized in several ways. How do individual child factors contribute to the risk of abuse or neglect and subsequent placement in foster care? Or, alternatively, how are the negative mental health and developmental outcomes associated with foster care mediated by individual factors within the child?

Children with disabilities are at higher risk for abuse and neglect (Horner-Johnson & Drum, 2006). The increased stress and parenting demands placed on parents appear to play a role in this heightened risk. Similarly, children with ADHD are at higher risk for abuse. This risk may be due in part to caretaker frustration around efforts to manage the child's impulsivity and hyperactive behavior. Sellinger (2006) reported that young age and temperamental factors (e.g., irritability, hyperactivity, difficult to soothe) elevate risk for typical as well as for disabled children.

Once a child has been abused or neglected and placed in foster care, certain individual factors can be protective against poor mental health outcomes. Intelligence has been recognized as a protective factor against a host of negative childhood outcomes (Rosenfeld et al., 1997). Intellectual capacity may support a wider array of coping strategies and problem-solving abilities and may impact social functioning in a manner that is protective. Similarly, physical attractiveness can be protective against the likelihood of abuse and negative outcomes associated with maltreatment, presumably due to the impact of physical appearance on adult's willingness to establish supportive relationships (ibid.). Dispositions that elicit positive responses, emotional ties with parent substitutes and the presence of an external support system can also mediate against the risk factors associated with abuse, neglect and foster care placement.

## FAMILY FACTORS INFLUENCING RISK AND RESILIENCY

Family factors can promote or protect against the risk of abuse, neglect and placement in foster care as well as mediate their impact. Maternal age (younger), extreme low income (participation in public income support programs), low maternal education, maternal depression, the presence of any other young children in the home and a mother's separation at age 14 years from her own mother significantly predict child maltreatment reports in the first year of life. Social isolation of the family and female-headed households also raised the risk of abuse or neglect and subsequent foster care (Coulton, Korbin, Su & Chow, 1995).

## SOCIAL AND COMMUNITY FACTORS INFLUENCING RISK AND RESILIENCY

Coulton, Korbin, Su and Chow (1995, p. 1065) found that rates of child maltreatment are related to "structural determinants of community social organization." They found that factors such as household age, household structure, economic resources, residential instability and proximity of neighborhoods to concentrated poverty predicted rates of child abuse and neglect. Other neighborhood indicators related to high risk for abuse or neglect included a low parent-to-child ratio, high rates of housing turnover and high numbers of single-parent families. In the absence of the stress-buffering effects of social support, economic resources and shared parenting, families may exhibit neglectful and abusive parenting practices.

## EVIDENCE-BASED TREATMENT INTERVENTIONS FOR CHILDREN IN FOSTER CARE

### What Works

There is a wide range of psychiatric disorders, developmental delays, behavioral problems, academic and learning difficulties and health issues present in the population of children in foster care. The range of potentially effective treatments is also vast, nearly encompassing the available literature on the treatment of psychiatric disorders in children. In contrast, there is relatively little research examining the impact of treatment or preventive interventions on a sample of children in foster care. To meet the highest standard of what works, interventions need to have demonstrated effectiveness across multiple clinical trials, be suitable for delivery to foster children and families and show evidence of effectiveness with a foster care or child welfare population. Multidimensional treatment foster care (MTFC), community wraparound and trauma-focused cognitive behavioral therapy (TF-CBT) meet these stringent criteria.

One of the most well-documented interventions for the treatment of behavioral and psychiatric disorders of children in foster care is MTFC (Chamberlain, 2003). Initially designed as a community-based alternative to residential care of adolescent delinquent males, MTFC has been expanded to serve adolescent females, young children (ages 3–5), and latency age children (6–11). MTFC views foster parents as the primary agents of therapeutic change and supports their work with a team of mental health and support staff. Key elements of MTFC include training of foster care parents in a home-based behavioral system with points and levels, support for foster parents, family therapy for biological parents (or other family), supportive therapy and skill training for children, school-based intervention and psychiatric medication management when needed. Like other successful evidence-based models, MTFC provides training, consultation and ongoing monitoring and support to providers implementing the model. Treatment procedures are manualized and well defined to promote model fidelity.

The original adolescent version of MTFC (Fisher & Chamberlain, 2000) is the best-documented of the program variations and the only version with sufficient randomized controlled studies to meet the standard of what works.

The community wraparound model has demonstrated effectiveness in helping to maintain community placement for foster children with emotional and behavioral disorders (Bruns, 2004; Hoagwood, Burns, Kiser, Ringeisen & Schoenwald, 2001; Kerker & Dore, 2006). First developed to serve children with serious emotional disturbance and their families, the application of wraparound has expanded to serve children and youth in the child welfare and juvenile justice arenas.

Wraparound is a value-based service-delivery system that emphasizes community-based care, family voice and choice, culturally competent services and a strength-based rather than deficit-oriented approach. It combines a comprehensive array of supportive and treatment interventions with case management and advocacy. In most applications, a wraparound facilitator or case manager works with families to identify strengths and needs and convenes a team composed of the child and family, community providers and natural supports. The team develops an individualized plan of care designed to improve functioning and to maintain community placement. A strong emphasis is placed on identifying and capitalizing on existing natural supports and fostering family competence and independence.

The evidence base supporting wraparound has been growing (Bruns, 2004; Burchard, Bruns & Burchard, 2002; Kamradt, 2000) despite features that challenge efforts to empirically validate the approach. Unlike most evidence-based treatment models, wraparound is not a single manualized treatment applied to a particular diagnosis. Instead, wraparound is designed to be a flexible, multifaceted approach to a range of complex problems encountered by children and families. In addition, wraparound has not been disseminated by a single model development team but has grown through a more organic grassroots process. As a result, fidelity to the core components of wraparound has been difficult to achieve (Bruns, Burchard, Suter, Leverentz-Brady & Force, 2004). However, when implemented with high fidelity, wraparound has been shown to improve child behavior, to reduce social problems, to improve school attendance, to decrease functional impairment and to reduce delinquency (Burchard et al., 2002).

The success of the approach is dependent on strong fidelity-based case management and a sufficient array of treatment and supportive services that can be reliably accessed and flexibly applied. The ability to provide intensive services that are matched to client and family needs while maintaining placement stability makes the wraparound approach particularly suited to children in foster care who typically present with complex disorders and whose problems are exacerbated by placement disruption.

TF-CBT is one of the best-documented and effective treatments for trauma-related disorders affecting children and youth (Cohen, Mannarino, Berliner & Deblinger, 2000). There is an extensive literature demonstrating the superiority of TF-CBT to "treatment as usual" for posttraumatic stress disorder (PTSD) and related conditions. Originally designed as an intervention to treat child victims of sexual abuse, the model has been expanded to treat symptoms resulting from a variety of traumatic experiences. Treatment can be as brief as 12 sessions or can be extended to meet child and family needs. The model uses four basic approaches to reduce trauma symptoms and to promote adaptive coping: (1) exposure; (2) cognitive processing and reframing; (3) stress management; and (4) parental treatment. The high rate of abuse and neglect and traumatic underpinnings of many of the behaviors and disorders prevalent among children in foster care makes this approach extremely well suited to this population.

## What Might Work

A number of evidence-based and promising practices have demonstrated effectiveness with the mental health disorders that are most common among foster care children (i.e., disruptive behavior disorders affective disorders) but have not been sufficiently tested with a foster care population. These include approaches to mental health assessment, family-based treatments, models of treatment foster care, parent-training approaches, selected school-based interventions and cognitive behavioral treatment for depression.

Psychiatric screening and assessment of children in foster care is not commonplace despite the high rate of psychiatric disorders in this population (Horwitz, Owens & Simms, 2000; Leslie et al., 2003;). According to Horwitz et al. (2000) more than 40% of child welfare agencies sampled did not have a policy to identify psychiatric or developmental problems at entry into care. Although some have argued that screening all children could result in overdiagnosis of psychiatric conditions, the high rates of disorder in this population appear to warrant an inclusive approach. If children entering foster care are not assessed and their treatment needs are not identified, it is unlikely that proper care will be obtained. Efforts to use community providers have had mixed results, as not all providers are sensitized to the special health-care and mental health needs of foster children. Horwitz et al. argued for the use of specialized foster care clinics for both assessment and treatment. Though such specialty clinics may improve problem detection and referral to care, their centralized location may be inconvenient to foster parents who may wish to bring their child to their provider of choice. Also, referral to a foster care clinic may inadvertently disrupt the continuity of care as children enter and then may leave the foster care system. Even though the preferred site of specialized evaluation may be unclear, the need for comprehensive screening and assessment for this vulnerable population is critical in linking to care.

Family-based treatments, including functional family therapy (Sexton & Alexander, 1999), multisystemic therapy (Henggeler, 1999) and multidimensional family therapy (Liddle et al., 2001) have demonstrated effectiveness with many of the behavioral and psychiatric problems typical of children in foster care (e.g., disruptive behavior disorders, juvenile delinquency, substance abuse disorders). They have also proven effective with children that have been in foster care or are at risk of placement. However, these interventions have not yet accumulated sufficient evidence to support their unquestioned efficacy with the foster care population, particularly when the intervention is provided while the child is in foster care placement. All of these evidence-based programs are family-based treatments that are often delivered in the home. A critical question concerns the degree to which the methods and practices employed in these approaches will need to be modified to fit a foster family ecology. Though there is substantial promise that these approaches can be adapted to serve children in the foster care system, further evidence is required before being touted as treatments of choice for the foster care population.

Several models of treatment foster care have demonstrated effectiveness, although most are not as well documented as MTFC (Reddy and Pfeiffer, 1997). Based on a meta-analysis of 40 outcomes studies evaluating treatment foster care, Reddy and Pfeiffer (1997) reported that foster family-based treatment (Hawkins, Meadowcroft, Trout &Art was here, but was deleted. Luster, 1985), Family-based residential treatment (Mikkelsen, Bereika & McKenzie, 1993) and foster family care (Reddy & Pfeiffer, 1997) achieved significant short-term outcomes with children and youth.

Treatment foster care is distinguished from specialized foster care by the focus on the foster parents as a primary agent of change rather than simply the custodial parent who cares for the child while clinical services are provided to the child. These approaches were found to have large positive effects on placement stability and children's social skills and medium effects on child behavior, discharge to a lower level of care and multiple indicators of the child's psychological adjustment. All outcome measures were assessed at the end of treatment. Reddy and Pfeiffer (1997) noted the need for long term follow-up to determine lasting impact and the need for more detailed explication of the essential training and support services provided to families. The review suggests that treatment foster care can be effective in helping children to be successful in family life and in assisting foster parents in providing an environment that supports healthy child development. Considering the economic costs of residential and group home care and the general lack of empirical support for institutional approaches (Hoagwood et al., 2001), treatment foster care should be disseminated as a viable cost-effective alternative.

Parent training is an extremely common intervention in child welfare practice, but only a few of the many programs offered qualify as best practices with strong empirical support (Barth et al., 2005). Most of the evidence-based parent training programs were developed for the treatment of early conduct or disruptive behavior disorders, but several have been used effectively with a population of abused and neglected children. The Incredible Years (Webster-Stratton & Hammond, 1997), parent–child interaction therapy (PCIT) (Eyberg

& Robinson, 1982) and parent management training (PMT) (Forgatch, Bullock & Patterson, 2004; Kazdin, 1997) are three of the most well-documented parent training curriculums.

Linares, Montalto, MinMin & Oza (2006) conducted a two-part intervention using the Incredible Years curriculum (Webster-Stratton & Hammond, 1997) with biological and foster parents. This intervention introduced co-parenting as a method of increasing consistency of approach between biological and foster parent homes, thus making the transition for children easier. At the end of the 12-week intervention, they noted greater improvements in co-parenting and positive parenting than was noted in a control group assigned to usual care. Follow-up also supported positive results for parenting behaviors and a trend toward fewer child-externalizing problems.

PCIT has been successfully used to treat externalizing behavior problems in young children but has recently been extended to serve children who have been abused and neglected (Herschell & McNeil, 2005). Noting the high level of externalizing behavior problems with children who have experienced abuse and neglect, it is not surprising that this approach has been successful with the population.

PCIT involves teaching parents two sets of skills that they apply in their interactions with children: (1) child-directed interaction, in which parents are taught to praise, reflect, imitate, describe and use enthusiasm during play-based interaction; and (2) learning about behavior modification techniques, such as effective commands, using time out and determining compliance thresholds. An innovative feature of PCIT is the use of "bug-in-the-ear" technology, which allows the parent to receive unobtrusive in-vivo coaching feedback while practicing skills with their child. PCIT is believed to operate by impacting children's emotion regulation and language development as well as altering coercive and inconsistent parenting that often underlies disruptive and oppositional behavior.

McNeil, Herschell, Gurwitch and Clemens-Mowrer (2004) developed a group-based version of PCIT for use with foster parents and followed outcomes over a five-month period. Although lacking randomized assignment and a comparison condition, the initial findings indicate that this group-based modification of PCIT can produce significant reductions in child disruptive behaviors and high satisfaction ratings from foster parents. The fact that this modified version can be delivered in only two days of focused training is encouraging given the many demands placed on foster parents and their limited availability for training or to participate in treatment.

PMT (Forgatch et al., 2004), is based on social interaction learning and a conceptualization that oppositional and defiant behavior are due to coercive and ineffective parenting processes. PMT teaches five core parenting techniques: (1) skill encouragement; (2) discipline; (3) monitoring; (4) problem solving; and (5) positive involvement. PMT has been incorporated into MTFC as the parent training approach for biological parents. As a component of MTFC it is difficult to determine if PMT would be effective on its own as an intervention targeting the parenting behaviors and parent–child interactions that occur within foster families. There is no reason to believe that foster parents would be likely to engage in the coercive and inconsistent parenting typical of families with conduct disordered youth. However, it is likely that the extremely challenging and persistent disruptive behaviors displayed by some foster children may evoke coercive or inconsistent responses from stressed and frustrated foster parents. An important research question remains: Does PMT applied to foster parents require modification to retain its effectiveness?

In a recent review of parent training programs in child welfare, Barth et al. (2005) described several other widely used but less well-documented parent training programs. These programs lack randomized controlled studies but have strong face validity and are supported by single case studies and quasi-experimental designs. The four Barth and colleagues recommend as promising practices are Parenting Wisely (Gordon, 2003), Nurturing Parent (Bavolek, 2002), Systematic Training in Effective Parenting (STEP) (Adams, 2001) and Project 12-Ways (Lutzker and Rice, 1984). The efficacy of these approaches with foster parents is unclear and requires further research.

A large number of mental health services for children are delivered at school (Hoagwood et al., 2001), and several school-based approaches have shown positive outcomes with children. Hoagwood et al. (2001) reported that contingency management for children with ADHD and conduct disorder reduces problem classroom behavior and aggression. Other school-based programs are reviewed following as preventive interventions.

Children in foster care often present with disorders (e.g., separation anxiety, school phobia, depression) that are amenable to outpatient psychotherapy. Meta-analyses of psychotherapy trials with children consistently demonstrate beneficial effects compared with no treatment (Hoagwood et al., 2001). Research on child psychotherapy as actually practiced in most community settings, however, does not support their effectiveness (ibid.). These effects may be due to the large variety of approaches used in community settings and the failure to match treatments to client needs or to maintain fidelity to prescribed models. If children in foster care are to benefit from outpatient psychotherapy, effective models must be selected, treatments must be matched to client needs, practitioners must be appropriately trained and supervised and monitoring of care must occur periodically throughout treatment to ensure fidelity to the defined model. One major advantage of outpatient approaches with a foster care population is that they are relatively short term (8–12 sessions) and require less involvement of parents than parent training or family-based interventions, thus fitting some of the practical challenges of delivering service to children in foster care.

Cognitive behavioral therapies are some of the most well-documented outpatient treatments for children and adolescents (Hoagwood et al., 2001; McClellan & Werry, 2003), particularly for anxiety disorders and depression. For depression, approaches incorporating self-control, behavioral and social problem solving and primary and secondary control enhancement (McClellan & Werry, 2003) have strong research support. For anxiety disorders (e.g., obsessive-compulsive disorder, overanxious, generalized, or separation anxiety disorder), self-instruction training methods are effective.

Interpersonal psychotherapy has demonstrated positive effects for the treatment of depression in adolescents (Burns, 2003). Children in foster care are especially prone to interpersonal difficulties, given the likelihood of attachment disruption, maladaptive responses to loss and separation and the negative impact of disruptive behaviors on relationships. Interpersonal psychotherapy may be particularly well suited to the needs of foster care children, but at this time there is insufficient evidence of its effectiveness with younger children.

## What Does Not Work

Interventions that are clearly not effective with children in foster care include orphanages, ending foster care at age 18, boot camps and long-term care in group homes or residential treatment centers. Orphanages are ineffective largely because they deny children the opportunity to develop long-term intimate relationships and adequate stimulation for necessary growth and development. Policies that required children to leave foster care at the age of 18 were abandoned after recognizing that most youth were woefully unprepared for life on their own. Most policies allow children to remain in foster care until they have completed their education or until they reach their 21st birthday. Boot camps, popular in the 1980s and 1990s as a treatment for juvenile delinquency, have been found to be ineffective and potentially harmful (Mihalic, Irwin, Elliott, Fagan & Hansen, 2001). The conclusion of Hoagwood et al. (2001) that residential and group home care is ineffective has raised considerable controversy, particularly since the largest portion of treatment dollars is spent at this level of care. The lack of evidence-based congregate treatment models has been a major impediment to improving care in this treatment setting.

## Overall Comment

The number of programs that work or might work is encouraging, given the tremendous needs of this population and the wide range of disorders for which they are at risk. Despite the significant array of programs the reality is that few have been implemented on a large enough scale to significantly impact the estimated 500,000 or more foster children that require effective treatments matched to their need.

There are many barriers to a more widespread implementation of effective services, including issues associated with the workforce, financing of training and quality assurance and provider readiness. Few graduate training programs adequately prepare students for evidence-based practice. As a result, the workforce issues are significant. Also, most rates of reimbursement for services do not adequately support the need for training, quality assurance and fidelity monitoring required by most evidence-based approaches. Finally, much has been written about the role of provider and organizational readiness and the need for leadership in the implementation of effective services (Fixsen, Naoom, Blasé, Friedman & Wallace, 2005).

## PSYCHOPHARMACOLOGY OF CHILDREN IN FOSTER CARE

The evidence base for pediatric psychopharmacology is quite limited. Ethical issues regarding informed consent, concerns about conducting medication trials with children and the lack of financial incentives for the drug industry to sponsor new studies on medications for which patents have already expired all contribute to the lack of empirical studies. In addition, the practice of evidence-based pediatric psychopharmacotherapy (i.e., using empirically based data to establish the efficacy, safety and tolerability of psychotropic medication for children) is roughly only three decades old (Connor & Meltzer, 2006). Despite this lack of data, the percentage of children that receive psychotropic medication and the prevalence of polypharmacy have grown considerably over recent years (Hoagwood et. al. 2001; Lyons et al., 2004). Concerns that children in foster care are overmedicated (Zima, Bussing, Crecelius, Kaufman & Belin, 1999) and that most psychopharmacological practice with children is driven by anecdotal rather than scientific evidence (Hoagwood et al., 2001) have led both the Academy of Child and Adolescent Psychiatry (AACAP) and individual states to develop psychopharmacological practice standards for children in foster care (AACAP, 2005).

Despite fears of overuse of medications and inappropriate prescribing practices, evidence suggests that the majority of children in foster care demonstrating treatable clinical symptoms do not receive the medication evaluation and treatment that is warranted (Zima et. al, 1999). This generally accepted observation, an awareness by the academic community of the importance of developing the evidence base for pediatric psychopharmacology plus legislative passage of the Food and Drug Administration Modernization Act in 1997 have led to a rapid expansion of clinical trials research in the last 10 years. Connor and Meltzer (2006) published a review summarizing the evidence on the efficacy of pediatric psychopharmacology by drug and disorder in children and adolescents. Medications that meet the highest standard of evidence for effectiveness with particular diagnoses include the following: atomexetine (Strattera), a newer nonstimulant, selective norepinephrine reuptake inhibitor for ADHD; fluoxetine (Prozac) for major depressive disorder and obsessive-compulsive disorder; and stimulants, which are dextroamphetamine preparations (e.g., Dexedrine, Adderall) or methylphenidate preparations (e.g., Ritalin, Concerta) for ADHD (Michelson et al., 2001).

ADHD is considered to be the most common medication-responsive diagnosis among children and youth in foster care. Recent developments in the use of stimulants for ADHD include the black-box warning in spring 2006 by the U.S. Federal Drug Administration (FDA) that stimulants as a class have a high potential for abuse and that misuse can cause sudden death and serious cardiovascular events. A positive development has been the publication of algorithms such as the recent revision of the Texas algorithm for treatment of ADHD in youth (Pliszka et al., 2006) and the soon-to-be published recommendations from the multisite, multimodal preschool ADHD treatment study (PATS). Stimulant medications have been shown to help children concentrate and perform better in school and to control hyperactive and impulsive behavior. Effective treatment with stimulants may promote placement stability by reducing the behavioral challenges facing children and their foster parents.

The other major class of psychiatric medications with demonstrated efficacy in children and youth is the selective serotonin reuptake inhibitors (SSRIs) (McClellan & Werry, 2003). Both fluoxetine (Prozac) and sertraline (Zoloft) have demonstrated effectiveness with children and adolescents in the treatment of anxiety disorders, and fluoxetine has been demonstrated to be effective for major depressive disorder. The use of these medications with children has been controversial, with some noting that the benefits outweigh the risks and others recommending the discontinuation of their use with children. Current practice suggests that these drugs can be very helpful to a large number of children and adolescents but that family members, practitioners and others should be educated about the risks of increased irritability and suicidality in a small number of users. A black-box warning was issued by the FDA in October 2004 for all antidepressant use in the pediatric age group. Though the link between increased suicidal activity and use of these medications was nonconclusive, the FDA did recommend increased physician monitoring of antidepressant side effects.

Risperidone (Risperdal) and other second-generation antipsychotic (SGA) medications have been shown to be effective in the treatment of behavioral disturbance in autism and mental retardation with externalizing symptoms (McClellan and Werry, 2003). Preliminary evidence also supports the use of SGAs in the treatment of childhood or adolescent onset schizophrenia (Hoagwood et. al., 2001).

In summary, there is clearly a need for additional controlled research regarding the safety and effectiveness of drugs with child and adolescent populations beyond what has been demonstrated for stimulants and antidepressants. Further study should also examine the differential effects within particular populations including children and youth in foster care.

## PREVENTION OF MENTAL HEALTH PROBLEMS OF CHILDREN IN FOSTER CARE

### What Works

The literature on intervention with high-risk groups is compelling regarding the value of early preventive intervention. It is also clear that no more than one third of all individuals in need of mental health care actually receive it (Durlak & Wells, 1997). These facts argue for the importance of prevention in the approach taken to meet the needs of children in foster care.

A number of the prevention programs described in this section do not specifically target children in foster care but are known to be effective with the kinds of disorders and risk factors that these children often face. Where interventions are directed specifically at children in foster care, they are best characterized as secondary or targeted prevention approaches. Early intervention foster care (EIFC) stands out as a well-defined intensive prevention program that targets young children in foster care and their foster and biological parents.

EIFC (Fisher et al., 2005) is an early childhood variant of MTFC, serving foster families with young children (ages 3–6). EIFC uses a team approach to provide training, education, support and consultation to foster parents, therapy services to children and parent training to birth parents (or other permanent resources). The program targets child behavior problems, emotional regulation and developmental delays (Fisher, Ellis, and Chamberlain, 1999). EIFC views the foster care setting as an active treatment environment rather than as a placement to hold the child until a more permanent placement can be obtained. By targeting and successfully impacting child behavior problems, this program helps to reduce one of the primary factors in placement disruptions. Early intervention helps to modify behaviors before they become ingrained styles that are more resistant to change.

In a randomized clinical trial, EIFC was found to significantly improve placement stability in comparison with a control condition of typical foster care. Stability in the treatment condition was 90% compared with 64% in the untreated population. This is a very significant and promising finding. In addition, follow-up analyses revealed that the effect of previous placement instability, a well-known risk factor for subsequent disruption, was essentially neutralized in the EIFC condition. The number of previous placements only predicted disruption in the control condition, not in the EIFC condition (Fisher et al., 2005). Although the EIFC approach is significantly more expensive than typical care, the ability to reduce disruptive behaviors and to reduce disruptions are likely to pay dividends well beyond the initial investment.

## What Might Work

Prevention as applied to foster care can focus on preventing the need for foster care placement or intervening early with children upon entry into foster care to reduce the risk for negative outcomes. A review of efforts to prevent foster care placement is beyond the scope of this chapter. This review of promising approaches will focus on prevention efforts directed at children in foster care or that children in foster care may benefit from if available in their school or community. Those that show promise include mentoring programs, school-based interventions, educational liaisons, use of early intervention services and nurse visiting programs.

The Big Brother Big Sister (BBBS) mentoring program has demonstrated positive results with at-risk groups (Burns, 2003; Hoagwood et al., 2001; Mihalic et al., 2001) but has not demonstrated its effectiveness with children in foster care. Targeted at families with single-parent households, BBBS provides positive modeling, support and experiences with positive leisure activities that can be protective against negative peer and antisocial influences. It is unclear how this model works in conjunction with foster care. Children in foster care have suffered considerable interpersonal losses and are typically struggling with issues of loyalty to their family of origin and the challenges of adjusting to a new family. The introduction of yet another adult figure in their life may not be advisable. Age, developmental and circumstantial factors are likely to play a significant role in the impact of a mentor on the child's well-being. On the other hand, if the mentor is able to remain continually involved with the child throughout the multiple changes in placement that are typical of children in foster care, he or she may be able to serve as a more reliable attachment figure than others likely to come in and out of the child's life. Further research is needed.

Schools are a primary site of mental health service delivery and a natural setting for prevention activities. All children, including those in foster care, must have an educational experience, and most attend public schools. One of the most strongly supported school-based preventive interventions is the Good Behavior Game (Hoagwood et al., 2001; Kellam, Rebok, and Ialongo, 1994). This program is a full classroom contingency management system that targets disruptive and aggressive behavior. The approach uses principles of functional behavioral analysis in promoting inhibition of aggression and substitution of more acceptable behavior. Multiple investigations of the program have shown strong effects on aggressive and disruptive behaviors and longer-term substance abuse and antisocial behaviors (Embry, 2002). This is a relatively low-cost intervention that specifically targets some of the most common behavioral disorders and risk factors associated with foster care.

Children in foster care are at high risk for poor educational outcomes stemming from their disadvantaged status and high rates of learning difficulties and behavioral problems. Effective advocacy within the educational system is often required to maximize their educational experience. Unfortunately, child welfare case workers and foster parents may lack the knowledge and skill to effectively advocate for their children on educational matters. The availability of educational advocates for consultation to social workers handling foster care cases was evaluated in a study of 120 children in foster care (Zeitlin et al., 2006). Results showed positive effects on social worker's involvement in children's educational programming and the children's educational performance. Additional studies with random assignment and clearer explication of liaison activities are needed.

Despite high rates of developmental delay and the particular vulnerability of young children to the impact of abuse or neglect and separation from family, children in foster care are seldom referred to or receive early intervention services. The Child Abuse and Prevention and Treatment Act was amended in 2003 to require states to refer any child under three who is involved in substantiated abuse or neglect to early intervention services funded under Part C of the of the Individuals with Disabilities Act (Dicker & Gordon, 2006). This legislation has removed major barriers to accessing early intervention services, but despite this change many children in foster care still do not receive the early intervention services they need.

Several states have developed models to integrate early childhood services into child welfare, foster care, and behavioral health delivery systems (Dicker & Gordon, 2006) to improve rates of referral to early childhood services. In Massachusetts, the Massachusetts Early Childhood Linkage Initiative forged a partnership between the agencies providing protective services and overseeing the early intervention programs. Vermont's Success by Six Initiative provides a home visit to every child born in the state and an early intervention referral of protective service cases, including children placed in foster care is facilitated by an automatic computer-based system. New York, through its Permanent Judicial Commission on Justice for Children, has promoted foster care referral to early childhood services through extensive educational efforts. Under this program, "many family court judges routinely order that every foster child younger than 3 be referred to Part C" (Dicker & Gordon, 2006, p. 176). The Dependency Court Intervention Program for Family Violence in Miami, Florida, facilitates an integration of domestic violence, child maltreatment and early intervention for mothers and their young children under 5. Not all of these state efforts are specifically focused on children in foster care; however, this approach of building relationships across provider systems and funding sources is a promising approach for improving the developmental status of children in foster care.

For many of the same reasons previously sited regarding early intervention services, prenatal and infancy home visiting programs hold promise for preventing foster care placement and the negative outcomes associated with children in foster care. This is particularly true when home visiting programs target young mothers that are at high risk for abuse or neglect. The Nurse Home Visitation (Mihalic et al., 2001) program has been selected as an exemplary practice in the Blueprints for Violence Prevention initiative. This program provides prenatal home visits by a nurse and follows mother and child through the child's second birthday. The program promotes the physical, cognitive and socioemotional development of children. Participation in the program has been associated with a 79% reduction in abuse and neglect among poor and unmarried mothers. Long-term 15-year follow-ups demonstrate impressive reductions in behavioral problems, arrests and criminal convictions as well as in maternal outcomes related to number of births, time between births and months on welfare (Mihalic et al., 2001).

## What Does Not Work

Although many prevention programs have yet to sufficiently demonstrate their effectiveness either in general or in regards to serving children in foster care, only a few can be put into this category. These include Scared Straight programs and earlier versions of the Drug Abuse Resistance Education (DARE) drug abuse prevention program.

## Overall Comment

The availability of effective prevention programs for children in foster care is critical given limited resources, the relatively low cost of most preventive interventions and the fact that few children with mental health problems ever receive appropriate treatment. The key factors for children in foster care are parenting behaviors, the impact of trauma, relational issues and support of healthy growth and development across multiple domains. In many ways these needs are not dissimilar from the needs of many high-risk populations of children and families. This suggests that many preventive interventions not specifically designed for foster care children may be applicable to this population. On the other hand, a unique feature of foster care is the child's separation from the family of origin and placement in an alternative family setting. This core feature of foster care can significantly affect the delivery and impact of preventive interventions.

EIFC stands out as a robust intervention specifically designed for young children in foster care. Other approaches, including traditional mentoring, educational advocacy, early intervention and prenatal and infancy home visiting programs, have shown positive outcomes with risk factors typical of children in foster care. Further research is needed to explore the effectiveness of these interventions with the specific population of children in foster care.

## RECOMMENDED BEST PRACTICE FOR CHILDREN IN FOSTER CARE

### Treatment

The problems faced by children in foster care are complex and multidetermined. A full array and continuum of effective services across multiple levels of care that is accessible to all who need it is required. No single treatment or category of intervention will be sufficient, and practice will need to be as varied as the problems faced by these children and their foster families. It is clear that the effective treatment of foster children will require the active engagement and participation of their foster parents. Each of the programs that work and the majority of those that might work either uses the family as the primary therapeutic agent or engages them as a component of the treatment process.

Other family-based treatments that were not specifically designed for the treatment of children in foster care (i.e., MST, FFT, and MDFT) show promise with this population but may need to be modified to match the unique ecology of the foster family system. Clearly, timely screening and assessment of mental health problems in this population are necessary first steps in adequately meeting children's needs. School-based and outpatient therapies that target specific symptom profiles (e.g., aggression and disruptive behaviors; anxiety and depressive symptoms) are needed and offer certain advantages (e.g., cost is low; relatively little is required from busy parents), but the trend is likely to be toward integrated combinations of treatments offering sufficient levels of treatment intensity and impact on multiple areas of dysfunction (e.g., developmental delay, disruptive behaviors, attachment and bonding, social problem solving, parent–child interaction). Intervention at the earliest point in time is highly recommended, and there is a great need for more evidence-based interventions with young children. In the future, those developing effective treatments of children in foster care will need to pay as close attention to issues of implementation, sustainability and funding mechanisms as is paid to the clinical model and outcomes.

## Pharmacology

The current state of psychopharmacologic treatment of children in foster care is a paradox. On the one hand, there are concerns of overmedication due to this population's disadvantaged status and high proportion of minority children. On the other hand, many children in foster care with disorders that would clearly benefit from psychotropic medication do not receive it. Similarly, there is little to no evidence for polypharmacy, but its use continues to grow at an alarming rate.

Stimulants and Strattera for the treatment of ADHD, SSRIs for the treatment of anxiety disorders and depression, and resperidone for the treatment of behavioral dyscontrol associated with autism, pervasive developmental disorder or mental retardation have the strongest empirical support. Although the class of newer antipsychotics may be effective in treating childhood onset psychosis, they are often prescribed to treat aggression and behavioral dyscontrol despite the lack of empirical evidence to support the latter. There is no doubt that many foster children with behavioral disorders can benefit from medication. It is equally true that care and caution should be exercised and that medication should only be used when clearly indicated.

## Prevention

Prevention programs are effective and cost-effective but are underused. The risk factors associated with children in foster care are prime candidates for targeted prevention. The ideal targeted prevention program for at risk foster children would screen and intervene at key transition points including pregnancy, birth, first removal and entry into foster care. Home visits would be used to screen children and families for risk factors, to identify supportive interventions and to implement early intervention services where needed. Programs should be intensive, multifaceted and capable of intervening around multiple risk factors or connecting with other service systems. Each intervention should be specifically tested and proven with a foster care population. Foster care itself should be redesigned as an active preventive and treatment intervention working to correct for earlier maltreatment and deprivation and to prevent poor health and mental health outcomes.

## REFERENCES

American Academy of Child and Adolescent Psychiatry (N.D.). AACAP Position Statement on Oversight of Psychotropic Medication use for Children in State Custody: A Best Principles Guideline. Retrieved January 17, 2007 from http://www.aacap.org/gagalleries/practiceinformation/fostercare/bestprinciples/final.pdf.

Adams, J. F. (2001). Impact of parent training on family functioning, *Child and Family Behavior Therapy, 23,* 29–42.

Barth, R., Landsverk J., Chamberlain, P., Reid J., Rolls, J., Hurlburt, M. et al. (2005, September). Parent-training programs in child welfare services: Planning for a more evidence-based approach to serving biological parents. *Research on Social Work Practice, 15*(5), 353–371.

Bavolek, S. J. (2002). *Research and evaluation report of the nurturing parenting programs.* Retrieved 16 September 2006 from http://www.nurturingparenting.com/npp/Research%20$%20Validation %20of%20NPP.pdf.

Bruns, E. J. (2004, October). *The evidence base and wraparound.* Unpublished manuscript, University of Maryland School of Medicine, Division of Child and Adolescent Psychiatry.

Bruns, E. J., Burchard, J. D., Suter, J. C., Leverentz-Brady, L. & Force, M. M. (2004). Assessing fidelity to a community based treatment for youth: The Wraparound Fidelity Index. *Journal of Emotional and Behavioral Disorders, 12,* 79–89.

Burchard, J. D., Bruns, E. J. & Burchard, S. N. (2002). The wraparound approach. In B. J. Burns and K. Hoagwood (Eds.), *Community Treatment for Youth: Evidence-based intervention for severe emotional and behavioral disorders* (pp. 3–15). New York: Oxford University Press.

Burns, B. J. (2003). Children and evidence based practice. *Psychiatric Clinics of North America, 26,* 955–970.

Chamberlain, P. (2003). The Oregon Multidimensional Treatment Foster Care model: Features, outcomes, and progress in dissemination. In S. Schoenwald & S. Henggeler (Series Eds.), Moving evidence-based treatments from the laboratory into clinical practice. *Cognitive and Behavioral Practice, 10*(4), 303–312.

Clausen, J., Landsverk, J., Ganger, W., Chadwick, D. & Litrownik, A. (1998). Mental health problems of children in foster care. *Journal of Child & Family Studies, 7*(3), 283–296.

Cohen, J. A., Mannarino, A. P., Berliner, L. & Deblinger, E. (2000). Trauma-focused cognitive behavioral therapy for children and adolescents: An empirical update. *Journal of Interpersonal Violence, 15,* 1202–1223.

Connor, D. F. & Meltzer, B. M. (2006). *Pediatric psychopharmacology—Fast facts.* New York: Norton.

Coulton, C. J., Korbin, J. E., Su, M. & Chow, J. (1995). Community level factors and child maltreatment rates. *Child Development, 66*(5), 1262–1276.

Dicker, S. & Gordon, E. (2006). Critical connections for children who are abused and neglected: Harnessing the new federal referral provisions for early intervention. infants & young children. *Interdisciplinary Journal of Special Care Practices, 19*(3), 170–178.

DiGiuseppe, D. & Christakis, D., (2003). Continuity of care for children in foster care. *Pediatrics, 111*(3), 208–213.

Duhaime, A., Christian, C. W., Rorke, L. B. & Zimmerman, R. A. (1998). Nonaccidental head injury in infants—The "shaken-baby syndrome." *New England Journal of Medicine 338*(25), 1822–1829.

Durlak, J. & Wells, A. (1997). Primary prevention mental health programs for children and adolescents: A meta-analytic review. *American Journal of Community Psychology, 25*(2), 115–152.

Embry, D. D. (2002). The good behavior game: A best practice candidate as a universal behavioral vaccine. *Clinical Child and Family Psychology Review, 5*(4), 273–297.

Eyberg, S. M. & Robinson, E. A. (1982). Parent-child interaction training: Effects on family functioning. *Journal of Clinical Child Psychology, 11,* 130–137.

Farmer, E., Burns, B., Chapman, M., Phillips, S., Angold, A. & Costello, E. (2001). Use of mental health services by youth in contact with social services. *Social Service Review, 75*(4), 605.

Fisher, P. A., Burraston, B. & Pears, K. (2005). The early intervention foster care program: Permanent placement outcomes From a randomized trial. *Child Maltreatment, 10*(1), 61–71.

Fisher, P. A. & Chamberlain, P. (2000). Multidimensional treatment foster care: A program for intensive parenting, family support, and skill building. *Journal of Emotional and Behavioral Disorders, 8*(3), 155–164.

Fisher, P., Ellis, B. & Chamberlain, P. (1999). Early intervention foster care: A model for preventing risk in young children who have been maltreated. *Children's Services: Social Policy, Research & Practice, 2*(3), 159.

Fixsen, D. L., Naoom, S. F., Blasé, K. A., Friedman, R. M. & Wallace, F. (2005). *Implementation research: A synthesis of the literature* (Louis de la Parte Florida Mental Health Institute, The National Implementation Research Network, FMHI Publication 231). Tampa: University of South Florida.

Forgatch, M. S., Bullock, B. M. & Patterson, G. R. (2004). From theory to practice: Increasing effective parenting through role-play: The Oregon model of parent management training (PMTO). In H. Steiner (Ed.), *Handbook of mental health interventions in children and adolescents: An integrated developmental approach* (pp. 357–365). San Francisco: Jossey-Bass.

Garland, A., Hough, R., McCabe, K., Yeh, M., Wood, P. & Aarons, G. (2001, April). Prevalence of psychiatric disorder in youths across five sectors of care. *American Academy of. Child and Adolescent Psychiatry, 40*(4), 409–417.

Gordon, D. A. (2003). Intervening with troubled youth and their families: Functional family therapy and parenting wisely. In J. McGuire (Ed.), *Treatment and rehabilitation of offenders* (pp. 193–220). Sussex, England: Wiley.

Halfon, N., Mendonca, A. & Berkowitz, G. (1995). Health status of children in foster care. *Archives of Pediatrics and Adolescent Medicine, 149,* 386–392.

Hawkins, R. P., Meadowcroft, P., Trout, B. A. & Luster, W. C. (1985). Foster family-based treatment. *Journal of Clinical Child Psychology 14*(3), 220–228.

Henggeler, S. W. (1999). Multisystemic therapy: An overview of clinical procedures, outcomes, and policy implications. *Child Psychology and Psychiatry Review, 4,* 2–10.

Herschell, A. & McNeil, C. (2005). Theoretical and empirical underpinnings of
parent–child interaction therapy with child physical abuse populations.
*Education & Treatment of Children, 28*(2), 142–162.

Hoagwood, K., Burns, B., Kiser, L., Ringeisen, H. & Schoenwald, S. (2001, September). Evidence-based practice in child and adolescent mental health
services. *Psychiatric Services, 52*(9), 1179–1189.

Horwitz, S., Owens, P. & Simms, M. (2000, July). Specialized assessments for
children in foster care. *Pediatrics, 106*(1), 59–66.

Horner-Johnson, W. & Drum, C. E. (2006). Prevalence of maltreatment of people
with intellectual disabilities: A review of recently published research.
*Mental Retardation and Developmental Disabilities Research Reviews,
12*(1), 57–69.

James, S. (2004). Why do foster care placements disrupt? An investigation of
reasons for placement change in foster care. *Social Service Review, 78*(4),
601–627.

Kamradt, B. (2000). Wraparound Milwaulkee: Aiding youth with mental
health needs. *Juvenile Justice, 7,* 14–23.

Kaplan, S. J., Pelcovitz, D. & Labruna, V. (1999). Child and adolescent abuse
and neglect research: A review of the past 10 years. Part I: Physical and
emotional abuse and neglect. *Journal of the American Academy of Child
and Adolescent Psychiatry, 38*(10), 1214–1222.

Kazdin, A. E. (1997). Parent management training: Evidence, outcomes, and
issues. *Journal of the American Academy of Child & Adolescent Psychiatry.* 36(10):1349-1356.

Kellam, S., Rebok, G. & Ialongo, N. (1994). The course and malleability aggressive behavior from early first grade into middle school: results of a developmental epidemiologically-based preventive trial. *Journal of Child
Psychology, Psychiatry, and Allied Disciplines, 35,* 259–281.

Kendler, K. S. (2001). Twin studies of psychiatric illness. *Archives of General
Psychiatry, 58*(11), 1005–1014.

Kerker, B. D. & Dore, M. M. (2006). Mental health needs and treatment of foster
youth: Barriers and opportunities. *American Journal of Orthopsychiatry,
76*(1), 138–147.

Leslie, L., Hurlburt, M. S., Landsverk, J., Rolls, J. A., Wood, P. & Kelleher, K. J.
(2003, July). Comprehensive assessments for children entering foster care:
A national perspective. *Pediatrics, 112*(1), 134–142.

Liddle, H. A., Dakof, G. A., Parker, K., Diamond, G. S., Barrett, K. & Tejeda,
M. (2001). Multidimensional family therapy for adolescent drug abuse:
Results of a randomized clinical trial. *American Journal of Drug and
Alcohol Abuse, 27*(4), 651–688.

Linares, l. O., Montalto, D., MinMin, L. & Oza, V. (2006). A promising parenting intervention in foster care. *Journal of Consulting & Clinical Psychology, 74*(1), 32–41.

Lutzker, J. R. & Rice, J. M. (1984). Project 12-ways: Measuring outcome of a
large in-home service for treatment and prevention of child abuse and
neglect. *Child Abuse and Neglect, 8,* 519–524.

Lyons, J., MacIntyre, J., Lee, M., Carpinello, S., Zuber, M. & Fazio, M. (2004). Psychotropic medications prescribing patterns for children and adolescents in New York's public mental health system. *Community Mental Health Journal, 40*(2), 101–118.

McClellan, J. & Werry, J. (2003, December). Evidence-based treatments in child and adolescent psychiatry: An inventory. *American Academy of. Child and Adolescent Psychiatry, 42*(12), 1388–1396.

McGloin, J. M. & Widom, C. S. (2001). Resilience among abused and neglected children grown up. *Development and Psychopathology. 13,* 1021–1038.

McNeil, C. B., Herschell, A. D., Gurwitch, R. & Clemens-Mowrer, L. (2004). *An evaluation of a modified training procedure for parent-child interaction therapy with foster parents.* Unpublished manuscript.

Michelson, D., Faries, D., Wernicke, J., Kelsey, D., Kendrick, K., Sallee, F. R. et al. (2001). Atomoxetine in the treatment of children and adolescents with attention-deficit/hyperactivity disorder: a randomized, placebo-controlled, dose-response study. *Pediatrics, 108*(5), e83.

Mick, E., Biederman, J., Faraone, S. V., Sayer, J. & Kleinman, S. (2002). Case-control study of attention-deficit hyperactivity disorder and maternal smoking, alcohol use, and drug use during pregnancy. *Journal of the American Academy of Child & Adolescent Psychiatry, 41*(4), 378–385.

Mihalic, S., Irwin, K., Elliott, D., Fagan, A. & Hansen, D. (2001). *Blueprints for violence prevention, juvenile justice bulletin.* Washington, DC: Office of Juvenile Justice and Delinquency Prevention, Department of Justice.

Mikkelsen, E. J., Bereika, G. M. & McKenzie, J. C. (1993). Short-term family-based residential treatment: An alternative to psychiatric hospitalization for children. *American Journal of Orthopsychiatry, 63*(1), 28–33.

Perry, B. (2002). Childhood experience and the expression of genetic potential: What childhood neglect tells us about nature and nurture. *Brain and Mind, 3,* 79–100.

Pilowsky, D. (1995, September). Psychopathology among children place in family foster care. *Psychiatric Services, 49*(9), 906–910.

Pliszka, S. R., Crismon, M. L., Huges, C. W., Corners, C. K., Emslie, G. J., Jensen, P. S. et al. (2006, June). The Texas consensus conference panel on pharmacotherapy of childhood attention deficit hyperactivity disorder. *Journal of the American Academy of Child & Adolescent Psychiatry, 45*(6), 642–657.

Reddy, L. & Pfeiffer, S. (1997). Effectiveness of treatment foster care with children and adolescents: A review of outcome studies. *American Academy of. Child and Adolescent Psychiatry, 36*(5), 581–587.

Rosenfeld, A., Pilowsky, D., Fine, P., Thorpe, J., Fein, E., Simms, M. et al. (1997, April). Foster care: An update. *Journal of American Academy of Child and Adolescent Psychiatry, 36*(4), 448–456.

Rubin, D., Alessandrini, E., Feudtner, C. & Localio, A. (2004, May). Placement stability and mental health costs for children in foster care. *Pediatrics, 113*(5), 1336–1341.

Sellinger, M. H. (2006). *An investigation of abuse in children with and without disabilities who are in or at risk for state custody.* Unpublished master's thesis, Vanderbilt University, Nashville, TN.

Sexton, T. L. & Alexander, J. F. (1999). *Functional family therapy: Principles of clinical intervention, assessment, and Implementation.* Henderson, NV: RCH Enterprises.

Simms, M. D., Dubowitz, H. & Szilagyi, M. (2000, October). Health care needs of children in the foster care system. *Pediatrics, 106*(4), 909–918.

Spitz, R. A. (1945). Hospitalism: An inquiry into the genesis of psychiatric conditions in early childhood. *Psychoanalytic Study of the Child, 1,* 53–74.

Spitz, R. A. (1946). Hospitalism: A follow-up report on investigation described in volume 1, 1945. *Psychoanalytic Study of the Child, 2,* 113–117.

U.S. General Accounting Office (GAO) (1994). *Foster care: Parental drug abuse has alarming impact on young children* (HEHS-94-89). Washington, DC.

Webster-Stratton, C. & Hammond, M. (1997). Treating children with early-onset conduct problems: A comparison of child and parent training interventions. *Journal of Consulting and Clinical Psychology, 65*(1), 93–109.

Zeitlin, A., Weinberg, L. & Shea, N. (2006). Improving educational prospects for youth in foster care: The education liaison Model. *Intervention in School & Clinic, 41*(5), 267–272.

Zima, B., Bussing, R., Crecelius, G. M., Kaufman, A. & Belin, T. R. (1999). Psychotropic medication use among children in foster care: relationship to severe psychiatric disorders. *American Journal of Public Health, 89*(11), 1732–1735.

Zima, B., Bussing, R., Freeman, S., Yang, X., Belin, T. & Forness, S. (2000). Behavior problems, academic skill delays and school failure among school-aged children in foster care: Their relationship to placement characteristics. *Journal of Child & Family Studies, 9*(1), 87–103.

Zimmer, M & Panko, L., (2006). Developmental status and service use among children in the child welfare system. *Archives of Pediatrics & Adolescent Medicine, 160*(2), 183–188.

# 11

# Children of Parents with
# Mental Illnesses

JOANNE NICHOLSON, JANICE COOPER,
RACHEL FREED AND MAREASA R. ISAACS

## INTRODUCTION

The mental health and well-being of children are intimately intertwined with the mental health and well-being of their parents (NFCMH, 2003). Given the prevalence of mental illnesses in the American population, and the prevalence of parenthood among those with mental illnesses, it is safe to conclude that millions of children will be affected at some point in their lives (Nicholson, Biebel, Williams & Katz-Leavy, 2004). Several decades of research suggest that these children are more likely to have developmental, behavioral and emotional difficulties than are children whose parents' functioning is not compromised by mental illnesses (e.g., Beardslee et al., 1996; Benjamin, Benjamin & Rind, 1998; Goodman & Gotlib, 1999, 2002; Hammen, 2003). Although there is a genetic component to many major mental illnesses, which increases the likelihood that children whose parents have mental illnesses will develop psychopathology, the impact of parental mental illness may be moderated by many factors—for example, individual characteristics of the child and parent as well as family, community and societal characteristics and conditions (Nicholson, Biebel, Hinden, Henry, & Stier, 2001). Given that only the minority of adults living with the symptoms of mental illnesses are diagnosed and receive appropriate treatment and rehabilitation, many children are likely to be impacted, negatively and unnecessarily, by parents' untreated illnesses. Appropriate treatment of parent and child, when indicated, and supportive and preventive interventions to promote healthy functioning and the achievement of desired goals may contribute to positive outcomes for all family members.

A commitment to the primary prevention of psychopathology and mental health promotion for school-age children in families living with parental mental illness is warranted for several reasons.

- Parental mental illness is prevalent (Nicholson et al., 2004).
- Parenting is a meaningful life role for many adults, including those with mental illnesses (Nicholson, Sweeney, & Geller, 1998a; Oyserman, Mowbray, Meares & Firminger, 2000).

- If parents function better, children will too (Weissman et al., 2006).
- There are effective treatment and rehabilitation strategies for adults living with mental illnesses (HHS, 1999).
- Because outcomes are multiply determined, there are ample opportunities for the prevention of problems and the promotion of resilience in children (Nicholson et al., 2001).
- Inattention or inappropriate attention to parental mental illness may have unfortunate and, in the most severe and tragic of cases, life-threatening consequences for children (Nicholson & Biebel, 2002).

## Diagnostic and Definitional Issues

A parent's mental illness is the primary diagnosable condition in this chapter. The parent with a diagnosis is the focus of traditional treatment interventions; the child is the focus if and when an emotional disturbance emerges. Parental mental illness may vary in severity, duration, impairment conferred on functioning, age at onset and treatability. Mental illnesses often co-occur with substance use disorders in adults and commonly accompany many medical illnesses (e.g., hypertension, arthritis, diabetes, cardiac illnesses) (HHS, 1999) that may further compromise an adult's ability to parent. Experiences of violence and related trauma may contribute to mental illness. In a recent study of adults with chronic major depression, for example, 45% experienced childhood physical abuse, 16% experienced childhood sexual abuse and 10% experienced neglect (Nemeroff et al., 2003). The characteristics of a parent's mental illness, the presence of co-occurring illnesses and a parent's experiences of violence and trauma are important factors in considering an adult's capacity to parent effectively and the impact of a parent's mental health on the child at any one point in time.

A parent's access to and participation in effective mental health treatment contribute to outcomes for children. Less than one third of adults with a diagnosable mental illness receive treatment in a year (HHS, 1999). Kessler and colleagues (HHS, 1999) reported that most of those with disorders who do not seek care believe their problems will go away by themselves or that they can handle them on their own. According to Sturm and Sherbourne (HHS, 1999), worry about costs and the inability to obtain an appointment soon enough are other reasons often cited by those not receiving care. Minority group members are less likely to have access to or to receive effective mental health services (HHS, 2001). The fear of losing custody of or contact with children may keep some adults with mental illnesses from seeking treatment in general or from obtaining help with parenting specifically (Nicholson et al., 1998a). However, the desire to parent as well as possible may motivate others to seek treatment (Nicholson et al., 1998a; Oyserman et al., 2000).

## Theoretical Perspectives

There are a number of transactional (biopsychosocial, ecological) models of parenting and parent–child relationships, and they are derived from several literatures: for example, the transactional model of children of depressed mothers (Van Doesum, Hosman, & Riksen-Walraven, 2005); the family model of adult and child development and mental health (Falkov, 2004); and the determinants of parenting process model (Belsky, 1984). Each emphasizes the reciprocity of relationships and multiple determinants of outcomes for parents and children. The parent–child relationship is built on continuous interactions, and the development of the child and the well-being of a parent are the product of these continuous interactions (Van Doesum et al., 2005). Adults and children bring their own characteristics to parent–child interactions, which are set in the context of the family, community and society. Individual and contextual factors serve as stressors or as supports to the relationship and contribute as risk or protective factors for both adults and children. In addition, attachment theory specifically speaks to the importance of a parent's emotional and physical availability in the child's early years, which may be compromised by a parent's disabling mental illness (Jacobsen, 2004).

Our framework for considering the issue of parental mental illness and its impact on children is developmental, multigenerational, family centered and culturally responsive. The strengths and needs as well as expectations and goals of family members change as they develop as individuals and in relation to each other. Parental mental illness may emerge before or after an individual becomes a parent and may occur or recur when children are at different ages and stages of development. Parenting experiences and family life have differing significance to and impact on individuals at different ages and stages. Parent–child relationships are reciprocal and dynamic; that is, the well-being of each affects the other. Parents and children must be viewed in the context of the family as defined by them and as influenced by gender, culture, ethnicity and race.

## Prevalence

One in five Americans has a mental disorder in any one year (HHS, 1999). The majority of adults meeting diagnostic criteria for disorders in the major categories of affective and anxiety disorders, posttraumatic stress disorder (PTSD) and nonaffective psychoses are parents with an average of approximately two children (Nicholson et al., 2004). Therefore, it is likely that many American children will be exposed to parental mental illness over the course of their lifetime.

Analyses of data from the National Co-Morbidity Survey indicate approximately 25% of mothers and 15% of fathers met criteria for affective disorder diagnoses (e.g., bipolar disorder type I, major depression, dysthymia) during their lifetime (Nicholson et al., 2004). Though women between the ages of 18 and 45 are particularly vulnerable to depression, men are by no means immune. More than 6 million men in the United States have depression each year (NIMH, 2005). Significant percents of women and men meeting diagnostic criteria for a range of disorders are parents: 68% of women with anxiety disorders are mothers and 56% of men are fathers; 73% of women with PTSD are mothers and 68% of men are fathers; and 62% of women with nonaffective psychotic disorders are mothers and 55% of men are fathers. The majority of women and men living in the community and meeting criteria for serious mental illness are parents as well (Nicholson et al., 2004).

Research studies provide evidence that from 30% to 50% of children whose parents have mental illness develop problems of their own (Nicholson et al., 2001); this is compared with an estimated rate of up to approximately 20% among the general child population (HHS, 1999). These difficulties range from developmental delays to behavioral and emotional difficulties to impaired functioning in school or relationships. The psychiatric diagnosis of a parent alone is not predictive of poor outcomes in offspring; that is, it does not automatically confer the risk of developing that specific disorder or symptoms severe enough to warrant psychiatric diagnosis in children. It is important to note that children may or may not have problems and that their problems may or may not fit a particular diagnostic category. Some children whose parents have mental illnesses may be quite resilient. Their coping strategies and the resources available to them may allow them to develop normally and even to excel.

Opportunities for the identification of children who would benefit from prevention and health promotion strategies are often overlooked. Strategies for identifying and addressing the mental health of parents and for enhancing the well-being of children are not routinely applied in settings in which adults who are parents and their children are frequently seen. For example, 48% of mothers and 18% of fathers with children in Early Head Start programs meet diagnostic criteria for depression at enrollment; though Early Head Start had no effect on parental depression or family use of mental health services, the program did have a positive impact on parent–child relationships (Early Head Start, 2003). Pediatric practitioners may not routinely inquire about parental well-being (Nicholson & Clayfield, 2004), though recent research suggests that brief screening for maternal depression, for example in pediatric settings, is feasible and that additional discussion time regarding depression and stress, though brief, leads mothers to seek support from primary care providers, social and community services, their spiritual communities, friends and spouses as well as mental health services (Olson, Dietrich, Prazar & Hurley, 2006). Mental health providers working with adults may not routinely inquire regarding the adult's roles and responsibilities as a parent (Aldridge & Becker, 2003; Biebel, Nicholson, Geller, & Fisher 2006; Nicholson, Geller, Fisher & Dion, 1993). Clinicians may feel they lack the skills to deal with child and family issues or that their adult clients may become upset when talking about child issues (Stallard, Norman, Huline-Dickens, Salter & Cribb, 2004). Mental health providers should be encouraged to ask adult clients about their goals and status as parents, to develop networks for the referral of identified family members to appropriate services and to educate their colleagues and other allied professionals regarding the needs of families living with parental mental illness.

## BIOLOGICAL AND GENETIC FACTORS

Research studies over the past several decades have demonstrated a significant genetic component in the development of mental illnesses. Family, twin and adoption studies reveal that particular psychiatric diagnoses aggregate in families and that parental mental illness is a critical risk factor for child psychiatric symptoms and disorders. The preponderance of research has focused exclusively on psychopathology in mothers as a risk factor for children, neglecting to account for psychopathology and other factors in fathers. The exclusion of paternal influences in the research is likely due to a variety of methodological and sociocultural factors: for example, the assumption that fathers are less willing to participate in research; the thought that certain forms of psychopathology, such as depression, are more prevalent among women; a higher likelihood that women with psychological disorders will be mothers than that men with psychological disorders will be fathers; and the high incidence of children living in homes with single mothers (Connell & Goodman, 2002). However, because children receive 50% of their genes from their fathers, paternal data is vital to understanding genetic transmission of mental illnesses.

More recently, researchers have increasingly begun to focus their research on children of both mothers and fathers with mental illness. However, it is unclear whether the genders confer equal genetic influence on offspring in terms of psychopathology. For this reason, some studies have examined the relative influences of maternal versus paternal psychopathology. For example, Connell and Goodman (2002) found that externalizing problems in children were equally related to the presence of psychopathology in mothers and fathers but that internalizing problems were more closely related to presence of psychopathology in mothers than in fathers.

The psychiatric illnesses listed in this section are prevalent among pediatric populations and are assumed to have a genetic component. This section describes what is known about the genetic transmission of these disorders and the relative risks to offspring.

## Schizophrenia and Psychotic Disorder

Extensive evidence from family, twin and adoption studies supports the role of genetic factors in the etiology of schizophrenia. First-degree relatives of persons with schizophrenia are significantly more likely to develop the disorder compared with the general population (HHS, 1999; Tsuang, Stone, & Faraone, 1999). Some estimates indicate that the risk of developing schizophrenia is as much as 10 times greater if an immediate biological relative has the disorder (HHS, 1999). Twin studies reveal a concordance rate of approximately 50% in monozygotic twins (Tsuang et al., 1999).

Most of the research on the heritability of schizophrenia has focused on adult offspring of parents with the disorder, as the onset of schizophrenia typically occurs in late adolescence and early adulthood. Childhood-onset schizophrenia (i.e., the onset of psychiatric symptoms by age 12) is extremely rare. However, people who develop schizophrenia during childhood appear to have a greater genetic vulnerability for the disorder than people who develop schizophrenia as adults (Kumra, Shaw, Merka, Nakayama & Augustin, 2001; Nicolson et al., 2003). Nicolson and colleagues (2003) found that parents of children with childhood-onset schizophrenia had a higher rate of schizophrenia spectrum disorders (e.g., schizophrenia, schizoaffective disorder, other nonaffective psychosis, schizotypal personality disorder) than parents of offspring with adult-onset schizophrenia.

Children of parents with schizophrenia are also at risk for a number of other maladaptive outcomes. Schizophrenia spectrum disorders tend to occur at higher rates in children of parents with schizophrenia than in the normal child population (Hans, Auerbach, Styr & Marcus, 2004; Kendler & Gardner, 1997; Niemi, Suvisaari, Haukka, Wrede & Lonnqvist, 2004). In addition, studies have shown that nonpsychotic offspring of parents with schizophrenia are at risk for developing thought disorder and mild to moderate cognitive impairment (Heydebrand, 2006; Tsuang et al., 1999). Specifically, this population has increased deficits in working memory, verbal memory and concept formation and has increased difficulty with tasks involving higher demand for effective encoding and increased memory load (ibid.).

## Depression

Studies have found that children of parents with depression are more than three times as likely as children with nondepressed parents to experience a depressive disorder (HHS, 1999). Although a number of environmental factors have been implicated in this association, genetic influences appear to be more important than environmental risk factors as a predictor of major depression in offspring (Fendrich, Warner & Weissman, 1990; Sullivan, Neale & Kendler, 2000). An estimated 20% to 50% of children and adolescents with depression have a family history of depression (HHS, 1999), and the degree of risk increases with the number of affected relatives (Goodman & Gotlib, 1999). Although the genetic influence on the development of depressive symptoms increases as children grow into adolescence (Scourfield et al., 2003), it appears that younger age of onset is associated with greater family occurrence of major depressive disorder (Lieb, Isensee, Hofler, Pfister, & Wittchen, 2002; Weissman et al., 1987). Weissman and colleagues (1987) found that early-onset depression in mothers is associated with a 14-fold increase in the risk of onset of major depression before age 13 in their children (Weissman, Warner, & Wickramaratne, 1988).

Children of parents with depression are also at risk for poor functioning in other areas. For example, a number of studies have linked parental depression with increased anxiety disorders in offspring (Foley et al., 2001; Lieb et al., 2002; Weissman et al., 1987). Research examining children of parents with depression has also revealed that this population is more likely to experience behavior and conduct disorders, substance abuse, poorer social functioning and worse academic performance (Anderson & Hammen, 1993; Foley et al., 2001).

## Bipolar Disorder

The most rigorous twin study reveals that the heritability of bipolar disorder is approximately 59% (HHS, 1999). Bipolar disorder in offspring tends to be associated with earlier parental symptom onset (Chang, Steiner, & Ketter, 2000). Children of parents with bipolar disorder are significantly more likely to develop mood and affective disorders (e.g., anxiety, unipolar depression, dysthymia, bipolar disorder) than the general child population (Chang et al., 2000; Delbello & Geller, 2001; Henin et al., 2005; Lapalme, Hodgins, & LaRoche, 1997). Interestingly, research by Hillegers and colleagues (2005) suggests that unipolar depression in bipolar offspring may actually be the first sign of the development of bipolar disorder.

Delbello & Geller (2001) found that rates of nonmood-disordered psychopathology in offspring of parents with bipolar disorder range from 5% to 52% compared with 0% to 25% in healthy volunteers. Offspring of parents with bipolar disorder have elevated rates of disruptive behavior disorders (Henin et al., 2005) and attention deficit hyperactivity disorder (ADHD) (Anderson & Hammen, 1993). However, the degree of dysfunction appears to be greater in children of mothers with unipolar depression than in children of mothers with bipolar disorder (Hillegers et al., 2005).

## Anxiety Disorder

Merikangas, Lieb, Wittchen and Avenevoli (2003) estimated that first-degree relatives of persons with any anxiety disorder have a three- to five-fold increased risk of developing anxiety disorders compared with the general population. The specificity of such associations is often difficult to interpret due to high comorbidity rates of anxiety and other affective disorders (Foley et al., 2001). Yet despite research challenges related to comorbidity, several researchers have shown that parental anxiety disorders are significantly associated with increased risk for anxiety disorders in offspring irrespective of co-occurring psychopathology (Beidel & Turner, 1997; Biederman et al., 2006). The picture becomes even more complex in light of studies showing a difference in genetic influence between mothers and fathers. For example, McClure, Brennan, Hammen and Le Brocque (2002) found that maternal—but not paternal—anxiety was significantly associated with the presence of anxiety disorders in children. Even so, risk appears to be highest when both parents have anxiety disorders, especially among offspring with childhood-onset anxiety disorders (Biederman et al., 2005).

All of the major subtypes of the anxiety disorders appear to aggregate in families. These include panic disorder, generalized anxiety disorder, social anxiety, phobias, separation anxiety and obsessive compulsive disorder (Bellodi, Sciuto, Diaferia, Ronchi, & Smeraldi, 1992; Biederman et al., 2005; Black, Gaffney, Schlosser & Gabel, 2003; Hettema, Neale, & Kendler 2001; Merikangas et al., 2003). However, panic disorder appears to have highest degree of familial loading compared with other anxiety subtypes (Hettema et al., 2001; Merikangas et al., 2003). In addition, children of parents with panic disorder have been found to exhibit more severe diagnoses and higher rates of comorbidity (Unnewhr, Schneider, Florin, & Margraf, 1998).

## Attention Deficit Hyperactivity Disorder

Although the research on ADHD is newer, a number of studies conducted over the past few decades reveal that ADHD has a significant genetic component (Biederman, Faraone, Keenan, Knee & Tsuang, 1990; Minde et al., 2003). Specifically, between 10% and 35% of children with ADHD have a first-degree relative with past or present ADHD (HHS, 1999). Research also shows that approximately 57% of parents with past ADHD have a child with the disorder (Biederman et al., 1995), and this association persists irrespective of environmental exposure to parental ADHD (Biederman, Faraone & Monuteaux, 2002). In addition, mothers and fathers appear to confer equal genetic risk on their sons and daughters (Biederman et al., 1990; Faraone et al., 2000).

## Eating Disorders

The two major forms of eating disorders—anorexia nervosa and bulimia nervosa—have been found to aggregate in families (Strober, Freeman, Lampert, Diamond & Kaye, 2000). This finding suggests that anorexia nervosa and bulimia nervosa may be linked genetically or, perhaps, that the predisposition to develop an eating disorder is inherited and may be expressed as one form of illness or the other. Studies have found between a 5- and 12-fold increase in occurrence of anorexia nervosa and bulimia nervosa in relatives of individuals with eating disorders compared with controls (Jacobi, Hayward, de Zwann, Kraemer, & Agras, 2004; Patel, Wheatcroft, Park, & Stein, 2002; Strober et al., 2000). Twin studies reveal a concordance rate of approximately 50% in monozygotic twins (Patel et al., 2002). Due to the disproportionate sex ratio for eating disorders, most of the research has focused on female participants; however, a study by Strober, Freeman, Lampert, Diamond and Kaye (2001) found that anorexia nervosa is also transmitted in families of males with the disorder.

Children of mothers with anorexia and bulimia have elevated rates of affective disorders (Jacobi et al., 2004; Patel et al., 2002). In addition, relatives of individuals with eating disorders are at increased risk for developing partial eating disorder syndromes (i.e., milder variations of anorexia nervosa and bulimia nervosa) (Strober et al., 2000). Full and partial syndromes often co-occur with symptoms of major depression in individuals, suggesting the two disorders share genetic risk factors (Wade, Bulik, Neale & Kendler, 2000; Walters & Kendler, 1995).

Although it is clear that certain mental illnesses run in families, twin studies reveal that genetic transmission alone cannot account for the occurrence of psychiatric symptoms and disorders. Other individual and environmental variables related to parenting, family relationships and sociocultural context are implicated in the development of psychopathology in children and youth. Family history may confer risk to a child, yet the development of psychiatric disorders likely involves a complex relationship between genes and environment. Researchers are still trying to understand the relative contributions of each.

## INDIVIDUAL FACTORS INFLUENCING RISK AND RESILIENCY IN CHILDREN WHOSE PARENTS HAVE MENTAL ILLNESS

Risk and resiliency are examined broadly here for two reasons: (1) The paucity of literature on individual factors that specifically contribute to resilience for children of parents living with mental illness; and (2) the overlap with risk and protective factors that influence adjustment for all youth (Hammen, 2003; Luthar, 2003; Radke-Yarrow, Zahn-Wexler, Richardson, Susman & Martinez, 1994). Researchers hone in on factors considered protective (i.e., indirect impact in the face of risk), promotive (i.e., direct link to resilience), compensory (i.e., deemed beneficial even in the absence of risk) and resourceful (i.e., benefit both high and low risk groups) (Fergusson & Harwood, 2003; Hammen, 2003; Sameroff, Gutman & Peck, 2003). Here the term *protective factor* is used throughout.

Individual factors contributing to risk and resilience for children and youth in general may have heightened implications for children living with the additional stressor of a parent whose functioning is actively impaired by mental illness. A child's inherent capacity for resilience may be influenced by a genetic predisposition to the development of mental health problems as well as by impairments in the parent's functioning over time. There is general agreement that risks have a multiplier effect; in the face of cumulative stressors for some youth, however, resilience is manifested, and they adjust well (Masten & Powell, 2003). Much of the research shows that individual factors lack primacy in their influence on resilience. Other factors, such as family functioning and community characteristics, often prove more critical (Cauce, Stewart, Rodriguez, Cochran, & Ginzler, 2003; Kumpfer, 1999). The impact of a parent's mental illness may be reflected in family, social and community factors such as the quality of the marital relationship and family supports available to the child or limited financial resources related to a parent's inability to sustain employment. Factors such as these are discussed in the next sections of this chapter.

Competence is the overarching quality associated with positive adjustment and resilience for all children (Masten & Powell, 2003; Wyman et al., 1999). Universally, youth are expected to meet a range of context-based, age-appropriate and community-determined developmental tasks associated with their school, with their relationships with friends and with their behavior in a range of settings, such as home, school and their community. With age, different social and cultural contexts and, therefore, different domains of competence become relevant (Masten & Powell, 2003). Individual attributes including mental health, intelligence and academic achievement, problem-solving skills, personality, social competence and engagement and self-esteem are important to competence and, hence, to resilience. Individual experiences of violence and trauma may compromise resilience.

The risks associated with mental health disorders are most evident in the genetic vulnerability posed to children of individuals with mental illness and in their heightened risk for the development of mental health problems (Hammen, 2003). Cuffe, McKeown, Addy, & Garrison's (2005) analysis of the impact of psychosocial stress on vulnerability to mental health disorders shows important racial, ethnicity and gender differences in the development of mental health disorders generally and in anxiety and affective disorders specifically. African American females are at lower risk than Whites or African American males for any disorders. More females are among youth with anxiety disorders and affective disorders (ibid.).

Intelligence promotes resilience. A multidirectional and dynamic factor, intelligence interacts with motivation and academic achievement (Luster, Lekskul, & Oh, 2004; Luthar & Zelazo, 2003; Masten & Powell, 2003). Youth of parents with mental illness with superior intelligence tend to adapt better than youth who are less intelligent (Luthar & Zelazo, 2003). Intelligence, though predictive of resilience, remains a weak estimator in comparison with environmental factors and individual attributes such as self-esteem (Sameroff et al., 2003). Indeed, irrespective of innate intellectual abilities, youth of parents with depression, who develop knowledge and understanding of parental illness and coping skills to be independent outside the home, adjust positively and have fewer mental health problems (Beardslee, Wright et al., 1997).

Linked to intelligence, school stands as a critical domain for youth resilience. Mental health and early learning are positively associated with resilience and a range of improved outcomes for adolescents in school, including eighth-grade reading level and high school completion, and in juvenile justice (Clements, Reynolds & Hickey, 2004; Gutman, Sameroff & Cole, 2003). Youth who succeed in school experience fewer symptoms of depression and exhibit fewer conduct problems (Gerard & Buehler, 2004). Academic achievement proves pertinent across the socioeconomic spectrum; among affluent suburban adolescents, it is protective against substance use (McMahon & Luthar, 2006).

Scholastic achievement is less protective for African American youth (Gerard & Buehler, 2004).

Although intelligence and knowledge foster competence, youth perception of peer relations and acceptance in peer groups contribute significantly to demonstrated competence in social contexts (Masten, 2005). Urban middle school students show clear links between perceived peer-group attributes and symptoms of mental health problems (Seidman & Pedersen, 2003). Youth who depict their peer affiliations as prosocial appear protected against depression and antisocial behavior. Although youth who describe their peer groups as antisocial and engaging or as disengaging and accepting are also protected against depressive symptoms, they are more likely to exhibit antisocial behavior (ibid.). African American youth are more likely to portray their peer profile as rejecting, and White youth represent theirs as antisocial and disengaging. Boys and younger youth connect with a disengaging and accepting profile (ibid.).

Personality traits can be protective in successful adaptation. Certain aspects of personality or temperament such as self-regulation, surgency or prosocial abilities support positive adjustments whereas others, including negative emotionality and impulsivity, can serve as risk factors for negative outcomes (Wyman et al., 1999). Self-regulation and emotionality are linked with both positive and negative adaptation in third to fifth graders (Lengua, 2002). Positive emotionality is associated with resilience, whereas negative emotionality leads to problems with adjustment. Youth with high self-regulation are more likely to have fewer problems adjusting, whereas youth with low levels of self-regulation are more vulnerable at even lower levels of risk (Jaser et al., 2005; Lengua, 2002). In the face of parental hostility and marital discord, adolescents with better emotional control are less likely to exhibit hostility (Schultz, Waldinger, Hauser & Allen, 2005). Emotional regulation also shields some youth exposed to violence from internalizing problems (Kliewer et al., 2004). For youth of parents with depression, self-regulation is linked to lower levels of depressive and anxiety-related symptoms and to a reduction of parental intrusion (Jaser et al., 2005). Conversely, lack of control in response to parent-induced stress leads to more symptoms of depression and anxiety. Boys are more likely to exhibit poor self-regulation than girls (Else-Quest, Hyde, Goldsmith & Van Hulle, 2006; Jaser et al., 2005).

Self-esteem proves one of the most sensitive predictors of youths' ability to rebound. A sense of self-worth is associated with an increased likelihood of adjustment in the face of adversity, with reduced depressive symptoms and with a lower likelihood of developing conduct-related problems (Gerard & Buehler, 2004). But racial, ethnic and gender-based differences characterize the intensity of the effect of self-esteem (Gerard & Buehler, 2004; McDonald et al., 2005). Hammen (2003) identified a number of studies in which positive self-worth is linked to positive adjustment for both children and youth whose mothers had depression and for those whose mothers did not have depression and who were deemed lower risk.

Engaged youth appear to possess enhanced self-esteem. Religiosity and spirituality are youth factors at the core of engagement for some youth. Participation in religious activities and saliency with religion are instrumental in shaping prosocial behaviors, in developing relationships with adults, in increasing self-esteem and in creating positive peer affiliation as well as reducing risky behaviors among African Americans at high risk (King & Furrow, 2004; Kogan, Luo, Murry & Brody, 2005). Engagement also surfaces as a protective factor in the form of racial, ethnic and cultural identity. Ethnic identity is associated with resilience against discrimination, substance abuse and violence for multiracial youth (Choi, Harachi, Gillmore & Catalano, 2006). Strong cultural affiliation moderates the relationship between low self-esteem and internalizing factors among primarily native-born Mexican American girls (McDonald et al., 2005). Collectively, positive youth experience in more than one setting increases the likelihood of fewer depressive symptoms and enhanced self-esteem (Seidman & Pedersen, 2003).

Risks associated with trauma and exposure to violence also present challenges for adjustment. For bereaved children, coping skills and the ability to interpret negative events relative to their own well-being are important personal attributes (Lin, Sandler, Ayers, Wolchik & Luecken, 2004). Youth exposed to violence experience more learning and academic problems and more externalizing and internalizing problems (Gorman-Smith & Tolan, 2003). High prosocial abilities prove protective for these youth against committing violence (Brookmeyer, Henrich, & Schwab-Stone, 2005). Similar studies of violence-exposed youth link individual factors such as temperament and external factors such as family functioning to youth's ability to rebound (Gorman-Smith & Tolan, 2003; Kliewer et al., 2004).

A variant of trauma, maltreatment places youth at increased risk for poor adjustment. Children who have been maltreated are at increased risk for mental health problems (Kaplan et al., 1998). The impact on psychological adaptation of child maltreatment is well documented (Cicchetti & Toth, 2005). Flores, Cicchetti and Rogosch (2005) demonstrated the differential impact on adaptive processes among Latino child survivors of maltreatment. In their study, maltreated Latino children had lower measures of resilience than nonmaltreated Latino children. Female status was positively related to high resilience functioning (ibid.).

## FAMILY FACTORS INFLUENCING RISK AND RESILIENCY

Although much of the increased vulnerability and risk for children is associated with genetic transmission of psychiatric conditions from parent to offspring (31% to 42%), more than 60% of the probability of children experiencing mental disorders under these circumstances depends on the family environment and community context that, unlike genetics, can be significantly modified (Beardslee, 2002; Goodman & Gotlib, 2002; Lorant et al., 2003; Seifer, 2003; Seifert, Bowman, Heflin, Danziger & Williams, 2000). The influence of parents, especially mothers experiencing depression, has been well documented in the research and treatment literature. Since depression is the most common and most widespread mental disorder, the findings from this body of research provide much of the context for examining family factors that influence risk and resiliency for children who live with parents with mental illness (Beardslee, 2002; Hammen, 1991).

Mental illness in family members, especially mothers, often increases vulnerability in children at all ages (Goodman & Gotlib, 1999, 2002; Seifer, 2003). Children with mothers who are depressed are four to six times more likely than children without depressed mothers to experience poor developmental outcomes (Goodman & Gotlib, 1999, 2002; Riley & Broitman, 2003). For instance, research on infants with depressed mothers find that the babies are often more fussy, obtain lower scores on measures of mental and motor development and are often reported by their mothers to have more difficult temperaments (Carro, Grant, Gotlib, & Compas, 1993; Goodman & Gotlib, 1999; Tarullo & Cohen, 2003). In school-age children, those with mothers with depression often have lower levels of academic achievement, exhibit more behavioral problems and have lower levels of social competence and poorer physical health (Isaacs, 2004; Riley & Broitman, 2003). Adolescents of mothers with depression are at a much higher likelihood of suffering from an affective disorder or other psychiatric disorder (Hammen & Brennan, 2001; Roberts, Roberts & Chen, 1997).

Studies have consistently indicated that parenting skills are the single most important way parental mental illness impacts children (Goodman & Gotlib, 2002; Heneghan, Mercer & DeLeone, 2004; Lovejoy, Graczyk, O'Hare & Neuman, 2000). Maternal sensitivity, levels of positive parenting and strong early mother–child attachment and bonding are critical aspects of parenting that are often impacted by parental mental illness. Strengthening parenting skills can be viewed as one strategy for reducing risks and increasing resiliency, especially for young children with depressed parents. Tarullo & Cohen (2003) found that depressed mothers who participated in the Early Head Start parenting skills program demonstrated improved parent–child relationships, especially in parent–child interaction and in consistent discipline.

Although various aspects of parenting, especially for young children, have been extensively studied, several other family factors also place children at increased risk for poor outcomes. Early stresses in the family environment (e.g., the presence of abuse or neglect, witnessing quarreling or violence, living with a substance abuser) are related to a greater risk of depressive symptomatology in young adults (Taylor et al., 2006). Taylor and colleagues (2006) report gene-by-environment interactions in that individuals who are homozygous carriers of the short allele of the serotonin transporter gene-linked polymorphic region exhibit greater depressive symptomatology as young adults if they experience early or recent adversity. A supportive early environment or recent positive experiences are related to less depressive symptomatology in these same young adults.

The presence of another parenting adult or caregiver in the household, most often a father, can mitigate any maternal parenting deficits. However, much of this depends on the quality of the marital or adult relationship and the availability of another supportive adult on a consistent basis. However, some parents with mental illness report that family members can undermine their efforts to parent, especially if they have negative attitudes about mental illness or treatment (Nicholson, Sweeney & Geller, 1998b). Thus, family members can be a source of strength or additional liability for children with parents suffering from mental illness.

Parental mental illness increases the likelihood of relationship and family disruptions, which may convey costs to children and parents alike. Children may be separated from parents who are hospitalized for mental illnesses. Though the prevalence of child abuse among parents with mental illness is unknown, parental mental illness poses a significant challenge to the child welfare system (i.e., in particular, the lack of mental health services for parents) (GAO, 2006). Mental illness is related to a higher likelihood of marital discord and divorce (Downey & Coyne, 1990; Fendrich et al., 1990; Weintraub, 1987). Parents with mental illnesses are vulnerable to custody loss, whether through the intervention of child protective services or through divorce proceedings (Nicholson et al., 2001). Though the safety and well-being of children are priorities, disrupted family relationships convey risk to children, parents and communities.

Family social supports and resources are also often related to the socioeconomic status of the family, with children growing up in poor families more likely to experience the negative side effects of parental mental illness (Lorant et al., 2003). Poverty and mental illness are highly correlated and often place increased stress and strain on families and children (Coiro, 2001; Costello, Compton, Keeler & Angold, 2003; Heneghan, Silver, Bauman, Westbrook & Stein, 1998; Seifert et al., 2000). Families experiencing poverty are less likely to have the financial resources to access mental health treatment, quality child care or other resources that often minimize the impact of parental mental illness in higher-income families (Beardslee et al., 1992; Beardslee, Keller, Lavori, Staley & Sacks, 1993).

The correlation between low income and mental disorders places many mothers and families of color at greater risk for negative child outcomes when children live with parental mental illness (Costello et al., 2003). For example, the prevalence of depression is twice as high among low-income mothers and mothers of color compared with their White counterparts—25% compared with 12% for the general female caregiver population in the United States (Coiro, 2001; Heneghan et al., 1998; Isaacs, 2004; Seifert et al., 2000). Families of color are also twice as likely to live in poverty (Heilemann, Frutos, Lee & Kury, 2004; Isaacs, 2004). Children are twice as likely to grow up in single-parent households or households where parents are separated, divorced or widowed. These families are likely to experience more adverse circumstances (e.g., discrimination, parental health problems, involvement with the criminal justice system, substandard housing, poor quality child care and health resources, limited employment opportunities) that complicate family life and place children at much higher risk. Parents in these circumstances are also more likely to experience comorbidities with mental illness that may include substance abuse, high levels of stress and anxiety, domestic violence and trauma, all of which exacerbate and exponentially increase risks to their children (Isaacs, 2004; Jones & Shorter-Gooden, 2003; Miranda & Green, 1999).

Thus, it is not parental mental illness alone but also the impact of poverty and other social factors that create the higher risk status of children of color. However, even in these circumstances, children show remarkable resiliency. Poor families with strong parenting skills, solid social supports and viable employment opportunities can protect their children from the impact of parental mental illness (Heilemann et al., 2004). However, the lack of access to mental health treatment for both parents and children and the poor quality of treatment that is often provided act as major impediments to building resiliency within families of color (Isaacs, 2004; Miranda & Cooper, 2004; Miranda & Green, 1999).

The impact of family factors varies across the developmental age spectrum of the child (Goodman & Gotlib, 2002; Wickramaratne & Weissman, 1998). Family factors place children most at risk in infancy and the early years of development when children are almost totally dependent on parental caregivers for the nurturing and supportive guidance needed for healthy development. Once children start school and grow into adolescence, other influences such as teachers, peers, other adult mentors, outside activities and academic achievement mitigate and moderate the potential risks from parental mental illness and support and strengthen resiliency (Fergusson & Harwood, 2003).

## SOCIAL AND COMMUNITY FACTORS

Bronfenbrenner (1981) highlighted the importance of social and community factors in his ecological model of human development. His model acknowledged that humans do not develop in isolation but in relation to their family and home, school, community and society. Each of these ever-changing and multilevel environments, as well as interactions among these environments, is key to healthy development. Blyth and Roelkepartian (1993) also acknowledged the importance of community in the healthy development of children and adolescents. They identified strengths in communities that support resiliency in youth: (1) opportunities to participate in community life; (2) avenues to contribute to the welfare of others; (3) opportunities to connect with peers and adults in the community; and (4) adequate access to community facilities and events. Despite the African proverb, "It takes a village to raise a child," the social and community factors acknowledged as important influences on the quality of life and well-being for children and adolescents in general and for those who reside with parents with mental illness in particular have not been sufficiently researched or used as resources by the mental health field (e.g., Earls & Carlson, 2001).

For the most part, mental health systems tend to focus on the characteristics of individuals suffering from mental disorders and on their interactions within family systems as the major locus of research and service intervention. In moving toward a public health model for mental health, it is increasingly important to understand the roles that community environment and context play in increasing or mediating risk or for strengthening and developing resiliency in children and youth (NFCMH, 2003).

Historically, empirical studies of community context tend to focus overwhelmingly on neighborhoods that are resource poor—that is, urban inner cities or rural areas where a multiplicity of factors, such as poverty, underemployment, inadequate housing, limited transportation, poor schools and other risks overdetermine great stress on families in their child-rearing roles and often limit access to needed resources and quality services. More recently, however, there has been a rekindled interest in understanding the impact of communities on child well-being and parental functioning. Recent studies provide increasing evidence that communities play a major role in supporting resiliency in youth, both directly and indirectly, and that some components of the community can also play a buffering role in reducing and mitigating risks (Garbarino, Dubrow, Kostelny, & Pardo, 1992; Gorman-Smith & Tolan, 2003; Sampson, 2001).

The relationship between community and mental illness is not entirely clear. However, we do know that living in poor, urban communities, being homeless or residing in substandard housing as well as resource-poor environments increase the likelihood of more severe disability from mental disorders.

Studies have consistently indicated that stress related to high-density urban environments tends to exacerbate risks for children and adolescents.

## EVIDENCE-BASED TREATMENT INTERVENTIONS

### What Works

A review of the literature did not uncover any intervention that met the criteria of three successful trials.

### What Might Work

### *What Children Whose Parents Have Mental Illness Need*

There are several sources of information about the impact of parental mental illness on children: (1) the reports of children themselves—that is, adult children who report retrospectively on their experiences growing up with parents who had mental illness—and study participants who are children at the time of research participation; (2) more recent work in Australia and the United Kingdom with young carers (i.e., children or youth caring for a parent compromised by illness); (3) the reports of parents with mental illness themselves; and (4) research studies of, typically, mothers who meet diagnostic criteria for specific mental illness diagnoses such as depression. Conclusions regarding the needs of these children and youth suggest targets for prevention, intervention and support strategies. Recommendations for what might work can be derived from these reports.

Diane Marsh and colleagues (see, e.g., Marsh, 1992; Marsh & Lefley, 1996; Marsh et al., 1993) wrote about the experiences of adult children of parents with mental illnesses. In interview and survey studies conducted by these authors and others, adult children report both negative and positive outcomes of having grown up with a parent with mental illness (Kinsella & Anderson, 1996). Negative consequences include feelings of isolation, poor self-esteem, anger, shame, anxiety and difficulty in relationships. Positive outcomes include the development of personal strength, resiliency and self-reliance; feelings of independence, compassion and empathy; sensitivity; resourcefulness; the ability to create and accomplish, along with other life skills; and the development of spiritual and life perspectives. Participants in these studies reported both subjective as well as objective burdens of having an ill parent and discussed the powerful impact of stigma and the effects of not understanding or being able to talk about their parents' illnesses. The authors made several recommendations for supports for children and families: (1) acknowledgement of the needs of all family members; (2) identification of resources outside the family; (3) adequate information and education about mental illness; (4) organized groups for children and teens that foster peer support, provide information and education, and reduce isolation; and (5) competency-based models that support resilience and alleviate burden to children through the development of coping skills and resource networks. It is important to remember that children who are adults at the time of research participation grew up in times when mental health treatment and rehabilitation strategies were not as effective as they are today and when the stigma associated with mental illness was, perhaps, even more pervasive.

Studies of children and youth themselves corroborate many of the positive and negative consequences of parental mental illness reported by adult children (e.g., Fudge & Mason, 2004; Garley, Gallop, Johnston & Pipitone, 1997; Riebschleger, 2004). Children and youth identify key issues, including (1) the lack of practical and emotional supports for children and families; (2) communication problems with service providers and family members and, therefore, the lack of information about mental illness; (3) the impact of hospitalizations and separations from ill parents; and (4) additional caregiving responsibilities. Children place the issues of living with parental mental illness in the larger context of ongoing family stress, including poverty, parental divorce and siblings running away from home (Riebschleger, 2004). They describe relationships with supportive adults, participation in activities, time out away from home and having someone to talk with as extremely helpful to coping. Children and youth recommend, and authors concluded the following (Fudge & Mason, 2004; Riebschleger, 2004):

1. Services should be family and child centered.
2. Inpatient psychiatric facilities should be more welcoming and family friendly.
3. Children should have personal care plans in place for times when parents are hospitalized or unable to care for them.
4. Extra help for families should include assistance with finances, transportation and domestic and emotional supports.
5. Social and recreational activities for parents and children together and separately would benefit families.
6. Peer supports are key.

Handley, Farrell, Josephs, Hanke and Hazelton (2001) recommended a programmatic focus on personal competency to promote social, emotional and cognitive development for children and the adoption of a family conference model to increase the competence of the extended family to provide support to parents with mental illness and their children.

Stallard and colleagues (2004) obtained both children's and parents' perspectives on the impact of parental mental illnesses and on the needs of children and families. Though the majority of parents reported their children are affected by their mental illnesses and half indicated their children worry about their illnesses, the majority did not feel their children understand about their illnesses. Nearly half of the children reported that no one talks with them about their parents' illnesses, though most of the parents thought it would be helpful and half the children wanted to know more. Almost one third of the parents and almost half the children felt that having more information, however, might have a negative effect (e.g., feel burdensome or confusing). Children worried about their parents and wished they would "get better."

Young carers of parents with mental illness have come to the attention of policy makers, providers and consumer advocates primarily in countries other than the United States (Aldridge & Becker, 2003). A young carer is defined in the United Kingdom as "a child or young person (under age 18) who is carrying out significant caring tasks and assuming a level of responsibility for another person which would usually be taken by an adult" (Falkov, 1998, p. 118). Though they acknowledge that there are age-appropriate roles for children in taking on household responsibilities and the significant cultural component to acceptable norms of care provided by children, children whose parents are compromised by mental illness may take on burdensome roles. The type and extent of the responsibilities of young carers whose parents have mental illness vary with the nature of the illnesses and impact on parents' functioning, and levels of care fluctuate over time (Aldridge & Becker, 2003). Their responsibilities may include personal care, paperwork, giving medicines, chores, looking after siblings and attending to the emotional well-being of their parents (e.g., keeping them company) and checking up on their parents (Falkov, 1998). Young carers may feel isolated from peers, extended family and school activities; may lag behind in school; and may experience conflict between caring for their parents and meeting their own needs. Young carers want many of the same things children and youth in other studies describe, including information about mental illness, practical and domestic help, a contact person in case of crisis and someone to talk to—though not necessarily a professional counselor (Aldridge & Becker, 2003; Falkov, 1998).

Parents with mental illness participating in interview studies provide insights into the needs of their children (Nicholson & Henry, 2003). Nurturance, discipline and encouragement to develop talents and interests are high on the list of children's needs reported by mothers with mental illness. Mothers report children benefit from positive role models and friends and prioritize a dependable home environment for their children, with safe places to go outside the home. Mothers are concerned that children suffer a "secondary stigma" because of their mothers' illnesses. According to mothers, children want to feel "normal" like "other families." Parents in studies from other countries corroborate these findings. Handley and colleagues (2001) indicated that parents reported children would benefit from respite services, information about mental illness and support groups.

Findings from studies of the impact of maternal mental illness—that is, mothers falling into particular diagnostic categories—are described in previous sections of this chapter. These studies, though they contribute significantly to our understanding of the impact of parental mental illness on children and their consequent needs, have several limitations. Often framed in a medical model type of research design, comparisons are typically made between groups of mothers with mental illness and groups of those without and the children of these mothers (Aldridge & Becker, 2003). The studies tend to be of White, married, middle-class mothers and their children, who are grouped by diagnostic category rather than mothers' functioning or extent of impairment. These women and their children are often interviewed or observed in research settings rather in their natural environments. The conclusions drawn from these studies suggest an inevitable causal relationship between parental impairment and the risk to children that does not necessarily take into consideration the diversity among mothers labeled with the same psychiatric diagnosis or the contexts or conditions of their lives. Key factors like presence or absence of a partner (e.g., spouse or father of the child) are not considered (Aldridge & Becker, 2003). In fact, the characteristics, role or impact of fathers with mental illness is largely unstudied (Nicholson, Nason, Calabresi & Yando, 1999).

### Innovative Interventions for Children and Youth

Although there is a dearth of rigorous data, both in the United States and abroad, on outcomes for school-age children or youth participating in treatment specifically designed for those whose parents have mental illness, several innovative approaches have been developed to provide support. The distinction between supportive interventions and interventions designed to prevent the development of psychopathology in children and youth is subtle and, perhaps, arbitrary. The following examples are framed as supportive interventions by their developers and the authors who write about them.

VicChamps peer-support programs for 5- to 12-year-olds children were begun in Victoria, Australia, in the mid 1990s (Maybery, Reupert, & Goodyear, 2006). Peer support is viewed as key to reducing isolation and to improving social connectedness and is developed in the context of school-holiday and after-school programs. Respite and education about mental illness and well-being are provided. Emphasis is placed on building on children's and families' strengths to promote resilience. Children who participate in the Vic Champs program have reduced emotional difficulties, fewer problems, and increased connections with family and peers and improved coping skills, self-esteem and resilience. As part of the VicChamps initiative, professional development packages were implemented, including half-day education programs for mental health and other workers, focusing on reducing stigma and building workers' knowledge and skills in dealing with children whose parents have mental illness. Champions were identified within organizations to advocate for the needs of these children.

Young carers projects have developed across the United Kingdom (Aldridge & Becker, 2003). Young carers project workers offer dedicated support to children and youth and their families, coordinate and facilitate access to other agencies and services and advocate for families. They help to maintain family relationships and stability and provide support to families in crises.

The SMILES Program is a three-day program for children with a parent or sibling with mental illness, implemented in Australia and Canada (Pitman & Matthey, 2004). The goal of the program is to increase children's knowledge of mental illness and to improve their coping skills. Data from 25 participating children indicate they achieved these aims.

BART's Place was developed at the Northcoast Behavioral Healthcare System in Cleveland, Ohio (Katz, Gintoli & Buckley, 2001). The program initially served hospitalized parents and their children, grandchildren and siblings under the age of 18. Family sessions in which the parent's mental illness is explained to children take place in a family-friendly playroom located on the ground floor of the psychiatric hospital and are supervised and facilitated by a psychologist. The community-based expansion of the program provides a five-week series of KidSupport groups to children aged 6 to 18 referred from the inpatient program or from schools or other community agencies.

### Interventions Targeted at Parents With Mental Illnesses and Their Children

A number of programs for parents with mental illnesses and their families have developed across the country, primarily in response to perceived community need rather than as research-based initiatives. Interventions were identified in a national survey and fell into three broad categories:

1. Inpatient programs for mothers designed to address both mental and reproductive health
2. Comprehensive community-based programs offering an array of essential services to families including case management or care coordination
3. Circumscribed community-based programs focusing on targeted treatment (e.g., dyadic therapy for parent and child) (Hinden, Biebel, Nicholson, Henry & Katz-Leavy, 2006).

Of the 20 programs providing data for the study, the majority were initiated to serve adults with mental illness who are parents, along with their children. In the study, 5 of the 20 were initiated by child-focused early intervention or child welfare providers targeting the high-risk group of families in which a parent has a mental illness. Two were developed by researchers and providers interested in risk and resilience processes among children of parents with mental illnesses. The largest number of interventions embraced a psychosocial rehabilitation orientation to parenting alone or in combination with a child development approach. A smaller number of programs identified child attachment or psychodynamic theory as the guiding framework, and three identified psychoeducational or child development approaches. Desired outcomes reflected program orientation and funding sources and the goals of parents and families. For example, the focus of inpatient programs included crisis stabilization and medication adjustment. The goal of comprehensive community-based interventions was to improve functioning across multiple domains for all family members. Circumscribed programs identified outcomes specific to the focus of the intervention, such as improved parent–child attachment and enhanced parenting skills. None of the programs were able to provide outcome data for parents or children at the time of the study.

### *Treatment of Parents*

The positive impact on children of the effective treatment of their mothers who were diagnosed with depression was shown in a recent study of mother–child pairs (Weissman et al., 2006). There was a significant decrease in the percent of psychiatric diagnoses in children whose mothers' depression remitted over a three-month time period. Children who were well at baseline were free of psychiatric disorders at three months if their mothers' depression remitted. Among children with mothers whose depression did not remit, there was an increase in rates of depressive, anxiety and disruptive behavior disorders at three months. The researchers suggest the possible preventive impact of effective treatment for mothers on outcomes for children, though they acknowledge they cannot demonstrate causality given their study design. They suggest a cycle in which maternal improvement may contribute to children's improvement, which in turn has positive impact on mothers.

### What Does Not Work

A review of the literature did not uncover any intervention that should not be used at the present time.

## Overall Comment

There is no evidence-based treatment or supportive intervention specifically targeted to school-age children or youth whose parents have mental illnesses. Parents and children who experience symptoms of diagnosable psychiatric disorders should be encouraged to seek effective treatment for those disorders. Better parental functioning most likely contributes to enhanced child functioning and vice versa. Therefore, participation in treatment and interventions that enhance the functioning of adults with mental illnesses who are parents should be encouraged. The support needs of children and youth whose parents have mental illnesses have been suggested in the literature. Innovative interventions, largely untested, have been developed, typically with the goals of addressing risk factors and of promoting resilience. To a large extent, the risk and protective factors for these children overlap with those of children in general. Parental mental illnesses do pose specific challenges, such as the lack of understanding or knowledge about mental illnesses and their impact on family relationships and family life, and interventions for these children typically take these into consideration.

## PSYCHOPHARMACOLOGY

Effective psychopharmacology for adults diagnosed with mental illnesses is likely to enhance their functioning as parents. No single, specific drug is used for difficulties children experience as a consequence of parental mental illness. Rather, if a child develops a particular psychiatric disorder, the appropriate evidence-based treatment regime, including psychopharmacology, should be followed.

## THE PREVENTION OF PSYCHOPATHOLOGY IN CHILDREN WHOSE PARENTS HAVE MENTAL ILLNESS

### What Works

There is broad support in the literature for family educational approaches for children and youth whose parents have a variety of conditions. A review of the literature did not uncover any relevant prevention intervention specifically for children whose parents have mental illnesses that met the criteria of three independent trials.

### What Might Work

Within the area of depression prevention, there are two prevention approaches with an evidence base: (1) Clarke et al.'s (2001) cognitive behavioral group prevention intervention for adolescents (age 13 to 18 years) of depressed parents; and (2) Beardslee, Gladstone, Wright and Cooper's (2003) family-based prevention approach for children (age 8 to 15 years) whose parents have depression.

Clarke and colleagues (2001) tested a manual-based, group psychoeducational intervention provided by master's-level therapists to adolescent offspring of parents with depression. The adolescents fell into low-, medium-, or high-severity depression groups, and the intervention dose was matched to the severity. Adolescents with medium-level severity depression (i.e., those with subsyndromal depression symptoms but no active depression episodes) were randomly assigned to experimental (intervention) or control (usual-care) conditions, in an intent-to-treat design. The prevention intervention consisted of 15 one-hour sessions for groups of 6 to 10 adolescents at health maintenance organization clinic offices, with youth attending an average of 9.5 sessions. Adolescents were taught cognitive restructuring techniques specially targeted to beliefs related to having a depressed parent. Parents were informed about the content and focus of the group intervention in general. Youth's episodes of major depression were the primary outcome at 12-, 18-, and 24-month follow-ups. Preventive effects of the intervention were clinically significant; that is, control group participants were more than five times as likely as experimental group participants to develop depression. Preventive effects faded over time, however, when measured at the two-year follow-up. The researchers recommended replication of the study by an independent group, with a more diverse sample. Participants in this study were overwhelmingly White youth, the majority of whose parents with depression were female, White, married and employed.

William Beardslee and colleagues evaluated the impact of two manual-based, preventive intervention strategies targeted to children living in homes with depressed parents (Beardslee et al., 2003; Beardslee, Wright, Rothberg, Salt & Versage, 1996; Beardslee, Salt, Versage et al., 1997; Beardslee, Versage et al., 1997). The interventions were family based, with goals of increasing positive interactions between parents and early adolescents and of increasing understanding of depression for everyone in the family. Families were assigned randomly to either a lecture or a clinician-facilitated intervention. Psychoeducation material was presented pertaining to mood disorders, risk and resilience. In the clinician-facilitated intervention, effort was made to link psychoeducation material to the family's life experiences. Parents were helped to build resilience and to decrease feelings of guilt and blame in children. Telephone contacts or refresher meetings were conducted at six- and nine-month intervals. Psychopathology and overall functioning were assessed in all family members in both groups at intake, one year postintervention and two and one-half years postintervention. Parents in both conditions reported significant positive change in their child-related behaviors and attitudes. Children in both conditions reported increased understanding of parental illness attributable to intervention participation. The clinician-facilitated intervention was more beneficial than the lecture program. In this study, as in the Clarke et al. study (2001), the sample was predominantly White and middle class. The investigators recommended further research with more diverse samples. They concluded that their results suggest that carefully delivered, cognitively oriented, family-based interventions can contribute to supporting resilience in relatively healthy children at risk of psychopathology due to parental depression.

## What Does Not Work

A review of the literature did not uncover any intervention that should not be used at the present time.

## Overall Comment

Well-defined preventive interventions offer the potential for significant impact on the mental health and well-being of children and youth whose parents have mental illnesses. Several have specifically shown promise in the prevention of depression in children and adolescents living with parents with depression. Preventive interventions must be targeted and tested with participants with diverse background, clinical and socioeconomic characteristics and replicated and tested by independent investigators to demonstrate effectiveness. Their potential value is undeniable.

## RECOMMENDED BEST PRACTICE

There is no specific or unique picture of the impact of parental mental illnesses on children. Parents and children may vary widely in individual characteristics, in mental health and functioning and in family and community circumstances. In addition, no treatment or supportive interventions or prevention approaches have been proven effective in three independent trials. Recommendations for the treatment of parents and children who meet criteria for psychiatric disorders and for supportive and preventive interventions for children and families living with parental mental illness can be drawn from the research literature.

### Treatment and Supportive Interventions for Parents and Children

- Adults with mental illnesses should receive effective treatment appropriate to their particular psychiatric diagnoses, clinical characteristics and current functioning. Treatment may include psychopharmacology, psychosocial, psychoeducational and rehabilitation interventions.
- Adults with mental illnesses should routinely be asked about their parenting status, their expectations and goals and the needs of their children. They may, too often, be seen as patients rather than as parents (Nicholson et al., 2001; Stallard et al., 2004). They may be contemplating becoming parents, may be providing full-time care for children or may be separated from children, temporarily or permanently, with whom they hope to maintain relationships. Adult mental health service providers who feel they do not have the time or skill to deal with adults' concerns regarding parenting and children must develop linkages with child providers. A family-centered approach requires overcoming the barriers between adult and child services and funding streams.
- Parents with mental illnesses should be assessed regarding their current capacity to function in the parenting role, and intervention and support strategies should be suggested to promote their parenting ability and to minimize the risk of psychopathology in their children.
- Interventions for adults can support parental functioning indirectly via incorporating consideration of the effects on parenting into all aspects of treatment or directly via psychosocial rehabilitation and support strategies targeted to parents and families (Nicholson & Miller, in press). Interventions may range from providing psychoeducation about the potential impact of parental mental illness on children or of parenting experiences on adult mental health and recovery to offering advice about how to communicate with children about mental illness and recommending referral to formal parent skills training or a support group.
- Families living with parental mental illness may need help identifying and accessing practical supports as well as benefits, entitlements and

other natural and professional supports. Identifying opportunities for respite for both parents and children may be critical. Parents and children who are old enough to have the conversation should be involved in preparing personal care plans (i.e., the identification of alternative care givers and supports for children in the event parents require hospitalization).

- Parents with mental illnesses and their children benefit from supportive relationships with other adults and children with peers. Opportunities should be sought for initiating and maintaining supportive relationships within families, among extended family members and in the community.

- Parents with mental illnesses and their children benefit from opportunities for success, whether in the work or home environment or at school, in academic efforts, in extracurricular activities or with peers. Parents and children may require support for identifying strengths and pursuing interests that contribute to feelings of competence and resilience.

- Barriers to treatment and intervention for family members living with parental mental illness must be overcome. Routine procedures and policies must be reviewed and modified to support family-centered care. For example, clinic waiting rooms can be made child friendly; psychiatric inpatient units can provide areas for safe, supported family interactions; eligibility requirements can be waived to reduce the barriers between adult and child services and funding streams.

## Psychopharmacology

- Parents with mental illnesses must receive adequate diagnostic services and psychopharmacology appropriate to their diagnoses, clinical characteristics, and conditions.

- Children and youth whose parents have mental illnesses, who met diagnostic criteria for mental health disorders, should be appropriately treated with effective medications when indicated.

## Prevention

- Interventions targeted to the prevention of psychopathology in school-age children and youth whose parents have mental illnesses that focus on psychoeducation regarding mental illness and its impact on parenting and family relationships as well as the development of coping skills and peer supports show great promise.

- Enhanced family communication regarding parental mental illness, couched in psychoeducation, with support for positive dialogue among family members, shows great promise in preventing the development of psychopathology in youth.

- Strategies must be implemented to identify the mental health needs of parents and children and to provide treatment and support in settings in which parents and children are routinely found (e.g., early intervention programs, pediatricians' offices, school settings, neighborhood centers).

- Strategies for supportive interventions, provided herein, may prove beneficial in prevention as well.

Given that outcomes for children and parents are multiply determined, there are many opportunities for treatment, intervention and prevention efforts to build competence and enhance resiliency in families living with parental mental illness. Appropriate, effective, natural and professional supports must be available to all family members—to support active participation in treatment and rehabilitation and to enhance the recovery of adults; to build resilience, to prevent the development of difficulties and to intervene early and appropriately with children; and, therefore, to optimize outcomes for all family members.

## REFERENCES

Aldridge, J. & Becker, S. (2003). *Children caring for parents with mental illness.* Bristol, England: The Policy Press.

Anderson, C. A. & Hammen, C. L. (1993). Psychosocial outcomes of children of unipolar depressed, bipolar, medically ill, and normal women: A longitudinal study. *Journal of Consulting and Clinical Psychology, 61*(3), 448–454.

Beardslee, W. R. (2002). *Out of the darkened room: Protecting the children and strengthening the family when a parent is depressed.* Boston: Little, Brown & Company.

Beardslee, W. R., Gladstone, T. R. G., Wright, E. J. & Cooper, A. B. (2003). A family-based approach to the prevention of depressive symptoms in children at risk: Evidence of parental and child change. *Pediatrics, 112,* 119–131.

Beardslee, W. R., Hoke, L., Wheelock, J., Rothberg, P. C., van de Velde, P. & Swarling, S. (1992). Initial findings on preventive intervention for families with parental affective disorders. *American Journal of Psychiatry, 149,* 1335–1340.

Beardslee, W. R., Keller, M. B., Lavori, P. W., Staley, J. E. & Sacks, N. (1993). The impact of parental affective disorder on depression in offspring: A longitudinal follow-up in a non-referred sample. *Journal of the American Academy of Child and Adolescent Psychiatry, 32,* 723–730.

Beardslee, W. R., Keller, M. B., Seifer, R., Podorefsky, D., Staley, J., Lavori, P. W. et al. (1996). Prediction of adolescent affective disorder: Effects of prior parental affective disorders and child psychopathology. *Journal of the American Academy of Child and Adolescent Psychiatry, 35*(3), 279–288.

Beardslee, W. R., Salt, P., Versage, E. M., Gladstone, T. R. G., Wright, E. J. & Rothberg, P. C. (1997). Sustained change in parents receiving preventive interventions for families with depression. *American Journal of Psychiatry, 154*(4), 510–515.

Beardslee, W., Versage, E., Wright, E., Salt, P., Rothberg, P. C., Drezner, K. et al. (1997). Examination of preventive interventions for families with depression: Evidence of change. *Development & Psychopathology, 9*(1), 109–130.

Beardslee, W. R., Wright, E. J., Rothberg, P. C., Salt, P. & Versage, E. M. (1996). Response of families to two preventive intervention strategies: Long-term differences in behavior and attitude change. *Journal of the American Academy of Child and Adolescent Psychiatry, 35*(6), 774–782.

Beardslee, W. R., Wright, E. J., Salt, P., Drezner, K., Gladstone, T. R. G., Versage, E. M. et al. (1997). Examination of children's responses to two preventive intervention strategies over time. *Journal of the American Academy of Child and Adolescent Psychiatry, 36*(2), 196–204.

Beidel, D. C. & Turner, S. M. (1997). *At risk for anxiety: I: Psychopathology in the offspring of anxious parents. Journal of the American Academy of Child and Adolescent Psychiatry, 36*(7), 918–924.

Bellodi, L., Sciuto, G., Diaferia, G., Ronchi, P. & Smeraldi, E. (1992). Psychiatric disorders in the families of patients with obsessive-compulsive disorder. *Psychiatry Research 42*(2), 111–120.

Belsky, J. (1984). The determinants of parenting: A process model. *Child Development, 55*(1), 83–96.

Benjamin, L. R., Benjamin, R. & Rind, B. (1998). The parenting experiences of mothers with dissociative disorders. *Journal of Marital and Family Therapy, 24*(3), 337–354.

Biebel, K., Nicholson, J., Geller, J. & Fisher, W. (2006). A national survey of State Mental Health Authority programs and policies for clients who are parents: A decade later. *Psychiatric Quarterly, 77*, 119–128.

Biederman, J., Faraone, S. V., Keenan, K., Knee, D. & Tsuang, M. T. (1990). Family-genetic and psychosocial risk factors in DSM-III attention deficit disorder. *Journal of the American Academy of Child and Adolescent Psychiatry, 29*(4), 526–533.

Biederman, J., Faraone, S. V., Mick, E., Spencer, T., Wilens, T., Kiely, K. et al. (1995). High risk for attention deficit hyperactivity disorder among children of parents with childhood onset of the disorder: a pilot study. *American Journal of Psychiatry, 152*(3), 431–435.

Biederman, J., Faraone, S. V. & Monuteaux, M. C. (2002). Impact of exposure to parental attention-deficit hyperactivity disorder on clinical features and dysfunction in the offspring. *Psychological Medicine, 32*(5), 817–827.

Biederman, J., Petty, C., Faraone, S. V., Hirshfeld-Becker, D. R., Henin, A., Dougherty, M. et al. (2005). Parental predictors of pediatric panic disorder/agoraphobia: a controlled study in high-risk offspring. *Depression and Anxiety, 22*(3), 114–20.

Biederman, J., Petty, C., Hirshfeld-Becker, D. R., Henin, A., Faraone, S. V., Dang, D. et al. (2006). A controlled longitudinal 5-year follow-up study of children at high and low risk for panic disorder and major depression. *Psycholological Medicine, 15*, 1–12.

Black, D. W., Gaffney, G. R., Schlosser, S. & Gabel, J. (2003). Children of parents with obsessive-compulsive disorder—a 2-year follow-up study. *Acta Psychiatrica Scandinavica, 107*(4), 305–313.

Blyth, D. A. and Roelkepartian, E. C. (1993). *Healthy communities, healthy youth*. Minneapolis: Search Institute.

Bronfenbrenner, U. (1981). *The ecology of human development: Experiments by nature and design*. Cambridge, MA: Harvard University Press.

Brookmeyer, K. A., Henrich, C. C. & Schwab-Stone, M. (2005). Adolescents who witness community violence: Can parent support and prosocial cognitions protect them from committing violence? *Child Development, 76*(4), 917–929.

Carro, M. G., Grant, K. E., Gotlib, I. H. & Compas, B. E. (1993). Postpartum depression and child development: An investigation of mothers and fathers as sources of risk and resilience. Milestones in the development of resilience. *Development and Psychopathology, 5,* 567–579.

Cauce, A. M., Stewart, A., Rodriguez, M. D., Cochran, B. & Ginzler, J. (2003). Overcoming the odds? Adolescent development in the context of urban poverty. In S. S. Luthar (Ed.), *Resilience and vulnerability: Adaptation in the context of childhood adversities* (pp. 343–363). New York: Cambridge University Press.

Chang, K. D., Steiner, H. & Ketter, T. A. (2000). Psychiatric phenomenology of child and adolescent bipolar offspring. *Journal of the American Academy of Child and Adolescent Psychiatry, 39*(4), 453–460.

Choi, Y., Harachi, T. W., Gillmore, M. R. & Catalano, R. (2006). Are multi-racial adolescents at greater risk? Comparisons of rates, patterns, and correlates of substance use and violence between monoracial and multiracial adolescents. *American Journal of Orthopsychiatry, 76*(1), 86–97.

Cicchetti, D. & Toth, S. L. (2005). Child maltreatment. *Annual Review of Clinical Psychology, 1,* 409–438.

Clarke, G. N., Hornbrook, M., Lynch, F., Polen, M., Gale, J., Beardslee, W. R. et al. (2001). A randomized trial of a group cognitive intervention for preventing depression in adolescent offspring of depressed parents. *Archives of General Psychiatry, 58,* 1127–1134.

Clements, M. A., Reynolds, A. J. & Hickey, E. (2004). Site-level predictors of children's school and social competence in the Chicago parent centers. *Early Childhood Research Quarterly, 19,* 273–296.

Coiro, M. J. (2001). Depressive symptoms among women receiving welfare. *Women's Health, 32,* 1–23.

Connell, A. M. & Goodman, S. H. (2002). The association between psychopathology in fathers versus mothers and children's internalizing and externalizing behavior problems: A meta-analysis. *Psychological Bulletin, 128*(5), 746–773.

Costello, E. J., Compton, S. N., Keeler, G. & Angold, A. (2003). Relationships between poverty and psychopathology: A natural experiment. *Journal of the American Medical Association, 290*(15), 2023–2030.

Cuffe, S. P., McKeown, R. E., Addy, C. L. & Garrison, C. Z. (2005). Family and psychosocial risk factors in a longitudinal epidemiological study of adolescents. *Journal of the American Academy of Child and Adolescent Psychiatry, 44*(2), 121–129.

Delbello, M. P. & Geller, B. (2001). Review of studies of child and adolescent offspring of bipolar parents. *Bipolar Disorder, 3*(6), 325–334.

Downey, G. & Coyne, J. C. (1990). Children of depressed parents: An integrative review. *Psychological Bulletin, 108*(1), 50–76.

Earls, F. & Carlson, M. (2001). The social ecology of child health and well-being. *Annual Review of Public Health, 22,* 143–166.

Early Head Start (2003). *Research to practice: Depression in the lives of Early Head Start families* (Early Head Start Research and Evaluation Project). Retrieved 20 October 2006 from http://www.afterschool.ed.gov/programs/opre/ehs/ehs_resrch/reports/dissemination/research_briefs/research_brief_depression.pdf.

Else-Quest, N. M., Hyde, J. S., Goldsmith, H. H. & Van Hulle, C. (2006). Gender differences in temperament. *Psychological Bulletin, 132*(1), 33–72.

Falkov, A. (Ed.) (1998). *Crossing bridges: Training resources for working with mentally ill parents and their children*. Brighton, England: Pavilion Publishing (Brighton) Limited.

Falkov, A. (2004). Training and practice protocols. In M. Gopfert, J. Webster & M. V. Seeman (Eds.), *Parental psychiatric disorder: Distressed parents and their families,* 2d ed. (pp. 375–392). Cambridge, England: Cambridge University Press.

Faraone, S. V., Biederman, J., Mick, E., Williamson, S., Wilens, T., Spencer, T. et al. (2000). Family study of girls with attention deficit hyperactivity disorder. *American Journal of Psychiatry, 157*(7), 1077–1083.

Fendrich, M., Warner, V. & Weissman, M. M. (1990). Family risk factors, parental depression, and psychopathology in offspring. *Developmental Psychology, 26*(1), 40–50.

Fergusson, D. M. & Harwood, J. L. (2003). Resilience in childhood adversity: Results of a 21-year study. In S. S. Luthar (Ed.), *Resilience and vulnerability: Adaptation in the context of childhood adversities* (pp. 130–155). New York: Cambridge University Press.

Flores, E., Cicchetti, D. & Rogosch, F. A. (2005). Predictors of resilience in maltreated and non-maltreated Latino children. *Developmental Psychology, 41*(2), 336–351.

Foley, D. L, Pickles, A., Simonoff, E., Maes, H. H., Silberg, J. L., Hewitt, J. K. et al. (2001). Parental concordance and comorbidity for psychiatric disorder and associate risks for current psychiatric symptoms and disorders in a community sample of juvenile twins. *Journal of Child Psychology and Psychiatry 42*(3), 381–394.

Fudge, E. & Mason, P. (2004). Consulting with young people about service guidelines relating to parental mental illness. *Australian e-Journal for the Advancement of Mental Health, 3*(2), 1–9.

Garbarino, J., Dubrow, N., Kostelny, K. & Pardo, C. (1992). *Children in danger.* San Francisco: Jossey-Bass.

Garley, D., Gallop, R., Johnston, N. & Pipitone, J. (1997). Children of the mentally ill: A qualitative focus group approach. *Journal of Psychiatric and Mental Health Nursing, 4,* 97–103.

Gerard, J. M. & Buehler, C. (2004). Cumulative environmental risk and youth maladjustment: The role of youth attributes. *Child Development, 75*(4), 1832–1849.

Goodman, S. H. & Gotlib, I. H. (1999). Risk for psychopathology in the children of depressed mothers: A developmental model for understanding mechanisms of transmission. *Psychological Review, 106*(3), 458–490.

Goodman, S. H. & Gotlib, I. H. (Eds.) (2002). *Children of depressed parents: Mechanisms of risk and implications for treatment.* Washington, DC: American Psychological Association.

Gorman-Smith, D. & Tolan, P. H. (2003). Positive adaptation among youth exposed to community violence. In S. S. Luthar (Ed.), *Resiliency and vulnerability: Adaptation in the context of childhood adversities* (pp. 392–413). New York: Cambridge University Press.

Gutman, L. M., Sameroff, A. J. & Cole, R. (2003). Academic growth curve trajectories from 1st grade to 12th grade: Effects of multiple social risk factors and preschool child factors. *Developmental Psychology, 39*(4), 777–790.

Hammen, C. (1991). *Depression runs in families: The social context of risk and resilience in children of depressed mothers.* New York: Springer-Verlag.

Hammen, C. (2003). Risk and protective factors for children of depressed parents. In S. S. Luthar (Ed.), *Resilience and vulnerability: Adaptation in the context of childhood adversities* (pp. 50–75). New York: Cambridge University Press.

Hammen, C. & Brennan, P. (2001). Depressed adolescents of depressed and non-depressed mothers: Tests of an interpersonal impairment of hypothesis. *Journal of Consulting and Clinical Psychology, 69,* 284–294.

Handley, C., Farrell, G. A., Josephs, A., Hanke, A. & Hazelton, M. (2001). The Tasmanian children's project: The needs of children with a parent/caregiver with a mental illness. *Australian and New Zealand Journal of Mental Health Nursing, 10,* 221–228.

Hans, S. L., Auerbach, J. G., Styr, B. & Marcus, J. (2004). Offspring of parents with schizophrenia: Mental disorders during childhood and adolescence. *Schizophrenia Bulletin, 30*(2), 303–315.

Heilemann, M., Frutos, L., Lee, K. & Kury, F. S. (2004). Protective strength factors, resources, and risks in relation to depressive symptoms among childbearing women of Mexican descent. *Health Care for Women International, 25*(1), 88–106.

Heneghan, A. M., Mercer, M. & DeLeone, N. I. (2004). Will mothers discuss parenting stress and depressive symptoms with their child's pediatrician? *Pediatrics, 113*(3), 460–467.

Heneghan, A. M., Silver, E. J., Bauman, L. J., Westbrook, L. E. & Stein, R. E. K. (1998). Depressive symptoms in inner-city mothers of young children: Who is at risk? *Pediatrics, 102,* 1394–1400.

Henin, A., Biederman, J., Mick, E., Sachs, G. S., Hirshfeld-Becker, D. R., Siegel, R. S. et al. (2005). Psychopathology in the offspring of parents with bipolar disorder: A controlled study. *Biological Psychiatry, 58*(7), 554–561.

Hettema, J. M., Neale, M. C. & Kendler, K. S. (2001). A review and meta-analysis of the genetic epidemiology of anxiety disorders. *American Journal of Psychiatry, 158*(10), 1568–1578.

Heydebrand, G. (2006). Cognitive deficits in the families of patients with schizophrenia. *Current Opinion in Psychiatry, 19*(3), 277–281.

Hillegers, M. H., Reichart, C. G., Wals, M., Verhulst, F. C., Ormel, J. & Nolen, W. A. (2005). Five-year prospective outcome of psychopathology in the adolescent offspring of bipolar parents. *Bipolar Disorder, 7*(4), 344–350.

Hinden, B., Biebel, K., Nicholson, J., Henry, A. & Katz-Leavy, J. (2006). A survey of programs for parents with mental illness and their families: Identifying common elements to build an evidence base. *Journal of Behavioral Health Services & Research, 33*(1), 21–38.

Isaacs, M. (2004). Community care networks for depression in low-income communities and communities of color: A review of the literature. A A working paper. Baltimore, MD: The Annie E. Casey Foundation.

Jacobi, C., Hayward, C., de Zwaan, M., Kraemer, H. C. & Agras, W. S. (2004). Coming to terms with risk factors for eating disorders: application of risk terminology and suggestions for a general taxonomy. *Psychological Bulletin, 130*(1), 19–65.

Jacobsen, T. (2004). Mentally ill mothers in the parenting role: clinical management and treatment. In M. Gopfert, J. Webster & M. V. Seeman (Eds.), *Parental psychiatric disorder: Distressed parents and their families,* 2nd ed. (pp. 112–122). Cambridge, England: Cambridge University Press.

Jaser, S. S., Langrock, A. M., Keller, G., Merchant, M. J., Benson, M. A., Reeslund, K. et al. (2005). Coping with the stress of parental depression II: Adolescent and parent reports of coping and adjustment. *Journal of Child and Adolescent Psychology, 34*(1), 193–205.

Jones, C. & Shorter-Gooden, K. (2003). *Shifting: The double lives of black women in America.* New York: HarperCollins Publishers.

Kaplan, S. J., Pelcovitz, D., Salzinger, S., Weiner, M., Mandel, F. S., Lesser, M. L. et al. (1998). Adolescent physical abuse: Risk for adolescent psychiatric disorders. *American Journal of Psychiatry, 155*(7), 954–959.

Katz, J. G., Gintoli, G. & Buckley, P. (2001). BART's Place for children and teenagers of parents with serious mental illness. *Psychiatric Services, 52,* 107.

Kendler, K. S. & Gardner, C. O. (1997). The risk for psychiatric disorders in relatives of schizophrenic and control probands: A comparison of three independent studies. *Psychological Medicine, 27*(2), 411–419.

King, P. E. & Furrow, J. L. (2004). Religion as a resource for positive youth development: Religion, social capital and moral outcomes. *Developmental Psychology, 40*(5), 703–713.

Kinsella, K. B. & Anderson, R.A. (1996). Coping skills, strengths, and needs as perceived by adult offspring and siblings of people with mental illness: A retrospective study. *Psychiatric Rehabilitation Journal, 20*(2), 24–32.

Kliewer, W., Cunningham, J. N., Diehl, R., Parrish, K. A., Walker, J., Atiyeh, C. et al. (2004). Violence exposure and adjustment in inner-city youth: Child and caregiver emotion regulation skill, caregiver-child relationship quality, and neighborhood cohesion as protective factors. *Journal of Clinical Child and Adolescent Psychology, 33*(3), 477–487.

Kogan, S. M., Luo, Z., Murry, V. M. & Brody, G. H. (2005). Risk and protective factors for substance use among African American high school dropouts. *Psychology of Addictive Behaviors, 19*(4), 382–391.

Kumpfer, K. L. (1999). Factors and processes contributing to resilience: The resilience framework. In M. D. Glanz & J. L. Johnson (Eds.), *Resilience and development: Positive life adaptation* (pp. 179–224). New York: Kluwer Academic/Plenum Publishers.

Kumra, S., Shaw, M., Merka, P., Nakayama, E. & Augustin, R. (2001). Childhood-onset schizophrenia: research update. *Canadian Journal of Psychiatry, 46*(10), 923–930.

Lapalme, M., Hodgins, S. & LaRoche, C. (1997). Children of parents with bipolar disorder: a metaanalysis of risk for mental disorders. *Canadian Journal of Psychiatry, 42*(6), 623–631.

Lengua, L. J. (2002). The contribution of emotionality and self-regulation to the understanding of children's response to multiple risk. *Child Development, 73*(1), 144–161.

Lieb, R., Isensee, B., Hofler, M., Pfister, H. & Wittchen, H. U. (2002). Parental major depression and the risk of depression and other mental disorders in offspring: A prospective-longitudinal community study. *Archives of General Psychiatry, 59*(4), 365–374.

Lin, K. K., Sandler, I. N., Ayers, T. S., Wolchik, S. A. & Luecken, L. J. (2004). Resilience in parentally bereaved children and adolescents seeking preventive services. *Journal of Child and Adolescent Psychology, 33*(4), 673–683.

Lorant, V., Deliege, D., Eaton, W. W., Robert, A., Phillippot, P. & Ausseau, M. (2003). Socioeconomic inequalities in depression: A meta-analysis. *American Journal of Epidemiology, 157*(2), 98–112.

Lovejoy, M. C., Graczyk, P. A., O'Hare, E. & Neuman, G. (2000). Maternal depression and parenting behavior: A meta-analytic review. *Clinical Psychology Review, 20*, 561–592.

Luster, T., Lekskul, K. & Oh, S. M. (2004). Predictors of academic motivation in first grade among children born to low-income adolescent mothers. *Early Childhood Research Quarterly, 19*, 337–353.

Luthar, S. S. (2003). Preface. In S. S. Luthar (Ed.), *Resilience and vulnerability: Adaptation in the context of childhood adversities* (pp. xxix). New York: Cambridge University Press.

Luthar, S. S. & Zelazo, L. B. (2003). Research on resilience: An integrative review. In S. S. Luthar (Ed.), *Resilience and vulnerability: Adaptation in the context of childhood adversity* (pp. 510–550). New York: Cambridge University Press.

Marsh, D. T. (1992). *Families and mental illness: New directions in professional practice*. New York: Praeger.

Marsh, D. T., Dickens, R. M., Yackovich, N. S., Wilson, J. M., Leichliter, J. S. & McQuillis, V. A. (1993). Troubled journey: Siblings and children of people with mental illness. *Innovations & Research, 2*(2), 17–28.

Marsh, D. T., & Lefley, H. P. (1996). The family experience of mental illness: Evidence for resilience. *Psychiatric Rehabilitation Journal, 20*(2), 3–12.

Masten, A. S. (2005). Peer relationships and psychopathology in developmental perspective: Reflections on progress and promise. *Journal of Child and Adolescent Psychology, 34*(1), 87–92.

Masten, A. S. & Powell, J. L. (2003). A resilience framework for research, policy and practice. In S. S. Luthar (Ed.), *Resilience and vulnerability: Adaptation in the context of childhood adversity* (pp. 1–28). New York: Cambridge University Press.

Maybery, D., Reupert, A. & Goodyear, M. (2006). *Evaluation of a model of best practice for families who have a parent with a mental illness* (Charles Sturt University, Wagga Wagga, Australia). Retrieved 20 October 2006 from http://www.quantifyingconnections.com/COPMIpage.htm.

McClure, E. B., Brennan, P. A., Hammen, C. & Le Brocque, R. M. (2002). Parental anxiety disorders, child anxiety disorders, and the perceived parent-child relationship in an Australian high-risk sample. *Journal of Abnormal Child Psychology, 29*(1), 1–10.

McDonald, E. J., McCabe, K., Yeh, M., Lau, A., Garland, A. & Hough, R. L. (2005). Cultural affiliation and self-esteem as predictors of internalizing symptoms among Mexican American adolescents. *Journal of Child and Adolescent Psychology, 34*(1), 163–171.

McMahon, T. J. & Luthar, S. S. (2006). Patterns and correlates of substance use among affluent, suburban high school students. *Journal of Clinical Child and Adolescent Psychology, 35*(1), 72–89.

Merikangas, K. R., Lieb, R., Wittchen, H. U. & Avenevoli, S. (2003). Family and high-risk studies of social anxiety disorder. *Acta Psychiatrica Scandinavica, 108*(Suppl. 417), 28–37.

Minde, K., Eakin, L., Hectman, L., Ochs, E., Bouffard, R., Greenfield, B. et al. (2003). The psychosocial functioning of children and spouses of adults with ADHD. *Journal of Child Psychology and Psychiatry, 44*(4), 637646.

Miranda, J. & Cooper, L. A. (2004). Disparities in care for depression among primary care patients. *Journal of General Internal Medicine, 19*(2), 120–126.

Miranda, J. & Green, B. L. (1999). The need for mental health services research focusing on poor young women. *Journal of Mental Health Policy and Economics, 2,* 73–80.

National Institute of Mental Health (NIMH) (2005). *Real men, real depression* (NIH Publication 05-4972). Retrieved 19 October 2006 from http://menand-depression.nimh.nih.gov.

Nemeroff, C. B., Heim, C. M., Thase, M. E., Klein, D. N., Rush, A. J., Schatzberg, A. F. et al. (2003). Differential responses to psychotherapy versus pharmacotherapy in patients with chronic forms of major depression and childhood trauma. *Proceedings of the National Academy of Sciences of the U.S.A. 100*(24), 14293–14296.

New Freedom Commission on Mental Health (NFCMH) (2003). Achieving the promise: Transforming mental health care in America. Final Report (DHHS Publication SMA-03-3832). Rockville, MD: Substance Abuse and Mental Health Services Administration.

Nicholson, J. & Biebel, K. (2002). The tragedy of missed opportunities: What providers can do. *Community Mental Health Journal, 38*(2), 167–172.

Nicholson, J., Biebel, K., Hinden, B., Henry, A. & Stier, L. (2001). *Critical issues for parents with mental illness and their families* (Rockville, MD: U.S. Department of Health and Human Services, Substance Abuse and Mental Health Services Administration, Center for Mental Health Services). Retrieved 28 April 2007 from http://www.mentalhealth.org/publications/allpubs/KEN-01-0109/default.asp.

Nicholson, J., Biebel, K., Williams, V. F. & Katz-Leavy, J. (2004). Prevalence of parenthood in adults with mental illness: Implications for state and federal policy, programs, and providers. In R. W. Manderscheid & M. J. Henderson (Eds.), *Mental health, United States, 2002* (pp. 120–137) (DHHS Publication SMA3938). Rockville, MD: U.S. Department of Health and Human Services, Substance Abuse and Mental Health Services Administration, Center for Mental Health Services.

Nicholson, J. & Clayfield, J. C. (2004). Responding to depression in parents. *Pediatric Nursing Journal. 30,* 136–142.

Nicholson, J., Geller, J. L., Fisher, W. H. & Dion, G. L. (1993). State policies and programs that address the needs of mentally ill mothers in the public sector. *Hospital and Community Psychiatry, 44,* 484–489.

Nicholson, J. & Henry, A. D. (2003). Achieving the goal of evidence-based psychiatric rehabilitation practices for mothers with mental illness. *Psychiatric Rehabilitation Journal, 27,* 122–130.

Nicholson, J. & Miller, L. J. (in press). Parenting with schizophrenia. In K. Mueser & D. V. Jeste (Eds.), *The clinical handbook of schizophrenia*. New York: Guilford Press.

Nicholson, J., Nason, M. W., Calabresi, A. O. & Yando, R. (1999). Fathers with severe mental illness: Characteristics and comparisons. *American Journal of Orthopsychiatry, 69*, 134–141.

Nicholson, J., Sweeney, E. M. & Geller, J. L. (1998a). Mothers with mental illness: I: The competing demands of parenting and living with mental illness. *Psychiatric Services, 49*, 635–642.

Nicholson, J., Sweeney, E. M. & Geller, J. L. (1998b). Mothers with mental illness: II: Family relationships and the context of parenting. *Psychiatric Services, 49*, 643–649.

Nicolson, R., Brookner, F. B., Lenane, M., Gochman, P., Ingraham, L. J., Egan, M. F. et al. (2003). Parental schizophrenia spectrum disorders in childhood-onset and adult-onset schizophrenia. *American Journal of Psychiatry, 160*(3), 490–495.

Niemi, L. T., Suvisaari, J. M., Haukka, J. K., Wrede, G. & Lonnqvist, J. K. (2004). Cumulative incidence of mental disorders among offspring of mothers with psychotic disorder: Results from the Helsinki High-Risk Study. *British Journal of Psychiatry, 185*, 11–17.

Olson, A. L., Dietrich, A. J., Prazar, G. & Hurley, J. (2006). Brief maternal depression screening at well-child visits. *Pediatrics, 118*, 207–216.

Oyserman, D., Mowbray, C. T., Meares, P. A. & Firminger, K. B. (2000). Parenting among mothers with a serious mental illness. *American Journal of Orthopsychiatry, 70*(3), 296–315.

Patel, P., Wheatcroft, R., Park, R. J. & Stein, A. (2002). The children of mothers with eating disorders. *Clinical Child and Family Psychology Review, 5*(1), 1–19.

Pitman, E. & Matthey, S. (2004). The SMILES program: A group program for children with mentally ill parents or siblings. *American Journal of Orthopsychiatry, 74*, 383–388.

Radke-Yarrow, M., Zahn-Wexler, C., Richardson, D. T., Susman, A. & Martinez, P. (1994). Caring behavior in children of clinically depressed and well mothers. *Child Development, 65*(5), 1405–1414.

Regier, D. A., Narrow, W. E., Rae, D. S., Manderscheid, R. W., Locke, B. Z. & Goodwin, F. K. (1993). The de facto US mental and addictive disorders service system. Epidemiological Catchment Area prospective 1-year prevalence rates of disorders and services. *Archives of General Psychiatry, 50*, 85–94.

Riebschleger, J. (2004). Good days and bad days: The experiences of children of a parent with a psychiatric disability. *Psychiatric Rehabilitation Journal, 28*, 25–31.

Riley, A. & Broitman, M. (2003). *The effects of maternal depression on the school readiness of low-income children* (Report for the Annie E. Casey Foundation). Baltimore, MD: Johns Hopkins University, Bloomberg School of Public Health.

Roberts, R., Roberts, C. & Chen, Y. (1997). Ethnocultural differences in prevalence of adolescent depression. *American Journal of Community Psychology, 25*, 95–110.

Sameroff, A. J., Gutman, L. M. & Peck, S. C. (2003). Adaptation among youth facing multiple risks: Prospective research findings. In S. S. Luthar (Ed.), *Resilience and vulnerability: adaptation in the context of childhood adversities* (pp. 364–391). New York: Cambridge University Press.

Sampson, R. J. (2001). How do communities undergird or undermine human development? Relevant contexts and social mechanisms. In A. Booth & A. C. Crouter (Eds), *Does it take a village? Community effects on children, adolescents, and families* (pp. 3–30). Mahwah, NJ: Erlbaum.

Schultz, M. S., Waldinger, R. J., Hauser, S. T. & Allen, J. P. (2005). Adolescents' behavior in the presence of interparental hostility: Developmental and emotion regulatory influences. *Developmental Psychopathology, 17,* 489–507.

Scourfield, J., Rice, F., Thapar, A., Harold, G. T., Martin, N. & McGuffin, P. (2003). Depressive symptoms in children and adolescents: changing aetiological influences with development. *Journal of Child Psychology and Psychiatry, 44*(7), 968–976.

Seidman, E. & Pedersen, S. (2003). Holistic contextual perspectives on risk, protection, and competence among low-income urban adolescents. In S. S. Luthar (Ed.), *Resilience and vulnerability: Adaptation in the context of childhood adversity* (pp. 318–342). New York: Cambridge University Press.

Seifer, R. (2003). Young children with mentally ill parents: Resilient developmental systems. In S. S. Luthar (Ed.), *Resiliency and vulnerability: Adaptation in the context of childhood adversities* (pp. 29–49). New York: Cambridge University Press.

Seifert, K., Bowman, P. J., Heflin, C. M., Danziger, S. & Williams, D.R. (2000). Social and environmental predictors of maternal depression in current and recent welfare recipients. *American Journal of Orthopsychiatry, 70*(4), 510–522.

Stallard, P., Norman, P., Huline-Dickens, S., Salter, E. & Cribb, J. (2004). The effects of parental mental illness on children: A descriptive study of the views of parents and children. *Clinical Child Psychology and Psychiatry, 9*(1), 39–52.

Strober, M., Freeman, R., Lampert, C., Diamond, J. & Kaye, W. (2000). Males with anorexia nervosa: A controlled study of eating disorders in first-degree relatives. *International Journal of Eating Disorders, 29*(3), 263–269.

Strober, M., Freeman, R., Lampert, C., Diamond, J. & Kaye, W. (2001). Controlled family study of anorexia nervosa and bulimia nervosa: Evidence of shared liability and transmission of partial syndromes. *American Journal of Psychiatry, 157,* 393–401.

Sullivan, P. F., Neale, M. C. & Kendler, K. S. (2000). Genetic epidemiology of major depression: review and meta-analysis. *American Journal of Psychiatry, 157*(10), 1552–1562.

Tarullo, L. B. & Cohen, C. (2003). Depression in the lives of Head Start and Early Head Start families. A presentation for the Foundations and Agencies Network for Children's Mental Health Annual Meeting, Washington, DC.

Taylor, S. E., Way, B. M., Welch, W. T., Hilmert, C. J., Lehman, B. J. & Eisenberger, N. I. (2006). Early family environment, current adversity, the serotonin transporter promoter polymorphism, and depressive symptomatology. *Biological Psychiatry, 60,* 671–676.

Tsuang, M. T., Stone, W. S. & Faraone, S. V. (1999). Schizophrenia: a review of genetic studies. *Harvard Review of Psychiatry, 7*(4), 185–207.

Unnewhr, S., Schneider, S., Florin, I. & Margraf, J. (1998). Psychopathology in children of patients with panic disorder or animal phobia. *Psychopathology, 31*(2), 69–84.

U.S. Department of Health and Human Services (HHS) (1999). *Mental health: A report of the surgeon general* (Rockville, MD: U.S. Department of Health and Human Services, Substance Abuse and Mental Health Services Administration, Center for Mental Health Services, National Institutes of Health, National Institute of Mental Health). Retrieved 15 May 2005 from http://www.surgeongeneral.gov/library/mentalhealth/home.html.

U.S. Department of Health and Human Services (HHS) (2001). *Mental health: Culture, race, and ethnicity—A supplement to mental health: A report of the surgeon general.* Rockville, MD: U.S. Department of Health and Human Services, Substance Abuse and Mental Health Services Administration, Center for Mental Health Services.

U.S. Government Accountability Office (GAO) (2006). *Child welfare: Improving social service program, training, and technical assistance information would help address long-standing service-level and workforce challenges* (GAO-07-75). Washington, DC: U.S. Government Accountability Office.

Van Doesum, K. T. M., Hosman, C. M. H. & Riksen-Walraven, J. M. (2005). A model-based intervention for depressed mothers and their infants. *Infant Mental Health Journal, 26,* 157–176.

Walters, E. E. & Kendler, K. S. (1995). Anorexia nervosa and anorexic-like syndromes in a population-based female twin sample. *American Journal of Psychiatry, 152*(1), 64–71.

Wade, T. D., Bulik, C. M., Neale, M. & Kendler, K. S. (2000). Anorexia nervosa and major depression: Shared genetic and environmental risk factors. *American Journal of Psychiatry, 157*(3), 469–471.

Weintraub, S. (1987). Risk factors in schizophrenia: The Stony Brook high-risk project. *Schizophrenia, 13*(3), 439–449.

Weissman, M. M., Gammon, G. D., John, K., Merikangas, K. R, Warner, V., Prusoff, B. A. et al. (1987). Children of depressed parents. Increased psychopathology and early onset of major depression. *Archives of General Psychiatry, 44*(10), 847–853.

Weissman, M. M., Pilowsky, D. J., Wickramaratne, P. J., Talati, A., Wisniewski, S. T., Fava, M. et al. (2006). Remissions in maternal depression and child psychopathology: A STAR*D report. *Journal of the American Medical Association, 295,* 1389–1398.

Weissman, M. M., Warner, V. & Wickramaratne, P. (1988). Early-onset major depression in parents and their children. *Journal of Affective Disorders, 15*(3), 269–277.

Wickramaratne, P. J. & Weissman, M. M. (1998). Onset of psychopathology in offspring by developmental phase and parental depression. *Journal of the American Academy of Child and Adolescent Psychiatry, 37,* 933–942.

Wyman, P. A., Cowen, E. L., Work, W. C., Hoyt-Meyers, L., Magnus, K. B., & Fagen, D. B. (1999). Caregiving and developmental factors differentiating young at-risk urban children showing resilient versus stress-affected outcomes: A replication and extension. *Child Development, 70*(3), 645–659.

# 12

# Physical Abuse in Childhood (Ages 5–13)

## SHARON G. PORTWOOD

## INTRODUCTION

In 2004, approximately 3 million American children were alleged to have been the victims of child abuse or neglect (HHS, 2006). Following investigation by state and local child protective agencies, an estimated 872,000 of these children were substantiated as victims. Physical abuse, which was experienced by 17.5% of victims, constituted the second most frequent type of maltreatment, following neglect (62.4% of victims).

Physical abuse is typically defined as nonaccidental injury to a child. These injuries are inflicted by punching, hitting, slapping, beating, kicking, biting or burning. The *Diagnostic and Statistical Manual of Mental Disorders*, 4th edition, text revised (*DSM-IV-TR*) (American Psychiatric Association, 2000, p. 738) lists physical abuse as a condition that may be the focus of clinical attention, but does not expressly define the term.

In addition to these clinical definitions, legal definitions of child abuse and physical abuse, in particular, may be found in states' criminal and child welfare laws. In general, state laws define physical abuse as injury caused by other than accidental means that results in a substantial risk of physical harm to the child; however, there is considerable variation across states in the specificity of the acts deemed to be physically abusive (Myers, 1992). Perhaps due to the fact that the primary purpose of relevant state laws is to guide official responses to child maltreatment in determining whether a particular act constitutes abuse, most legal definitions emphasize the overt consequences of abuse, such as bruises or broken bones, which constitute the most compelling evidence of abuse in a courtroom setting.

Despite the fact that child physical abuse is expressly defined within multiple domains (e.g., child welfare, criminal law, clinical practice, research), it remains an elusive construct, and there is no clear consensus on such fundamental questions as the role of intent (to cause harm) or consequences in defining abuse. Since 1979, U. S. Congress has commissioned three National Incidence Studies (NIS-1, NIS-2, and NIS-3) to provide official estimates of child maltreatment. Each of these studies used both a harm standard and an endangerment standard in categorizing children as abused. In NIS-3, which reported data from 1993 child welfare cases, 1,553,800 children were classified as abused under the harm standard compared with 2,815,600 under the endangerment standard (Sedlak & Broadhurst, 1996). This differential illustrates the constraints imposed by the lack of consistent definitional standards. In fact, the lack of a definitional consensus impacts not only prevalence estimates but also empirical examinations of child abuse, its consequences, treatment and prevention (Portwood, 1998).

Arguably, an all-inclusive definition of child physical abuse should include sibling abuse, bullying and disorders such as Munchausen syndrome by proxy,[1] which can result in physical harm to a child. However, consistent with the *DSM-IV-TR* definition previously cited, the scope of this chapter is limited to physical abuse perpetrated by a child's caregiver. Such abuse constitutes the vast majority of documented child maltreatment cases, with national statistics consistently reflecting that most children who are physically abused are victimized by their parents. According to 2004 figures, approximately 40% of victims of child physical abuse were abused solely by their mothers; 19% were abused solely by their fathers, and 19% were abused by both parents. Approximately 13% were abused by a nonparental perpetrator (Children's Bureau, 2004).

Within the family context, abuse may be viewed as the extreme end of a continuum of parenting behavior. However, there is considerable debate as to what constitutes appropriate parenting, based in large part on social, cultural and historical factors. Put simply, whether physical acts constitute abuse is, in large part, a social judgment. The valuative nature of labeling certain acts as abuse is perhaps nowhere better demonstrated than in the continuing debate on spanking. Although the use of corporal punishment in school settings in no longer sanctioned,[2] there is no clear consensus on the propriety of employing corporal punishment in the home. Researchers and other experts contest not only whether corporal punishment has negative effects on children but also whether negative effects are substantial or minimal (see Friedman & Schonberg, 1996; Kahneman, 2003). At the same time, in a 1995 national survey, more than 90% of American parents reported using corporal punishment on their young children (Straus & Stewart, 1999). Beyond spanking, other acts of parent-to-child physical aggression, such as slapping a child's hand, are not typically considered abusive (Black, Heyman & Slep, 2001).

Multiple theories and models have been offered in an effort to explain child physical abuse. These have focused on the individual victim, the individual perpetrator, parent–child interaction, family dynamics, interactions between individuals and their environment and sociocultural factors. Early theories of child physical abuse were based on a psychiatric model, which typically viewed child maltreatment as the result of parent psychopathology. However, more recent theories of abuse in childhood have moved away from these individual level approaches, instead recognizing that abuse is better explained through a complex interaction of individual, family, system and social factors (Belsky, 1993). Today, there is increasing recognition that child maltreatment results from the interaction of multiple factors across multiple domains, consistent with Bronfenbrenner's (1986) ecological model of family functioning. Nonetheless, individual and family-oriented theories continue to underlie most current prevention efforts, including therapy for parents with certain psychological characteristics, home visiting programs, parent support groups and parent education programs.

## BIOLOGICAL AND GENETIC FACTORS

Researchers have investigated a variety of factors with biological or genetic components among both perpetrators and victims of child abuse, with mixed results as to whether these factors contribute to the occurrence of child maltreatment. A majority of these studies have focused on perpetrators and, more specifically, on abusive parents.

A growing body of research indicates that biological factors (e.g., neuropsychological factors, hyperactivity) may increase individuals' risk for committing child abuse. For example, physically abusive individuals have shown hyperresponsive physiological activity to child stimuli such as crying, which may prompt increased negative responses in stressful situations involving children (Milner & Chilamkurti, 1991). Others have found data to support the hypothesis that deficits in cognitive processing may impair a parent's coping abilities and thus may increase the risk for child physical abuse (Milner, 1998). Still other studies have found that abusive adults report more health problems and physical disabilities than do nonabusers (Miller-Perrin & Perrin, 1999). The genetic nature of these factors, if any, is as yet unclear.

Though not solely biological or genetic in nature, parental substance abuse, which is reported to be a contributing factor in cases involving between one third and two thirds of children in the child welfare system, has been of particular interest to researchers (Kumpfer & Bayes, 1995). Relevant to child physical abuse is the finding that substance abuse can influence caregivers' parenting and discipline. More directly, prenatal exposure of children to drugs or alcohol poses a very real threat of physical harm, affecting an estimated 550,000 to 750,000 children each year (Goldman, Salus, Wolcott & Kennedy, 2003).

In regard to victims, it has been theorized that certain biological or genetic factors, including temperament and physical disability, may predispose a child toward abuse, primarily due to the increased stress these conditions present to parents. Primary among the child characteristics that have been associated with maltreatment are having a disability, a difficult temperament, psychiatric symptoms or behavioral problems (Brown, Cohen, Johnson & Salzinger, 1998). In 1993, the National Center on Child Abuse and Neglect (NCCAN) released a study representing the first national effort to assess the incidence of abuse among children with disabilities. This study indicated that the rate of abuse in this population is approximately double that found among children without disabilities. Earlier studies (see, e.g., Baladerian, 1990) found that the risk of abuse among children with disabilities was between 4 and 10 times greater than that of their counterparts without disabilities. Overall, however, it is unclear to what extent disabilities precede physical abuse. Moreover, the question of directionality—that is, does negative parenting behavior produce negative behavior from the child or vice versa?—has not been resolved.

## INDIVIDUAL FACTORS INFLUENCING RISK AND RESILIENCY

Although there is general agreement that demographic factors, while correlated with abuse, are not causal in nature, they have nonetheless been the subject of extensive empirical inquiry. Nonetheless, the nature of their association with risk and resiliency remains unclear. For example, some data support a slightly higher risk for physical abuse among males compared with females (Miller-Perrin & Perrin, 1999). NIS-3 data indicated that this heightened risk was limited to more severe cases of abuse (Sedlak & Broadhurst, 1996). However, in their review of relevant studies, Black and colleagues (2001) found that, overall, the empirical evidence did not suggest that child gender is a risk factor for parent-to-child physical aggression. There was more persuasive evidence to demonstrate a relationship between physical aggression toward the child and the child's socialized aggression, attention and internalizing and externalizing behaviors (as reported by the abusive parents). Similarly, the impact of race and ethnicity on risk for child physical abuse is uncertain. Using NIS-2 data, Sedlak (1997) found an age × race interaction whereby Hispanic and Black children were at increased risk for parent-to-child physical aggression as they aged. However, as discussed more fully herein, the effects of race are no doubt confounded with socioeconomic status.

Rather than focusing on the characteristics of victims, the vast majority of the literature examining risk factors for child maltreatment has examined perpetrators and, in the case of physical abuse, the child's parents. Overall, investigations into mothers' demographic characteristics, which far outnumber studies of fathers' characteristics, do not evidence clear associations between child physical abuse and maternal age, education and marital status (Black et al., 2001). However, Connelly and Straus (1992) did find a weak association between maltreatment rates and maternal age at the time of the child's birth; the younger a woman was when her child was born, the more likely she was to engage in abusive behavior. Clearly, any link between maternal age and child physical abuse may be a function of the relationship between age and other factors that impact risk of maltreatment, including lower socioeconomic status, lack of social support and resultant higher levels of stress.

Similar to age, studies examining the role of race have produced mixed results, leaving open the question of whether there is a racial difference in perpetration of child physical abuse (Black et al., 2001). Although minority race children are consistently overrepresented in child welfare reports (Cappalleri, Eckenrode & Powers, 1993), Berger and Brooks-Gunn (2005) found that the increased risk for physical abuse by African American mothers disappeared after controlling for socioeconomic status.

More promising as risk factors for identifying potentially abusive parents are factors related to mothers' dysphoria, such as unhappiness, emotional distress, anxiety, loneliness and isolation, depression, stress and coping (Berger, 2005; Berger and Brooks-Gunn, 2005; Black et al., 2001). Substance abuse and lack of involvement in community activities have also been associated with increased risk for abusive behavior (Brown et al., 1998).

As noted, relatively little research has examined risk and resiliency factors among fathers, despite the fact that they are overrepresented as perpetrators in cases of severe child physical abuse. In their review of the literature examining potential pathways for child physical abuse, Guterman and Lee (2005) identified a set of possible sociodemographic risk factors among fathers, including fathers' absence, age, employment status and economic contributions to the family. Other potential risk factors included paternal substance abuse, a history of maltreatment as a child, the nature of the father's relationship with the child's mother and the father's level of involvement with the child.

In examining individual level factors that impact risk and resiliency for child physical abuse, primary attention has been paid to characteristics related to individuals' parenting and discipline practices. Five areas that have been significantly associated with abusive parenting are (1) cognitive disturbances, (2) deficits in parenting skill, (3) problems with impulse control, (4) difficulties with stress management and (5) social skill problems (Azar & Twentyman, 1986). Deficits in any of these areas, alone or in combination, can play a role in more systemic difficulties that increase the risk of abuse; for example, a parent's poor social skills may result in a smaller support network that, in turn, heightens his or her risk for abusive parenting. The dominant perspective, which is grounded in learning and behavioral theories, focuses on lack of parent knowledge or lack of parenting skills. Studies indicate that abusive parents can be distinguished from nonabusive parents based on social-cognitive and affective processes tied to the parents' perceptions of their child and the parent–child relationship (Erickson & Egeland, 1996). More specifically, abusive parents often have difficulty putting their child's behavior in context, with regard for his or her developmental level. Abusive parents tend to have inappropriate expectations for their children that do not comport with the child's abilities or level of understanding and that, in turn, may lead the parent to make negative attributions about the child's behavior or the motives for that behavior. These attributions may also reflect parents' own childhood experiences and level of cognitive functioning. Consistent with cycle of violence theories, abusive parents tend to report more violence in their family of origin than do nonabusing parents (Milner, 1998). Nonetheless, the majority of individuals abused as children (about 70%) do not grow up to be abusers (Miller-Perrin & Perrin, 1999).

Studies have also found parents who abuse their children to be less supportive, affectionate, playful and responsive to their children than nonabusive parents (Bousha & Twentyman, 1984). Abusive parents tend to communicate with their child less frequently, and they demonstrate fewer positive parenting behaviors (Azar & Twentyman, 1986). Research on maltreating parents, particularly physically abusive mothers, evidences that they are both more likely to use harsh discipline strategies (e.g., physical punishment) and verbal aggression and less likely to use positive parenting strategies (e.g., the use of time-outs, reasoning with the child, acknowledging and encouraging the child's successes) (Trickett & Kucynski, 1986; Whipple & Webster-Stratton, 1991).

## FAMILY FACTORS INFLUENCING RISK AND RESILIENCY

Beyond and in conjunction with risk factors at the individual level, the family setting may contribute to risk and resiliency. In their review of risk factors for child physical abuse, Black and colleagues (2001) identified three family variables that, from adolescents' reports, were moderately to strongly associated with physical abuse: (1) high levels of family stress; (2) being less adaptive; and (3) being less cohesive. Other studies have identified high levels of family conflict and lack of expressiveness as risk factors for child physical abuse. Moreover, compared with nonabusive parents, abusive parents report more conflict and less support in their own families of origin (Milner, 1998).

Not only the dynamics of family interactions but also the situations in which families find themselves may impact the potential for child physical abuse. These factors include domestic violence, social isolation, illness, death of a family member and financial stress (Miller-Perrin & Perrin, 1999; Milner, 1998). Some studies (see, e.g., Sedlak & Broadhurst, 1996) indicate that children living with single parents are at higher risk of physical abuse than are those children living with two biological parents. It has been proposed that this heightened level of risk may be tied to the higher levels of stress experienced by single parents, who are more likely to experience financial stress and social isolation (Goldman et al., 2003).

Partner aggression has also been identified a significant risk factor for abuse (Black et al., 2001). Although intimate partner violence is not limited to male-to-female aggression, approximately 85% of victims are women, a rate that is five times that of males. Moreover, Black women experience domestic violence rates 22 times those for women of other races and 35% higher than the rate for White women in particular (Rennison & Welchans, 2000).

Research demonstrating a high co-occurrence of spousal battering and child maltreatment points to a serious risk to the physical safety of children in these violent homes (Appel & Holden, 1998). In fact, based on his review of 36 studies, Edleson (2001) estimated that 30% to 60% of children whose mothers are abused are themselves subjected to abuse. Intimate partner violence and child maltreatment have also been linked in terms of their severity and frequency.

As described by Edleson (2001), spousal violence and child maltreatment can interact in a number of ways: The same perpetrator may target both his spouse and children, a child may simply become caught up in a domestic assault or intervene to protect his or her mother or a battered mother may abuse or neglect her child as a result of her experiences. Maternal reciprocity, in which a mother responds to her battering with violence against her child, is, however, controversial and poorly understood. Further, data indicating that much of the violence committed by women can be categorized as self-defense has prompted some researchers to suggest that mothers may use violence against their children as a way of preventing more serious injury to the child at the hands of her male partner (Edleson, 2001).

As noted, overall, theoretical approaches to physical abuse in childhood have moved toward more ecological approaches, which recognize that multiple factors, contexts and systems contribute to this phenomenon. Wolfe (1987) proposed a transitional model of abuse that conceptualizes parents moving through three stages along a continuum that culminates in abusive parenting. At each stage, a variety of destabilizing and compensatory factors—including characteristics of the parents, the parent–child relationship, the family and the broader social context—may operate to move a parent toward abusive parenting. In the initial stage, the parent experiences a general reduction in tolerance for stress and disinhibition of aggression; in the second stage, the parent manages acute crises and provocation poorly; and in the final stage, the parent exhibits habitual patterns of arousal and aggression with family members.

## SOCIAL AND COMMUNITY FACTORS INFLUENCING RISK AND RESILIENCY

Like the individual, the family cannot be viewed in isolation; rather, it is important to consider the broader context in which the family operates. As indicated in the preceding sections, one factor that has been the subject of fairly intense research scrutiny is the level of stress that a family or its members experience as well as the link between stress and societal and cultural conditions such as poverty, social isolation, racism, sexism and tolerance of violence and child maltreatment. Some theorists propose that there is a spillover effect from acceptable forms of violence (e.g., violence on television) to unacceptable forms of violence (e.g., child physical abuse), whereas others link abuse to the implicit acceptance of violence against children in our society.

Several theories have been proposed in an effort to elucidate the association between poverty and child maltreatment, perhaps the predominant one of which links the two through stress (i.e., poverty leads to higher levels of stress, which, in turn, lead to higher risk of child physical abuse). Some have proposed that characteristics that make parents vulnerable to poverty, such as substance abuse, also make them vulnerable to perpetrating abuse. For example, there are data to suggest that maltreating parents, compared with their nonabusive counterparts, report experiencing great social isolation and less social support (Chan, 1994; Thompson, 1994). Environmental theories propose that maltreatment would be decreased if resources (e.g., money, information) and supports (e.g., social support) for parents were increased and systemic changes were made (Daro, 1988).

A number of community socioeconomic characteristics are associated with increased levels of child maltreatment (Garbarino, Kostelny & Grady, 1993). For example, in their analysis of 185 different neighborhoods in Missouri, Drake and Pandey (1996) found that communities with greater poverty and a lower percentage of two-parent families had significantly higher rates of child physical abuse. Overall, data confirm that communities with a larger proportion of residents living in poverty experience higher rates of abuse; however, the reasons for this association are unclear. For example, parents in poverty are more likely to live in communities with high levels of violence, which some contend may predispose these parents to view violence as an acceptable response or behavior. In fact, children living in high-violence neighborhoods have been found to be at higher risk for physical abuse than children from safer neighborhoods (Cicchetti, Lynch & Manly, 1997). However, violence is certainly not characteristic of all poor families, indicating that other factors are also involved.

As noted, empirical data evidence a significant relationship between child maltreatment and social bonding and social isolation (Thompson, 1994). Clearly, levels of social bonding may be influenced by community, as well as individual-level variables. In fact, child maltreatment rates tend to be low even in high-poverty neighborhoods when residents know one another, when there is a sense of community pride, when people are involved in community organizations and when residents feel that they can ask their neighbors for help (Emery & Laumann-Billings, 1998). Nonetheless, this dynamic may explain why communities with more female-headed households, a higher unemployment rate, a lower percentage of wealthy residents, a lower median education level, more overcrowding and a higher percentage of new residents tend to have higher rates of maltreatment (Garbarino et al, 1993). For example, as of March 2003, 28% of female-headed households lived below the poverty line compared with 13.5% of male-headed households with no wife present and 5.4% of married couples. In fact, the national poverty rates for children and other individuals living in single-mother households has always been higher than the overall national poverty rate (U.S. Census Bureau, 2003). Similarly, interrelationships among these factors may explain why communities with a larger proportion of African American or Hispanic residents experience higher rates of maltreatment. U.S. Census data from 2003 indicated that 24.4% of Blacks and 22.5% of those of Hispanic origin lived below the poverty line compared with 8.2% of White non-Hispanic individuals.

## EVIDENCE-BASED TREATMENT INTERVENTIONS FOR PHYSICAL ABUSE IN CHILDHOOD

### What Works

Treatment for child physical abuse often consists of intensive case management, through which a professional, typically a social worker, oversees the provision of services to the family, including both the child and the parents. In the vast majority of identified cases of child physical abuse, treatment begins with social service system intervention, the immediate goal of which is to end the physical abuse and thus routinely involves the child's removal from the home. The next step is to ensure that the necessary services are provided to ensure that a safe environment is provided for the child, ideally within the parental home. The specific services provided, as well as the family's response, vary considerably. Accordingly, the length of treatment is also highly diverse. However, treatment has been conceptualized as moving through three distinct phases:

1. Crisis (initial period up to four months), in which the primary goal is to establish trust between the professional and his or her clients
2. Dependence (4–12 months after implementation of treatment), in which offending parents develop a dependence on the professional for support, encouragement and practical assistance
3. Open acknowledgment of dependence between worker and client (13–24 months).

Only after parents have become aware of their needs and have developed alternative ways of coping, as well as strategies for seeking any necessary help in the future, are services terminated.

In most states, although child protective services assumes primary responsibility for case management, recommended services (e.g., parenting education, mental health services) are provided through outside contractor agencies. The fundamental question, then, is, which services are effective in treating child physical abuse? As with the other topics covered in this chapter, this question requires the consideration of both parents and children. Generally, treatment services for parents are aimed at changing potentially abusive parenting behaviors, whereas child services target abuse-specific symptoms (Kees & Bonner, 2006).

Treatment of physically abusive parents occurs primarily in outpatient settings, and there is wide variation in the curriculum and content offered through psychoeducational or parenting programs. The fact that minimal data are available in support of the effectiveness of any particular program content in regard to its impact on child physical abuse severely limits the ability to identify effective programs. Likewise, following Kempe, Silverman, Steele, Droegemueller and Silver's (1962) initial identification of the battered child syndrome, child treatment services centered on the long-term medical consequences of the child's injuries, such as brain damage, improperly healed fractures and losses in sensory capacity. Only later did attention turn to the psychological consequences of these injuries, which accounts, in part, for the lack of data to inform treatment interventions. Nonetheless, there is emerging evidence to suggest that some innovative approaches may be effective in responding to child physical abuse by working with both children and parents. Foremost among these is abuse-focused cognitive behavior therapy (AF-CBT).

AF-CBT has been acknowledged as an evidence-based practice that effectively assists school-age children and their parents in overcoming the impact of child physical abuse (Kolko, 2002). AF-CBT represents an integration of cognitive and learning and behavioral interventions with traditional child abuse and family-systems therapies. The intervention, which is delivered primarily in outpatient settings, can also be delivered on an individual basis in alternative residential settings by a trained mental health professional. The treatment typically involves 12 to 18 hours of service over a period of 10 to 12 weeks, with components directed to the child, the parent and the parent–child dyad or family system. Overall, the approach emphasizes education in specific intrapersonal and interpersonal skills aimed at encouraging prosocial behavior and at discouraging coercive or aggressive behavior at the individual and family level (Kolko & Swenson, 2002).

An increasing number of studies evidence the effectiveness of AF-CBT in connection with the treatment of child physical abuse victims. Studies have shown AF-CBT to be more effective in decreasing symptomatology when compared with no treatment as well as with standard community treatment (Cohen, Berliner & Mannarino, 2003). In a randomized controlled trial, Kolko (1996b) compared AF-CBT provided individually with child and parent, family therapy, and standard community care. He found that both CBT and family therapy produced more improvement in the areas of child-to-parent violence, child externalizing behavior, parental distress and abuse risk and family conflict and cohesion than did standard community care (Kolko, 1996a). Participants receiving CBT or family therapy were also less likely to experience repeat acts of abuse.

Another well-researched program that integrates both treatment and prevention components focused on parents is Project 12-Ways (Lutzker & Newman, 1986). Project 12-Ways provides in-home treatment in an effort to improve parents' ability to generalize skills learned as well as to reduce the potential stigma of clinic-based programs. Among the services provided are training in parenting, assertiveness, self-control, employment, money management, health and nutrition, home safety and stress reduction. Program evaluation data have demonstrated reductions in repeat reports of child abuse for program participants compared with a matched comparison group (Lutzker, Bigelow, Doctor, Gershater & Greene, 1998; Lutzker & Rice, 1987).

## What Might Work

Another treatment intervention for which there are data available to support a positive impact on abusive behavior is parent–child interaction therapy (PCIT). Originally developed as a treatment for children ages 2 to 7 years with externalizing behavior problems (e.g., oppositional and defiant disorder), PCIT has recently been adapted for use with victims of child physical abuse. Based on the work of Sheila Eyberg (Eyberg & Boggs, 1989), PCIT is a parent-training program in which therapists provide parents with specific behavioral skills through direct coaching by way of a wireless device. The primary modification of PCIT for child abuse populations is an increased focus on the parent; selection for treatment is based on the parent's demonstrating aggressive or abusive behavior toward his or her children (Herschell & McNeil, 2005). The program consists of two phases, child-directed interaction and parent-directed interaction, which together typically extend over 10 to 14 weeks. In the first phase, parents learn play therapy skills (e.g., PRIDE skills [praise, reflection, imitation, description and enthusiasm]) as well as how to apply these skills by attending to positive child behavior. Parents are then taught relaxation skills. In the parent-directed interaction phases, parents are taught behavior modification principles (e.g., effective use of time-outs), with attention to adapting skills to the specific needs of the particular parent and child. As parents interact with their child, they are instructed on how to integrate relaxation and child behavior management skills. Parents are encouraged not to use physical discipline and are coached on self-control and the development of appropriate expectations for their child.

Initial studies examining the use of PCIT as a response to child physical abuse have produced promising results. In a randomized clinical trial, a group receiving combined PCIT and motivation intervention for physically abusive parents demonstrated significantly lower physical abuse recurrence at the three-year follow-up than did a community parenting group (Chaffin et al., 2004). In a study of 136 biological parents and their children, Timmer, Urquiza, Zebell and McGrath (2005) found decreases in child behavior problems, parent stress, and abuse risk following the PCIT intervention.

Day and residential treatment programs represent an early response to child victims of abuse. Such programs have been directed primarily at preschoolers and have shown some evidence of success (Kolko, 1996a); however, whether these programs' combination of group activities, peer interaction and individual treatment generalizes successfully to older children remains an open question.

Play therapy approaches have also been popular among providers working with victims of child abuse; however, the effectiveness of these approaches has not been well supported empirically (Kaplan, Pelcovitz & Labruna, 1999). Instead, emerging research indicates that treatment interventions that focus on the child's specific symptoms and are guided by the clinical research literature on evidence-based treatments for those particular symptoms are more effective than general approaches. For example, exposure-based therapy has demonstrated effectiveness for posttraumatic stress and anxiety symptoms, as have cognitive interventions for depression and behavioral parent training for children with behavior problems (Chaffin, 2000).

## What Does Not Work

A number of attachment-based treatment and parenting interventions have been developed that aim to assist children who, as a result of abuse, exhibit behavioral and relationship disturbances that place them at risk for negative outcomes. Although several of these interventions show promise, a particular subset of therapies aimed at attachment disorder or other attachment problems have been connected to a number of child deaths and thus raise serious concern; notable among these is a technique known as attachment parenting. In contrast with interventions designed to improve early childhood attachment by focusing on the parent–child relationship and by teaching positive parenting skills, which have been show effective in enhancing children's attachment security (Bakermans-Kranenburg, van IJzendoorn & Juffer, 2003), attachment parenting focuses on what is characterized as the individual child's pathology.

Central to these conceptualizations is a focus on the concept of suppressed rage as an explanation of the behavior of children, typically foster, adoptive, deprived or traumatized children. Deviating from traditional attachment theory, proponents of these controversial attachment therapies propose that young children who experience adversity, including child physical abuse, become enraged at a deep, primitive level, which precludes them from developing healthy attachments or being genuinely affectionate with others. Further, behavior problems result when the child's rage erupts into unchecked aggression. Such children are described as highly manipulative and resistant to authority, leading them to engage in continuing power struggles. Importantly, most attachment researcher agree that rage theory is not well supported, either theoretically or empirically (Chaffin et al., 2005).

Many controversial attachment therapies maintain that for the child to function normally, his or her rage must be released. Accordingly, a primary feature of many of these therapies is the use of psychological, physical or aggressive means, including scheduled holding, binding and rib-cage stimulation (e.g., tickling), to provoke the child into ventilating his or her rage. However, when tested empirically, encouraging physical ventilation of anger has been found to increase rather than to decrease levels of anger and aggression toward others. In addition, children who respond to abuse by expressing or ventilating anger appear to have poorer adaptation (Chaffin et al., 2005).

## Overall Comment

Research has established that the successful treatment of physically abusive parents is elusive, particularly in regard to altering persistent parenting patterns (Geeraert, Van den Noortgate, Grietens & Onghena, 2004). Moreover, only in the past two decades has there been a sustained effort to develop empirically supported treatments directed at the child victims of physical abuse. Recent innovations do offer encouraging results. Among these innovations, AF-CBT appears to be particularly promising; however, additional research is needed to identify its critical components as well as optimal dosage (Cohen et al., 2003). Future research may also serve to document positive outcomes related to child physical abuse among programs that target parents and their children with behavior disorders, including, most notably, PCIT.

## PSYCHOPHARMACOLOGY AND PHYSICAL ABUSE IN CHILDHOOD

Generally speaking, there is no direct support for the use of psychopharmacology in responding to child physical abuse. Rather, as noted by Cohen et al. (2003), psychopharmacological agents may be prescribed for child victims who develop particular symptomatology (e.g., depression, anxiety disorders, panic attacks, posttraumatic stress disorder [PTSD], behavioral disorders) in an effort to address those specific symptoms. Because children's responses to physical abuse vary widely, it is difficult to link any particular medication to their experience of abuse. Although there has been some systematic study of the use of psychotropic medication (i.e., selective serotonin reuptake inhibitors such as sertraline or paroxetine) for children with symptoms of PTSD, clear evidence of its effectiveness, if any, is not currently available.

## THE PREVENTION OF PHYSICAL ABUSE IN CHILDHOOD

### What Works

Efforts to enhance parental capacity, which constitute the most prevalent and best-researched methods to prevent physical child abuse, fall into three broad categories: public education and awareness efforts; home visitation programs; and parenting education and support services directed to at-risk parents (Daro & Connelly, 2002). Parent education models are grounded in the belief that lack of knowledge about child development and inadequate parenting skills are primary causes of child maltreatment (Cowen, 2001; Wolfe, 1985). The focus of these programs is on teaching parents new skills beyond and, in many situations in contrast with, those learned during their own upbringing that will improve their resources, coping skills and parenting competencies (Reppucci, Britner & Woolard, 1997). Despite the prevalence of parent education programs, few have been evaluated for their specific impact, if any, on child maltreatment. Empirical evaluations have produced evidence of positive gains in overall parenting skill, an increase in positive parent–child interactions, more extensive use of social supports, less use of corporal punishment, higher self-esteem, personal functioning and, for teenage mothers, fewer subsequent births, higher employment rates and less welfare dependency (Daro, 1988; Daro & Connelly, 2002). However, positive outcomes have not been consistent across programs. Moreover, most programs for which empirical evidence of effectiveness is available target first-time parents or parents of very young children. Little is know about preventing the physical abuse of children once they enter their elementary school years.

Among the large number of parent education and support programs that have been developed, two have proliferated and are widely recognized as the most prominent across research and practice:

1. The Olds model, the central feature of which is nurse home visitation (Holden, Willis & Corcoran, 1992)
2. The Healthy Families model, a paraprofessional model developed from Hawaii Healthy Start

By late 2004, there were approximately 170 nurse–family partnership programs and 430 Healthy Families program sites in operation (Leventhal, 2005). Fundamental components of both the Olds model and the Healthy Families model include early and frequent home visits, the provision of care within the context of a therapeutic and supportive relationship, an established curriculum, modeling effective parenting and connecting families to appropriate community services. However, there are also important distinctions between the two models, the primary one of which relates to the individual providing the intervention—that is, the home visitor. As noted, the Olds' model uses nurses, reasoning that their professional health training and experience has prepared them to make clinical assessments and to offer guidance to clients. The Healthy Families model employs paraprofessionals, reasoning that although they are less skilled at making assessments and have less training in regard to health and development issues, as community members they are nonetheless better able to establish strong personal connections with families at risk. Although there are also distinguishing features to the selection criteria employed to identify families for service provision, both models target first-time mothers from families perceived as at high risk and thus are not specifically directed at children in the age range covered by this chapter (i.e., 5–13 years). In fact, although there are data demonstrating the positive impact of the Olds model (see, e.g., Kitzman et al., 1997, 2000) and the Healthy Families model (Duggan et al., 1999) on factors including parenting attitudes and behavior as well as reports of child maltreatment, the impact of these strategies on reducing the physical abuse of older children has not been documented empirically.

## What Might Work

New approaches to parent education hold promise for the effective prevention of child physical abuse. Among the better known is Project Safe Care (Gershater-Molko, Lutzker & Wesch, 2002), a highly structured, skill-based protocol that provides home-based parent training focused on parent–child interaction training, home safety and child health. The program is currently being offered to families with parenting risk factors and at least one comorbid problem (e.g., parental substance abuse) and evaluated through a randomized trial in Oklahoma.

Other programs have taken a more universal approach to prevention, seeking to educate parents on stress management, coping and parenting skills, appropriate discipline, child development and safety issues. Illustrative of this approach is the Adults and Children Together (ACT) Against Violence Parents Raising Safe Kids program. Developed by the American Psychological Association in collaboration with the National Association for the Education of Young, ACT is a national antiviolence initiative that emphasizes the critical role that parents and other adult caregivers can play in providing a learning environment for young children that helps to protect them from violence and injury. The overarching goals of ACT are (1) to make early violence prevention a central and ongoing part of the community and (2) to educate adults about their important role in creating healthy and safe environments for children that will protect them from violence. The program can be implemented in diverse settings (e.g., schools, community agencies) and can be integrated into the broader community framework of services for parents (e.g., Head Start, Healthy Families, general education development [GED] courses), regardless of their level of risk for abuse. In fact, one of the strengths of ACT is its ability to be administered to all parents in an efficient and economical manner, such that the prevention of violence against children becomes an important piece of a public health approach to violence within the community. However, efforts to evaluate the outcomes of ACT are in their early phases.

Other parent education programs may also contribute to the prevention of child physical abuse, despite a focus on other goals. For example, Parenting Wisely is a self-administered, interactive CD-ROM program offered as an alternative or complement to family interventions. Originally developed at Ohio University, the program was specifically geared toward low-income, single-parent families (Gordon & Stanar, 2003). Parenting Wisely has demonstrated positive outcomes for parents including increased knowledge and use of effective parenting skills, enhanced problem solving, establishing clear expectations and reductions in violence and is recognized as a model program by the U.S. Department of Health and Human Services Substance Abuse Mental Health Services Administration (O'Neill & Woodward, 2002; see also studies cited at http://www.parentingwisely.org). Although not yet implemented or evaluated with child abuse populations specifically, some efforts to examine the generalizability of programs such as Parenting Wisely are currently under way.

Family support models that emphasize family strengths in an effort to increase the capabilities of individuals and families are also gaining in popularity among service providers. Such programs, which are typically voluntary, are based on the philosophy that services to children and families should do the following (Kagan, 1994):

1. Be offered to the family as a whole rather than to children and parents separately
2. Build on family strengths
3. Empower families to make decisions regarding the extent and type of services they receive
4. Include an array of comprehensive services
5. Incorporate a prevention component

Despite the rapid expansion of family support models nationally, empirical evidence of their effectiveness is, as yet, minimal (Kees & Bonner, 2006). Moreover, research has identified engagement and retention of participants as well as lack of consistency as challenges to the success of these programs (Daro & Connelly, 2002). However, recent data indicate that high-risk families remained in family support programs longer and received more kinds and more intensive services than did low-risk families (Green, Johnson & Rodgers, 1999).

One promising prevention program that employs a combined parenting education and family support strategy is the Triple P-Positive Parenting

Programme, developed by Sanders, Cann and Markie-Dadds (2003) in Australia and currently under evaluation in the United States. Triple P employs a multilevel system designed to prevent severe behavioral, emotional and developmental problems as well as child maltreatment by enhancing protective factors and reducing risk factors. The objectives of the program are as follows:

1. To enhance the knowledge, skills, confidence, self-sufficiency, coping skills and resourcefulness of parents
2. To promote nurturing, safe, engaging, nonviolent and low-conflict environments
3. To promote children's social, emotional, linguistic, intellectual and behavioral competencies through positive parenting practices

Triple P encompasses five levels of intervention, based on a tiered continuum reflecting varying levels of family risk and protective factors and the accompanying type and intensity of intervention required. The program is further tailored to the developmental level of the child (i.e., infancy, toddlerhood, preschool age, preadolescence, adolescence). Because development of the parent's capacity for self-regulation is viewed as a central skill to promoting parental competence, Triple P focuses on giving parents the skills necessary to be independent problem solvers (i.e., self-sufficiency, self-efficacy, self-management, personal agency). Other parenting skills are centered on five core principles: (1) ensuring a safe and engaging environment for the child; (2) creating a positive learning environment; (3) using assertive discipline; (4) formulating realistic expectations of children; and (5) caring for oneself as a parent.

There is increasing acknowledgment that community-based models that incorporate multiple intervention components are the most promising means of reducing child physical abuse; however, few such programs have been implemented or evaluated. In South Carolina, Melton and colleagues are testing Strong Communities, which incorporates a community-based approach to prevention. The goal of Strong Communities (http://www.clemson.edu/strongcommunities) is to strengthen neighborhoods and to build parent leadership capacity through outreach workers, volunteers and community organizations, all of whom serve as partners in efforts to make child protection an integral part of daily life and to facilitate informal and reciprocal social support within the community. This initiative also integrates home visiting and other supports into pediatric well-child visits, community policing and school-based early childhood programs.

Other models for integrating multiple interventions may also prove successful. For example, Parent Child Development Centers, which consist of comprehensive parent education for mothers, including information on child development and effective parenting, home management, nutrition and health, mothers' personal development and awareness of resources along with programs for children and other supports, could incorporate successful elements of parenting education more generally. Similarly, programs that help build parents' social support networks may reduce the stresses that lead to abuse (MacLeod & Nelson, 2000). To the extent that the Healthy Families model incorporates multiple program components, its positive benefits may well extend to children in the range of 5 to 13 years. Disseminated by Prevent Child Abuse American since 1992, programs based on the Healthy Families model today frequently develop collaborative partnership with other service providers in their communities and incorporate additional training or hire specialists to meet particular family needs, factors that may well enhance their impact. Nonetheless, both retention and fidelity have presented continuing challenges to Healthy Families, with studies indicating that the model is rarely implemented as designed (Duggan et al., 1999). The retention problem, in particular, may limit the impact of the program for older children. For example, in the original Hawaii Healthy Start Program, only 49% of eligible families were still actively participating in the program by the time the child was 1 year of age (Leventhal, 2005).

Given that factors at multiple levels contribute to the occurrence of child physical abuse, it follows that prevention efforts should also target multiple levels, including social and system level reform. However, as a number of commentators (e.g., Garbarino & Collin, 1999) have noted, society has tended to neglect not only children but also whole segments of the population (e.g., the poor), such that efforts at this level—along with any research to inform these efforts—are rare. For example, there are few interventions that seek to prevent child abuse by helping families to escape poverty. Some programs encourage teen parents to return to school or to obtain further training, outcomes that, in turn, may contribute to increasing their self-sufficiency; however, this component is frequently lacking in programs aimed at older parents, even though they also face significant economic hardships. Initial evaluations of programs developed to help parents obtain financial self-sufficiency suggest that they may be helpful in improving the economic situation of poor families; however, they require an intensive and long-term approach and careful evaluation is necessary to determine their effect, if any, on preventing child physical abuse (Hay & Jones, 1994).

Similarly, the potential impact of public policy on child physical abuse has not been well explored, in large part because there is relatively little policy that addresses prevention directly. This is perhaps best illustrated at the federal level, where the Child Abuse Prevention and Treatment Act (CAPTA) remains the sole federal program aimed specifically at child abuse prevention. Originally enacted in 1974, CAPTA defined child abuse and neglect, established the National Center on Child Abuse and Neglect (NCCAN), established basic state grants for prevention and treatment, provided money for demonstration grants to prevent, to identify and to treat child abuse and neglect; and founded an advisory board to coordinate the federal response to maltreatment. The Community-Based Family Resource and Support (CBFRS) program is the major prevention component of CAPTA, providing funding for various community-based family support programs designed to prevent child abuse, including parenting classes, substance abuse treatment, mental health services, respite care and domestic violence services. CAPTA has been reauthorized several times since 1974. However, to date, the Act has yet to be fully funded, making it impossible to measure the potential impact of its provisions (Portwood, 2006).

Other federal policies may impact child abuse prevention, albeit less directly. For example, as noted by Hay and Jones (1994), welfare policy that seeks to keep children out of poverty and ensures the availability of affordable, quality child care could assist in reducing child physical abuse. Provision of high-quality care for children could also help to prevent child abuse both directly and indirectly by reducing parental stress. However, the current trend is toward increasing responsibility for child-related programs at the state level—at the same time most states have less funds available or are directing less funds to support social programs.

The media is another promising outlet for promoting positive parenting and FOR reducing child physical abuse. Illustrative of this potential are the results of mass education efforts on the dangers of shaking a baby (Showers, 1992). A campaign in the Netherlands designed to encourage abused children to disclose abuse also produced positive results (Hoefnagels & Baartman, 1997). At a community level, the Mayor's Office for Children and Youth and the Baltimore City Commission for Children and Youth documented a reduction in observed incidents of child abuse associated with receiving a bad report card following implementation of a school-related child abuse prevention initiative that included televised public service announcements prior to and during the week of report card distribution, along with informational inserts in report cards (Mandell, 2000). Taken together, these studies suggest that the media may be a powerful tool for public health education on the topic of child physical abuse.

## What Does Not Work

Although some child physical abuse prevention programs have demonstrated success, many fail to provide evidence of program effectiveness (Gomby, Culross & Behrman, 1999). Though some programs are most likely better than others, few empirical studies have attempted to identify those factors that increase a program's likelihood of success. However, researchers have identified components of particular child abuse prevention programs that are not successful. For example, in their meta-analysis of 56 home visitation programs designed to promote family wellness and to prevent child maltreatment, MacLeod and Nelson (2000) found the lowest effect sizes for those programs that involved 12 or fewer visits and continued for less than six months. Despite this finding, almost 40% of the interventions examined were less than six months in duration, raising concern that as implemented, a substantial number of such programs are not effective.

Although there are some encouraging data on the ability of parent education interventions to reduce child abuse and, more frequently, to enhance positive parenting practices, overall the research establishes that there is no single cure-all, particularly for those families facing multiple challenges, including domestic violence (Eckenrode et al., 2000). Likewise, attempts to educate parents dealing with severe depression and substance abuse have shown limited success (Daro & Cohn, 1988). Arguably, the primary limitation to the existing child abuse prevention programs appears is not their approach, per se, but the degree to which they can be effective with a particular subpopulation (Daro, 1988). For example, research indicated that current parent training programs are less effective with disadvantaged parents and low-income single mothers in particular (Webster-Stratton, 1998). However, few of the hundreds of parent education and support programs that have been developed have been tailored for use with specific groups, which may impact not only their effectiveness in general but also other specific factors that can affect their impact. For example, Daro and Connelly (2002) proposed that the high attrition rates in most programs—between 30% and 50%—is attributable to a mismatch between what is offered and what is needed.

## Overall Comment

Strikingly little empirical data are available to inform efforts to prevent the physical abuse of children ages 5 to 13 years. Though not decisive, a considerably larger body of research addresses prevention efforts with parents of young children (i.e., below the age of 5 years). The extent to which these findings can be generalized to older children is, for the most part, untested. Though there is widespread agreement that intervention efforts should begin as early in a child's life as possible, from a theoretical perspective efforts to provide support and education for parents and other caregivers at any point in a child's life would appear to be have some positive impact on the prevention of abusive behaviors. Nonetheless, overall the record of child abuse prevention programs has been mixed, owing to multiple factors, including a failure to implement programs as designed or to adhere to quality controls and an inability to be as comprehensive as necessary. In addition, the general lack of availability of prevention programming and, more specifically, programs' inability to target those parents most in need of prevention services have limited the success of current prevention efforts.

There is increasing acknowledgement that prevention efforts must extend beyond parents to communities and society at large. Among the range of programs that have yet to be fully evaluated are increasing the economic self-sufficiency of families, enhancing communities and their resources, discouraging excessive use of corporal punishment and other forms of violence, making health care more accessible and affordable, expanding and improving coordination of social services, improving treatment for alcohol and drug abuse, improving the identification and treatment of mental health problems, increasing the availability of affordable child care and increasing the value that society places on children (Bethea, 1999).

## RECOMMENDED BEST PRACTICE

### Treatment

Given that there is no single cause of child physical abuse, it follows that there will be no single treatment solution; rather, interventions must address a range of treatment targets (Herschell and McNeil, 2005). In doing so, the following best practices are recommended:

- A preliminary assessment should focus on the characteristics of the child, the parent and the broader parent–child or family context. Not only the family's various clinical problems but also their strengths should be identified (Kolko, 2002).
- Appropriate treatment should focus on the parent to eliminate abusive behavior as well as on the child to reduce symptomatology and to promote healthy psychosocial development (Kolko, 2002).
- Among the treatments developed for child physical abuse, AF-CBT is recognized as an evidence-based practice, with empirical study documenting positive outcomes for both physically abusive and aggressive

parents and their school-age children. Another promising intervention, PCIT, which was originally developed as a treatment for children ages 2 to 7 years with externalizing behavior problems, has recently been adapted for use with victims of child physical abuse and has demonstrated some positive effects.

## Prevention

The most common approaches to child abuse prevention involve providing education or support to parents (Gomby et al., 1999). Ideally, interventions can be initiated early in the child's life, even before his or her birth. However, in the case of older children, positive results may still obtain from prevention efforts that impact the parent–child relationship before abuse occurs or parents have established negative patterns of parenting.

Though research supporting the effectiveness of particular programs is sparse, there is a considerably body of data (e.g., Bethea, 1999; Daro, 1996; Guterman, 1997; MacLeod & Nelson, 2000) to support the following best practices:

- Overall, programs should emphasize and seek to expand on family strengths.
- Both instruction and services should focus on the child's particular developmental level.
- Programs should be interactive, providing opportunities for parents to model the behaviors being promoted.
- An emphasis on social supports and developing the skills required to access these supports is another important component of successful prevention programs. Similarly, there must be a broad network of support services, with special supports for those requiring more intensive services.
- In-home services, as well as case-management support, are particularly promising components of parent education and support programs. However, home visitation components must be of sufficient duration (i.e., more than six months in length).
- Programs must recognize cultural differences in family functioning and the nature of parent–child interactions and be responsive to this diversity.
- There must be careful attention to fidelity of program implementation.
- Prevention efforts should also include an evaluation component to inform program processes and outcomes. Current evaluations of prevention programs frequently do not include measures related to child abuse, making it difficult to determine what, if any, impact the program has on the occurrence of child physical abuse as well as to distinguish effective and promising programs and their essential components.
- Given the complex nature of the origins and consequences of child maltreatment, to prevent abuse multiple strategies must be employed, with different approaches tailored to the unique features of specific types of abuse.

Overall, as noted by Daro and Connelly (2002), future prevention efforts need to offer communities flexible alternatives for constructing prevention programs tailored to their specific needs and resources from empirically based components.

In addition to the need to incorporate best practices at the program level, communities must begin to examine strategies for integrating programs into a comprehensive system of support and effecting reforms at broader levels of society. Even well-designed and well-implemented programs are unlikely to lead to substantial change unless they are supported by their context. To prevent all forms of child abuse, communities must acknowledge that parenting is an extremely important and difficult job and make a real and sustained commitment to supporting children and their families.

## ENDNOTES

1. Munchausen-by-proxy is a pattern of behavior in which a parent, typically the mother, intentionally falsely reports, exaggerates or induces illness in her child. DSM-IV-TR refers to this disorder as "factitious disorder by proxy." (See American Psychiatric Association, 2000, pp. 281–283.)
2. The American Academy of Child and Adolescent Psychiatry, sponsored by the American Psychiatric Association, stated its opposition to corporal punishment in schools in a 1989 position statement. In doing so, the Academy acknowledged that it was aligning itself with the National Congress of Parents and Teachers, the American Medical Association, the National Association of School Psychologists, the National Education Association, the American Bar Association, and the American Academy of Pediatrics. Similar position statements opposing corporal punishment in schools have been passed by the American Psychological Association and the National Association for the Education of Young Children.

## REFERENCES

American Psychiatric Association (2000). *Diagnostic and Statistical Manual of Mental Disorders* (4th ed., text revision). Washington, DC: American Psychiatric Association.

Appel, A. E. & Holden, G. W. (1998). The co-occurrence of spouse and physical child abuse: A review and appraisal. *Journal of Family Psychology, 12,* 578–599.

Azar, S. T. & Twentyman, C. T. (1986). Cognitive behavioral perspectives on the assessment and treatment of child abuse. In P. C. Kendall (Ed.), *Advances in cognitive behavioral research and therapy,* vol. 5 (pp. 237–267). New York: Academic Press.

Bakermans-Kranenburg, M. J., van IJzendoorn, M. H. & Juffer, F. (2003). Less is more: A meta-analyses of sensitivity and attachment interventions in early childhood. *Psychological Bulletin, 129,* 195–215.

Baladerian, N. (1990). *Overview of abuse and persons with disabilities.* Culver City, CA: Disability, Abuse and Personal Right Project, SPECTRUM Institute.

Belsky, J. (1993). Etiology of child maltreatment: A developmental-ecological analysis. *Psychological Bulletin, 114,* 413–434.

Berger, L. (2005). Income, family characteristics and physical violence toward children. *Child Abuse & Neglect, 29,* 107–133.

Berger, L. & Brooks-Gunn, J. (2005). Socioeconomic status, parenting knowledge and behaviors, and perceived maltreatment of young low-birth-weight children. *Social Service Review, 79,* 237–268.

Bethea, L. (1999). Primary prevention of child abuse. *American Family Physician, 59,* 1577–1590.

Black, D. A., Heyman, R. E. & Slep, A. M. (2001). Risk factors for child physical abuse. *Aggression and violent behavior, 6,* 121–188.

Bousha, D. M. & Twentyman, C. T. (1984). Mother-child interactional style in abuse, neglect, and control groups: Naturalistic observations in the home. *Journal of Abnormal Psychology, 93,* 106–114.

Bronfenbrenner, U. (1986). Ecology of the family as a context for human development: Research perspectives. *Developmental Psychology, 22,* 723–742.

Brown, J., Cohen, P., Johnson, J. & Salzinger, S. (1998). A longitudinal analysis of risk factors for child maltreatment. *Child Abuse and Neglect, 22,* 1065–1078.

Cappalleri, J., Eckenrode, J. & Powers, J. (1993). The epidemiology of child abuse: Findings from the Second National Incidence and Prevalence Study of Child Abuse and Neglect. *American Journal of Public Health, 83,* 1622–1624.

Chaffin, M. (2000). What types of mental health treatment should be considered for maltreated children? In H. Dubowitz & D. DePanfilis (Eds.), *Handbook for child protection practice* (pp. 409–413). Thousand Oaks, CA: Sage.

Chaffin, M., Hanson, R., Saunders, B., Nichols, T., Barnett, D., Zeanah, C. et al. (2005). Report of the APSAC Task Force on Attachment Therapy, Reactive Attachment Disorder and Attachment Problems.

Chaffin, M., Silovsky, J., Funderburk, B., Valle, L. A., Brestan, E. V., Balachova, T. et al. (2004). Parent–child interaction therapy with physically abusive parents: Efficacy for reducing future abuse reports. *Journal of Consulting and Clinical Psychology, 72,* 491–499.

Chan, Y. C. (1994). Parenting stress and social support of mothers who physically abuse their children in Hong Kong. *Child Abuse and Neglect, 18,* 261–269.

Children's Bureau (2004). Child maltreatment. Washington, DC: U.S. Department of Health and Human Services.

Cicchetti, D., Lynch, M. & Manly, J. T. (1997). *An ecological developmental perspective on the consequences of child maltreatment.* Washington, DC: U.S. Department of Health & Human Services, National Center on Child Abuse and Neglect.

Cohen, J. A., Berliner, L. & Mannarino, A. P. (2003). Psychosocial and pharmacological interventions for child crime victims. *Journal of Traumatic Stress, 16,* 175–186.

Connelly, D. C. & Straus, M. A. (1992). Mother's age and risk for physical abuse. *Child Abuse & Neglect, 16,* 709–718.

Cowen, P. S. (2001). Efectiveness of a parent education intervention for at-risk families. *Journal for Specialists in Pediatric Nursing, 6,* 73–82.

Daro, D. (1988). *Confronting child abuse: Research for effective program design.* New York: Free Press.

Daro, D. (1996). Preventing child abuse and neglect. In J. Briere, L. Berliner, J. A. Bulkley, C. Jenny & T. Reid (Eds.), *The APSAC handbook on child maltreatment* (pp. 343–358). Thousand Oaks, CA: Sage.

Daro, D. & Cohn, A. H. (1988). Child maltreatment efforts: What have we learned? In G. T. Hotaling, D. Finkelhor, J. T. Kirkpatrick & M. A. Straus (Eds.), *Coping with family violence: Research and policy perspectives* (pp. 275–287). Thousand Oaks, CA: Sage Publications.

Daro, D. & Connelly, A. C. (2002). Child abuse prevention: Accomplishments and challenges. In J. E. B. Meyers, L. Berliner, J. Briere, C. T. Hendrix, C. Jenny & T. A. Reid (Eds.), *The APSAC handbook on child maltreatment,* 2d ed. (pp. 431–448). Thousand Oaks, CA: Sage.

Drake, B. & Pandey, S. (1996). Understanding the relationship between neighborhood poverty and specific types of child maltreatment. *Child Abuse & Neglect, 20,* 1003–1018.

Duggan, A., McFarlane, E., Windham, A., Rohde, C., Salkever, D., Fuddy, L. et al. (1999). Evaluation of Hawaii's Healthy Start program. *Future of Children, 9,* 66–90.

Eckenrode, J., Ganzel, B., Henderson, C. R., Smith, E., Olds, D. L., Powers, J. et al. (2000). Preventing child abuse and neglect with a program of nurse home visitation: The limiting effects of domestic violence. *Journal of American Medical Association, 284,* 1385–1391.

Edleson, J. L. (2001). Studying the co-occurrence of child maltreatment and woman battering in families. In S. A. Graham-Bermann & J. L. Edleson (Eds.), *Domestic violence in the lives of children: The future of research, intervention and social policy* (pp. 91–110). Washington, DC: American Psychological Association.

Emery, R. E. & Laumann-Billings, L. (1998). An overview of the nature, causes, and consequences of abusive family relationships: Toward differentiating maltreatment and violence. *American Psychologist, 44,* 121–135.

Erickson, M. F. & Egeland, B. (1996). Child neglect. In J. Biere, L. Berliner, J. A. Bulkley, C. Jenny & T. Reid (Eds.), *The APSAC handbook on child maltreatment* (pp. 4–20). Thousand Oaks, CA: Sage.

Eyberg, S. M. & Boggs, S. R. (1989). Parent training for oppositional-defiant preschoolers. In D. E. Schaefer & J. M. Briesmeister (Eds.), *Handbook of parent training: Parents as co-therapists for children's behavior problems* (pp. 105–132). Oxford: John Wiley & Sons.

Friedman, S. B. & Schonberg, S. K. (1996). Proceedings of a conference on "The short- and long-term consequences of corporal punishment." *Pediatrics, 98,* 803–860.

Garbarino, J. & Collin, C. C. (1999). Child neglect: The family with a hole in the middle. In H. Dubowitz (Ed.), *Neglected children: Research, practice, and policy* (pp. 1–23). Thousand Oaks, CA: Sage.

Garbarino, J., Kostelny, K. & Grady, J. (1993). Children in dangerous environments: Child maltreatment in the context of community violence. In D. Cicchetti & S. Toth (Eds.), *Child abuse, child development, and social policy* (pp. 167–189). Norwood, NJ: Ablex Publishing.

Geeraert, L., Van den Noortgate, W., Grietens, H. & Onghena, P. (2004). The effects of early prevention programs for families with young children at risk for child physical abuse and neglect: A meta-analysis. *Child Maltreatment, 9,* 277–291.

Gershater-Molko, R. M., Lutzker, J. R. & Wesch, D. (2002). Using recidivisim data to evaluate Project Safe Care: Teaching bonding, safety, and health care skills to parents. *Child Maltreatment, 7,* 227–285.

Goldman, J. Salus, M. K., Wolcott, D. & Kennedy, K. Y. (2003). *A coordinated response to child abuse and neglect: The foundation for practice.* Washington, DC: U.S. Department of Health & Human Services, Office on Child Abuse and Neglect. Retrieved 27 October 2006 from http://www.childwelfare.gov/pubs/usermanuals/foundation.

Gomby, D., Culross, P. & Behrman, R. (1999). Home visiting: Recent program evaluations—Analysis and recommendations. *Future of Children, 9,* 4–26.

Gordon, D. A. & Stanar, C. R. (2003). Lessons learned from the dissemination of Parenting Wisely, a parent training CD-ROM. *Cognitive and Behavioral Practice, 10,* 312–323.

Green, B. L., Johnson, S. A. & Rodgers, A. (1999). Understanding patterns of service delivery and participation in community-based family support programs. *Children's Services: Social Policy, Research, and Practice, 2,* 1–22.

Guterman, N. (1997). Early prevention of child physical abuse and neglect: Existing evidence and future directions. *Child Maltreatment, 2,* 12–34.

Guterman, N. B. & Lee, Y. (2005). The role of fathers in risk for child physical abuse and neglect: Possible pathways and unanswered questions. *Child Maltreatment, 10,* 136–149.

Hay, T. & Jones, L. (1994). Societal interventions to prevent child abuse and neglect. *Child Welfare, 73,* 379–403.

Herschell, A. D. & McNeil, C. B. (2005). Theoretical and empirical underpinnings of parent–child interaction therapy with child physical abuse populations. *Education and Treatment of children, 28,* 142–162.

Hoefnagels, C. & Baartman, H. E. M. (1997). On the threshold of disclosure—The effects of a mass media field experiment. *Child Abuse & Neglect, 18,* 349–356.

Holden, E., Willis, D. & Corcoran, M. (1992). Preventing child maltreatment during the prenatal/postnatal period. In D. Willis, E. Holden & M. Rosenberg (Eds.), *Prevention of child maltreatment: Developmental and ecological perspectives* (pp. 193–224). New York: John Wiley & Sons, Inc.

Kagan, S. L. (1994). *Putting families first: America's family support movement and the challenge of change.* San Francisco: Jossey-Bass.

Kahneman, D. (2003). Experiences of collaborative research. *American Psychologist, 58,* 723–730.

Kaplan, S. J., Pelcovitz, D. & Labruna, V. (1999). Child and adolescent abuse and neglect research: A review of the past 10 years. Part I: Physical and emotional abuse and neglect. *Journal of the American Academy of Child & Adolescent Psychiatry, 38,* 1214–1222.

Kees, M. R. & Bonner, B. L. (2006). Child abuse prevention and intervention services. In R. G. Steel & M. C. Roberts (Eds.), *Handbook of mental health services of children, adolescents, and families* (pp. 151–166). New York: Academic/Plenum Publishers.

Kempe, C. H., Silverman, F., Steele, B., Droegemueller, W. & Silver, H. (1962). The battered child syndrome. *Journal of the American Medical Association, 181,* 17–24.

Kitzman, H., Olds, D. L., Henderson, C. R., Hanks, C., Cole, R., Tatelbaum, R. et al. (1997). Effect of prenatal and infancy home visitations by nurses on pregnancy outcomes, childhood injuries, and repeated child bearing: A randomized controlled trial. *Journal of the American Medical Association, 278,* 644–652.

Kitzman, H., Olds, D. L., Sidora, K., Henderson, C. R., Hanks, C., Cole, R. et al. (2000). Enduring effects of nurse home visitation on maternal life course: A 3-year follow-up of a randomized trial. *Journal of American Medical Association, 283,* 1983–1989.

Kolko, D. J. (1996a). Clinical monitoring of treatment course in child physical abuse: Psychometric characteristics and treatment comparisons. *Child Abuse & Neglect, 20,* 23–43.

Kolko, D. J. (1996b). Individual cognitive behavioral therapy and family therapy for physically abused children and their offending parents: A comparison of clinical outcomes. *Child Maltreatment, 1,* 322–342.

Kolko, D. J. (2002). Child physical abuse. In J. E. B. Meyers, L. Berliner, J. Briere, C. T. Hendrix, C. Jenny & T. A. Reid (Eds.), *The APSAC handbook on child maltreatment,* 2d ed. (pp. 21–54). Thousand Oaks, CA: Sage.

Kolko, D. J. & Swenson, C. C. (2002). *Assessing and treating physically abused children and their families: A cognitive behavioral approach.* Thousand Oaks, CA: Sage Publications.

Kumpfer, K. L. & Bayes, J. (1995). Child abuse and drugs. In J. H. Jaffe (Ed.), *The encyclopedia of drugs and alcohol,* vol. 1 (pp. 217–222). New York: Simon & Shuster.

Leventhal, J. D. (2005). Getting prevention right: Maintaining the status quo is not an option. *Child Abuse & Neglect, 29,* 209–213.

Lutzker, J. R., Bigelow, K. M., Doctor, R. M., Gershater, R. M. & Greene, B. G. (1998). An ecobehavioral model for the prevention and treatment of child abuse and neglect: History and applications. In J. R. Lutzker (Ed.), *Handbook of child abuse research and treatment* (pp. 239–266). New York: Plenum Press.

Lutzker, J. R. & Newman, M. R. (1986). Child abuse and neglect: Community problem, community solutions. *Education and Treatment of Children, 9,* 344–354.

Lutzker, J. R. & Rice, J. M. (1987). Using recidivism data to evaluate Project 12-Ways: An ecobehavioral approach to the treatment and prevention of child abuse and neglect. *Journal of Family Violence, 2,* 283–290.

MacLeod, J. & Nelson, G. (2000). Programs for the promotion of family wellness and the prevention of child maltreatment: A meta-analytic review. *Child Abuse & Neglect, 24,* 1127–1149.

Mandell, S. (2000). Child abuse prevention at report card time. *Journal of Community Psychology, 28,* 687–690.

Miller-Perrin, C. & Perrin, R. (1999). *Child maltreatment: An introduction.* Thousand Oaks, CA: Sage Publications.

Milner, J. S. (1998). Individual and family characteristics associated with intrafamilial child physical and sexual abuse. In P. K. Trickett & C. J. Schellenbach (Eds.), *Violence against children in the family and the community* (pp. 141–170). Washington, DC: American Psychological Association.

Milner, J. S. & Chilamkurti, C. (1991). Physical child abuse perpetrator characteristic: A review of the literature. *Journal of Interpersonal Violence, 6,* 336–344.

Myers, J. E. B. (1992). *Legal issues in child abuse and neglect.* Thousand Oaks, CA: Sage Publications.

O'Neill, H. & Woodward, R. (2002). Evaluation of the Parenting Wisely CD-ROM Parent-Thinking Programme. *Irish Journal of Psychology, 23,* 62–72.

Portwood, S. G. (1998). Factors influencing individuals' definitions of child maltreatment. *Child Abuse and Neglect, 22,* 437–452.

Portwood, S. G. (2006). What we know—And don't know about preventing child maltreatment. *Journal of Aggression, Maltreatment, and Trauma, 12,* 55–80.

Rennison, M. & Welchans, W. (2000). *Intimate partner violence* (NCJ 178247). Washington, DC: U.S. Department of Justice, Office of Justice Programs, Bureau of Justice Statistics.

Reppucci, N. D., Britner, P. A. & Woolard, J. L. (1997). *Preventing child abuse and neglect through parent education.* Baltimore: Paul H. Brooks.

Sanders, M. R., Cann, W. & Markie-Dadds, C. (2003). The Triple-P Positive Parenting Programme: A universal population-level approach to the prevention of child abuse. *Child Abuse Review, 12,* 155–171.

Sedlak, A. J. (1997). Risk factors for the occurrence of child abuse and neglects. *Journal of Aggression, Maltreatment & Trauma, 1,* 149–187.

Sedlak, A. & Broadhurst, D. (1996). *Third National Incidence Study of Child Abuse and Neglect.* Washington, DC: U.S. Government Printing Office.

Showers, J. (1992). "Don't shake the baby": The effectiveness of a prevention program. *Child Abuse & Neglect, 16,* 11–18.

Straus, M. A. & Stewart, J. H. (1999). Corporal punishment by American parents: National data on prevalence, chronicity, severity, and duration in relation to child and family characteristics. *Clinical Child and Family Psychology Review, 2,* 55–70.

Thompson, R. A. (1994). Social support and the prevention of child maltreatment. In G. B. Melton & F. D. Barry (Eds.), *Protecting children from abuse and neglect: Foundations for a new national strategy* (pp. 40–130). New York: Guilford Press.

Timmer, S. G., Urquiza, A. J., Zebell, N. M. & McGrath, J. M. (2005). Parent–child interaction therapy: Application to maltreating parent-child dyads. *Child Abuse & Neglect, 29,* 825–842.

Trickett, P. K. & Kucynski, L. (1986). Children's misbehaviors and parental discipline strategies in abusive and non-abusive families. *Developmental Psychology, 22,* 115–123.

U.S. Census Bureau (2003). *Income, poverty, and health insurance coverage in the United States: 2003.* Retrieved 26 October 2006 from http://222.census.gov/prod/2004pubs/p60-226.pdf.

U.S. Department of Health and Human Services (HHS) (2006). Child Maltreatment 2004. Washington, DC: U.S. Government Printing Office, Administration on Children, Youth and Families.

Webster-Stratton, C. (1998). Parent training in low-income families: Promoting parental engagement through a collaborative approach. In J. R. Lutzker (Ed.), *Handbook of child abuse research and treatment* (pp. 183–210). New York: Plenum.

Whipple, E. E. & Webster-Stratton, C. (1991). The role of parental stress in physically abusive families. *Child Abuse & Neglect, 15,* 279–291.

Wolfe, D. (1985). Child-abusive parents: An empirical review and analysis. *Psychological Bulletin, 97,* 462–482.

Wolfe, D. A. (1987). *Child abuse: Implications for child development and psychopathology.* Newbury Park, CA: Sage Publications.

# 13

# Sexual Abuse in Childhood: *The Abused Child*

JOSH S. SPITALNICK, SINEAD N. YOUNGE,
JESSICA M. SALES AND RALPH J. DICLEMENTE

## INTRODUCTION

Recent media attention, such as the lawsuits and admissions within the Catholic Church, school teachers found having sex with their students, revelations by Hollywood members such as Oprah Winfrey, Teri Hatcher and Carlos Santana (to name a few) regarding their own experiences of victimization as well as a new wave of predators via the Internet and on-line chat rooms, all serve as reminders to the public that childhood sexual abuse (CSA) continues to be epidemic in the United States. CSA remains a serious issue that impacts all children, regardless of race, ethnicity, age or socioeconomic status (SES) (Sapp & Vandeven, 2005). CSA victims often go untreated for years due to a lack of disclosure and then present for therapy or to medical doctors as adults for a variety of problems associated with psychological, physical and relational difficulties (Berman, Berman, Bruck, Pawar & Goldstein, 2001). Recurring CSA reports also serve as a reminder to the legal, medical and mental health communities that more efforts are needed to treat current victims, to advocate for their needs and to prevent future victimizations from occurring.

### Prevalence of Child Sexual Abuse

In 1997, a meta-analysis of studies conducted in North American between 1969 and 1991 found that about 22% of women and 8.5% of men reported being a victim of CSA (Gorey & Leslie, 1997). In 2000, CSA represented 10% of the reported cases of child abuse (HHS, 2002). Recent estimates have led researchers to speculate that one of every four girls and 1 of every ten boys has experienced sexual abuse as a child (Fieldman & Crespi, 2002). An examination of the CSA literature, however, yields notable inconsistencies with regard to prevalence estimates. A variety of factors have been put forth to explain such varying rates, including methodological variations between studies (e.g., definition of CSA, method of data collection, sampling and population variations) and the notable occurrence of underreporting.

## Definitional Issues of Child Sexual Abuse

One problem that contributes to the marked discrepancy in prevalence estimates is the variability of definitions of sexual abuse used in CSA research and by professionals who work with victims. Some researchers employ more restrictive definitions that only include sexual penetration, some use any form of sexual contact, whereas others rely on a broader definition that includes nonphysical forms of sexual abuse (e.g., exposure to pornography). Definitions also have varied according to what age is considered the cut-off for nonconsensual sexual contact. Some studies require multiple sexual contacts as a component of the definition whereas others include single incidents.

Despite these variabilities, many researchers and clinicians employ some variation of Finkelhor's (1984) definition of CSA. This definition stipulates the use of force or coercion of a sexual nature when either the victim is under the age of 13 and the perpetrator is at least 5 years older or the victim is between 13 and 16 and the perpetrator is at least 10 years older.

## Underreporting of Child Sexual Abuse

In addition to the lack of standardized CSA definition, underreporting also contributes to variability of CSA prevalence estimates. As a result, most researchers and health-care providers believe that estimates should be considered only conservative approximations. In fact, CSA has been considered the most underreported form of abuse (Finkelhor, 1984). Retrospective reports of CSA reveal that only 3% to 6% of adults who were sexually abused as children ever reported the abuse (Russell, 1983; Timnick, 1985). Widom and Morris (1997) found that only 42% of CSA victims who were court identified as experiencing CSA before the age of 12 reported experiencing any such events. Additionally, research indicates that noncontact sexual abuse is reported less often that contact sexual abuse (Wilcox, Richards & O'Keeffe, 2004).

Understandably, many children are often reluctant to report abuse or might lack the verbal clarity to explain the experience, especially if the abuse occurred at an early age. Children may also be reticent to report CSA if they think that they will not be believed or if they perceive a lack of support from family and friends (Watkins & Bentovim, 1992). Other factors contributing to underreporting include the fact that some "victims" do not experience the abuse as negative, or, as some researchers have revealed, they do not seem to develop any clinically significant symptomology that would lead them to seek help (Dhaliwal, Gauzas, Antonowicz & Ross, 1996; Rind, Tromovitch & Bauserman, 1998).

## Sequalae of Child Sexual Abuse

As the experience and events surrounding CSA are complex, so too are its sequalae. Researchers have found that victims of CSA can experience a variety of short- and long-term difficulties. However, since no single symptom or cluster of symptoms can fully define the sequalae of CSA, it does not correspond with any particular psychological diagnosis. Additionally, comorbidity is a significant issue with children and adolescents who have been victims of trauma, including CSA (AACAP, 1998).

Although no psychological syndrome has been identified that reliably occurs following CSA, researchers have found that 20% to 57% of children with a history of CSA meet partial or full criteria for posttraumatic stress disorder (PTSD) (Ackerman, Newton, McPherson, Jones & Dykman, 1998; Gianconia et al., 1995). Based on the *DSM-IV-TR* (APA, 2000) criteria, PTSD is the result of actually experiencing, witnessing or being confronted by an event that involves actual or threatened death or serious injury and then reacting to the event in a manner consistent with intense fear, hopelessness or horror. The *DSM-IV-TR* outlines three primary clusters of PTSD symptoms: (1) reexperiencing the traumatic event; (2) avoidance of stimuli related to the trauma; or (3) numbing associated with the trauma, hyperarousal or hypervigilant behavior. Child-specific stipulations are also outlined in the *DSM-IV-TR* (ibid.) that acknowledge the presence of disorganized or agitated behavior rather than experiencing intense fear, hopelessness or horror.

Several psychological disorders have been identified to be comorbid with childhood PTSD, including major depression, dysthymia, other anxiety disorders, attention deficit hyperactivity disorder (ADHD), conduct disorder, oppositional defiant disorder and substance abuse and dependence (Weller, Shlewiet & Weller, 2003). Given the nature of sexual abuse, it is not surprising that CSA victims, in addition to PTSD, suffer from other psychological difficulties. Depressive syndromes represent some of the most likely emotional difficulties, particularly among CSA victims who have been sexually abused more than once (Cheasty, Clare & Collins, 2002). When PTSD is not present, other areas of difficulty can include the following:

1. Anxiety (Kolko, Moser & Weldy, 1988)
2. Inappropriate sexual behavior or sexual difficulties (Hornor, 2004; Olsson et al., 2000; Wilcox et al., 2004)
3. Relationship difficulties (Wekerle et al., 2001)
4. Substance abuse (Hibbard, Ingersoll & Orr, 1990)
5. Eating disorders (Jones & Emerson, 1994)
6. Shame and self-doubt (Seymour et al., 2000; Sgroi, 2000)
7. Self-esteem or identity difficulties (Hotte & Rafman, 1992; Wozencraft, Wagner & Pellegrin, 1991)

Younger CSA victims can experience difficulties, such as attachment disorders, impaired social skills and severe oppositional and conduct disordered behavior (Donnelly & Amaya-Jackson, 2002). Victims of CSA have also been found to experience physical symptoms, including headaches and stomachaches (Kimerling & Calhoun, 1994), as well as pain disorders (Beautrais, 2000).

Despite the growing number of studies that report significant mental and medical health sequalae of CSA, it must be noted that some research, including a prominent and well-publicized meta-analysis, have suggested that CSA does not have negative, lasting sequalae (Rind et al., 1998; Steel, Sanna, Hammond, Whipple & Cross, 2004). Moreover, it has been found that most CSA victims who present as asymptomatic remain without notable serious mental health issues (70%), though some (30%) do develop symptoms later (Kendall-Tackett, Williams & Finkelhor, 1993). It is unclear, however, whether CSA victims truly do not develop symptoms or whether they develop them following a particular assessment (i.e., clinical or research), leading some to speculate a "sleeper effect," with more serious mental health issues developing years after abuse (Saywitz, Mannarino, Berliner & Cohen, 2000).

## Major Theoretical Perspectives

Several theories have been used to explain the short- and long-term sequalae of CSA, including the PTSD formulation outlined by the *DSM-IV-TR,* developmental theories that highlight the interaction between developmental milestones and serious mental health needs and Briere's (1996) self-trauma model that includes empirically based principles of cognitive-behavioral and psychodynamic therapy to explain the experience of the victims. Due to the complexity of CSA, most agree that CSA is not to be understood by a single theoretical model (Ross & O'Carroll, 2004). Thus, Finkelhor's (1987) traumagenic dynamic theory is one that incorporates aspects of several theories and has been seen as useful in understanding the sequalae of CSA.

### *Traumagenic Dynamic Theory*

Finkelhor's (1987, p. 354) model posits that four dynamic qualities account for the general sequalae of CSA in that traumagenic dynamics serve as an experience "that alters a child's cognitive or emotional orientation to the world and causes trauma by distorting the child's self-concept, worldview, or affective capacities." There are four traumagenic dynamics: (1) traumatic sexualization; (2) Stigmatization; (3) Betrayal; and (4) Powerlessness, and they are influenced by the child's level of adjustment before the abuse and can be influenced by the response of others once the victim has disclosed the abuse. These dynamics have been used to explain how the victim's sexuality can be shaped in ways that are both developmentally and interpersonally dysfunctional (e.g., sexual preoccupations, compulsive sexual behavior, sexual aggressive behavior), how the negative messages associated with sexual abuse impact one's sense of self, how betrayal leads to distrust and fear of safety and how a loss of a sense of power can be damaging. As a theoretical approach to understanding the sequalae of CSA, traumagenic dynamics helps to explain the symptoms associated with sexual abuse, the learning process that occurs during and following the abuse, the influence of the victim's level of developmental maturity and the traumatic experience itself.

## BIOLOGICAL AND GENETIC CHILD SEXUAL ABUSE RESEARCH

Few studies have examined the role of genetic factors in individuals with a history of CSA. As genetic research has been linked to increases in one's vulnerability to serious mental health issues, several studies have explored whether genetic factors are implicated in the development of dysfunctional behavior in victims of CSA. Specifically, studies investigating the role of CSA on mental disorders in twins have found that CSA was associated with a variety of psychological disorders (Dinwiddie et al., 2000; Kendler et al., 2000; Nelson et al., 2002). These studies observed a significant relationship between CSA and depression, and, similarly to nontwin studies, one's risk for a depressive disorder significantly increased when the abuse included contact and penetration. Moreover, discordant twin analyses in Nelson et al.'s (2002) study revealed that CSA was associated with the development of depression; similar findings were reported in Dinwiddie et al. (2000) and Kendler et al. (2000), but only when the CSA involved intercourse. Overall, the results of these twin studies support the relationship between depression and CSA, particularly when sexual intercourse occurs.

Another emerging area of inquiry investigates neurochemical changes in the brain in people with a history of CSA. The rationale for examining neurobiological factors following CSA is based on research examining conditioned fear, with an emphasis on the functioning of the hypothalamic-pituitary-adrenal (HPA) axis, an identified neurochemical axis implicated in the stress response (Gilbert, Greening & Dollinger, 2001). In their longitudinal study comparing girls with and without a history of CSA (five years after sexual abuse), De Bellis, Chrousos, et al. (1994) found that the sexually abused girls demonstrated dysregulation of the HPA axis as evidenced by attenuated adrenocorticotropic hormone (ACTH) levels in response to ovine corticotropin-releasing hormone (CRH) and did not have higher levels of cortisol secretion. It was hypothesized that the previous stress of the abuse had caused prior CRH hypersecretion, resulting in the HPA axis reducing its typical regulatory response. Putnam and Trickett (1997) also found changes in stress responses in a series of studies with a prospective, longitudinal sample of CSA females ages 6 to 15. Their results suggest that, in contrast to nonabused girls, sexually abused girls have more dysregulation of the HPA axis, sympathetic nervous system and immune system, resulting in differences in their hormonal and neurochemical stress responses and regulation of their neuroendocrine systems. Furthermore, in a study conducted within six months of disclosure of abuse, CSA victims were found to have increased morning cortisol levels as compared with the nonabused control group, which was matched on several variables, including age, ethnicity and socioeconomic status (De Bellis & Putnam, 1994). Contrary to this finding, King, Mandansky, King, Fletcher & Brewer (2001) reported lower morning cortisol in CSA girls abused in the past two months when compared with a matched control sample.

In addition to studies of the HPA axis, researchers have studied levels of urinary catecholamine excretion in child PTSD samples given that the adult literature has found increased levels of catecholamine in populations with PTSD (Southwick et al., 1993). In a longitudinal study measuring urinary catecholamine excretion, 12 sexually abused girls were found to secrete significantly greater amounts of the dopaminergic metabolite, homovanillic acid, as compared with the control group, suggesting increased catecholamine activity (De Bellis, Lefter, Trickett & Putnam, 1994).

Taken together, these findings suggest that children with a history of CSA are likely to experience dysregulation of the HPA axis. It is unclear whether the attenuation of the HPA axis found in several studies might be considered a protective factor for the brains of children who are understandably vulnerable or whether it represents a muted response due to the brains' familiarity with stress (Glaser, 2000). Additionally, the majority of findings suggest that children with a history of CSA continue to respond neurochemically to the stressful trauma well after the abuse as evidenced by their increased levels of cortisol and catecholamine. Therefore, the results of these studies identified neurophysiological changes that may represent an organic marker for PTSD in sexually abused female children. It remains unclear, however, whether these biological changes represent a risk factor for the development of PTSD or whether exposure to a traumatic stress, such as CSA, produced these effects (Weller et al., 2003).

## RISK AND RESILIENCE

### Individual Factors Influencing Risk

A culmination of individual, relational, community and cultural factors contribute to the risk and resiliency of CSA survivors. Although children are not responsible for the harm inflicted upon them, a number of characteristics are associated with a child's risk of being sexually abused.

### *Gender and Age*

CSA generally occurs early in life with gender playing a significant role in the reported incidence and prevalence of abuse. Of CSA cases, 78% occur among females in comparison with males who comprise approximately 22% of CSA cases (Tjaden & Thoennes, 2000). Early female sexual maturation may be associated with increased vulnerability to abuse. More than half of all rapes of females (54%) occur before age 18, and 22% of these rapes occur before age 12. For males, 75% of all rapes occur before age 18, and 48% occur before age 12 (ibid.).

### *Race and Ethnicity*

The incidence and prevalence of reported CSA rates vary across racial and ethnic groups with marked variability. Several national studies reported that African American and Caucasian children experience near-equal levels of sexual abuse (Sedlak & Broadhurst, 1996). In contrast, other studies identified both African American and Latino children as having an increased risk for sexual victimization (Finkelhor, Hotaling, Lewis & Smith, 1990; Mennen, 1995). Siegel, Sorenson, Golding, Burnam and Stein (1987) studied non-Hispanic Whites and Latinos in Los Angeles and found that Whites were twice as likely as Latinos to have experienced CSA. Interestingly, there has been little research on CSA for Asian Americans. The U.S. Department of Health and Human Services (HHS) National Center on Child Abuse and Neglect (1998) reported that Asians comprise approximately 1% of reported CSA cases. This low prevalence among Asian Americans conflicts with studies undertaken outside the United States that report a CSA prevalence of 4.9% (Ima & Holm, 1991) and 10% (Kitahara, 1989). The discrepancies in CSA prevalence among various racial and ethnic groups were attributed to methodological differences in data collection that result in overrepresentations of particular groups and to the reluctance of some groups to use mental health services and public agencies (Kenny & McEachern, 2000).

With the use of self-report surveys, abuse may be underreported among the general population because individuals are afraid or ashamed to reveal the abuse, have repressed memories of abuse and refuse to participate in studies or deny that what happened was "real" abuse (Advocates for Youth, 1995). Among racial and ethnic minorities, African American women have been found to be less likely than their White counterparts to report incidents of abuse to the police and social service agencies (Abney & Priest, 1995). This difference might, in part, be due to African Americans' more frequent negative experiences that lead to distrust of the social service system (Klonoff & Landrine, 1997). The problem of underreporting abuse may be further compounded by the considerable diversity in child-rearing practices and disciplinary practices among various cultures and by their definitions ascribed to maltreatment within cultural groups and the social norms around help-seeking behavior. Consequently, a child's race or ethnicity may influence the way the experience of sexual abuse is processed, the meaning of the abuse to the victim and the severity and kinds of symptoms that may later develop.

## *Mental and Physical Disability*

Another population receiving increasing attention around issues of CSA is children and adolescents with physical or intellectual disabilities. It is difficult to estimate the prevalence of CSA among children with disabilities because states do not collect data about abused children with disabilities in the same way as CSA victims without disabilities. Many cases of sexual abuse go undocumented because children with disabilities may not have the ability or desire to inform anyone of the abuse, particularly when family members are perpetrators. In other instances, even if the children do recognize behaviors as wrong, the victims may not attempt to stop the abuse or neglect because they fear losing the relationship with their caretaker, on whom they are emotionally and physically dependent (National Research Council, 1994). A national study (Crosse, Kaye & Ratnofsky, 2001) found that children with disabilities were 1.7 times more likely to be abused than children without disabilities. Similar to children without disabilities, most abuse is perpetuated by people who know the victim, such as family members, acquaintances, residential care staff, personal care attendants and transportation providers. Research suggests that up to 95% of abusers of children with disabilities are known and trusted by their victims (Crosse et al., 2001; Sullivan & Knutson, 2003). Because the care required by some children with disabilities is critical to their survival, many have been taught to obey those in authority and to comply with their caretakers' requests or demands (National Research Council, 1994; Steinberg & Hylton, 1998).

## *Socioeconomic Status and Family Environment*

Family characteristics associated with CSA include, but are not limited to, marital dysfunction including parental separation and domestic violence and parental serious mental health issues (Fergusson, Lynskey & Horwood, 1996; Fleming, Mullen & Bammer, 1997; Mullen, Martin, Anderson, Romans & Herbison, 1996). Another factor indirectly associated with CSA is SES. Poverty makes children more susceptible to dangerous situations (e.g., walking alone at night, less parental supervision, family disorganization) and coercive rewards (e.g., food, money, toys) by perpetrators. Studies have also reported increased sexual assault and sexual abuse among children from lower SES backgrounds.

Parent-related risk factors have also been linked to increased likelihood of incidences of CSA. Parents with poor coping skills, with diminished impulse control and with a history of violence have children who are more likely to be sexually abused (Ammerman & Baladerian, 1993). Parents with low self-esteem or who are diagnosed with chronic depression may be at greater risk for abusing their children (Mitchell & Buchele-Ash, 2000). Studies have found that CSA is often associated with other family problems including parental alcoholism, parental rejection and parental marital conflict (Vogeltanz et al., 1999). Miller, Maguin and Downs (1997) found that parental alcohol abuse may leave children more vulnerable to sexual abuse by others because parental alcohol abuse may interfere with the parents' ability to provide a supportive, nurturing and protective environment.

## Intrafamilial versus Interfamilial Perpetrators

Most children are abused by someone they know and trust. Depending on the perpetrator's relationship with the child, adults who may be aware of the sexual abuse may not disclose or intervene for fear of disrupting and destroying the family unit (Conte, 1995). Data on the perpetrators of child sexual abuse are somewhat inconsistent. One report in 2001 found that 80.9% of perpetrators were parents and that 15.9% were nonparents (e.g., other caregivers, babysitters, extended family members) (American Humane, 2001). Perpetrators in remaining cases (3.2%) were missing or unknown. Females were more often perpetrators than males (59.3% females, 40.7% males) (ibid.). However, other reports have found that approximately 60% of perpetrators are nonrelative acquaintances, such as a friend of the family, babysitter or neighbor (Whealin, 2006). It is worth noting that boys are more likely than girls to be abused by a perpetrator outside of the family (AMA, 1992).

Recently, the percentage of perpetrators who do not know their victims regardless of gender is on the rise. With the popularity and accessibility of the Internet, child pornographers and other perpetrators, who are strangers, make contact with children using the Internet. Fleming et al. (1997) reported that girls who were socially isolated with few friends of their own age were almost twice as likely to report having been sexually abused. Subsequently, an unhappy social or family life may contribute to the risk for abuse outside as well as inside the family for two reasons. First, children in such families probably receive poorer supervision when out of the home, and second, such children, who may have particularly strong needs for positive attention and affection, may be more vulnerable to the ploys of nonfamily perpetrators who offer attention and affection as a lure, as previously noted (Finkelhor & Baron, 1986). The perpetrator, even at the time of abuse, may be the person who most meets the needs of that child for attention, affection and nurturing.

## Individual Factors for Resiliency

There is a limited amount of research on positive adaptation following CSA, and typically such resilience has been explored primarily in the intrapersonal domain. The term *resilient* has been applied to individuals who have the ability to withstand the expected negative sequalae of childhood trauma. More specifically, resilience has been defined as the ability to cope, or to adapt and even to thrive, following a negative experience (National Clearinghouse on Child Abuse and Neglect, 2005). The protective factors that may increase resiliency include individual characteristics such as optimism, self-esteem, a sense of control and an ability to place the responsibility of the abuse with the abuser and not themselves. The family or social environment (e.g., access to social support), community well-being, including neighborhood stability, and access to health care have also all been identified as protective factors (Thomlison, 1997).

It is important to assess resilience in CSA survivors across multiple domains of functioning. The majority of extant research on resilience have examined developmental outcome in a single domain of functioning. However, the processes underlying resilience may build over time and across domains (i.e., psychological well-being, physical health, romantic relationships, work competence, and parental competence); thus, there may be considerable variability in functioning across domains. A person may function well in one domain at the expense of functioning well in other salient domains (Lyons, 1991). When multiple adaptational domains are assessed, individuals often show significant discrepancies in how adequately they function across domains, and many individuals who are successful in one domain may not be successful in another (O'Dougherty, Fopma-Loy & Fischer, 2005).

## Resilience and the Family

The impact of CSA is not solely an individual phenomenon, as it impacts both the child and his or her family. The response a child receives when disclosing his or her abuse has long-term consequences. Prior investigations have shown that supportive family environments can reduce the risk of negative outcomes in individuals who are victims of CSA (Romans, Martin, Anderson, O'Shea & Mullen, 1995; Spaccarelli & Kim, 1995). When children who disclose abuse are believed and supported, the consequences are often less severe than when disclosure is met with disbelief, blame or rejection. Unfortunately, for many children at risk for CSA, this type of supportive family dynamic may not have existed prior to the onset of abuse; therefore, it may not exist after the child discloses the abuse. In cases of incestuous abuse, the support of the nonoffending parent is critical. Although studies have demonstrated that satisfying interpersonal relationships may buffer the sequalae of CSA on subsequent mental health adjustment (Banyard, 1999; Feinauer, Callahan & Hilton, 1996), parents of CSA survivors are also confronted with a variety of stressors including possible separation from a perpetrator spouse, loss of resources, disruption of the family and feelings of guilt, all of which may place a strain on interpersonal relationships and the necessary support for the child.

## SOCIAL AND CULTURAL FACTORS

Cultural factors may play a role in moderating the long-term impact of CSA. Ethnically based variables such as religiosity, social and family support, coping strategies and treatment seeking have the potential to help or hinder long-term adjustment. Specifically, religion and spirituality play a central role in the lives of many African American and Latino families. Religion may help to provide a protective environment and to encourage a perception of community support of the survivor of CSA. However, Sanders-Phillips, Moisan, Wadlington, Morgan and English (1995) found that Hispanic girls had significantly higher levels of depression following CSA in comparison with their African American counterparts. This finding may be attributed to the high regard for virginity in Hispanic culture, which has a significant impact on the reaction from young Hispanic female victims of CSA. Above and beyond inherent cultural characteristics, some have argued that parental support (particularly maternal) following disclosure has been identified as a prominent mediating factor in a child's adjustment to abuse. African American mothers have been found to be more supportive of their children following the disclosure of abuse in comparison with their Caucasian, Hispanic and Asian counterparts (Pierce & Pierce, 1984; Rao, DiClemente & Ponton, 1992). It should be noted that the study of ethnic minority populations and CSA are conducted with a number of limitations that may explain the reported discrepancies.

The use of culturally insensitive measures often fails to capture the cultural nuances and may erroneously lead to the belief that particular ethnic or cultural groups are asymptomatic or overly symptomatic following CSA. A culturally tailored approach to examining the psychological outcomes of CSA in diverse populations is warranted.

## SERIOUS MENTAL HEALTH ISSUES AND CHILD SEXUAL ABUSE

Despite 30 years of research examining incidence and prevalence of CSA, risk and resilience factors and sequalae of CSA, empirical investigations of treatment efficacy for CSA, particularly psychotherapeutic interventions, continues to lag behind other areas of research. However, researchers are beginning to demonstrate the clinical efficacy of some treatment modalities and have identified others that have produced promising results. Literature reviews over the past 20 years have synthesized findings from numerous interventions for CSA populations (see Finkelhor and Berliner, 1995; Jones & Ramchandani, 1999; O'Donohue & Elliott, 1992; Ross & O'Carroll, 2004; Saywitz et al., 2000). Thus, the following represents the most current and comprehensive review of intervention research with an emphasis on the statistical and clinical significance of psychotherapeutic treatments for sexually abused child and adolescent populations.

### Treatment That Works
#### *Cognitive-Behavioral Therapy (CBT)*
CBT, an empirically based, problem-focused and solution-oriented psychotherapeutic approach, includes both structured and supportive techniques. Several well-controlled studies have demonstrated the effectiveness of CBT as a first-line approach to treating children and adolescents who have been sexually abused and experienced difficulties (e.g., PTSD) associated with the abuse. Its application to CSA populations is likely due to the empirical success with adult populations who struggle with serious mental health issues following a traumatic experience.

In one of the first published clinical trials for sexually abused children, 100 CSA victims (83 girls and 17 boys ages 7–13) and their nonoffending mothers were randomly assigned to one of four possible treatment conditions (Deblinger, Lippman & Steer, 1996):

1. Child-only CBT
2. Mother-only CBT
3. Child-and-mother CBT
4. Community-control condition

Assessments occurred both pre- and posttreatment and included several methods, such as clinical interviews, parenting techniques, self-reports of anxiety and depression and parent reports of child behaviors. CBT techniques for the children included gradual exposure, modeling, psychoeducation and coping techniques. Parental behavior management was taught to parents to deal with their child's dysfunctional behaviors resulting from the abuse. Overall, the CBT treatments were superior to the community control condition. Treatment specific results revealed that for the children receiving CBT alone or with their parents, PTSD symptoms improved significantly when compared with the parents-only CBT group. For treatments involving the parent (i.e., child and parent, parent only), parents reported improved parenting skills as well as decreased child externalizing and depressive symptoms, with these reductions maintained two years later (Deblinger, Steer & Lippman, 1999).

Cohen and Mannarino (1996, 1998) conducted two studies examining the efficacy of CBT versus nondirective supportive therapy for CSA victims and their nonoffending parents. In the first study (Cohen & Mannarino, 1996), 67 3- to 7-year-olds and their parents were randomly assigned to either a structured, abuse-specific CBT intervention or to a nonspecific supportive intervention. The CBT intervention included techniques such as thought stopping, activation of positive imagery, cognitive reframing, contingency reinforcement, problem solving and parent training. The nonspecific supportive intervention constituted nonspecific play therapy for the children and supportive counseling for the parent. Assessments were conducted pre- and posttreatment and at a 12-month follow-up. Results revealed that children in the CBT treatment exhibited significantly greater improvement in PTSD symptoms, reduction of sexualized behaviors and improvement in their internalizing symptoms and other disordered behaviors. Additionally, most of these differences were maintained at a 12-month follow-up and were both statistically and clinically significant (Cohen & Mannarino, 1997; Ramchandani and Jones, 2003).

In a second study (Cohen & Mannarino, 1998), 49 7- to 14-year-olds and their parents were randomly assigned to either the structured, manualized abuse-specific CBT intervention or to the manualized, nonspecific intervention. For the children and adolescents, the CBT intervention focused on reducing problematic behavior associated with the abuse, as well as symptoms of depression and anxiety. Additionally, they incorporated CBT techniques that emphasized the interaction among thoughts, emotions and behaviors. For parents, intervention techniques focused on coping with the negative emotions related to the abuse, on learning how to more effectively support their child and on managing their child's problematic behaviors. The nonspecific supportive intervention constituted nonspecific play therapy for the children and supportive counseling for the parent. Assessments were conducted pre- and posttreatment and at a 12-month follow-up. Results revealed that the CBT intervention was superior with regard to treating depression and to improving social competence, though differences were not significant related to sexualized behavior, to other problematic behavior or to anxiety.

Farrell, Hains, and Davies (1998), using a multiple baseline design, examined the effectiveness of CBT with four CSA victims (ages 8–10) experiencing PTSD. For this intervention, CBT consisted of training of relaxation skills, positive self-talk and cognitive restructuring with assessment points before and after treatment, and at a three-month follow-up. This study found that all four participants reported decreases in PTSD symptoms and three of the participants, who initially had increased levels of depression and anxiety at baseline, reported decreases following treatment.

In a clinical investigation of the efficacy of CBT, 36 CSA victims, ages 5 to 17, who suffered from PTSD symptoms were randomized to one of three treatments: CBT for only the child, family CBT, or a wait-list control condition (King et al., 2000). Assessment was conducted before and after treatment and at a three-month follow-up. Results revealed that children in either treatment group experienced significant improvements in PTSD symptoms as well as self-reported fear and anxiety when compared with the control group. For those children diagnosed with PTSD, significantly more of CBT-treated children no longer met diagnostic criteria for PTSD than the control participants. This study also identified significant improvements related to the parent-completed PTSD measure and clinician ratings of global functioning.

Only two published studies have failed to demonstrate CBT superior treatment efficacy. In a randomized study of 80 CSA victims, researchers found only small differences between the two treatment groups (i.e., traditional group therapy v. group therapy plus CBT) (Berliner & Saunders, 1996). In this study, the added CBT components that failed to differentiate the treatment groups consisted of stress inoculation and graded exposure. Several explanations, however, were offered by the researchers to account for a lack of treatment efficacy, including the fact that the CSA victims did not have to be symptomatic, could have already had psychotherapy with a child mental health professional before enrolling in the study, both of which might have contributed to low symptom scores thereby reducing the likelihood of group differences post-treatment (Ramchandani and Jones, 2003). Moreover, Deblinger, Stauffer and Steer's (2001) investigation found that CBT group therapy only yielded small benefits over supportive group in their investigation with children 2 to 8 years of age and their nonoffending mothers.

Overall, these studies provide empirical support for the use of CBT when treating CSA victims with various serious mental health issues. Given that victims of sexual abuse and those exposed to traumatic events typically avoid the distressing event or reminders of the event and that they often experience significant cognitive, emotional, behavioral and physiological disruption, it is not surprising that CBT interventions increasing one's sense of coping, safety and self-efficacy have been proven effective forms of treatment.

## Treatment That Might Work

### The Role of the Parent

Although the inclusion of the nonoffending parent is not considered as a specific treatment orientation, the participation of a caregiver does have consistent empirical support and has been found to contribute to improve parenting techniques and increased support for the child (e.g., Cohen & Mannarino, 1996; Deblinger et al., 1996, 2001; King et al., 2000). In a study randomly assigning 32 sexually abused African American girls and their parents to either a CBT intervention or a nonspecific treatment (eight sessions), researchers found that the CBT participants reported significant reductions of parental negative expectations of the abuse and self-blame among parents, as well as significant improvements related to parental support for the children (Celano, Hazzard, Webb & McCall, 1996). Despite these positive results, this study failed to find that CBT girls exhibited more PTSD-related improvements than the control group. From the studies reviewed by O'Donohue and Elliott (1992), they found that the primary caregiver was identified not only as important in their ability to inform the researchers and clinicians about their child but also as influential in their child's ability to change. For young children specifically, parental support has been identified as the best predictor of positive outcome for the child (Cohen & Mannarino, 1998). However, despite the evidence supporting the positive role of the nonoffending parent in treatment, it has yet to be formally investigated with a randomized trial, pointing to a need for such an investigation. Additionally, it is unclear whether including the nonoffending parent for children from all racial and ethnic backgrounds is supported (Ramchandani and Jones, 2003).

## Peer Support Groups

For older adolescents, the use of peer support groups has received some empirical support. An investigation of the efficacy of peer support groups for female CSA victims ages 15 to 20 found them to be effective at decreasing psychosocial difficulties, general health issues and the victims' sense of social isolation as well as effective in preventing future victimizations (Norring & Walker, 2001).

## Eye Movement Desensitization and Reprocessing (EMDR)

A study of 14 CSA Iranian girls ages 12 to 13 years were randomly assigned to either and EMDR or CBT treatment (12 sessions) (Jaberghaderi, Greenwald, Rubin, Zand & Dolatabadi, 2004). Pretreatment and two-week posttreatment assessments were conducted for PTSD symptoms and behavioral problems. Though statistically significant effect sizes were reported for both interventions related to the PTSD and behavioral outcome, the researchers reported a nonsignificant trend on self-reported PTSD symptoms in favor of EMDR.

EMDR, developed by psychologist Dr. Francine Shapiro in the 1980s, uses bilateral stimulation (i.e., right/left eye movement and tactile or auditory stimulation) to activate opposite sides of the brain in an attempt to release traumatic emotional memories kept in the nervous system. Proponents of EMDR have suggested that traumatic events and their subsequent emotions negatively affect the biochemical equilibrium in the brain and interrupt information from being processed and addressed in an adaptive manner.

After identifying the specific trauma, gathering a detailed history and preparing the client for the trauma work, EMDR typically begins (Shapiro, 2001). According to Lee, Taylor and Drummond (2006), EMDR consists of two separate processes: distancing and free association. First, the client is encouraged to take the role of an observer of experiences in the session, an approach similar to mindfulness techniques. In doing so, the client is becoming aware of the traumatic experience in the past while also remaining aware of the present situation; this is a technique aimed at keeping a balance between attention to the trauma and actively distancing oneself from the trauma. Following the ability to be dually attentive, the client is encouraged to experience associations to the identified trauma while eye movements are elicited. This technique includes the therapist being open to such associations with the focus shifting to helping the client develop responses that are more adaptive (Lee et al., 2006). New associations become the focus of intervention according to structured protocols until the client's distress is significantly reduced or eliminated (Silver, Rogers, Knipe & Colelli, 2005). Target of intervention then becomes any continued physical sensations until no further change occurs (ibid.). Despite the specific techniques developed by Shapiro (2001) and tested by other researchers, some have argued that the mechanisms that underlie EMDR's effectiveness remain controversial and unidentified (Cahill, Carrigan & Frueh, 1999).

### Treatments That Do Not Work

Although a review of the literature did not reveal any published studies that should not be considered for use in treating CSA victims, the abundance of empirical evidence from the aforementioned studies reveals that nonspecific supportive therapy delivered via individual, family or group format does not seem to represent an effective treatment approach.

## PSYCHOPHARMACOLOGY AND CSA

Research investigating psychopharmacological clinical trials for CSA populations is still in its infancy. Since CSA is not a psychological disorder and since researchers have examined the use of psychotropic agents to treat disorders that have previously been cited to occur among CSA populations (e.g., PTSD, depression), the following summarizes drug efficacy studies for child and adolescent populations affected by the most commonly occurring serious mental health issues in CSA populations: (1) PTSD and (2) depression.

### Posttraumatic Stress Disorder

### *Medications That Work to Treat PTSD in CSA Populations*

In their search of 20 years of clinical trials, Donnelly and Amaya-Jackson (2002) found that from 1980 and 2000 14 studies were published investigating psychopharmacological treatments for PTSD in children but that none employed a double-blind, randomized, placebo-controlled trials (RCT). To date, no RCT psychopharmacological trials have been published or replicated. Thus, currently no psychopharmacological treatments for childhood PTSD can considered statistically and clinical significant. It is worth noting, however, that the antidepressant sertraline (Zoloft) has been used to treat PTSD in adult populations (Williams & Miller, 2003).

### *Medications That Might Work to Treat PTSD in CSA Populations*

#### *Selective Serotonin Reuptake Inhibitors (SSRIs)*

For children and adolescents, SSRIs are prescribed for anxiety disorders more than any other class of psychotropics (Emslie, Weinberg & Mayes, 1998). The high frequency of SSRI prescriptions for anxiety disorders, and specifically PTSD, is likely due to its broad spectrum of activity through the serotonin neurotransmitter system, a system implicated in anxiety, depression, compulsive behaviors, impulsivity and arousal (Friedman, 1990; Williams & Miller, 2003).

Though several case studies, open trials and RCTs have been published demonstrating the effectiveness of SSRIs related to the treatment of adult

PTSD (Connor & Davidson, 1998; Hidalgo & Davidson, 2000), notably fewer studies have been published investigating the treatment of child and adolescent PTSD, with a notable absence of RCT studies. In a study of 24 children and adolescents and 14 adults with PTSD, citalopram (Celexa) was given to treat symptoms of PTSD (Seedat, Lockhat, Kaminer, Zungu-Dirwayi & Stein, 2001). Symptoms were significantly reduced in all age groups. Moreover, this study found that children and adolescents improved more than the adults with regard to hyperarousal symptoms. In a reported case study of an 8-year-old girl with comorbid anxiety disorders, including PTSD, Good and Peterson (2001) reported that after she initially responded to fluvoxamine (Luvox) and then relapsed, mirtazapine (Remeron) was also taken, with overall symptoms reduction. In an open-label trial of nefazadone (Serzone) at an average effective dose of 200 mg twice daily, Domon and Andersen (2000) reported effectiveness in treating hyperarousal symptoms, anhedonia and insomnia and concentration difficulties related to adolescent PTSD. However, in June 2004 the U.S. Federal Drug Administration (FDA) added a warning with nefazadone (Serzone) related to risk of increased liver failure.

### Tricyclic Antidepressants (TCAs)

In a study of 25 children ages 2 to 19 years, Robert, Blakeney, Villarreal, Rosenberg & Meyer (1999) randomized participants to either chloral hydrate or imipramine (1 mg/kg) (both TCAs) for seven days to treat symptoms of acute stress disorder (ASD) in children with burn injuries. Of the 12 participants receiving imipramine, 10 experienced from half to full remission of their trauma symptoms, whereas only 5 of 13 chloral hydrate participants experienced reduction of symptoms. This study also highlighted the effectiveness of TCAs in treating sleep-related flashbacks and insomnia. However, due to notable side effects of TCAs and reported lack of effectiveness in treating childhood depression, the utility of TCAs is questionable for children and adolescents (Donnelly & Amaya-Jackson, 2002).

### Adrenergic Agents and Antagonists

Given the clusters of PTSD symptoms, which include sympathetic arousal and mood dysregulation, it is not surprising that medications such as clonidine (adrenergic agent) and propranolol (adrenergic antagonist), medications used to reduce sympathetic arousal, have received some support in their treatment of PTSD symptoms in children (De Bellis & Putnam, 1994). In an open-label investigation of 17 children with PTSD, the use of low-dose clonidine (0.05 to 0.1 mg twice daily) was found to significantly reduce anxiety, arousal and impulsivity (Perry, 1994). In another open-label investigation of seven preschool children ages 3 to 6 with a history of severe sexual or physical abuse, Harmon and Riggs (1996) found that treatment with clonidine resulted in moderate or greater improvement in targeted PTSD symptoms in all patients. In a five-week uncontrolled A-B-A investigation of 11 children with PTSD, propranolol (2.5 mg/kg per day) was found to significantly reduce PTSD symptoms (e.g., arousal, intrusive symptoms) in 8 of the patients (Famularo, Kinscherff & Fenton, 1988).

*Anticonvulsants*

The use of carbamazepine (300 to 1200 mg per day, serum levels 10 to 11.5 µg/ml) was examined in 28 children and adolescents ages 8 to 17 with sexual abuse histories (Loof, Grimley, Kuller, Martin & Shonfield, 1995). However, half of the sample had comorbid conditions and required additional psychotropic medications. Results revealed that 22 of 28 experienced complete remission of symptoms, whereas the other 6 experienced significant improvement in most PTSD symptoms except for abuse-specific nightmares.

### Medications That Do Not Work to Treat PTSD in CSA Populations

A review of the literature revealed no psychotropic trials designed to treat PTSD in children or adolescents that failed to demonstrate symptoms reduction.

## Depression

### Medications That Work to Treat Depression in CSA Populations

*Selective Serotonin Reuptake Inhibitors (SSRIs)*

Fluoxetine (Prozac) has received FDA approval for treating depression in children and adolescents following three positive clinical trials for adolescent depression (Emslie et al., 1997, 2002; March et al., 2004). In all three trials, the Clinical Global Impressions (CGI-I) level of improvement in the "much or very much improved" classification for fluoxetine was 52% to 61% compared with 33% to 37% for those receiving placebo (Bridge, Salary, Birmaher, Asare & Brent, 2005).

### Medications That Might Work to Treat Depression in CSA Populations

*Selective Serotonin Reuptake Inhibitors (SSRIs)*

In their published study of two RCTs examining the effectiveness of sertraline (Zoloft) to treat child and adolescent major depression, Wagner et al. (2003) found a 10% difference in symptom reduction between sertraline and placebo when the two studies were combined. However, results disappeared when each study was analyzed separately. In a study examining the effectiveness of citalopram (Celexa) in treating childhood depression, Wagner et al. (2004) reported a 12% difference between drug and placebo when assessing depression with the Children's Depression Rating Scale-Revised (CDRS-R).

### Medications That Do Not Work to Treat Depression in CSA Population

In a meta-analysis by Whittington et al. (2004), five published RCTs were compared with unpublished reports found in the U.K. Committee on Safety of Medicines review. Based on the results of the meta-analysis, the authors recommended that, despite the previous data that once favored the effectiveness for paroxetine (Paxil), sertraline (Zoloft) and venlafaxine (Effexor) in treating child and adolescent depression, these medications should be considered unfavorable. They came to this decision based on the evidence that suggests an increased risk of suicidal ideation and other serious negative events (Weller, Kang & Weller, 2004).

## THE PREVENTION OF CHILD SEXUAL ABUSE

As the prevalence of CSA remains high, with typical estimates indicating that 20% of children will be sexually assaulted before age 18 (Sandberg, Lynn & Green, 1994), child sexual abuse has received a great deal of research attention, and many prevention programs have been developed and implemented over the past two decades. Unlike the prevention efforts to combat physical abuse or neglect of children, which focus on modifying adult behavior, the focus of CSA prevention programs has been aimed toward altering the knowledge and skills of children during group-based lessons, usually conducted in school (preschool or elementary) settings.

### School-Based CSA Prevention Programs

School-based CSA prevention programs, focused on teaching children to avoid and report abuse, have been widely used throughout the United States. A survey of school administration from 400 school districts in the United States found that more than 85% had offered a CSA prevention program in the past year and that 64% required districts to offer the programs (Daro, 1994). Additionally, random telephone sampling of children in the United States found that 67% of them had participated in a CSA prevention program (Finkelhor & Dziuba-Leatherman, 1995). Given that school-based CSA prevention programs appear to be pervasive and that the apparent method of choice implemented by communities to protect children from being sexually abused, it is imperative to understand the strengths and limitations of this approach.

The major goal of school-based CSA prevention is on primary prevention, whereby they aim to improve children's ability to recognize and resist assault. These programs also have a secondary prevention focus to encourage victims of CSA to disclose the abuse to a trusted adult so that abused children can receive protection and early intervention to reduce the negative consequences of abuse. Specifically, most programs have four objectives in common:

1. Assisting children in recognizing potentially abusive situations
2. Instructing children to resist and remove themselves from potentially dangerous situations
3. Encouraging children to report abuse (current or previous) to an authority figure
4. Reassuring children that abuse is not their fault (Wurtele, 1998)

Despite their common goals, school-based programs vary widely on several dimensions. Specifically, they vary in terms of program length, age and group of children targeted, occupation of instructors and presentation format (i.e., films/videos, theater productions, group-based discussions, behavioral skills training, and role playing). Recent reviews have explored how these programmatic variations impact the efficacy of school-based programs (Davis & Gidycz, 2000; Rispens, Aleman & Goudena, 1997; Wurtele, 1998). Based on these reviews and meta-analyses, several key components of school-based CSA interventions have been identified that contributed to the success of such programs.

### What Works

#### Programs With Active Participant Involvement

School-based interventions that incorporate behavioral skills components into their programs produced significantly higher knowledge and skills gains than did programs that only employed education-only strategies (Wurtele, Marrs & Miller-Perrin, 1987). Examples of successful behavioral skills training include active skills rehearsal, shaping and reinforcement. Additionally, programs that included more active program activities such as role plays and participant rehearsal were more effective than less active programs (i.e., lectures or films) (Blumberg, Chadwick, Fogarty, Speth & Chadwick, 1991; Wurtele, Saslawsky, Miller, Marrs & Britcher, 1986). Corroborating these findings, a recent meta-analysis of CSA prevention programs concluded that child participation level was an important factor predicting participants' knowledge gains, with programs where children actively participated in activities producing effect sizes three times larger than programs without active child participation (Davis & Gidycz, 2000).

Programs incorporating active participation by the child and behavioral skills training may be effective because the active involvement of participants increases attention levels and allows children the opportunity to practice skills with adult supervision and feedback (Davis & Gidycz, 2000). Thus, the prevention tool of education is strengthened with the additional tools of competency enhancement and social support. From a developmental perspective, children's stage of cognitive development makes active learning strategies ideal as the physical involvement in the tasks makes the information and skills being taught more salient and concrete for young children.

#### Programs with Multiple Sessions

In their meta-analysis of school-based CSA prevention programs, Davis and Gidycz (2000) found that programs delivered over the course of four sessions or more were more effective than those programs presented in one, two or three sessions. They concluded that this effect was not the result of increased hours spent learning about prevention; rather, it was due to segmenting and delivering the material in smaller, spaced doses that may be more appropriately matched to children's attention spans and may provide opportunities for repetition to better facilitate learning.

#### Programs Tailored to the Age of Participants

Young children are at particularly high risk for sexual abuse, yet many critics of CSA prevention programs have claimed that preschoolers and kindergarteners cannot learn CSA prevention strategies due to limited cognitive resources (Reppucci & Haugaard, 1989). However, research demonstrates that children as young as 3 1/2 years of age show significant gains in CSA prevention knowledge and skills after participating in CSA programs, especially when those programs teach concrete concepts, include active learning activities (rehearsal, role-plays), are spaced over multiple sessions to increase repetition and match attention span, employ evaluation instruments that are developmentally appropriate for participants age and include teacher–parent education (see Wurtele, 1998, for a detailed review). Thus, school-based prevention programs for young children do work, but they must be tailored to the developmental level of the target population.

### Home Visitation Programs

The goal of home visitation programs is to reduce child abuse and neglect by providing knowledge, skills and support to parents and families identified as at risk for abuse. A recent meta-analysis examining the effects of family wellness promoting programs on the prevention of child abuse demonstrates that these general family wellness programs are able to prevent child abuse, with more programmatically comprehensive and intense programs having the greatest effects (MacLeod & Nelson, 2000). An example of such a program that has been evaluated and well documented is the Nurse Home Visitation Program by Olds, Henderson, Chamberlin and Tatelbaum (1986), in which high-risk families were visited by nurses in their homes approximately 9 times during pregnancy and 23 times following the birth of the child until their second birthday. In a 15-year follow-up of the families in the original Nurse Home Visitation Program, children in the control group, whose families never received home visitations, showed abuse rates twice as high as the children whose families received the nurse home visitations in their early years (Olds, Eckenrode & Henderson, 1997). Thus, high-quality home visitation programs targeting high-risk families may play a significant role in the primary prevention of child abuse, including sexual abuse.

## What Might Work

### Programs for Special Needs Children

Children with special needs (e.g., mental retardation, physical disabilities) may be particularly vulnerable to sexual abuse for several reasons including their increased dependency on care providers, inability to protect themselves, desire to be accepted by others and exceptional compliance with adult requests (Sobsey & Mansell, 1990). CSA prevention programs have been developed for children with special needs, yet the effectiveness of such programs is rarely assessed (Dreyer & Haseltine, 1986; LaBarre, Hinkley & Nelson, 1986). One program conducted by Haseltine and Miltenberger's (1990), a nine-week behavioral skills training CSA prevention program, was demonstrated to be effective in teaching such skills to mild to moderately mentally retarded young adults. This suggests that CSA prevention programs may be effective for special needs youth as well. However, more research is needed with children with special needs to more precisely quantify program efficacy.

### Programs That Involve Parents

Often, CSA prevention efforts are aimed exclusively toward children though it is believed by many that parental involvement in prevention efforts is a potentially important prevention strategy (Daro, 1994; Wurtele & Miller-Perrin, 1992). Indeed, Finkelhor, Asdigian and Dziuba-Leatherman (1995) found that children who participated in school-based CSA prevention programs, as well as received prevention instruction from parents, had significantly more knowledge about CSA, were more likely to use self-protection strategies, were more capable of alluding attackers attempts and were more likely to disclose victimization. These findings suggest that involving parents in CSA prevention efforts, especially when coupled with other prevention programs (i.e., school-based curriculum), is likely to be a successful strategy if employed by future prevention programs.

## What Does Not Work

A review of the literature did not identify any prevention efforts that should not be used at the present time. For the most part, several meta-analyses on CSA prevention have indicated that CSA prevention programs are generally effective in terms of increasing participating children's knowledge and skill gains (Berrick & Barth, 1992; Davis & Gidycz, 2000; Rispens et al., 1997).

## RECOMMENDED BEST PRACTICE

Childhood sexual abuse can be a traumatic event that affects an individual in so many destructive ways. Fortunately, researchers and clinicians have developed and evaluated interventions, leading to the identification of effective psychotherapeutic and pharmacological interventions. Though it is unlikely that any one treatment will ever be effective for all CSA victims due to its complexity, working from a conceptual framework, such as PTSD formulation, might be valuable for treatment planning. Much of the recent, empirically supported treatment efficacy literature incorporates the PTSD formulation as a conceptual basis for CSA interventions, as noted in the emphasis of intervention components and targets for symptom reduction. Thus, a PTSD case formulation can be particularly important when determining whether abuse-specific treatments (e.g., CBT) will be used (Ross & O'Carroll, 2004). The primary goal of any clinician working with a CSA victim will be to develop an individualized treatment plan that is based on evidence-based practices which meet the needs of the child and his or her family.

## Treatment

- Given that not all CSA victims experience significant difficulties associated with the abuse, specific psychological services may not be initially warranted. Moreover, given the complexity and diverse sequalae of CSA, no one intervention is considered universally applicable or effective for all CSA victims (Saywitz et al., 2000). Regardless, upon suspecting or identifying a CSA victim, the child's safety becomes of utmost priority, which often includes removal of the child from the environment in which the abuse has occurred. If a parent or professional believes that the child does require psychological services, effective treatment options have been developed to specifically target serious mental health issues likely to develop in the aftermath of CSA. Despite the concerns of some who have suggested that discussing or reliving the abuse only hurts the child, the treatment research refutes these concerns and demonstrates that CSA victims and their nonoffending caregivers can benefit from specific therapeutic interventions (King et al., 1999). Therefore, the following recommendations, based on the most recent empirical support, should be considered the first-line approach to treating CSA victims (Donnelly & Amaya-Jackson, 2002):

- Individualize treatment planning based on the child's needs, the family's needs, the child's presenting difficulties and abuse-specific events.
- Use direct and supportive techniques since more passive and nonspecific approaches can encourage silence and avoidance that is too often experienced during the abusive experience.
- Include the nonoffending caregiver whenever possible, especially when skills are being taught that the caregiver can use to help the child.
- Employ cognitive-behavioral techniques (e.g., gradual exposure, desensitization, stress inoculation and relaxation training) for PTSD-related symptoms (e.g., reexperiencing the event, intrusive thoughts and flashbacks, avoidant behaviors, hyperarousal).
- Employ cognitive-behavioral techniques (e.g., coping-skills training, cognitive restructuring) for depression, anxiety or other affective dysregulation.
- Employ cognitive-behavioral techniques (e.g., behavioral management, parent training) that decrease externalizing (e.g., aggression) or inappropriate sexualized behaviors.
- Consider other treatments to treat the emotional difficulties and PTSD symptoms associated with CSA (e.g., EMDR, interpersonal therapy, supportive group psychotherapy, psychoeducation).
- Consider play-based exposure therapy as a possible alternative treatment approach for CSA victims who are particularly young or cognitively delayed.

## Pharmacology

The use of psychopharmacological interventions should be considered in conjunction with psychotherapy. More often, however, psychopharmacological treatments are often employed when there is a notable severe or acute presentation of serious mental health needs and the CSA victim experiences partial or no response to psychotherapeutic interventions (Donnelly & Amaya-Jackson, 2002). When psychopharmacological treatments are used, it is important to insure that psychosocial supports and psychoeducation services are available for both the victim and any nonoffending family members involved in treatment.

The following recommendations are based on the most recent empirical evidence and are considered a second-line or additive approach to treating mild to moderate CSA sequalae. When the child is experiencing significantly disabling serious mental health issues that are unlikely to initially be alleviated with psychotherapy, psychopharmacology is likely to be the first-line treatment approach. The following empirically based treatment recommendations are for the most commonly occurring sequalae of CSA (e.g., PTSD, depression, anxiety):

- In a recent survey of psychiatrists asked about interventions for childhood PTSD, 95% endorsed the use of medications such as SSRIs, alpha-agonists, tricyclic antidepressants, and anxiolytics (Cohen & Mannarino, 1996).
- Several SSRIs (e.g., Citalopram (Celexa), fluoxetine (Prozac)), have received empirical support and should be considered the first-line

psychopharmacological treatment for symptoms of depression, anxiety and PTSD, such as hyperarousal, depressed affect, anhedonia, concentration difficulties, worry, anxious affect, numbing and avoidant symptoms.

- Medication such as clonidine, imipramine and carbamazepine might also be considered if insomnia, hyperstartle or hyperarousal symptoms, and nightmares are problematic and not resolved with SSRIs.
- Other commonly prescribed adult psychotropics, such as paroxetine (Paxil), sertraline (Zoloft), escitalopram (Lexapro), venlafaxine (Effexor) and mirtazapine (Remeron) have limited support for their use in treating PTSD, depression and anxiety in children and adolescents and should be used cautiously, if at all, especially due to reports of increased risk of suicidal ideation (e.g., paroxetine, sertraline, venlafaxine) or increased risk of liver failure (i.e., nefazodone).

## Prevention

Evidence indicates that school-based CSA prevention programs have been widely implemented in schools across the United States, and these programs appear to be successful at enhancing children's knowledge about sexual abuse and strategies to prevent it. In support of these findings, a recent long-term follow-up survey of 825 female undergraduate students found that those who had participated in a school-based CSA prevention program were significantly less likely to have been the victims of sexual abuse (Gibson & Leitenberg, 2000). However, a national telephone survey of 2,000 young people between 10 and 16 years old found that victimized and threatened children were more likely to use self-protection strategies if they had participated in a CSA prevention program that used active learning activities and multiple sessions and included materials to take home and share with parents (Finkelhor et al., 1995). Thus, future school-based CSA prevention efforts should incorporate all of prevention's technology (i.e., education, competency, promotion, natural caregiving and system change). Further, it should actively engage participants, be delivered over multiple sessions, and be tailored to the age of participants to enhance their effectiveness. Last, for families already identified as at risk for abuse, comprehensive home visitation programs appear to be effective in terms of decreasing risk factors for CSA.

## Conclusion

Prevention and intervention efforts are the most effective ways to safeguard future generations of children from being sexually abused and to spare current victims from ongoing victimization. Given the complexity of CSA and its sequalae, the treatment of victims requires a multidimensional, multidisciplinary and multimodal treatment approach to provide the most comprehensive yet victim-specific intervention. As researchers and clinicians embark on the next generation of CSA prevention research, particular attention must focus on the new vehicle of child victimization, the Internet. This medium provides an unfortunately high level of accessibility to sexual predators who seek their next victim. Therefore, mental health, social service and law enforcement communities need to continue efforts aimed at increasing our understanding of CSA sequalae (both short term and long term) and accuracy of identifying at-risk children, as well as to ensure the continued availability of prevention and intervention services if we are to reduce the epidemic of childhood sexual abuse.

## REFERENCES

Abney, V. D. & Priest, R. (1995). African American and sexual child abuse. In L. Fontes (Ed.), *Sexual abuse in nine north American cultures* (pp. 11–30). Thousand Oaks, CA: Sage.

Ackerman, P., Newton, J., McPherson, W., Jones, J. & Dykman, R. (1998). Prevalence of post traumatic stress disorder and other psychiatric diagnoses in three groups of abused children (sexual, physical, and both). *Child Abuse & Neglect, Volume 22,* 759–774.

Advocates for Youth (1995). Child sexual abuse I: An overview: Fact sheet (Ed. S. K. Flinn). Washington, DC: Advocates for Youth. Retrieved 18 May 2006 from http://www.advocatesforyouth.org/PUBLICATIONS/factsheet/fsabuse1.htm.

American Academy of Child and Adolescent Psychiatry (AACAP) (1998). Practice parameters for the assessment and treatment of children and adolescents with posttraumatic stress disorder. *Journal of the American Academy of Child and Adolescent Psychiatry, 37,* 4S–26S.

American Humane (2001). *Child abuse and neglect in America: What the data say: Fact sheet.* Retrieved 18 May 2006 from http://www.americanhumane.org/.

American Medical Association (AMA) (1992). *Diagnostic and treatment guidelines on child sexual abuse.* Chicago: Author.

American Psychological Association (APA) (2000). *Diagnostic and statistical manual of mental disorders,* 4th ed. (text revised). Washington, DC: Author.

Ammerman, R. T. & Baladerian, N. J. (1993). *Maltreatment of children with disabilities.* Chicago: National Committee to Prevent Child Abuse.

Banyard, V. L. (1999). Childhood maltreatment and the mental health of low-income women. *American Journal of Orthopsychiatry, 69,* 161–171.

Beautrais, A. (2000). Risk factors for suicide and attempted suicide among young people. *Australian and New Zealand Journal of Psychiatry, 34,* 420–436.

Berliner, L. & Saunders, B. (1996). Treating fear and anxiety in sexually abused children: Results of a controlled 2-year follow-up study. *Child Maltreatment, 1,* 294–310.

Berman, L., Berman, J., Bruck, D., Pawar, R. & Goldstein, I. (2001). Pharmacotherapy or psychotherapy?: Effective treatment for FSD related to unresolved childhood sexual abuse. *Journal of Sex & Marital Therapy, 27,* 421–425.

Berrick, J. D. & Barth, R. P. (1992). Child sexual abuse prevention: Research review and recommendations. *Social Work Research and Abstracts, 28,* 6–15.

Bridge, J. A., Salary, C. B., Birmaher, B., Asare, A. G. & Brent, D. A. (2005). The risks and benefits of antidepressant treatment for youth depression. *Annals of Medicine, 37,* 404–412.

Blumberg, E., Chadwick, M., Fogarty, L., Speth, T. & Chadwick, D. (1991). The touch discrimination component of sexual abuse prevention training. *Journal of Interpersonal Violence, 6,* 12–28.

Briere, J. (1996). A self-trauma model for treating adult survivors of severe child abuse. In J. Briere, L. Berliner, J. A. Bulkley, C. Jenny & T. Reid (Eds.), *The APSAC handbook on child maltreatment* (pp. 140–157). Thousand Oaks, CA: Sage.

Cahill, S. P., Carrigan, M. H. & Frueh, B. C. (1999). Does EMDR work? And if so, why? A critical review of controlled outcome and dismantling research. *Journal of Anxiety Disorders, 13,* 5–33.

Celano, M., Hazzard, A., Webb, C. & McCall, C. (1996). Treatment of traumagenic beliefs among sexually abused girls and their mothers: An evaluation study. *Journal of Abnormal Child Psychology, 24,* 1–17.

Cheasty, M., Clare, A. & Collins, C. (2002). Child sexual abuse: A predictor of persistent depression in adult rape and sexual assault victims. *Journal of Mental Health, 11,* 79–84.

Cohen, J. A. & Mannarino, A. P. (1996). A treatment outcome study for sexually abused preschool children: Initial findings, Journal of the American Academy of Child Adolescent Psychiatry, 35, 42–50.

Cohen J. A. & Mannarino A. P. (1997). A treatment study for sexually abused preschool children: Outcome during a one-year follow-up. Journal of the American Academy of Child Adolescent Psychiatry, *36,* 1228–1235.

Cohen, J. A. & Mannarino, A. P. (1998). Interventions for sexually abused children: Initial treatment outcome findings. *Child Maltreatment, 3,* 17–26.

Connor, K. & Davidson, J. (1998). The role of serotonin in posttraumatic stress disorder: neurobiology and pharmacotherapy. CNS Spectrum, 3, *43–51.*

Conte, J. (1995). Assessment of children who may have been abused: The real world context. In T. Ney (Ed.), *True and false allegations of child sexual abuse: Assessment and case management* (pp. 290–302). New York: Brunner/Mazel.

Crosse, S. B., Kaye, E. & Ratnofsky, A. C. (2001). *A report on the maltreatment of children with disabilities.* Washington DC: National Center on Child Abuse and Neglect.

Daro, D. (1994). Prevention of child sexual abuse. *Future of Children, 4,* 198–123.

Davis, M. K. & Gidycz, C. A. (2000). Child sexual abuse prevention programs: A meta-analysis. *Journal of Clinical Child Psychology, 29,* 257–265.

De Bellis, M., Chrousos, G., Dorn, L., Burke, L., Helmers, K., Kling, M., et al. (1994). Hypothalamic-pituitary-adrenal axis dysregulation in sexually abused girls. *Journal of Clinical Endocrinology and Metabolism, 7,* 249–255.

De Bellis, M., Lefter. L., Trickett, P. & Putnam, F. (1994). Urinary catecholamine excretion in sexually abused girls. *Journal of the American Academy of Child and Adolescent Psychiatry, 33,* 320–327.

De Bellis, M. & Putnam, F. (1994). The psychobiology of childhood maltreatment. *Child & Adolescent Psychiatric Clinics of North America, 3,* 1–16.

Deblinger, E., Lippman, J. & Steer, R. (1996). Sexually abused children suffering posttraumatic stress symptoms: Initial treatment outcome findings. Child Maltreatment, 1, 310–321.

Deblinger, E., Stauffer, L. B. & Steer, R. A. (2001). Comparative efficacies of supportive and cognitive behavioral group therapies for young children who have been sexually abused and their nonoffending mothers. *Child Maltreatment: Journal of the American Professional Society on the Abuse of Children, 6,* 332–343.

Deblinger, E., Steer, R. & Lippman, J. (1999). Two year follow-up study of cognitive behavioral therapy for sexually abused children suffering post-traumatic stress symptoms. *Child Abuse and Neglect, 23,* 1371–1378.

Dhaliwal, G., Gauzas, L., Antonowicz, D. & Ross, R. (1996). Adult male survivors of childhood sexual abuse: Prevalence, sexual abuse characteristics, and long-term effects. *Clinical Psychology Review, 16,* 619–639.

Dinwiddie, S., Heath, A. C., Dunne, M. P., Bucholz, K. K., Madden, P. A., Slutske, W. S. et al. (2000). Early sexual abuse and lifetime psychopathology: a co-twin-control study. *Psychological Medicine, 30,* 41–52.

Domon, S. & Anderson, M. (2000). Nefazodone for PTSD. *Journal of the American Academy of Child and Adolescent Psychiatry, 39,* 942–943.

Donnelly, C. L. & Amaya-Jackson, L. (2002). Post-traumatic stress disorder in children and adolescents: Epidemiology, diagnosis and treatment options. *Pediatric Drugs, 4,* 159–170.

Dreyer, L. B. & Haseltine, B. A. (1986). *The Woodrow Project: A sexual abuse prevention curriculum for the developmentally disabled.* Fargo, ND: Rape and Abuse Crisis Center.

Emslie, G. J., Heiligenstein, J. H., Wagner, K. D., Hoog, S. L., Ernest, D. E., Brown, E., et al. (2002). Fluoxetine for acute treatment of depression in children and adolescents: A placebo-controlled, randomized clinical trial. *Journal of the American Academy of Child and Adolescent Psychiatry, 41,* 1205–1215.

Emslie, G. J., Rush, A. J., Weinberg, W. A., Kowatch, R. A., Hughes, C. W., Carmody, T., et al. (1997). A double-blind, randomized, placebo controlled trial of fluoxetine in children and adolescents with depression. *Archives of General Psychiatry, 54,* 1031–1037.

Emslie, G. J., Weinberg, W. A. & Mayes, T. L. (1998). Treatment of children with antidepressants: Focus on selective serotonin reuptake inhibitors. *Depression and Anxiety, 8*(Suppl 1), 13–17.

Famularo, R., Kinscherff, R. & Fenton, T. (1988). Propranolol treatment for childhood posttraumatic stress disorder, acute type: A pilot study. *American Journal of Diseases of Children, 142,* 1244–1247.

Farrell, S. P., Hains, A. A. & Davies, W. H. (1998). Cognitive behavioral interventions for sexually abused children exhibiting PTSD symptomatology. *Behavior Therapy, 29,* 241–255.

Feinauer, L. L., Callahan, E. H. & Hilton, H. G. (1996). Positive intimate relationships decrease depression in sexually abused women. *American Journal of Family Therapy, 24,* 99–106.

Fergusson, D. M., Lynskey M. T. & Horwood, L. J. (1996). Childhood sexual abuse and psychiatric disorders in young adulthood: Part I: The prevalence of sexual abuse and the factors associated with sexual abuse. *Journal of the American Academy of Child and Adolescent Psychiatry, 35,* 1355–1365.

Fieldman, J. P. & Crespi, T. D. (2002). Child sexual abuse: Offenders, disclosure, and school-based initiatives. *Adolescence, 37,* 151–160.

Finkelhor, D. (1984). *Child sexual abuse: New theory and research.* New York: Free Press.

Finkelhor, D. (1987). The trauma of child sexual abuse: Two models. *Journal of Interpersonal Violence, 2,* 348–366.

Finkelhor, D., Asdigian, N. & Dziuba-Leatherman, J. (1995). The effectiveness of victimization prevention instruction: An evaluation of children's responses to actual threats and assaults. *Child Abuse & Neglect, 19,* 141–153.

Finkelhor, D. & Baron, L. (1986). Risk factors for child sexual abuse. *Journal of Interpersonal Violence, 1,* 43–71.

Finkelhor, D. & Berliner, L. (1995). Research on the treatment of sexually abused children: A review and recommendations. *American Academy of Child and Adolescent Psychiatry, 34,* 1408–1423.

Finkelhor, D. & Dziuba-Leatherman, J. (1995). Victimization prevention programs: A national survey of children's exposure and reactions. *Child Abuse and Neglect, 19,* 129–139.

Finkelhor, D., Hotaling, G., Lewis, I. & Smith, C. (1990). Sexual abuse in a national survey of adult men and women: Prevalence, characteristics, and risk factors. *Child Abuse and Neglect, 1,* 19–28.

Fleming, J., Mullen, P. E. & Bammer, G. (1997). A study of potential risk factors for sexual abuse in childhood. *Child Abuse and Neglect, 21,* 49–58.

Friedman, M. J. (1990). Interrelationships between biological mechanisms and pharmacotherapy of post-traumatic stress disorder. In M. E. Wolfe & A. D. Mosnian (Eds.), *Posttraumatic stress disorder: Etiology, phenomenology, and treatment* (pp. 204–225).Washington, DC: American Psychiatric Press.

Giaconia, R., Reinherz, H., Silverman, A., Pakiz, B., Frost, A. & Cohen, E. (1995). Trauma and posttraumatic stress disorder in a community population of older adolescents. *Journal of the American Academy of Child and Adolescent Psychiatry, 34,* 1369–1380.

Gibson, L. & Leitenberg, H. (2000). Child sexual abuse prevention programs: Do they decrease the occurrence of child sexual abuse? *Child Abuse & Neglect, 24,* 1115–1125.

Gilbert, B. O., Greening, L. & Dollinger, S. J. (2001). Neurotic disorders of children: Obsessive-compulsive, somatoform, dissociative and post-traumatic stress disorders. In C. E. Walker & M. C. Roberts (Eds.), *Handbook of clinical child psychology,* 3d ed. (pp. 414–431). New York: Wiley.

Glaser, D. (2000). Child abuse and neglect and the brain—A review. *Journal of Child Psychology and Psychiatry, 41,* 97–116.

Good, C. & Peterson, C. (2001). SSRI and mirtazapine in PTSD. *Journal of the American Academy of Child and Adolescent Psychiatry; 40,* 263–264.

Gorey, K. & Leslie, D. (1997). The prevalence of child sexual abuse: Integrative review adjustment for potential response and measurement biases. *Child Abuse & Neglect, 21,* 391–398.

Harmon, R. & Riggs, P. (1996). Clinical perspectives: Clonidine for posttraumatic stress disorder in preschool children. *Journal of the American Academy of Child and Adolescent Psychiatry, 35,* 1247–1249.

Haseltine, B. & Miltenberger, R. (1990). Teaching self-protection skills to persons with mental retardation. *American Journal on Mental Retardation, 95,* 188–197.

Hibbard, R., Ingersoll, G. & Orr, D. (1990). Behavioral risk, emotional risk and child abuse among young adolescents in a nonclinical setting. *Journal of Pediatrics, 86,* 896–901.

Hidalgo, R. & Davidson, J. (2000). Selective serotonin reuptake inhibitors in post-traumatic stress disorder. *Journal of Psychopharmacology, 14,* 70–76.

Hornor, G. (2004). Ano-genital warts in children: sexual abuse or not? *Journal of Pediatric Health Care, 18,* 165–170.

Hotte, J. & Rafman, S. (1992). The specific effects of incest on prepubertal girls from dysfunctional families. *Child Abuse & Neglect, 16,* 273–283.

Ima, K. & Hohm, C. F. (1991). Child maltreatment among Asian and Pacific Islander refugees and immigrants: The San Diego case. *Journal of Interpersonal Violence, 6,* 267–285.

Jaberghaderi, N., Greenwald, R., Rubin, A., Zand, S. O. & Dolatabadi, S. (2004). A comparison of CBT and EMDR for sexually abused Iranian girls. *Clinical Psychology and Psychotherapy, 11,* 358–368.

Jones, D. P. H. & Ramchandani, P. (1999). *Child sexual abuse: Informing practice from research.* Oxford: Radcliffe Medical Practice.

Jones, W. P. & Emerson, S. (1994). Sexual abuse and binge eating in a nonclinical population. *Journal of Sex Education and Therapy, 20,* 47–55.

Kendall-Tackett, K. A., Williams, L. M. & Finkelhor, D. (1993). Impact of sexual abuse on children: A review and synthesis of recent empirical studies. *Psychological Bulletin, 113,* 164–180.

Kendler, K. S., Bulik, C. M., Silberg, J., Hetteman, J. M., Myers, J. & Prescott, C. (2000). Childhood sexual abuse and adult psychiatric and substance use disorders: An epidemiological and cotwin control analysis. *Archives of General Psychiatry, 57,* 953–959.

Kenny, M. & McEachern, A. (2000). Racial, ethnic, and cultural factors of child sexual abuse: A selected review of the literature. *Clinical Psychology Review, 20,* 905–922.

Kimerling, R. & Calhoun, K. S. (1994). Somatic symptoms, social support, and treatment seeking among sexual assault victims. *Journal of Consulting and Clinical Psychology, 62,* 333–340.

King, J., Mandansky, D., King, S., Fletcher, K. & Brewer, J. (2001). Early sexual abuse and low cortisol. *Psychiatry of Clinical Neuroscience, 55,* 71–74.

King, N. J., Tonge, B., Mullen, P., Myerson, N., Heyne, D. & Ollendick, T. H. (1999). Cognitive-behavioral treatment of sexually abused children: Review of research. *Behavioural and Cognitive Psychotherapy, 27,* 295–309.

King, N., Tonge, B. J., Mullen, P., Myerson, N., Heyne, D., Rollings, S., et al. (2000). Sexually abused children and post-traumatic stress disorder. *Counselling Psychology Quarterly, 13,* 365–375.

Kitahara, M. (1989). Childhood in Japanese culture. *Journal of Psychohistory, 17,* 43–72.

Klonoff, E. A. & Landrine, H. (1997). Distrust of Whites, acculturation, and AIDS knowledge among African Americans. *Journal of Black Psychology, 23,* 50–57.

Kolko, D. J., Moser, J. T. & Weldy, S. R. (1988). Behavioral/emotional indicators of sexual abuse in psychiatric inpatients: A controlled comparison with physical abuse. *Child Abuse & Neglect, 12,* 529–541.

LaBarre, A., Hinkley, K. R. & Nelson, M. F. (1986). *Sexual abuse! What is it? An informational book for the hearing impaired.* St. Paul, MN: St. Paul-Ramsey Foundation.

Lee, C. W., Taylor, G. & Drummond, P. D. (2006). The active ingredient in EMDR: Is it traditional exposure or dual focus of attention? *Clinical Psychology and Psychotherapy, 13,* 97–107.

Loof, D., Grimley, P., Kuller, F., Martin, A. & Shonfield, L. (1995). Carbemazepine for PTSD [letter]. *Journal of the American Academy of Child and Adolescent Psychiatry, 34,* 703–704.

Lyons, J. A. (1991). Strategies for assessing the potential for positive adjustment following trauma. *Journal of Traumatic Stress, 4,* 93–105.

MacLeod, J. & Nelson, G. (2000). Programs for the promotion of family wellness and the prevention of child maltreatment: a meta-analytic review. *Child Abuse & Neglect, 24,* 1127–1150.

March, J., Silva, S., Petrycki, S., Curry, J., Wells, K., Fairbank, J., et al. (2004). Fluoxetine, cognitive-behavioral therapy, and their combination for adolescents with depression: Treatment for Adolescents With Depression Study (TADS) randomized controlled trial. *Journal of the American Medical Association, 29,* 807–820.

Mennen, F. E. (1995). The relationship of race/ethnicity to symptoms in childhood sexual abuse. *Child Abuse Neglect, 19,* 115–24.

Miller, B. A., Maguin, E. & Downs, W. R. (1997). Alcohol, drugs, and violence in children's lives. In M. Galanrer (Ed.), *Recent developments in alcoholism: Alcoholism and violence,* vol. 13 (pp. 357–385). New York: Plenum Press.

Mitchell, L. M. & Buchele-Ash, A. (2000). Abuse and neglect of individuals with disabilities: Building protective supports through public policy. *Journal of Disability Policy Studies, 10,* 225–243.

Mullen, P. E., Martin, J. L., Anderson, J. C., Romans, S. E. & Herbison, G. P. (1996). The long-term impact of the physical, emotional and sexual abuse of children: a community study. *Child Abuse and Neglect, 20,* 7–22.

National Clearinghouse on Child Abuse and Neglect Information (2005). Long-term consequences of child abuse and neglect. Retrieved 18 May 2006 from http://nccanch.acf.hhs.gov/pubs/factsheets/long_term_consequences.cfm.

National Research Council (1994). *Understanding child abuse neglect.* Washington, DC: National Academy Press.

Nelson, E. C., Heath, A. C., Madden, P. A., Cooper, M. L., Dinwiddie, S. H., Bucholz, K. K. et al. (2002). Association between self-reported childhood sexual abuse and adverse psychosocial outcomes: Results from a twin study. *Archives of General Psychiatry, 59,* 139–145.

Norring, F. & Walker, R. (2001). Support and group therapy for adolescents with a history of sexual abuse. *Medicine & Hygiene, 59,* 2022–2026.

O'Donohue, W. & Elliott, A. (1992). The treatment of the sexually abused child. *Journal of Clinical Child Psychology, 21,* 218–228.

O'Dougherty, M., Fopma-Loy, J. & Fischer, S. (2005). Multidimensional assessment of resilience in mothers who are child sexual abuse survivors. *Child Abuse and Neglect, 29,* 1173–1193.

Olds, D., Eckenrode, J. & Henderson, C. (1997). Long-term effects of home visitation on maternal life course and child abuse and neglect: 15-year follow-up of a randomized trial. *Journal of the American Medical Association, 278,* 637–643.

Olds, D., Henderson, C. Chamberlin, R. & Tatelbaum, R. (1986). Preventing child abuse and neglect: A randomized trial of nurse home visitation. *Pediatrics, 78,* 65–78.

Olsson, A., Ellsberg, M., Berglund, S., Herrera, A., Zelaya, E., Pena, R. et al. (2000). Sexual abuse during childhood and adolescence among Nicaraguan men and women: A population-based anonymous survey. *Child Abuse & Neglect, 24,* 1579–1589.

Perry, B. (1994). Neurobiological sequelae of childhood trauma: PTSD in children. In M. M. Murburg (Ed), *Catecholamine function in post-traumatic stress disorder: Emerging concepts* (pp. 233–255). Washington, DC: American Psychiatric Press.

Pierce, L. & Pierce, R. (1984). Race as a factor in the sexual abuse of children. *Social Work Research and Sexuality, 4,* 9–14.

Putnam, F. & Trickett, P. (1997). Psychobiological effects of sexual abuse. *Annals of the New York Academy of Sciences, 821,* 150–159.

Ramchandani, P. & Jones, D. P. H. (2003). Treating psychological symptoms in sexually abused children: From research findings to service provision. *British Journal of Psychiatry, 183,* 484–490.

Rao, K., DiClemente, R. & Ponton, L. (1992). Child sexual abuse of Asians compared with other populations. *Journal of the American Academy of Child and Adolescent Psychiatry, 31,* 880–886.

Reppucci, N. D. & Haugaard, J. J. (1989). Prevention of child abuse: Myth or reality? *American Psychologist, 44,* 1266–1275.

Rind, B., Tromovitch, P. & Bauserman, R. (1998). A metal-analytic examination of assumed properties of child sexual abuse using college samples. *Psychological Bulletin,* 124, 22–53.

Rispens, J., Aleman, A. & Goudena, P. P. (1997). Prevention of child sexual abuse victimization: A meta-analysis of school programs. *Child Abuse & Neglect, 21*(10), 975–987.

Robert, R., Blakeney, P., Villarreal, C., Rosenberg, L. & Meyer, W. J. (1999). Imipramine treatment in pediatric burn patients with symptoms of acute stress disorder: A pilot study. *Journal of the American Academy of Child and Adolescent Psychiatry; 38,* 873–82.

Romans, S., Martin, J., Anderson, J., O'Shea, M. & Mullen, P. (1995). Factors that mediate between child sexual abuse and adult psychological outcome. *Psychological Medicine, 25,* 127–142.

Ross, G. & O'Carroll, P. (2004). Cognitive behavioural psychotherapy intervention in childhood sexual abuse: Identifying new directions from the literature. *Child Abuse Review, 13,* 51–64.

Russell, D. (1983). The incidence and prevalence of intrafamial and extrafamilial sexual abuse of female children. *Child Abuse & Neglect, 7,* 133–146.

Sandberg, D., Lynn, S. & Green, J. (1994). Sexual abuse and revictimization: Mastery, dysfunctional learning, and dissociation. In S. Lynn & J. Rhue (Eds.), *Dissociation: Clinical and theoretical perspectives* (pp. 242–267). New York: Guilford.

Sanders-Phillips, K., Moisan, P. A., Wadlington, S., Morgan, S. & English, K. (1995). Ethnic differences in psychological functioning among Black and Latino sexually abused girls. Child Abuse and Neglect, 19, 691–706.

Sapp, M. & Vandeven, A. (2005). Update on childhood sexual abuse. *Current Opinion in Pediatrics, 17,* 258–164.

Saywitz, K. J., Mannarino, A. P., Berliner, L. & Cohen, J. A. (2000). Treatment of sexually abused children and adolescents. *American Psychologist, 55,* 1040–1049.

Sedlak, A. J. & Broadhurst, D. D. (1996). *First national incidence study of child abuse and neglect.* Washington, DC: U.S. Department of Health and Human Services.

Seedat, S., Lockhat, R., Kaminer, D., Zungu-Dirwayi, N. & Stein, D. (2001). An open trial of citalopram in adolescents with post traumatic stress disorder. *International Clinical Psychopharmacology, 16,* 21–25.

Seymour, A., Murray, M., Sigmon, J., Hook, M., Edmunds, C., Gaboury, M. et al. (Eds.) (2000). *2000 National Victim Assistance Academy.* Retrieved 19 December 2005 from http://www.ojp.usdoj.gov/ovc/assist/nvaa2000/academy/welcome.html.

Sgroi, S. (2000). *Discovery, reporting, investigation, and prosecution of child sexual abuse* (Sexuality Information and Education Council of the United States [SIECUS] Report, 29), 5–10.

Shapiro, F. (2001). *Eye movement desensitization and reprocessing: Basic principles, protocols and procedures,* 2d ed. New York: Guilford Press.

Siegel, J. M., Sorenson, S. G., Golding, J. M., Burnam, M. & Stein, J. (1987). The prevalence of childhood sexual abuse. *American Journal of Epidemiology, 126,* 1141–1153.

Silver, S., Rogers, S., Knipe, J. & Colelli, G. (2005). EMDR therapy following the 9/11 terrorist attacks: A community-based intervention project in New York City. *International Journal of Stress Management, 12,* 29–42.

Sobsey, D. & Mansell, S. (1990). The prevention of sexual abuse of people with developmental disabilities. *Developmental Disabilities Bulletin, 18,* 51–66.

Southwick, S., Krystal, J., Morgan, A., Johnson, D., Nagy, L., Nicolaou, A. et al. (1993). Abnormal noradrenergic function in post-traumatic stress disorder. *Archives of General Psychiatry, 50,* 266–274.

Spaccarelli, S. & Kim, S. (1995). Resilience criteria and factors associated with resilience in sexually abused girls. *Child Abuse and Neglect, 19,* 1171–1182.

Steel, J., Sanna, L., Hammond, B., Whipple, J. & Cross, H. (2004). Psychological sequelae of childhood sexual abuse: abuse-related characteristics, coping strategies, and attributional style. *Child Abuse & Neglect, 28,* 785–801.

Steinberg, M. A. & Hylton, J. R. (1998). *Responding to maltreatment of children with disabilities: A trainer's guide.* Portland, OR: Oregon Institute on Disability and Development, Child Development & Rehabilitation Center, Oregon Health Sciences University.

Sullivan, R. M. & Knutson, J. F. (2003). Maltreatment and disabilities: A population-based epidemiological study. *Journal of Early Intervention, 1,* 21–33.

Thomlison, B. (1997). Risk and protective factors in child maltreatment. In M. W. Fraser (Ed.), *Risk and resilience in childhood: An ecological perspective* (pp. 50–72). Washington, DC: NASW Press.

Timnick, L. (1985, August 15). The Times poll: Twenty-two percent in survey were child abuse victims. Los Angeles Times, p. 1.

Tjaden, P. & Thoennes, N. (2000). Extent, nature, and consequences of intimate partner violence: Findings from the national violence against women survey (NCJ187867). Washington, DC: U.S. Department of Justice.

U.S. Department of Health and Human Services (HHS) (2002). *Administration on Children, Youth and Families: 11 years of reporting: Child maltreatment 2000*. Washington, DC: U.S. Government Printing Office.

U.S. Department of Health and Human Services, National Center on Child Abuse and Neglect (1988). Child Maltreatment (1996): Reports from the states in the National Child Abuse and Neglect Data System. Washington, DC: U.S. Government Printing Office.

Vogeltanz, N. D., Wilsnack, S. C., Harris, T. R., Wilsnack, R. W., Wonderlich, S. A. & Kristjanson, A. F. (1999). Prevalence and risk factors for childhood sexual abuse in women: National survey findings. *Child Abuse & Neglect, 23*, 579–592.

Wagner, K. D., Ambrosini, P., Rynn, M., Wohlberg, C., Yang, R., Greenbaum, M. S. et al. (2003). Efficacy of sertraline in the treatment of children and adolescents with major depressive disorder—two randomized controlled trials. *Journal of the American Medical Association, 290*, 1033–1041.

Wagner, K. D., Robb, A. S., Findling, R. L., Jin, J., Gutierrez, M. M. & Heydorn, W. E. (2004). A randomized, placebo-controlled trial of citalopram for the treatment of major depression in children and adolescents. *American Journal of Psychiatry, 161*(6), 1079–1083.

Watkins, B. & Bentovim, A. (1992). The sexual abuse of male children and adolescents: A review of current research. *Journal of Child Psychology and Psychiatry, 33*, 197–248.

Wekerle, C., Wolfe, D. A., Hawkins, D. L., Pittman, A. L., Glickman, A. & Lovald, B. E. (2001). Childhood maltreatment, posttraumatic stress symptomatology, and adolescent dating violence: Considering the value of adolescent perceptions of abuse and a trauma mediation model. *Development & Psychopathology, 13*, 847–871.

Weller, E. B., Kang, J. & Weller, R. A. (2004). How the evidence tipped SSRIs' risk-benefit balance. *Current Psychiatry, 3*, 12–23.

Weller, E. B., Shlewiet, B. & Weller, R. A. (2003). Traumatized children: Why victims of violence live out their nightmares. *Current Psychiatry, 2*, 30–39.

Whealin, J. (2006). *A National Center for PTSD Fact Sheet*. Retrieved 18 May 2006 from http://www.ncptsd.va.gov/facts/specific/fs_child_sexual_abuse.html.

Whittington, C., Kendall, T., Fonagy, P., Cottrell, D., Cotgrove, A. & Boddington, E. (2004). Selective serotonin reuptake inhibitors in childhood depression: Systematic review of published versus unpublished data. *Lancet, 363*, 1341–1345.

Widom, C. & Morris, S. (1997). Accuracy of adult recollections of childhood victimization: Part 2. Childhood sexual abuse. *Psychological Assessment, 9*, 34–46.

Wilcox, D., Richards, F. & O'Keeffe, Z. (2004). Resilience and risk factors associated with experiencing childhood sexual abuse. *Child Abuse Review, 13*, 338–352.

Williams, T. & Miller, B. (2003). Pharmacologic management of anxiety disorders in children and adolescents. *Current Opinion in Pediatrics, 15,* 483–490.

Wozencraft, T., Wagner, W. & Pellegrin, A. (1991). Depression and suicidal ideation in sexually abused children. *Child Abuse and Neglect, 15,* 505–511.

Wurtele, S. (1998). School-based child sexual abuse prevention programs: Questions, answers, and more questions. In J. R. Lutzker (Ed.), *Handbook of child abuse research and treatment* (pp. 501–516). New York: Plenum Press.

Wurtele, S., Marrs, S. & Miller-Perrin, C. (1987). Practice makes perfect? The role of participant modeling in sexual abuse prevention programs. *Journal of Consulting and Clinical Psychology, 55,* 599–602.

Wurtele, S. & Miller-Perrin, C. (1992). *Preventing child sexual abuse: Sharing the responsibility.* Lincoln: University of Nebraska Press.

Wurtele, S., Saslawsky, D., Miller, C., Marrs, S. & Britcher, J. (1986). Teaching personal safety skills for potential prevention of sexual abuse: A comparison of treatments. *Journal of Consulting and Clinical Psychology, 54,* 688–692.

# Epilogue, or Final Credits

We opened this volume with an allusion to the cinema and the multi-episode serial, in particular. You might imagine each of the chapters in this book as a part in that story, and, in a sense, this epilogue represents the rolling of the final credits. Although we will not be sharing the names of the typists whose keystrokes formed the words on this page, nor will we be disclosing the typeface and font size of the print before you, we will share our impressions of the themes that emerged from this volume and where those themes should lead practice in the coming decade.

First, the concept of family is dynamic rather than static in form, function and operation. Granted, in the past, community involvement was evident, and the biological nuclear family was not the dominant child-rearing entity. Still, the complexity of relationships between individuals and society is historically unique. We do not see this evolving situation changing. Rather, we see laws creating rules that will eventually morph into norms of behavior. For example, in cases of adoption the open process of biological and adoptive parents knowing one another and the continued relationship of biological parents to the child whose parental rights were surrendered were unheard of when Tom Gullotta adopted Bernie 20-some-odd years ago. Likewise, the growing frequency of coparenting, joint custody, and visitation in families where a divorce has occurred is quite recent.

Next, family issues are mostly problems in living. That said, readers might wonder why we insisted on the talented teams of scholars writing these chapters to address questions of genetics and psychopharmacology in each of the topical chapters in this book. We did so because we wanted readers to see if certain behavioral family patterns were in part genetic. Not surprisingly, only a few are, and our suspicion was confirmed both for us and for you that no silver bullet in the form of a pill for family distress existed.

The majority of the distressful issues in this chapter are relational. The screenplay writer—be it known as life, fate, karma, God, or bad luck—scripted a family dissolved by divorce, with a mentally ill parent, a seriously ill child or a remarriage. The characters—son, daughter, wife, in-laws and others—behave to the circumstances found before them, and in all, save a blessed few, there are pain, hurt and wounds that heal ever so slowly. This process of moving on is a reference to the muddling observation made in the opening remarks of this book. To be blunt, shit happens. When it does, there is no purifying ritual that will return one to a presoiled state of cleanliness. No, one will need to drag oneself out of that manure pit and crawl away. With luck, a shower of social support may wash away some of the night soil, or the sun with its ability to bring intrapersonal clarity to the situation may enable one to brush off the caked-on remains of the pit immersion. Regardless, one will be soiled and somewhat uncertain about the next step, and rightfully so. It is at this moment that this book has a use for those seeking help and for those who would extend that helping hand.

For the soiled individual looking to muddle forward through counseling for themselves and family members, there are several promising paths to encouraging healthier behavior. Interestingly, these paths emerge from social learning theory more than any other school of thought. Presently, the why of this reality can be accounted for by the lack of research on other theories. We are able to say that social learning theories, especially those with cognitive elements, are helpful in easing the distress of many adverse family situations, but they do not allow us to categorically reject other approaches. This presents a dilemma. If the science of social science is to advance, other counseling approaches must be studied planfully and either verified or rejected. Yet there appears to be no concerted effort to undertake this vital work. In a previous volume, the editors offered this proposal to resolving this problem (Gullotta & Blau, 2007). Graduate schools of clinical psychology, social work, marriage and the family, psychiatric nursing and psychiatry should establish centers of practice to evaluate two counseling approaches. In addition to cognitive behaviorism, the center might choose gestalt, analytically oriented therapy or a transpersonal approach to evaluate its usefulness in a variety of clinical circumstances.* The doctoral student enrolled in these programs can choose the traditional dissertation pathway to a diploma or work in the center. As the answer to the question of whether a particular therapeutic technique has use could take several years to answer, the center doctoral student would not be able to offer a dissertation as finished as another. Nevertheless, in our opinion, the value of their center work likely will exceed the minor advances that even the best dissertations of today make to the social sciences. If this plan were embraced, within a decade or so significant progress in advancing clinical practice would be made.

For the individual who would like to see others avoiding, if possible, the distress of many of the life events discussed in this volume, this book offers several promising approaches. Indeed, the research literature in support of preventive interventions is superior to the clinical literature for two reasons. The first is that 95% of prevention research has appeared in the past 30 years (Durlak, 2003). This research has benefited from advances in design methodology and statistical analysis. The second is the clinical professional reticence to admit that health can be promoted and, in many instances, distress prevented. This rejection by clinicians motivated prevention scholars to build programs not just on theory but also on theory and research. As with our suggestion for centers of clinical practice, we urge graduate schools of community psychology, public health and social work to establish research centers for prevention science. Considerable work remains in integrating prevention's technology of social competency, natural care-giving, community organization, systems intervention and education into effective interventions. The field of health promotion and prevention remains in its infancy in systematically applying these tools to nurture healthier behavior.

---

* If you wonder why we would insist on cognitive behavioral theory, it is presently the intervention with the strongest empirical support. We want to be sure those graduate students have a job should that other counseling intervention fail miserably.

Finally, in our opinion, a bio-psycho-social-environmental approach is a superior construction to understanding the problems in living of families and the individuals in those families. It is not that person-in-the-environment (Germain & Bloom, 1999) and an ecological framework (Bronfenbrenner, 1979) are theoretically weaklings. They are not. Rather, the visual and vocal articulation of bio-psycho-social-environmental forces the reader to acknowledge that biology + psychology + social relations + environmental factors create a dynamic ever-changing set of circumstances that shape and reshape the family and the individuals in those families for better and for worse. As mental health professionals who have chosen a life of helping others to address their problems in living and to prevent the development of those problems whenever possible, we have a responsibility "to interfere, for good, in human matters" using our best skills developed by a process that relies on fact rather than fiction (Dickens, 1843, p. 37).

## REFERENCES

Brofenbrenner, U. (1979). *The ecology of human development.* Cambridge, MA: Harvard University Press.

Dickens, C. (1843). *A Christmas carol.* London, England: Chapman and Hall.

Durlak, J. A. (2003). Effective prevention and health promotion programming. In T. P. Gullotta and M. Bloom (Eds.), *Encyclopedia of primary prevention and health promotion* (pp. 61–68). New York: Kluwer/Academic Press.

Germain, C. B. & Bloom, M. (1999). *Human behavior in the social environment: An ecological view.* New York: Columbia University Press.

Gullotta, T. P. & Blau, G. A. (2007). *Handbook of childhood behavioral issues: Evidence based approaches to prevention and treatment.* New York: Taylor & Francis.

# Index